# Culture and the State in Late Chosŏn Korea

Harvard
East
Asian
Monographs
182

*The Harvard-Hallym Series on Korean Studies*

The Harvard-Hallym Series on Korean Studies, published by the Harvard University Asia Center, is supported by the Korea Institute of Harvard University and by Hallym University in Korea. It is committed to the publication of outstanding new scholarly work on Korea, regardless of discipline, in both the humanities and the social sciences.

Professor Carter J. Eckert
Director
Korea Institute, Harvard University

Dr. Dahl-Sun Han
President
Hallym University

# Culture and the State in Late Chosŏn Korea

JAHYUN KIM HABOUSH &
MARTINA DEUCHLER, editors

Published by the Harvard University Asia Center
and distributed by Harvard University Press
Cambridge, Massachusetts, and London
1999

Printed in the United States of America

The Harvard University Asia Center publishes a monograph series and, in coordination with the Fairbank Center for Chinese Studies, the Korea Institute, the Reischauer Institute of Japanese Studies, and other faculties and institutes, administers research projects designed to further scholarly understanding of China, Japan, Vietnam, Korea, and other Asian countries. The Center also sponsors projects addressing multidisciplinary and regional issues in Asia.

Library of Congress Cataloging-in-Publication Data

Culture and the state in late Chosŏn Korea / JaHyun Kim Haboush &
    Martina Deuchler, editors.
            p.    cm.
    Includes bibliographical references and index.
    ISBN-13: 978-0-674-17982-0 (cl: alk. paper)  ISBN-10: 0-674-17982-X (cl: alk. paper)
    ISBN-13: 978-0-674-00774-1 (pbk: alk. paper) ISBN-10 0-674-00774-3 (pbk: alk. paper)
    1. Confucianism and state--Korea--History.  2. Neo-Confucianism--Korea.  3.
Korea--Politics and government--1392–1910.    I. Haboush, JaHyun Kim.  II.
Deuchler, Martina, 1935–  .
BL1842.C85      1999
951.9' 02--dc21                                                    99-24738
                                                                        CIP


Index by Martina Deuchler

⊗    Printed on acid-free paper

Last figure below indicates year of this printing
18  17  16  15  14  13  12  11  10  09

# Contents

*Reference Matter*

# Preface

This volume grew out of the conference "Confucianism and Late Chosŏn Korea" held at the University of California, Los Angeles, in 1992. This conference was broadly conceived as a follow-up to one on Neo-Confucianism in Korea, held in Bellagio, Italy, in 1981, on which *The Rise of Neo-Confucianism in Korea* (Columbia University Press, 1985) is based. *The Rise of Neo-Confucianism in Korea* focuses on the period from the fourteenth to the seventeenth centuries; we start where that volume left off. In recent years, there has been a growing awareness that late Chosŏn Korea was a vibrant period and that it should be studied in its own right rather than in terms of the long-accepted view as a time of continual decline sandwiched between an early period of vigor and the eventual loss of sovereignty to Japan in 1910. The conference in Los Angeles was an attempt to begin serious inquiries into this period. We had a lively discussion on a wide range of topics. We were both exhilarated by interesting possibilities of approach and humbled by the realization of how little we knew of the period and how much work was ahead of us. In our discouraging moments, however, we kept reminding ourselves of the Korean adage "The beginning is half way to accomplishment."

Considerably more papers were delivered at the conference than are collected in this volume. We have narrowed our concentration and decided to include only those papers devoted to problems pertaining to the relationship of intellectual or religious communities to the state. Thus, papers dealing with the history of ideas, popular culture, and rural societies have been omitted. We are, however, deeply indebted to the insights and knowledge we acquired from these contributions. Participants in the conference whose work is not included here were Chai-Sik Chung, Dieter Eikemeier, Michael Kalton, Fujiya Kawashima, Oak-sook Chun Kim, and Mark Setton. We are also immensely inspired by the discussants, who shared valuable ideas and expertise, which they brought from their own disciplines and areas of specialization. Peter Bol, Willem Jan Boot, Wm. Theodore de Bary, John Duncan, Benjamin Elman, Laurel Kendall, Peter Nosco, Herman Ooms, and James Palais joined us as discussants. We are grateful to all of them.

We also thank John R. Ziemer of the Harvard University Asia Center. We are deeply indebted to him for his encouragement and meticulous care of the manuscript.

We would also like to thank the National Endowment for the Humanities for providing a grant in support of the conference and the Center for Korean Studies at the University of California, Los Angeles, for making its facilities available to us.

# Contributors

Don Baker teaches Korea at the University of British Columbia, where he holds the Canada-Korean Business Council Chair of Korean Studies. His recent publications include *Sourcebook of Korean Civilization* (co-editor), *Chosŏn hugi Yugyo wa Ch'ŏnjugyo ŭi taerip* (Confucians confront Catholicism in Chosŏn Korea), and "World Religions and National States: Competing Claims in East Asia."

Robert E. Buswell, Jr., is Professor of Buddhist Studies at the University of California, Los Angeles, where he also serves as chair of the Department of East Asian Languages and Cultures and director of the Center for Korean Studies. His books include *The Korean Approach to Zen* (reprinted in a paperback abridgment as *Tracing Back the Radiance: Chinul's Korean Way of Zen*), *The Formation of Ch'an Ideology in China and Korea*, and *The Zen Monastic Experience: Buddhist Practice in Contemporary Korea*.

Yŏng-ho Ch'oe is Professor of Korean History at the University of Hawaii. His publications include *The Civil Examinations and the Social Structure in Early Yi Korea*, and *Sourcebook of Korean Civilization* (co-editor).

Martina Deuchler is Professor of Korean Studies at the School of Oriental and African Studies, University of London. She specializes in the social and intellectual history of Chosŏn Korea. Her publications include *Confucian Gentlemen and Barbarian Envoys* and *The Confucian Transformation of Korea: A Study of Society and Ideology*.

JaHyun Kim Haboush is Professor of East Asian History and Culture at the University of Illinois, Urbana-Champaign. Her publications include *The Rise of Neo-Confucianism in Korea* (co-editor), *A Heritage of Kings: One Man's Monarchy in the Confucian World*, and *The Memoirs of Lady Hyegyŏng: The Autobiographical Writings of a Crown Princess of Eighteenth-Century Korea.*

Boudewijn Walraven is Professor of Korean Language and Culture at Leiden University, the Netherlands. He has written widely on popular religion. He is the author of *Songs of the Shaman: The Ritual Chants of the Korean Mudang.* He has also translated several stories from the Chosŏn period.

*Culture and the State in Late Chosŏn Korea*

# Introduction

## JAHYUN KIM HABOUSH &
## MARTINA DEUCHLER

SCHOLARSHIP ON KOREAN HISTORY, especially of the premodern period, stands at crossroads in the English-speaking world. A full generation of scholars has paved the way before us, and much interesting work has been done in the past few decades. Nonetheless, the field is still young, and since only a small number of us are engaged in it, research leaves many important areas, periods, and issues unattended. At the same time, we feel that we are part of the historical scholarly endeavor and that our work acquires meaning in the context of current discourse in history. This realization leads us to aim for several objectives in our work. We wish to bring light to neglected but important areas and periods of Korean history, as well as to offer new and comparative insights and directions. This volume has been conceived with these aspirations.

The first objective of this volume is to offer an alternative approach to the study of the late Chosŏn period. Although a few book-length studies in Western languages on this period have appeared in recent years,[1] the late Chosŏn period remains one of the less studied periods in Korean history. Research conducted on this period in Korea mostly falls under the rubrics of "post-colonial" historiography and modernization theory. Countering the deterministic historical visions expressed in these works, we present the late Chosŏn as a vibrant time responding to challenges of its own and generating new

agendas. The Chosŏn dynasty (1392–1910) had exceptional longev-
ity, spanning two dynasties in China and two shogunates in Japan.
A great deal of change occurred both within and outside Korea
during this period, and many differences distinguish the late Chosŏn period from the earlier period.

This book investigates interactions among the state, Confucian
communities, and various religious communities and the way the
boundaries separating them had to be redrawn from the late sixteenth to the nineteenth centuries. The contributors to this volume
argue that the power and influence each group exercised were determined by a dynamic interactive relationship among ideology,
government policies, and the self-perceptions and social adjustments
of each group, and that each relationship had to be continuously recalibrated and renegotiated. The volume thus challenges a static
view of the Korean Confucian state and suggests new approaches to
the complex ways in which intellectual and religious communities
negotiated and adjusted their ideologies and practices in the late
Chosŏn period.

The early Chosŏn can be seen as a time when the state attended to
the task of establishing Neo-Confucian hegemony. The Chosŏn is
often cited as one of the rare instances before the modern era in
which a polity was proclaimed on the basis of a specific ideology.
The state and the ruling elite had to cope with instituting Neo-
Confucianism as political, social, ritual, and intellectual orthodoxy.
Since this task involved, at the very least, a contest over worldviews,
familial and social structure, and the institutions of authority, the
policies and the rhetoric that accompanied them were forceful and
polemical. A number of studies are devoted to the ensuing meta-
morphoses. *The Confucian Transformation of Korea* by Martina Deuchler discusses the processes through which Confucian norms were
adopted as social and ritual orthodoxy, especially in the construction
of a Confucian patriarchy and patrilineal descent groups.[2] The
chapters in *The Rise of Neo-Confucianism in Korea*, edited by Wm.
Theodore de Bary and JaHyun Kim Haboush, discuss the particular
ways in which Buddhism, which had long enjoyed unrivaled su-
premacy, was marginalized and Chosŏn Korea came to possess Neo-
Confucianism and to shape it into the main ingredient of its intellectual and political culture from the fifteenth to the seventeenth
centuries.[3]

Korean Confucian orthodoxy received its lasting philosophical contours from T'oegye Yi Hwang (1501–70) and Yulgok Yi I (1536–84) in the sixteenth century. Both defined orthodoxy according to their understanding of the Ch'eng-Chu school of Neo-Confucianism. For T'oegye, self-cultivation constituted the core of a generative process of self that would eventually lead to harmonization of the human order with the cosmic order. It required intellectual discipline and an ascetic way of life — two premises that grew out of his rather pessimistic view of human nature — and demanded close interpretation of the Neo-Confucian textual tradition.[4] Yulgok, in contrast, seems to have understood the Neo-Confucian agenda as calling for a personal effort to comprehend the canon and to actualize its teachings in everyday life.[5] Although Yulgok fully acknowledged the textual authority of the Ch'eng-Chu school, his insistence on independent exploration precluded a narrow definition of the orthodox. It was Yulgok more than T'oegye, however, who endorsed an activist government to formulate and implement Confucian policies.

Korean orthodoxy received its institutional underpinnings when, in 1610, five Korean scholars were enshrined in the Shrine of Confucius (Munmyo) in Seoul.[6] This act had far more than a mere symbolic significance for the history of Korean Confucianism. It was a major assertion of Confucian orthodoxy in itself. By securing for themselves a permanent and recognized place within the wider context of Confucian civilization, Korean Confucians placed themselves on the same level as their intellectual forebears of Sung China; at times they even professed a belief that they were more faithful keepers of orthodoxy than the erring Ming Chinese. This enshrinement affirmed the Korean Confucians' sense of their place, both diachronic and synchronic, in the Neo-Confucian tradition and the Neo-Confucian world.

Still, it would be a mistake to assume that homogeneity reigned either within the Confucian community or outside it in the second half of the Chosŏn dynasty. That community was marked by factional affiliations, regional distinctions, and divergent views on the propriety of holding government office. In the capital, the Sŏnggyun'gwan (Confucian Academy), as a part of the central administration, represented state hegemony and catered principally to the interests of the capital elite. Although some individuals spent time at the academy but never served in the government, it mostly educated and prepared the younger generation of the ruling establishment for the higher civil service examinations (*munkwa*), which assured entry into the officialdom. Hence, the academy spoke with the voice of power.

The intellectual strongholds of the rural elite were the private academies (sŏwŏn), which embodied the independent spirit of the scholarly community and were often in an ambiguous relationship to the state. They were based on the notion that moral philosophy was the source of the moral order of society. This was reflected in their history and their sense of mission. The earliest academies, built in the second half of the sixteenth century, were founded in an atmosphere of enthusiastic belief in the transformatory force of Neo-Confucianism. This optimistic view was shared by all parties—the local scholarly communities as well as the central government. Private academies were regarded as sanctuaries where the study of scholarship and moral tenets could be pursued without the pressures of preparing for a civil service career. Besides fulfilling their role as teaching institutions, private academies were also symbolic centers in which earlier worthies and local personalities, who were revered for their services to their localities, were enshrined. The expansion and proliferation of the private academies in the seventeenth and eighteenth centuries led to great variety in intellectual and political orientation and outlook, but the initial conception of the academies as harbingers of moral transformation persisted.

Given the rather diverse constituents of the Confucian community, the lack of a consensus with regard to orthodoxy is not surprising, and this uncertainty manifested itself in disagreements within the hegemonic group itself. Was the "orthodox" what was sanctioned by the state? To what extent did the state have the authority to interfere in the process of definition? Where was the boundary between what was tolerable and what had to be censured as a threat to the existing order? Such boundaries obviously shifted according to the definition of the space within which certain kinds of activities, ideas, and behavior were permitted. When it came to non-hegemonic religious groups such as Buddhism, shamanism, and later, Catholicism, this question of the sphere of permissibility was felt even more acutely.

This book also seeks to place Korea in a larger framework of forces that interacted with outside influences and contributed to shaping and constructing policies and images. A major element that distinguished the late Chosŏn from the earlier period was the reconstitution of the world order in East Asia in the late sixteenth and early seventeenth centuries and the consequent changes in Korean perceptions of the world and self. Korea was viscerally affected by the great sweep of political realignments that passed through East Asia during this period. Japan launched full-scale invasions of Korea twice in the 1590s, and there were Manchu attacks in 1627 and 1636. However much the war with Japan challenged the Korean assumptions on which national security policy had been based and created a sense of insecurity, it was the Korean capitulation to the Manchus and the subsequent fall of the Ming to these "barbarians" in 1644 that threatened the very basis of Korean cultural identity. Since Koreans viewed the Manchu conquest of China as nothing less than the loss of the center of civilization to barbarians, the world order as they had known it was completely in chaos. The world changed from a benign place of order and peace in which the hierarchy among countries corresponded to their degree of civilization to a lopsided and disorderly one in which power was divorced from legitimacy, creating suspicion and contempt.

These changes in the world order had tremendous repercussions for the entire East Asian region in the seventeenth century. A number of studies have focused on reactions in China and Japan. Benjamin Elman's study of philosophical and scholastic changes[7] and Kaiwing Chow's discussion of ritual and social redirection in China[8] are but two noteworthy examples. Nowhere else, however, did the discourse circle so closely around the throne as it did in Korea. It is remarkable that the Korean search for a new identity took the form it did. The scholarly debates surrounding monarchical legitimacy vividly illustrated the powerful role the scholar-official elite played in the formation of identity. Concerns extended far beyond the discourse of power, however, and permeated every aspect of the restructuring of identity. The new order challenged their epistemological foundations, and hence Koreans had to construct a new episteme of the world and the self, one that allowed them to sustain their political beliefs and to maintain their cultural identity. It is our contention that much of the intellectual and political turmoil of the seventeenth century was embedded in an acute sense of crisis and the consequent quest for a new episteme.

Another and, perhaps, the ultimate objective of this volume is to suggest a new way of conceptualizing the political, academic, and religious culture of late Chosŏn Korea. Factionalism is a good example. Factionalism has long been viewed as an unallayed evil in

Korean history responsible for every possible problem ranging from corrupt government to lack of unity and loss of sovereignty. A new wave of studies has argued that it had "positive" effects but still approaches the subject of factionalism from the stance of determining whether it was "positive" or "negative."[9] We take a different approach. We study factionalism as an ingredient of the political culture of a certain historical period in constant interaction with issues of the time, shaping and being shaped by them. Although none of the chapters in this volume is devoted solely to factionalism, several discuss the way in which factions interacted with intellectual issues, such as the ritual controversy, the Classics controversy, and the debate over academies.

Similarly, we do not evaluate the scope of tolerance or intolerance for "heterodoxy" or nonhegemonic religions. Rather we wish to bring a new perspective to the discussion of religious culture. Nonhegemonic religious practices were not "persecuted," but this tolerance differed from the religious freedom found in a modern society.[10] We draw attention to how the discourse on these issues was conducted and how it was applied in practice. How was the question of "heterodoxy" or "heterodox" religion conceptualized, what were the boundaries of acceptability and unacceptability, and when and in which spheres did these apply? Several chapters employ the public/private binary as a heuristic device to come to terms with this question.

A good example is the case of Pak Sedang, discussed at length in this volume. Were Pak Sedang's papers safe from "public" scrutiny as long as they remained invisible in a box stored in the "private" sphere of a scholar's study? Pak's ideas came to be judged by "public" opinion only when his commentaries on the Classics became "visible," that is, when they entered the public domain. At the same time, Pak's devious ritual behavior came to light, making him a "despoiler" of the Confucian tradition in a double sense in the eyes of those who at that time styled themselves guardians of orthodoxy. If the desire to preserve and exhibit "right learning" by staking out definite, yet faction-oriented boundaries had not been so acute, Pak Sedang might never have been put on trial. His trial, however, became a test case that climaxed in a definition of the "heterodox" even within the hegemonic group.

The binary of public and private also offers a useful frame for conceptualizing the question of tolerance for nonhegemonic religions. At the beginning of the dynasty, the Neo-Confucians adopted harsh measures to curb the power of Buddhists and shamanic practitioners. Both groups were driven from the capital and banned from participating in state rituals as well as in the life-cycle rituals of the people. The Buddhists were confined to a few dozen monasteries in the mountains.[11] Because of its amorphous nature, native popular religion appears to have fared a little better than Buddhism. In the absence of an organized ecclesiastical community and a well-defined body of scriptures, shamanic beliefs were more difficult to expurgate from popular religiosity and ritual. Although the state left little space for shamans in the public domain, shamanism persisted by avoiding direct contests with the state and by specializing in those private rituals outside Confucian concerns. It was consequently gender-based and practiced mainly by women in the inner quarters in connection with childbearing and childrearing. In this capacity it in fact supported the Confucian patriarchy.

Thus whereas the public space was occupied by what was manifest, orthodox, and legitimate, marginalized groups, such as Buddhists and practitioners of popular religion, were tolerated as long as they remained "invisible," that is, as long as they did not claim part of the public space. By the late Chosŏn period, diminished and consigned to "invisible" spaces in their spheres of activity, neither Buddhism nor popular religions were perceived as threatening the existing socio-religious order, and the state felt no need to persecute them. Both religions, however, even in reduced form, continued to play an important part in the popular imagination. In fact, Buddhist and shamanic motifs and conceptions were conspicuous in popular literature and art in the late Chosŏn. Nevertheless, Confucian hegemony reigned large and was supported by a state based squarely on the premise that the political and social order had to be sustained by the moral and ritual concepts of Ch'eng-Chu philosophy.

The strength of such convictions was gravely tested by the introduction of Catholicism in the late eighteenth century. News about the new creed had reached Korea a century earlier and stimulated curiosity about the Western science that was transmitted along with religious tracts and paraphernalia. Certain Confucian circles conducted intense debates about the acceptability of the new religion within the framework of the Confucian tradition. There were conversions, but they were perceived as subversive. Moreover, practicing their creed with the zeal of the newly converted, the Christians' open display of contempt for ancestor worship was construed as a direct challenge to orthodoxy. The state authorities were soon alerted to the incompatibility of Christianity with the Confucian moral order and to the threat the new religion posed to the Confucian polity. Neither the state nor the Christians were equipped with the experience or the determination to devise a formula for acceptable and unacceptable categories by assigning practices to "visible" and "invisible" space. The state resorted to suppression and persecution, and many Christians responded with defiance. Unlike the cases of Buddhism and popular religion, it was a story of confrontation and conflict.

The first three chapters in this volume discuss the processes through which the roles of the state and of the community of Confucian scholars were redefined and the boundaries between them redrawn in the second half of the seventeenth century. Yŏng-ho Ch'oe suggests that the academies' relationship to the state evolved within the rhetorical frame of fulfilling a mission to transform the individual and society. But how autonomous were these institutions? Studies of academies in China have shown that the relative degree of state control versus autonomy for the academies was determined through a complex mechanism.[12] In discussing academies during the Ch'ing dynasty, Alexander Woodside points out that private scholars actively sought to reform schools in such a way as to bring them under governmental control rather than to leave them in the hands of private interests, although their initiatives coincided with government reform programs as well.[13] Ch'oe believes that Chosŏn academies sought independence from rather than submission to state leadership. As far as pedagogical methods and the publication of scholars' writings were concerned, the academies enjoyed virtually complete independence. This may mean that individual pursuit of knowledge was in fact less under the control of state ideology than is often suggested.

Ch'oe, moreover, shows that the choice of worthies for enshrinement and veneration in private academies was largely and increasingly determined by localization and stress on family ties. The way in which localization took place in Chosŏn Korea makes an interesting comparison to the situation in Sung China. In a study of the changing patterns of enshrinement of worthies during the Sung dynasty, Ellen Neskar concludes that the worthies chosen for veneration changed from persons of national prominence to those of a more modest local and individual accomplishment, and from persons with heroic attributes to those of civil and intellectual virtue. She sees this as a sign that leading intellectuals had lost faith in the central government and were instead stressing individual and local efforts in transforming society in the Southern Sung.[14] Robert Hymes has suggested that much local activity concerning academies was family-based.[15] In Korea, the emphasis seems to have been more on the local connections of the chosen rather than his service to the local community. It appears that the relationships of regions to the state varied considerably.

The state's policies concerning local autonomy seem to have been contradictory, as exemplified by an incident involving the proposed construction of an academy to honor Kim Sanghŏn in Andong. As Ch'oe explains, the state was unwilling to override local sentiment. However, around the same time, King Yŏngjo (r. 1724–76) enforced state control by various means, including the destruction of a large number of shrines built without prior permission from the government. Here, then, the state and the local communities were locked in conflict over control of the symbols of the Confucian orthodox tradition. The state's approach to individual cases appears to have differed from its pursuit of general policies toward the large local scholarly community. The last point discussed by Ch'oe is the growing participation in politics of students and scholars at the private academies. Such participation followed factional affiliation, and as a result, the treatment of individual academies varied sharply. Nevertheless, a new mode of political discourse seems to have developed in the late seventeenth century. This theme is taken up by Haboush.

JaHyun Kim Haboush focuses on the ritual controversy surrounding the question of how to mourn King Hyojong (r. 1649–59) as a site for examining the meaning of scholarly discourse on the state. Perhaps one of the most celebrated events in late Chosŏn history, this seventeenth-century ritual controversy has regularly been interpreted within the context of ritual scholarship and/or factionalism.[16] Haboush, in contrast, argues that the ritual controversy was a point on which the scholarly community's search for a new identity for Korea converged and clashed.

During the past few decades, historians of Chosŏn Korea have generally come to accept the proposition that seventeenth-century

Korea emerged with a new sense of mission as the last bastion of Confucian civilization, yet no detailed study has explored this theme. Haboush approaches it in two separate, though related, ways. One is to discuss and analyze the rhetorical tropes of the rites controversy to show how Koreans constructed a new episteme of the world and self. The other is to examine the controversy in relation to the emerging consciousness of national identity. She argues that de- spite a shared belief within the scholarly community that Korea was the last bastion of Confucian civilization, there was a deep cleavage in the community concerning the meaning of this role, and that this division was marked by differing perceptions of self and the bound- aries between self and the other. One group of scholars subscribed to the view that Korea was a discrete body in which various parts were inextricably integrated into one another and that, as such, it had an autonomous and separate existence distinct from its previous mem- bership in the fallen civilization. Another group saw Korea as con- sisting of divisible political and cultural entities; the latter were in- extricably linked to this bygone civilization and, in fact, were its only surviving fragment. The two groups consequently differed on what Korea should perpetuate, how it should do it, and what the spiritual sources of authority for this process should be.

Haboush maintains that this difference in views over the issue of whether the cultural could be separated from the political, and if so, which had hierarchical priority, extended to conceptions of the sov- ereign and scholars. The beliefs that a scholar could (or could not) act as a cultural self apart from his political self or evaluate the oc- cupant of the throne on purely cultural grounds directly influenced stances on whether one could and should act as an arbiter of royal legitimacy. It was these points that most closely determined concep- tions of the boundaries between the state and the scholarly commu- nity and over which the opposing factions clashed.

The shifting of boundaries between the state and the scholarly community also constitutes the main theme of Martina Deuchler's discussion of the debate on the role of the state in determining an individual scholar's mode of inquiry and the right of the state to limit the range of scholarship within the context of Neo-Confucian orthodoxy. How can one explain the several cases of state censorship of scholarship that arose in the seventeenth century and remained a focal point of contention at the court for several decades? The cen- sorship question was raised in the same atmosphere of tension and uncertainty that had produced the ritual controversy. In fact, it began with the same group of people, although it came to involve other scholars. The issue was embedded in the same concern for the redefinition of civilization and Korea's role in it but concentrated on the question of canonical tradition and hermeneutics. The controversy evolved around such questions as the rigidity or openness of the canonical tradition, the proper relationship of the individual scholar to the scholarly tradition, and the state's role in regulating the individual scholar's mode of acquiring knowledge and the scope of his scholarship.

The Korean state maintained a close relationship to the scholarly establishment yet, on the whole, did not dictate the course of scholarship. The three cases studied by Deuchler, which culminated in the burning of a book and its printing blocks, were isolated incidents, but they illustrate that although the role of the state was discussed and the final decision needed royal approval, the scholarly establishment initiated and carried out the debates. In this sense, these cases epitomized the extremely politicized culture of that time rather than a fundamental rearrangement of the boundary between the state and the scholarly community.

Deuchler places the three scholars accused of heterodoxy at an intellectual crossroads. Although they, especially Yun Hyu (1617–80), did not discard the critical methods used by Sung Neo-Confucians, by refusing to accept as truth anything other than what they themselves had researched, they presaged the "evidential research" (*kojŭng*; Chin. *k'ao-cheng*) scholarship of eighteenth-century Korea—a century in which Korea displayed a greater sense of intellectual confidence and diversity.[17]

The next three papers, devoted to three different religious communities, discuss the meaning of tolerance and persecution of non-hegemonic religions in Confucian Korea. What did it mean to be a marginalized group in a Confucian state? Robert Buswell discusses the way in which the strategies of later Buddhists differed from the strategies the Buddhist ecclesiastical community had adopted to survive when Neo-Confucianism became the state ideology at the beginning of Chosŏn and the state expelled Buddhism from public ground. It was not the rhetorical topoi of the Buddhist apologia that altered—the Buddhists continued to evoke a vision of fundamental harmony between Buddhism and Confucianism. Rather, it was the audience at which it was directed that changed. Whereas in early

Chosŏn such a vision was produced as a defense against Confucian oppression, by the time of Hyujŏng (1520-1604), the principal defender of Buddhism in the sixteenth century, it had become an inward-directed, protective strategy of survival. Interestingly, Hyujŏng turned to the indigenous ecumenical tradition, developed in the mid-Koryŏ period (twelfth century), and emphasized the interdependence of doctrinal study and meditative practice.

Boudewijn Walraven probes the domain of popular religion, in particular shamanic rituals, against the background of Korea's Confucianization, which he terms a "civilizing" process. What elements in this process made Confucians so sensitive and even hostile to popular religion? To answer this question, he studies the Confucians' attitudes toward spirits and suggests that rather than the shamans' views of spirits, it was their freewheeling practices that ran counter to the Confucians' insistence on social values and hierarchy and led to their eventual expulsion from the public realm. Yet, even popular religion absorbed elements of Confucian ritualism, and it was the increasing Confucianization of men, Walraven thinks, that left shamanic rituals in the hands of women. The feminization of shamanism may thus have been the product of a gender-segregated society in which practitioners and clients tended to be of the same sex.

The last chapter discusses the persecution of Catholics in the late eighteenth and early nineteenth centuries. Unlike the cases of Buddhism and popular religion, this persecution is a story of confrontation and conflict. Why could the Chosŏn state not accommodate Christianity, as it had Buddhism and popular religion? By the same token, why could Catholics not negotiate with the Confucian state? Don Baker probes these questions and seeks an answer in the framework of ideological assumptions of what was acceptable and what not. He sees this struggle as a collision between two fundamentally different philosophical systems, one of which stressed orthodoxy, and the other orthopraxis. As Baker makes clear, the Confucians and the Catholics operated with different philosophical systems of signification.

Baker discusses at length Chinese and Korean Confucian attitudes toward heterodox thought (*idan*) and shows that both the early critics of and the early converts to Catholicism emerged from T'oegye's school, the Namin. He probes the thought of Yi Ik (1681-1763) and Chŏng Yagyong (1762-1836), both of whom, although committed

Neo-Confucian scholars, showed themselves open to certain aspects of the new creed. Whereas Yi Ik remained skeptical, Chŏng Yagyong was willing to incorporate into his thought some theistic notions, although he, too, never abandoned the Confucian Classics. Beyond conceptual and rhetorical themes, the story of Korean Catholicism in the late Chosŏn is a remarkable chapter in the annals of church history. The first few converts were intellectuals, but soon, without benefit of missionaries, the new creed spread to all social classes. Despite repeated and severe government persecutions in the nineteenth century, the Catholic community persevered and survived into the twentieth century. To date, Korean Catholics boast 103 canonized saints, the fourth largest number after Italy, France, and Spain. The Confucian-Catholic collision that Baker discusses reveals an intriguing sociology of religious interaction, especially in view of the current popularity of Christianity, Protestant Christianity in particular, and its increasingly prevalent domestication of ritual in South Korea.

These six chapters were brought together here in the hope that each would shed light not only on its specific topic but also on the general intellectual and religious culture of late Chosŏn Korea. We, the authors of these essays, are aware that these contributions are preliminary inquiries. Nor do we, coming from different disciplines, claim consistency of approach. Rather, we have attempted to convey the notion that the late Chosŏn period was not a time of continuous decline but a time in which vigorous debates were conducted at various intellectual levels and in different quarters of society. We will be content if this volume spurs greater interest in late Chosŏn Korea.

# Private Academies and the State in Late Chosŏn Korea

## YŎNG-HO CH'OE

THE PRIVATE ACADEMIES (*sŏwŏn*) of Chosŏn Korea have received considerable scholarly attention in the past several decades. Most studies have concentrated on these academies as centers of Neo-Confucian scholarship and strongholds of scholars in rural areas. Since the private academies emerged in the mid-sixteenth century and prospered through the late nineteenth century under the auspices of the Neo-Confucian scholarly community, it is not surprising that they were studied in terms of the intellectual and social makeup of this community and their role in it.

The major studies of private academies offer different views on the subject. Yu Hongnyŏl, who pioneered the study of this topic in the 1930s, sees their development largely as the result of the withdrawal of the Confucian literati collectively known as the *sarim* (the forest of scholars) from national politics to avoid persecution. He cites three main reasons for the rise of the academies. First, a significant decline in the state educational system gave rise to a movement to revitalize education through private initiatives. Second, one strategy for Confucianizing Chosŏn society was to enshrine loyal and martyred officials who had become popular among the Neo-Confucian literati (as explained below, the enshrinement of distinguished Confucian personalities was a main feature of private academies). Third, a series of four purges of literati carried out during and after King Yŏnsan's (1494–1506) reign discouraged many Confucian scholars from seeking public office in the capital. Instead they chose a quiet life in rural surroundings and pursued their studies of Neo-Confucian sages.[1]

Yi T'aejin, on the other hand, views the rise of private academies more as a manifestation of the growth of the *sarim*. A new breed of scholar-officials, the *sarim* were more ideologically committed to the cause of Neo-Confucianism and were determined to realize the goals of the Confucian sages. In spite of setbacks suffered as the results of the four literati purges, *sarim* scholar-officials continued to gain political strength, and they founded private academies to further their ideological and political objectives.[2] Unlike Yu Hongyŏl, who in work published in the 1930s saw the private academies as a site of withdrawal from active political life, Yi T'aejin explains them as the locus for active promotion of ideological visions. More recently, Chŏng Manjo has argued that private academies developed as part of a conscious attempt by *sarim* scholars to further the Neo-Confucianization of Chosŏn society by "rectifying the mores of the scholar-officials" (*chŏng sasŭp*).[3]

The private academies, however, were not merely isolated places of learning; they functioned in a complex web of social and political relations and interacted constantly with the state at one extreme and local society on the other. Their relationship with the state was particularly complex. Although they shared a commitment to the Neo-Confucian vision of society, each operated with different notions of the public and private roles of scholars and scholarship and the relationship between scholarship and politics. Thus, although mutually supportive, they were also jealous of their respective powers, and they constantly negotiated the boundary between autonomy and control. They competed with each other for spheres of influence and hegemony over orthodoxy. The relative degree of autonomy and control as well as the relationship between scholarship and politics constantly shifted in response to social and political changes. What were these changes and what is their historical significance? In this chapter, I hope to show that these shifts represent negotiating points between the state and academies over their differing perceptions of the roles of scholars and scholarship. I discuss several areas in which these shifts occurred both in rhetoric and in practice from the mid-sixteenth century when the academies first appeared to the end of the eighteenth century, and their historical and cultural significations.

## The Rise of the Private Academies

The private academies were conceived in terms of and defined by the idea and rhetoric that Neo-Confucian scholarship was the moral foundation of society, and hence a sanctuary for its pursuit safe from outside intrusions should be provided. The first private academy, the Paegundong Academy, was founded by Chu Sebung (1495–1554), who left this account:

On the fourth day of the seventh month, in autumn, in the year [1541], I arrived at P'ungsŏng [P'unggi] [to take office as its magistrate]. That year, there was a great drought. The next year [in 1542], there was a great famine. In that same year, I set up a shrine for Hoehŏn [An Hyang (1243–1306)] at Paegundong. In the following year [1543], I had the [county] school building removed to the northern part of the county and established a private academy separately in front of the shrine to Hoehŏn.[4]

Establishing an academy at a time of economic hardship elicited criticism. In his defense, Chu Sebung cited the example of Chu Hsi (1130–1200), who, he said, had repaired the White Deer Grotto Academy (Pai-lu-tung shu-yüan) and established shrines for several former masters when the Sung was at war with the Chin. Chu Sebung then went on to explain:

Heaven produced a multitude of people. What makes them human beings is that they have education (*kyo*). Without education, [there can be no five cardinal principles]. . . . [Without education,] the three human bonds will decline, the nine rules [of governance] will decay, and the human race will perish forever. [Therefore,] all education must begin with venerating the sages. It is for this reason that the shrine was set up to respect virtue and the private academy was established to promote learning. Indeed, education is needed more urgently than famine relief in troubled times.[5]

It is significant that Chu justified academies as the font of morality and knowledge and that he made the enshrinement of a former sage an integral part of them. The Paegundong Academy became the model for other private academies, and it became customary for a new academy to establish a shrine for a noted worthy. An Hyang, the sage enshrined at the Paegundong Academy, was a famous scholar-official of the Koryŏ period and is credited with introducing the teachings of the Sung master Chu Hsi to Korea. Paegundong was his birthplace, and his ancestors and descendants had lived there for many generations. An Hyang thus represented both Confucian scholarship and local interests, a conjunction not always present in later instances of shrines to worthies.

Although Chu Sebung was a magistrate when he founded the academy, he was committed to the idea that the academy should enjoy autonomy. He also believed that it should possess the resources to choose students without being constrained by the financial status of applicants, and he began a campaign to secure an endowment for it.[6] After Chu left P'unggi, his successors as magistrate and the local people continued the campaign, and as a result, the academy received a large number of contributions in the form of land, books, precious metals, food products, and slaves from many different regions over many years, making it one of the richest private academies in Korea.[7] In 1550, while serving as magistrate of P'unggi country, Yi T'oegye (Hwang, 1501–70), the great Neo-Confucian scholar, formally requested that the throne grant a royal charter to the Paegundong Academy.[8] The charter, which was accompanied by a plaque bearing the name Sosu Academy, books, and several other additional items, signified state support for the academy's claim that it was a place for independent scholarship rather than a place where interference or control was executed.[9] The account in the *Myŏngjong sillok*, the Veritable Records for the reign of Myŏngjong (1545–67), which describes the establishment of the Sosu Academy, is explicit on this issue: "In order for Confucian scholars to pursue their scholarship, it is essential that they do so in surroundings of peace and quiet. If the provincial governor or the county magistrate, wishing to exalt study, prescribes restrictive rules for these scholars, it will only deprive them of their freedom and lead them astray from the proper way of cultivation. There should be no interference from outside."[10]

Following this recognition of the Sosu Academy, private academies were organized in many parts of the country either by important scholars or by groups of local scholars. Major academies founded before 1600 include the Imgo Academy, established in 1553 at Yŏngch'ŏn (Kyŏngsang province), which enshrined Chŏng Mongju (1337–92); the Tosan Academy, which was started by Yi T'oegye in 1574 in Yean (Kyŏngsang province) and where he himself was later enshrined; the Oksan Academy, founded in 1573 near Kyŏngju to enshrine Yi Ŏnjŏk (1491–1553); and the Todong Academy. The Todong Academy was first organized in 1564 as the Ssang-gye Academy at Hyŏnp'ung (Kyŏngsang province) and enshrined Kim Koengp'il (1454–1504). It was renamed Todong in 1604 when it was re-established at a new location, after the original academy had been destroyed during Hideyoshi's invasion of 1592–98.[11]

By the end of the sixteenth century, the private academy had struck deep roots in Korea and was accepted as an educational institution essential to the state and society. The importance of the academies was recognized and furthered even during the national crisis of Hideyoshi's invasion. In 1595, confronted with a desperate military situation caused by the Japanese invasion, King Sŏnjo (r. 1568–1608) ordered the conversion of what he called "nonessential private academies" to military training grounds.[12] This, however, met with strong opposition from the Office of the Censor-General (Saganwŏn), which insisted that "even in the midst of a war we must continue to nurture and train [scholars]. [Adherence to] the Way alone will sustain us, and now more than ever is it time to restore the Way."[13] The king in the end concurred with this request and rescinded his order.

### Rules and Regulations

From the beginning, it was assumed that each academy would draw up its own rules and regulations. These rules fell largely into two categories—those defining the principal objectives of the institution and those concerned with more practical issues, such as the criteria for admission and regulations for the students' daily life. For their larger objectives, almost all academies followed the lead of the Sosu Academy and adopted the "Articles of Learning" (*hsüeh-kuei*) prepared by Chu Hsi for his White Deer Grotto Academy.[14] Chu Hsi's "Articles of Learning," which Wing-tsit Chan describes as an excellent "summary of Confucian morality,"[15] consist of five basic principles of learning. The first article cites the five cardinal principles as the basis of instruction. The second reads: "Study extensively, inquire accurately, think it over carefully, sift it clearly, and practice it earnestly. This is the order of study." The third emphasizes sincerity and truthfulness in one's deeds and words as the bases for self-cultivation, and the fourth stresses the rectification of moral principle. The fifth draws on quotations from Confucius and Mencius. It reads: "Do not do to others what you do not wish them to do to you. If you do not succeed in your conduct, turn inward and seek for its cause there."[16] Yi T'oegye's later inclusion of Chu Hsi's "Articles of Learning" in his *Sŏnghak sipto* (Ten diagrams on sage learning) made it even more familiar to Korean scholars.[17] These articles were prominently displayed in the main study halls of academies as constant admonitions to the scholars who studied there.[18]

There was more variation in the rules and regulations concerning academic standards and codes of conduct for students. T'oegye and Yi I (Yulgok, 1536–84), two seminal Neo-Confucian scholars of the sixteenth century, were active in shaping private academies. Both established academies and wrote regulations for them.[19] Their rules became models for many other private academies in Korea and indicate their conceptions of what students' life in private academies should be.

Who was admitted to the private academies is of great significance. Admission standards varied considerably. Both the Sosu Academy and the Sŏak Academy (near Kyŏngju) had the same criteria for admission. First consideration went to those who had already obtained the *saengwŏn* (Classics licentiate) or *chinsa* (literary licentiate) degrees by passing the lower-level civil examination. Second priority was given to those who had passed the preliminary examination (*ch'osi*) in the lower-level civil examination. Finally, those who had not passed the preliminary examination were admitted if they could demonstrate a serious commitment to scholarship and good conduct and if they were recommended by recognized scholars.[20] These were very high criteria for admission and were obviously designed to attract elite scholars in the countryside. Since these admission qualifications were almost the same as those for Sŏnggyun'gwan, the government's Confucian Academy in the capital, these private academies apparently intended their academic programs to operate at the same level as the Confucian Academy.

Unlike the Sŏak and Sosu academies, which stressed the high academic standards for admission, the Ŭnbyŏng Study Hall (later reorganized as the Sohyŏn Academy) and the Munhŏn Academy, both in the Haeju area, emphasized a strong commitment to scholarship. The Munhŏn Academy specified that "all those who have a firm determination to pursue scholarship, regardless of whether they are old or young, are admitted subject to the approval of academy scholars [provided that] the reputation and conduct of the candidate are free from blame."[21]

Whether private academies admitted students of the commoner class is a subject of heated debate among historians studying the academies. The admission rules of the Munhŏn Academy indicate nothing on the matter, but those of the Ŭnbyŏng Study Hall stipulate: "As for rules of admission, all those who have a firm determination for scholarship are qualified for admission regardless of whether they are of scholar families (*sajok*) or commoners (*sŏryu*). Before admission, however, they must receive the approval of those who had previously been admitted."[22] This rule allowing commoners to enroll was apparently adopted by other private academies as well. The rules of admission for the Sŏksil Academy, founded in 1656 in Yangju to enshrine the Kim brothers Sangyong (1561–1637) and Sanghŏn (1570–1652), state that "anyone—regardless of whether he is old or young, of high birth (*kwi*) or low (*ch'ŏn*)—who has a firm determination to study will be admitted."[23] *Ch'ŏn* usually refers to men of low birth status such as slaves, but it is believed that here it indicates "men of lower status" in relation to the *yangban*—namely commoners, not slaves or others of low birth status. The same rules were adopted by the Musŏng Academy at Chŏngŭp in Chŏlla province.[24]

Pak Sech'ae (1631–95), an influential scholar-official, wrote the rules governing the Munhoe Academy, which enshrined Chu Hsi along with Yi Yulgok, Sŏng Hon (1535–98), and others at Paech'ŏn in Hwanghae province. Its admission rule is basically the same as that of the Sŏksil and Musŏng academies; it was open to committed scholars "without regard for their high or low birth." Pak Sech'ae later added an explanatory note: " 'Men of high birth' (*kwi*) refers to members of scholar families (*sajok*), and 'men of low birth' (*ch'ŏn*) refers to *kyosaeng* and *sŏp'a chi ryu*."[25] *Kyosaeng* refers to Confucian students in the public schools in the county seats (*hyanggyo*). These were mostly commoners after the mid-seventeenth century. *Sŏp'a chi ryu* here means commoners. Pak Sech'ae later explained that he had added this gloss after a group of *kyosaeng* in Paech'ŏn county formally complained to the local office that the use of the term "low birth " in the admission rules might be interpreted as suggesting that they were lowborn.[26]

Did these rules signify flexibility concerning the social class of students or were they used more metaphorically to stress the serious commitment of students? There is no evidence that the relatively open admission rules were ever observed. Thus, until the social backgrounds of students enrolled at the academies are known, there is no way of gauging how open admissions were. What is observable is that academies had different admission rules and that these rules were stipulated by the individual academies without guidance from the central government.

## Curriculum and Publication of Books

What subjects did students study? What were the curricula of the Korean academies? Were they different or similar to the one at the public schools? Was there variety or uniformity among academies? Who decided the curriculum of the academy? Fortunately, the survival of a few academy regulations gives a general picture of what the Korean students studied at these private academies.

As far as I can determine, there is no information available on the subjects studied at the Sosu Academy, the oldest in Korea. However, the collected works of Yi T'oegye contain his Rules of the Isan Academy (Isan wŏn'gyu), which reflect his ideas of what a Korean academy ought to offer. The first article prescribes the basic subjects to be studied as well as the objectives of the academy.

For all students, the Four Books and the Five Classics should be studied as the roots and origins [of all things], and the *Elementary Learning (Sohak)* and the *Family Ritual (Karye)* should be studied as the door. While observing the state policy of nurturing talent, they should uphold the meticulous teachings of the sages and worthies. Aware that all the goodness is endowed within us, we firmly believe that the old way can be realized today. [Therefore,] everyone should exert his utmost effort to comprehend in his mind and heart the essence and usefulness of learning. Although it is necessary to study various histories, philosophies, collective writings, literary works, prose, and poems and also to prepare for the civil examinations, these should be studied as things of secondary importance. . . . One should constantly exhort oneself lest one becomes indolent. Books that are depraved, insidious, or licentious are not allowed into the academy lest one's pursuit of the Way be disturbed and one's determination confused.[27]

The Sŏak Academy, which was founded in 1561 in Kyŏngju, used this same article verbatim as its rules.[28] This is not surprising since Yi T'oegye was closely associated with the founding of this academy as well. The curricula at these academies were similar to that at the public schools, which also consisted of the Four Books and the Five Classics and the philosophical works of the Sung masters.[29]

Yi Yulgok did not prescribe a specific curriculum for either the Ŭnbyŏng Study Hall or the Munhoe Academy. For the Ŭnbyŏng Study Hall, the rule states only that "any writing or thought that is not the work of the sages and worthies is not allowed within the academy."[30] Instead, Yulgok wrote the *Important Methods of Eliminating Ignorance (Kyŏngmong yogyŏl)* in 1577 and *A Model for Schools (Hakkyo mobŏm)* in 1582. *Important Methods* was meant for students of all ages; *A Model* includes recommendations for the running of schools, but a larger portion is devoted to the instruction of students. Eventually *A Model* came to be widely used as a basic guide for students in both public schools and private academies. Both works provide extensive guidelines on how to study, the core curriculum, and the sequential order in which the books should be studied. Both are more or less the same, but the list in *Important Methods* is a little more detailed: the *Elementary Learning*, the *Great Learning*, the *Analects*, the *Mencius*, the *Doctrine of the Mean*, and the *Odes*, followed by the ritual texts, the *History*, the *Changes*, and the *Spring and Autumn Annals*. Then Yulgok recommends various Sung philosophical works such as *Reflections on Things at Hand (Chin-ssu lu)*, and the *Heart Classic (Hsin ching)*.[31] The core curriculum that Yulgok proposed is quite similar to the one at the public schools and to those prescribed by Yi T'oegye. However, its significance lies in the sequence of the books he sets forth. JaHyun Kim Haboush attributes this to the mentality of sixteenth-century Korea, a conviction that there was a right way to do things and a determination to find and follow it.[32] In any case, many private academies adopted this practice, and it became customary for each academy to prescribe a sequence of books. Pak Sech'ae's curriculum for the Munhoe Academy[33] and Kim Wŏnhaeng's (1702–72)[34] for the Sŏksil Academy show a similar concern for the core curriculum and the sequential order in which it was to be studied.

As can be seen from the curricula, almost all Korean private academies placed a great emphasis on the study of the School of Nature and Principle (Sŏngnihak) of Sung China. The academies seem to have adopted core curricula from the beginning, although it was Yi Yulgok who first prescribed an exact order. Although neither the curriculum nor the sequence varied greatly, this uniformity was self-imposed. As academies became more self-consciously zealous in their role of defining Neo-Confucian orthodoxy, they required students to devote their full attention to the study of Neo-Confucian teachings and did not permit them to read unrelated materials. Thus, both the Sŏksil and the Musŏng academies, echoing the rule at the Ŭnbyŏng Study Hall, stipulated that "any book that is not by the sages and worthies and any idea that does not deal with Neo-Confucian teachings are not allowed within the academy."[35]

Private academies also promoted active scholarship by their students and scholars, and they emerged as centers for the publication of scholarly books. The *Nup'an ko* (Bibliography of printed books) of Sŏ Yugu (1764–1845) lists 167 different titles published by 78 different academies.[36] These publications dealt mostly with the philosophy of the School of Nature and Principle. Academies seem to have enjoyed complete autonomy in choosing which books to publish and the manner in which they distributed these publications. They customarily exchanged publications with one another.

### Life in a Private Academy

The private academies seem to have placed a great emphasis on maintaining their schools as an autonomous and sacred space in which students were to pursue their studies with no interference or interruption. This began with the regulation of students' lives. The Sŏksil and Munhoe academies prescribe a rather strict regimen.[37] Students were to arise at daybreak and clear their bedding. Younger members were to clean the rooms in which they slept. After washing, they put on their formal caps and gowns and went to the shrine to pay homage to the enshrined worthies. They then exchanged bows before returning to their rooms to study. Seniority played an important role in the interaction among students, and the younger ones were required to yield in most things from seating arrangements for meals to housecleaning chores. Students appear to have studied individually most of the time. They were expected to devote their entire hearts and minds to their books while maintaining proper posture and decorum at all times. They were not allowed to talk during study hours. In leisure periods after meals and in between studies, they were permitted to exchange views on issues concerning righteousness and principle, to compose prose and poetry or practice calligraphy, to examine books in the library, or to walk around the courtyard. After supper, they resumed their studies, continuing until late at night.

There was a monthly lecture and discussion session, which was held on the sixteenth day of every month in the case of the Sŏksil

Academy. For this session, each student attending the academy was assigned certain chapters to study beforehand; those under thirty years of age had to recite the assigned passage from memory and discuss it before the instructor. Older students could use the text. Their recitations and discussions were evaluated and graded into four categories. Older scholars who did not wish to recite the text were also allowed to participate and were encouraged to take part in the discussion. Visitors were also permitted to attend the lecture session.

Discussion was an important part of the academy life. The gist of the monthly discussions was recorded, and some of these records indicate that these sessions were extremely lively; students raised many serious questions, pointing out ambiguities and apparent inconsistencies in the writings of former worthies. For example, one topic discussed in a session at the Sŏksil Academy concerned the nature of men and material objects. A student, Yu Hŏnju, cited Chu Hsi's remark in his discussion of the *Doctrine of the Mean* that the natures of men and material objects are the same. Then he asked, "Why is it that Master Chu speaks of the nature of humanity, and the righteousness, propriety, and wisdom that are parts of human nature, but he does not extend this nature as an inherent aspect of material objects?" Another student, Chŏng Yŏngŭi, pointed out that the passages on the inherent goodness of men in the *Great Learning* and the *Elementary Learning* contain no reference to the nature of material objects. Yu Hanjŏng, a third student, commented by citing passages from the *Doctrine of the Mean*. At another session, more than one hundred topics were discussed by Kim Wŏnhaeng, the instructor, and the students.[38] This was indeed an impressive academic meeting. Records of lectures given by Pak Sech'ae at the Munhoe and Hwagok academies suggest equally serious debates on various philosophical issues.[39]

In addition to the regular monthly lecture session, students at private academies pursued academic inquiries by sending written questions to distinguished scholars to solicit their views on issues that had arisen in discussion. The collected works of Kim Wŏnhaeng and Pak Sech'ae include responses to inquiries from students at several academies.[40] This suggests that students at private academies were encouraged to seek guidance from scholars of repute.

Private academies apparently sought independence from state control by remaining aloof from the civil service examinations.

Although academies probably had different views on the matter, preparations for the civil service examinations were generally discouraged. As noted above, in the rules of the Isan and Sŏak academies, Yi T'oegye placed study for the civil service examinations secondary to the study of Neo-Confucian teachings. Subsequently, other influential scholars much more actively discouraged the use of the academies to prepare for the examinations. Yi Yulgok unequivocally stated in his prescriptions for the Ŭnbyŏng Study Hall, "Anyone who wants to study for the civil service examinations must do so somewhere outside [the academy]."[41] This same rule was adopted by both the Sŏksil and the Musŏng academies.[42] Pak Sech'ae was even more emphatic in discouraging study for the civil service examinations:

The reason that former sages required that private academies be independent of public schools was that students at public schools studied for the civil service examinations, and this prevented them from devoting their effort to the study of [sagely] learning. If private academies were to continue this obsolete practice, in the end there would be no place to study [sagely] learning and the root [of all learning] would be eradicated. Therefore, it would be better to build a separate hall outside the private academy for those who wish to prepare for the civil service examinations, and these people should not be allowed to enter the lecture hall [of the academy].[43]

This view was affirmed by others. The great seventeenth-century scholar of practical learning Yu Hyŏngwŏn (1622–73) wrote:

The private academies of today did not exist in ancient times. As education declined in later generations, the public schools were reduced to a place where people sought personal fame and selfish interest through the civil service examinations. Those scholars who possessed righteous ambition were compelled to seek quiet places elsewhere in remote regions where they built study facilities to pursue scholarship. This is how the private academies originated.[44]

Despite this disclaimer, however, it would be premature to conclude that the academies did not prepare students for the examinations. There were hundreds of academies throughout Korea, including many in the region near the capital, and there must have been geographical and temporal variation in their practices. Suffice it to say that the academies thought of themselves not as playing a supporting role in the training of personnel for the state bureaucracy but as upholding Neo-Confucian orthodoxy and advancing scholarship.

In fact, the academies made every attempt to stay out of politics by prohibiting students from speaking about such matters. Both the Sŏksil and the Musŏng academies stipulated that "one should not speak for or against court affairs and government appointments" and that "one should not speak for or against the local magistrate and his staff, nor of their deeds, good or mistaken."[45] Similarly, Pak Sech'ae emphatically prohibited Munhoe Academy students from even visiting the local magistrate on matters concerning their academy.[46] The government also favored this separation between politics and scholarship. As noted above, King Myŏngjong ordered that the governor and the local magistrates not interfere with the affairs of academies.[47]

## The Proliferation of Private Academies

The concept of the private academy as a center of Neo-Confucian scholarship and moral cultivation caught the imagination of Neo-Confucian scholars in Korea, who established them in all parts of the country during the seventeenth and eighteenth centuries. By the middle of the seventeenth century, there was virtually no administrative district without a private academy, and many counties had two or more. The private academy movement became so popular in fact that, according to Right State Councilor Min Am (1636–94), "scholars in various regions regarded it as shameful if their counties did not have a private academy."[48] Maintaining a private academy in one's home county became a matter of pride for local scholars, and they competed to establish them.

As the private academies came to be accepted as important educational institutions, their numbers grew by leaps and bounds. Chŏng Manjo has made a careful study to determine the number of academies and shrines (*sau*) established during the reign of each king (see Table 1).[49] The number of newly organized academies increased steadily during the seventeenth century, rising sharply during the reigns of Sukchong (r. 1674–1720) and Kyŏngjong (r. 1720–24). Chŏng Manjo also gives a breakdown of the number of academies established in the various provinces from 1609 till 1800 (see Table 2).[50] Private academies were largely concentrated in the three southern provinces of Kyŏngsang, Chŏlla, and Ch'ungch'ŏng; these provinces accounted for nearly 70 percent of the total number. Kyŏngsang province, with 257, alone had more than one-third of the

Table 1
*Number of New Private Academies by Reign*

| Rulers | Number | Per Year |
|---|---|---|
| Myŏngjong (1545–67) | 17 | 0.8 |
| Sŏnjo (1569–1608) | 82 | 2.1 |
| Kwanghae (1608–22) | 38 | 2.9 |
| Injo (1623–49) | 55 | 2.1 |
| Hyojong (1649–59) | 37 | 4.1 |
| Hyŏnjong (1659–74) | 72 | 5.1 |
| Sukchong (1674–1720) | 327 | 7.3 |
| Kyŏngjong (1720–24) | 29 | 9.7 |
| Yŏngjo (1724–76) | 159 | 3.1 |
| Chŏngjo (1776–1800) | 7 | 0.3 |
| TOTAL | 823 | 3.2 |

Table 2
*The Number of Private Academies and*
*Shrines by Province, 1609–1800*

| Province | Number | Percent of total |
|---|---|---|
| Kyŏngsang | 257 | 35.5% |
| Chŏlla | 142 | 19.6 |
| Ch'ungch'ŏng | 101 | 14.0 |
| Kyŏnggi | 53 | 7.3 |
| Hwanghae | 39 | 5.4 |
| Kangwŏn | 43 | 5.9 |
| P'yŏngan | 56 | 7.7 |
| Hamgyŏng | 33 | 4.6 |
| TOTAL | 724 | 100.0% |

total. But even Hamgyŏng province, a remote border region, had 33 academies. Since there were eighteen counties in Hamgyŏng province, many counties had more than one academy.

If the emergence of academies in all parts of the country had a significant effect on disseminating and popularizing Neo-Confucian teachings in rural Korea, their drastic increase in number seems to have presented serious problems. In 1657, the first systematic criticism was leveled against private academies by Sŏ P'irwŏn (1614–71), the governor of Ch'ungch'ŏng province. Sŏ pointed out what he regarded as four grave deficiencies resulting from the growing popularity of private academies. The first was a general neglect of the public schools.

A difference in degree of importance between public schools and private academies has arisen. All the rural members of scholar families who have some talent and literary skills are registered with private academies, and they are called academy scholars (*wŏnyu*). They regard public schools as if they are inns and treat the public school students as if they are slaves. In places of sacrificial offerings to former sages [i.e., the *hyanggyo*] weeds and grass grow, and the places designated by the state to promote scholarship [*hyanggyo*] have been reduced to wasteland.

The second was the loss of men who would otherwise serve military duties for the state.

[Private academies] actively recruit idle men regardless of whether they are commoners or lowborn to keep them as *pono* [auxiliary slaves]. [Private academies] use them at will as servants and take possession of whatever they produce. Such practices deprive [the state] of men for the military tax, and thus a multitude of men clamor [to work for private academies in order to avoid the military tax] until they get what they wish.

Private academies became places of refuge from the burdensome military duties, thus depriving the state of badly needed male adults. As we shall see below, this became a serious problem for the Chosŏn government.

The third point concerned abuses in the selection of persons enshrined in private academies: "The individuals enshrined for reverence have not been selected through open discussion. Instead, some [have been chosen merely because] they are either descendants [of worthies] or ancestors of [the organizers], and some [were chosen] only to flatter favorites." Sŏ maintained that since the individuals honored at private academies were often not well qualified, disputes and even brawls sometimes arose. He insisted that such situations harmed mores and morality. The fourth point was that the sacrificial rites offered in spring and autumn by the private academies imposed heavy expenses on the local governments since local magistrates were obliged to provide provisions and supplies.

Governor Sŏ proposed that because of these abuses, the state should intervene in two areas. He suggested that those enshrined individuals whose merits rendered them unworthy of enshrinement at academies should be honored instead at village shrines (hyangsa), and that village shrines in which unsuitable individuals were enshrined should be abolished. He also pointed out that the same individual was frequently enshrined at more than one academy, and he proposed an honoree be limited to enshrinement in at most one private academy within each province. He also recommended that the government scrutinize the qualifications of prospective candidates and approve their enshrinement before allowing the construction of a new academy to begin. He then suggested punishments for those who violated these rules. His second item called for refraining from the use of all auxiliary slaves: "All the so-called wŏnno . . . should be released from service to the academies and reassigned to military ranks so as to bring them under state control."[51]

Sŏ P'irwŏn's memorial set off a long and heated debate. The Ministry of Rites opposed Sŏ's proposal to abolish shrines, but it agreed that some form of state control was in order. The ministry resoundingly seconded the proposal requiring permission to establish a new academy or village shrine, terming it "an extremely good idea," as well as the suggestion that violators be punished. It recommended that the number of the auxiliary slaves be limited to seven for a chartered academy, five for an unchartered academy, and two for a village shrine and that all other servants be returned to their villages to pay the military tax. Finally, it endorsed Sŏ's proposal that the government not provide material assistance for the sacrificial rites of private academies. King Hyojong (r. 1649–59) approved these recommendations.[52]

Two officials in the Office of Special Advisers, Yi Chŏngyŏng (1616–86) and Min Chŏngjung (1628–92), however, vehemently opposed Sŏ P'irwŏn's proposal, labeling it "useless words." They acknowledged that there might have been one or two problems, but maintained that private academies were "the fountainhead of the nation's morality" and that the worthies enshrined in the academies inspired later generations to emulate them. Therefore, there should be no attempt to abolish any of them. They then demanded the dismissal of Sŏ P'irwŏn from office and the removal of the senior officials in the Ministry of Rites for endorsing Sŏ's proposal.[53] This controversy was taken up by high state councilors and other officials, but no clear-cut resolution was reached.[54]

## Private Academies and State Control

Sŏ P'irwŏn's critique of the private academies was based on the perception that academies encroached upon a space that should fall under state control—hegemony over orthodox education, appropriation of taxable manpower, and the selection of worthy individuals for enshrinement. The disagreement among government agencies and officials manifested in the debate seems to have been embedded more in differing views of the roles of the state and academies than in different assessments of the situation. From some time in the mid-seventeenth century, the perception that academies were proliferating too rapidly seems to have become widespread. An examination of documents such as the *Records of the Private Academies* (*Sŏwŏn tŭngnok*) reveals that this was viewed as a serious problem and that warnings were constantly issued against their excessive number.[55] In the face of the continued proliferation of academies and the problems they posed, the state was perforce compelled to confront the question of adopting some measure of control. The question was what it should check and how.

The state seems to have been unconcerned that it was the private academies rather than public schools that defined Neo-Confucian scholarship and education in rural areas. This may have been due to the fact that the Confucian Academy in the capital remained the ultimate symbol of state orthodoxy. In any case, there seems to have been a clear demarcation in prestige and quality between the private academies and the public schools—students of the yangban class and/or of serious intentions went to private academies, and those enrolled at public schools lacked prestige and were deficient in scholarship. This trend was observed as early as the sixteenth century,[56] and by the seventeenth century everyone seems to have accepted it as a given.[57]

The state was willing to acknowledge the prestige of private academies and, in matters considered to be the privileges that accrued to superior scholarship, to extend preferential treatment to them. Exempting the students at academies from paying the military tax was one such perquisite. The exemption was perhaps the most coveted privilege of late Chosŏn society, and soon it was felt that the academies were being used as havens for military dodgers. A comparison of the different ways the state handled this problem for academies and for public schools is revealing. Before the emergence of private academies, all students enrolled at public schools were exempted from the military tax.[58] It was felt that because of this privilege, many students flocked to the public schools to escape the tax, causing a significant decline in academic standards. In order to screen military tax dodgers, the so-called *kogang* test system was devised at the public schools to detect delinquency and to determine if students met minimum academic standards. Students who failed this test became liable for the military tax. This rule, however, was not applied to academy students. In 1644, the Ministry of Rites specified that "ever since the beginning, the private academies have not been the same as the public schools, and therefore the system of requiring those who fail the periodic test (*kogang*) to bear the military tax is not applied [to academy students]."[59]

This preferential treatment made enrollment at private academies even more desirable, and from the mid-seventeenth century, concern over the abuse of this privilege grew. In an instruction issued in 1675, the Border Defense Council declared: "The non-quota students of all public schools today are dodgers of the [military] tax. They do not attend public schools. Instead they try to enroll in private academies in order to avoid the annual *kogang* test given by the provincial inspectors. This abuse has become a serious problem, a situation that is truly deplorable."[60] According to the Ministry of Rites, this situation was especially bad in the southern provinces, where the private academies were filled by many who were merely avoiding military obligations.[61] On another occasion in 1707, Yun Segi (1647–1712), then the minister of rites, stated that "because the students of the academies are given preferential treatment over those of the public schools, people compete with each other to gain admission to academies. Academies thus have become a haven for dodgers of the military tax."[62]

Concerns about private academies soon grew to include the deterioration of academic standards and the scholarly atmosphere at the academies. In 1675, an official observed, "Since the morality of the country has deteriorated, people have no respect for the law. They have built so many private academies without scruple that nowadays there is hardly any empty space left in the country. Students of public schools who are not literate vie with each other to gain admission as academy students to avoid the military tax."[63] In 1738, Pak Munsu (1691–1756), the minister of military affairs, leveled an even harsher criticism against the academies.

Private academies nowadays are established with magnificent structures by the sons of former high ministers and by wealthy individuals who try to avoid their military obligations. . . . Several hundred treacherous individuals belong to one academy simply to escape their military tax. They collect money and grain as if they were tax officials. They have made the academy into a place where they cook chickens, slaughter animals, and make themselves drunk. Fearful of these people, the local magistrates avoid them.[64]

Similar accounts abound. In a memorial presented in 1793, Yi Pokhyu, an official in the Ministry of Rites, stated:

Private academies are places for the promotion of scholarship. But lately the practice of scholarly exchanges among students has wholly been neglected [at academies]. Private academies have been reduced to places for drinking and eating by loafers. As many as several hundred people at each academy are exploiting them to escape their military tax. A severe drain on the number of military tax bearers in various counties is caused by this phenomenon.[65]

Even if both Yi Pokhyu and Pak Munsu exaggerated the number of tax avoiders at private academies, the unrestrained growth in the number of students was increasingly viewed as a serious problem. The state attempted to classify students at academies as resident and nonresident students, just as in the case of public schools. In 1699, Yu Sangun (1636–1707) proposed returning all the nonresident students of academies to the military registers. King Sukchong approved Yu's proposal,[66] although it is not clear how effective this measure was. Another device the government introduced to deal with this problem was to limit the number of students admitted to academies by setting up quotas. In 1710, King Sukchong issued a decree prescribing the maximum number of students as 30 for academies whose enshrined worthies were included in the shrine of the Confucian Academy, 20 for academies that had received a royal charter, and 15 for the academies that had no royal charter.[67] It is notable that the state made no attempt to administer the *kogang* at private academies or to interfere with admission criteria.

Another area of contestation between the state and the academies concerned enshrinement. Ever since Chu Sebung had established a shrine for An Hyang as an integral part of the Sosu Academy, virtually every private academy in Korea had established a shrine for a Confucian worthy or worthies within its compound. Originally there was a difference in the roles and functions of academies and shrines. The academy was a place where scholars gathered for the purpose of pursuing scholarship; a shrine was a structure that honored certain worthies whose distinguished scholarship served as an ideal that academy scholars strove to emulate.[68] To renew their commitment to the ideals of the enshrined worthies, academy members made sacrificial offerings in spring and autumn. However, although all private academies maintained a shrine, not all shrines were attached to academies.[69] These independent shrines proliferated.

The sort of individuals selected for enshrinement seems to have changed over time as well. In the earlier period, enshrinement was based on distinguished scholarly achievement. Most academies established during the sixteenth century chose to honor individuals known for their scholarship in Neo-Confucian teachings, such as An Hyang at Sosu, Chŏng Mongju at Imgo, Yi T'oegye at Tosan, Yi Ŏnjŏk at Oksan, Kim Koengp'il at Okch'ŏn, and Ch'oe Ch'ung (984–1068) at Munhŏn. Notable individuals who had had distinguished careers in government service were not eligible for enshrinement unless they had attained equal distinction for their scholarship. Yi Sik (1584–1647), the minister of rites, confirmed this in a memorial he submitted in 1644: "Initially, the private academy was established as the site where scholars could cultivate their scholarship in quiet surroundings. Those honored by enshrinement were always selected from those who were well-known in their times as men of exemplary scholarship and virtue."[70]

During the seventeenth and eighteenth centuries, enshrinement was no longer limited to men of scholarly achievement. Those selected were frequently individuals who had served as government officials and had no notable academic distinction. In 1700, Right State Councilor Sin Wan (1646–1707) commented on this change:

[In the past,] all those who were enshrined in private academies were chosen from those who distinguished themselves in Confucian scholarship. Recently, however, this has not been the case. Those who, while serving as provincial governors and county magistrates, exerted great influence upon Confucian students and made notable achievements in their public careers are also permitted to be enshrined. Not all those who are enshrined are men of scholarship. Even such individuals as the late prime ministers Yi Wŏnik [1547–1634], Yi Hangbok [1556–1618], and Yi Tŏkhyŏng [1561–1613], who were not primarily known for their scholarship, are now enshrined.[71]

In some cases the enshrined included native sons of little or no significant achievement, and in other cases wealthy and influential families sought to honor their own ancestors with enshrinement.

More significantly, however, as factional conflict intensified, partisan considerations played an increasingly important role.

In a study of those responsible for organizing new academies and shrines as well as their motivations, Chŏng Manjo has divided the organizers of shrines into two categories. The first were local officials who set up shrines, mostly for martyred individuals such as Yi Sunsin (1545–98) and Chŏng Mongju, to honor their loyalty to country and principle. Such cases, however, were small in number and unimportant. Most shrines were erected by private individuals, who were divided into three subgroups. The first consisted of descendants of the enshrined worthy. To have a family member enshrined as a worthy enhanced the pride and prestige of the kin group and helped to bring about kin harmony and solidarity. The second group consisted of disciples of the enshrined individual. In the hope of continuing the academic and political precepts of their teacher, disciples often organized an academy with a shrine for their teacher. Since the philosophical views of influential individuals were invariably tied to the political debates of the time, these academies often became involved in factional conflict. The third group consisted of local individuals who attempted to gain political influence in their region by establishing an academy in the name of a well-known personage. By identifying themselves with the enshrined worthy, these local leaders hoped to gain the political support of members of the lineage of the enshrined, who were usually influential and powerful.[72] My examination of virtually the same materials that Professor Chŏng used has led me to similar conclusions.

Let us look at some examples of enshrinement. First, lineage affiliation was an important factor. The Anbong yŏngdang in Sŏngju in Kyŏngsang province is a good example. Anbong yŏngdang enshrined eighteen notable members of the Sŏngsan Yi, spanning fourteen generations from Yi Changgyŏng, a Koryŏ official, to Yi Kwangjŏk (1628–71). (Sŏngju is the ancestral seat of the Sŏngsan Yi.) Founded in 1581, Anbong yŏngdang was destroyed during the Hideyoshi invasion, but was rebuilt in 1606 by the provincial governor, Yi Tŏgon, who was a nonagnatic descendant of the Sŏngsan Yi. Afterwards it was maintained and protected by both the agnatic and the nonagnatic descendants of the Sŏngsan Yi.[73] Another example is the Samgang Academy at Miryang in Kyŏngsang province, first established in 1563, which enshrined five Min brothers. Not much is known about these brothers except that they lived during the reign of King Chungjong (r. 1504-44) and spent their lives together amicably at Samgang. Apparently they held no governmental office, nor were they known for scholarship. Their fraternal affection was a good enough reason to immortalize them.[74]

Other academies were organized by the disciples of those enshrined or by those who followed their teachings in the hope of promoting those teachings. Oksan Academy was founded in 1572 to enshrine Yi Ŏnjŏk at An'gang, near Kyŏngju in Kyŏngsang province, by his disciples,[75] and Tŏkch'ŏn Academy, which enshrined Cho Sik (1501-72), was founded in 1576 at Chinju in Kyŏngsang province by Cho's followers.[76] Hwangsan Academy in Ch'ungch'ŏng province was established to enshrine Kim Changsaeng (1548-1631) by his disciples because Kim often visited Hwangsan.[77] Hwayang Academy is a classic example of an academy organized by disciples of the enshrined. Founded in 1695, Hwayang Academy enshrined Song Siyŏl (1607-89) in the scenic valley of Hwayangdong, near Ch'ŏngju in Ch'ungch'ŏng province. Song's faithful disciples Kwŏn Sangha (1641-1721), Chŏng Ho (1648-1736), and others were responsible for starting this academy. Hwayangdong was chosen because it was Song Siyŏl's favorite place of retreat, where he meditated and taught his followers.[78]

Third, geographic connections with the worthy to be enshrined also led to the establishment of an academy. The birthplace of a distinguished individual was often a favorite site for an academy dedicated to his honor. As we have seen earlier, Sosu Academy, the first private academy in Korea, was organized at Sunhŭng, where the enshrined worthy An Hyang was born and where his descendants lived for many generations. Chŏng Mongju, whom many Chosŏn scholars regarded as the father of Neo-Confucianism in Korea, was born in Yŏngch'ŏn, Kyŏngsang province. In 1553, local scholars, officials, and others pooled their resources to organize a private academy on the site where Chŏng Mongju had been born and where he had studied in his youth. This academy was later named the Imgo Academy.[79] The place at which a worthy attained a notable achievement was also a favorite site for enshrinement. Both Noryang and T'ongyŏng on the southern coast were important places for Yi Sunsin, the great naval hero of the Japanese invasion, the former being the place where he was killed in his last battle and the latter where he had his naval command. At both places, a shrine was established for Yi Sunsin by local people, and King Hyŏnjong granted both a charter with the same title, "Loyal and Brave" (Ch'ungnyŏl), in 1663.[80] A visit by an eminent person could also result in enshrinement. Set up initially as a study hall, Kosan Academy in Kyŏngsang province was elevated to an academy after a visit by Yi T'oegye. After its destruction during the Japanese invasion, it was rebuilt in 1690 to enshrine Chŏng Kyŏngse (1563–1633), who had visited there while serving as governor of the province.[81] A place of exile was often selected for an enshrinement. Kim Ch'angjip (1648–1722), a powerful leader of the Noron, was briefly exiled to remote Puryŏng in Hamgyŏng province. In 1771, a group of scholars in Puryŏng circulated a letter proposing to establish an academy in honor of Kim Ch'angjip. The letter stated that "it would be a shame for our community" if an academy was not organized for this "great worthy" at the site where he spent his exile. This private academy was named Ch'unghyŏn Academy.[82] Sometimes marriage with a local woman was considered adequate grounds. Kim Ilson (1464–98), a victim of the Literary Purge of 1498, was widely admired by *sarim* scholars for his uprightness and courage. Among the many shrines that honored him, one at Mokch'ŏn in Ch'ungch'ŏng province was unique in that it enshrined Kim Ilson because "he, a man of Yŏngnam, married a local woman."[83]

As private academies and shrines grew popular, their founders grew quite resourceful in finding reasons for enshrinement. But as the number of academies and shrines proliferated, there were bound to be abuses. For example, in 1645, the governor of Chŏlla province reported that a Sin Kyŏngjik and a Sŏng Kyŏngch'ang had established an academy enshrining their grandfather, who did not meet any qualification, next to a public school. When, following public outcries, the county magistrate, Pak Changwŏn, had the building destroyed, they started a campaign to remove the magistrate and even mobilized a mob to destroy one of the buildings attached to the magistrate's office.[84] It was against this background that Sŏ P'irwŏn urged King Hyojong in 1657 that organizers be required to obtain the state's approval before constructing shrines or academies.

Private academies represented multiple interest groups, however, and there were many instances in which state approval of the enshrined had no effect in reducing tensions stemming from conflicts of interests among these groups. Since the reasons for constructing academies were diverse, there were instances in which different groups competed for the same site. Perhaps the most serious incident arose in the mid-eighteenth century when members of the Sŏin faction attempted to establish an academy for Kim Sanghŏn in the city of Andong.[85]

The Andong region in Kyŏngsang province was known during the later part of the Chosŏn dynasty as the heartland of the Yŏng-nam school of Neo-Confucianism. The proposed site was Yean, near Andong, where Yi T'oegye had been born and had spent much of his long scholarly life. Influenced by the teachings of T'oegye, scholars in this region generally adhered to his philosophy in the academic debates on such issues as the primacy of principle over material force (*i-ki*) that raged in Korea during the seventeenth and eighteenth centuries. In the factional politics of the late Chosŏn dynasty, the followers of Yi T'oegye's philosophy were usually identified with the Namin.[86] In the struggle for power, however, the Namin were constantly outmaneuvered by the Sŏin except on a few brief occasions and were forced into retirement most of the time. As the sense of alienation grew pervasive among scholars in Kyŏngsang province, Andong became the center of the embittered Namin, who harbored resentment toward their political opponents, who controlled the central government.[87]

In 1738, with the support of the provincial governor and the county magistrate, several local persons headed by one An T'aek-chun attempted to establish an academy to enshrine Kim Sanghŏn. A moral purist known for his dedication to principle and loyalty, Kim Sanghŏn was a leader of the Sŏin in his lifetime and was the grandfather of Kim Suhang (1629–89) and the great-grandfather of Kim Ch'angjip, both of whom were powerful leaders of the Noron faction, an offshoot of the Sŏin. Andong was the Kim family's ancestral seat and also the place to which Kim Sanghŏn retired after Korea's humiliating defeat in the Manchu invasion of 1637.[88] (He had advocated fighting the Manchu to the last man rather than surrendering.) Hence there was ample justification in prevailing practice for establishing an academy dedicated to him, even though there were no less than twelve academies within the county of Andong at the time.[89]

But the plan provoked a violent reaction in Andong. More than a thousand angry people surrounded the magistrate's office, heaping insults on the officials there and then destroying the shrine to Kim.[90] The construction of an academy in honor of Kim Sanghŏn in Andong was regarded by the local people as a politically motivated action by the Noron to secure a foothold in the heartland of the Namin. This incident in turn touched off an angry debate within the court between the Noron and Soron factions that threatened King Yŏngjo's (r. 1724–76) policy of "grand harmony" (*t'angp'yŏng*).[91] (A split within the Sŏin had led to the formation of the Noron and the Soron factions in the late seventeenth century; the Noron in general pursued an uncompromising position toward the Namin, whereas the Soron sought more lenient measures during Yŏngjo's reign.)

Representing the Noron position, Kim Chaero (1682–1759), the second minister in the Office of Ministers-Without-Portfolio, deplored the decline in morality among the people of Kyŏngsang province:

The late upright Minister Kim Sanghŏn is a great worthy whose dedication to the cause of justice and loyalty will be adored by hundreds of generations. Unable to find fault to criticize him, those in the Yŏngnam region who disagreed with him could not help but admire him. They fear that the construction of an academy [after him] would threaten their control of local power (*hyanggwŏn*) and thus oppose it. The opposition comes from a vicious heart. If they had disagreed [with the establishment of the academy], they still could have appealed to the court. [Instead,] they destroyed the shrine for the former upright minister . . . and this is an act of robbery. If this act is not stopped now, the country will face unending worries in the future. . . . Those who are guilty of this crime must be punished severely, and only then can we expect that they will develop a sense of fear [toward authority] and reform themselves.[92]

A Soron member, Pak Munsu, the minister of military affairs, disagreed, however, criticizing those who were attempting to establish an academy for Kim Sanghŏn in Andong as the troublemakers. Praising Kim as an exemplary worthy, Pak Munsu admitted there were good reasons for establishing a shrine for him. He then went on to say:

When one organizes a [new] academy, [it is customary that] one first listens to the opinions of local scholars [before undertaking construction], irrespective of whether the scholars' views are right or wrong. This has been the correct practice generally followed in our country. Therefore, one of his descendants, [a great-grandson] Kim Ch'angjip, even though his power could have moved heaven at his time, did not build a shrine [to Kim Sanghŏn] in the end when the general opinion of local people opposed it. Presently, the local opposition still persists, and yet An T'aekchun and his gang, relying on the power of the magistrate, built a shrine suddenly [without following proper procedures]. Truly, is this the way to honor Kim Sanghŏn?

Their intent is to slander. . . . There are numerous scholars in Andong, and all of them are descendants of prominent officials who served under former rulers, and they have maintained their own points of views for many generations. How can it be possible to change their hearts overnight just because they are pressured to do so?[93]

Concerned about the alienation of the Andong populace, Pak Munsu was calling for a more cautious approach so as not to offend the sensibilities of local people. He then concluded, "If the government or any family sets up an academy against the will of the local people, it is not the way and principle of the academy."[94]

The underlying issue in the heated debates that followed is that the Kim Sanghŏn academy had challenged local power in Andong.[95] Kim Chaero and his colleagues blamed the people of Andong for the trouble and attributed their violent actions to the potential threat the Kim Sanghŏn academy would have posed to local power. Pak Munsu, on the other hand, interpreted the attempt to organize a Kim Sanghŏn academy as an unnecessary intrusion of an outside force into Andong, which constituted an act of provocation. Thus, the academy issue became embroiled in a conflict between the central government and the local populace.

The governor of Kyŏngsang province, Yun Yangnae (1673–1751), assessed the situation as follows:

The state wanted to lessen the control of the local powers in Andong but was unable to do so. The Sŏin people were unable to put their feet into the public schools. As the situation developed to their dislike, they wanted to establish a place of their own [by building an academy]. But the Namin were not willing to share their wealth. This is how the present situation developed.[96]

As the people of Yŏngnam resisted, there were those who wanted to reform them by teaching them a lesson. In a memorial, Yi Suhae, a censor, stated that the people of Yŏngnam often committed flagrant crimes with no sign of repentance and that a Kim Sanghŏn academy would be a good influence in "transforming" the people through proper teaching.[97] As Chŏng Manjo points out, the incident of the Kim Sanghŏn academy was compounded because it involved both factional politics and a conflict over local control between the central government and local elites.

In the end, anxious to maintain his policy of grand harmony, King Yŏngjo adopted a middle ground and blamed both sides. He ordered the dismissal of the governor and the magistrate for permitting the construction of the academy in spite of the existing prohibition against a new one. At the same time, he decreed the banishment of those responsible for instigating the violence against the Kim Sanghŏn academy. As for the academy itself, the king withheld permission to rebuild it.[98] This incident demonstrates the complex issues that the state had to consider in negotiating with the academies between control and autonomy.

## The Politicization of Private Academies

Contrary to the stated wish of the private academies to remain apart from politics, they grew increasingly politicized during the seventeenth and eighteenth centuries, particularly through factional affiliation, which coincided with scholarly lineage. The factional alignments of late Chosŏn dynasty politics in general followed the scholastic lineages of Yi T'oegye and Yi Yulgok: the Sŏin followed the philosophical beliefs of Yulgok, and the Namin embraced the philosophical precepts of T'oegye. Because of this, the academies' factional affiliations can be seen as an extension of their commitment to scholarship rather than a deviation from it.

As factional conflict intensified, it had a significant effect upon the establishment of private academies. When one faction gained power, it encouraged its followers to organize new academies while denying its opponents the right to do the same. Such politicization is clearly demonstrated in Chŏng Manjo's study on the number of royal charters granted to private academies during the reign of King Sukchong, a period known for its partisan politics (see Table 3).[99] The extremely partisan nature of such charters is apparent. Such politicization had a serious impact on the standards, objectives, and orientations of academies as centers of academic pursuit.

The politicization of academies often led to bitter fighting among political factions over the authorization of a new academy and the destruction of existing ones. The issue surrounding the enshrinement of Song Siyŏl as the "co-deity" at the Tobong Academy in Kyŏnggi province is a case in point. As leader of the Noron, Song Siyŏl long dominated the politics of the Chosŏn court, until he was forced to take poison in 1689 at the age of 82. A formidable scholar with a single-minded dedication to causes he considered just, he commanded unflinching loyalty from his followers before and after

Table 3
*Number of Royal Charters Granted*

| Span | In power | Namin | Sŏin | No faction | Total |
|------|----------|-------|------|------------|-------|
| 1674–80 | Namin | 13 | 1 | 3 | 17 |
| 1680–89 | Sŏin | 0 | 19 | 4 | 23 |
| 1689–94 | Namin | 13 | 1 | 1 | 15 |
| 1694–1720 | Sŏin | 2 | 55 | 19 | 76 |
| TOTAL | | 28 | 76 | 27 | 131 |

his death. If he was a paragon of virtue in the eyes of his admirers, he was seen by his opponents as an evil man who ruthlessly persecuted his political enemies. In 1694, when the Namin, who had forced the death of Song Siyŏl, lost power, the Sŏin gained control of the government, and as a result honor and prestige were restored to Song Siyŏl and a posthumous title was conferred upon him. Thereafter, as many as 70 private academies throughout the country enshrined him as their guardian worthy; of these no less than 37 were honored with royal charters.[100]

Since Song Siyŏl's honor had been restored under the Sŏin administration, a scholar, Yi Suk (1626–88), proposed in 1694 to enshrine Song as the "co-worthy" in the prestigious Tobong Academy,[101] which was founded in 1573 to enshrine Cho Kwangjo (1482–1519). The main victim of the 1519 purge, Cho Kwangjo was universally respected as a martyr in a just cause by Neo-Confucian literati in Korea, and enshrinement of Song Siyŏl in the Tobong Academy would elevate Song's stature to the level of Cho Kwangjo's. Song's admirers did in fact compare his life and achievements with those of Cho Kwangjo.[102] His opponents, however, vehemently opposed his enshrinement on the grounds that Song was "a man who promoted only the partisan interest of his political party and who brought harm to the state and ruin to the government." In spite of this opposition, Song's enshrinement at the Tobong Academy was approved by the king in late 1694,[103] and in the following year he was formally honored at the Tobong Academy.[104] But, in 1721, when the Noron lost power to the Soron, the enshrinement of Song in the Tobong Academy came under criticism, and in 1723 Song's tablet was removed.[105] With the enthronement of King Yŏngjo in 1724, the Soron was once again placed in a defensive position, as the Noron demanded reprisals.[106] This shift in political fortunes prompted the followers of Song Siyŏl to initiate a campaign to restore Song's enshrinement in the Tobong Academy,[107] and he was once again enshrined there in 1725, this time for good.[108] There are many similar cases in which enshrinement became entangled with factional issues.

With the intensification of factional conflict, many private academies came to be identified with political factions. According to Yi Suhwan's dissertation on the structure of private academies, most of the academies organized after the seventeenth century were associated either with the Namin or the Sŏin—based on the intellectual lineages of the guardian worthies or the founders. The Namin academies were concentrated largely in Kyŏngsang province, and the Sŏin academies in Kyŏnggi and Ch'ungch'ŏng provinces.[109] Moreover, there was a difference in the backgrounds of the officers and administrators of the academies. Most of the directors and officers of the Namin academies were locally distinguished scholars with few if any ties to the central government.

The Sŏin academies, on the other hand, typically appointed a high official in the central government as director while assigning locally distinguished scholars to positions as deputy director in charge of the actual day-to-day management of the academy. For example, directors of the Tonam Academy, founded at Yŏnsan in 1634 to enshrine Kim Changsaeng, included such individuals as Song Chun'gil (1606–72), sixth state councilor; Yi Chae (1680–1764), minister of personnel; Pak P'ilchu (1665–1748), fourth state councilor; and Yi Kijin (1687–1755), minister of personnel.[110] The Tonam Academy later added Kim Chip (1574–1656), Song Chun'gil, and Song Siyŏl, all powerful leaders of the Sŏin, to its honored roll of enshrined. At the Sŏksil Academy, founded at Yangju in 1656 to enshrine the two brothers Kim Sangyong and Kim Sanghŏn, academy regulations stipulated that the director was to be "a person of high position and moral virtue who is widely admired by the scholars of his time."[111] At the time the Musŏng Academy received a royal charter in 1696, its director was Nam Kuman (1629–1711), the chief state councilor and the leader of the Sŏin.[112] The regulations of the Musŏng Academy stipulated that its director was to be "an official of the third grade or higher with a high reputation of virtue."[113] Thus, the Sŏin academies usually maintained close political connections with the central government, which was largely dominated by the Sŏin during the seventeenth and eighteenth centuries. This situation in turn made the academies in the countryside an important basis of power for the political factions.

The factional affiliations of academies are further revealed by their library holdings. As mentioned above, it was customary for academies to exchange their publications, but this was done only among academies affiliated with the same faction. In 1968–69, Yi Ch'unhŭi conducted an inventory of the books preserved by 33 surviving academies in South Korea and discovered that none of the libraries of Namin-sponsored academies in Kyŏngsang had the works of Yi Yulgok or Song Siyŏl, and that the Sŏin-sponsored academies did not possess any works of Yi T'oegye, Yi Ŏnjŏk, or Yu Sŏngnyong (1542–1607).[114] Factional rivalry apparently prevented scholars at the private academies from openly reading the works of opponents.

Another manner in which the academies were politicized was through students' active participation in political discourse. Students both at public schools and at private academies enjoyed the privilege of sending memorials to the throne on political matters. Students at the Confucian Academy availed themselves of this entitlement from early on and frequently voiced their views in joint memorials. Perhaps because of the self-imposed ideal of separation between scholarship and politics, students and scholars at the private academies refrained from engaging in overtly political discourse. Until the mid-seventeenth century, memorials by students of private academies were largely confined to sectarian matters such as endorsing or opposing the enshrinement of specific persons.[115] As Haboush observes in her chapter in this volume, this changed during the period of ritual controversy. In 1666, a memorial from a thousand students and scholars at private academies in Kyŏngsang province marked the beginning of private academies' participation in national political discourse.[116] Afterwards, students at private academies periodically sent joint memorials to the throne on matters considered to be of national significance, and these memorials were often signed by students from several provinces.

Apparently procedures evolved and a network developed among private academy students that allowed them to address matters they thought required attention. In addition to political issues, the memorials dealt with a wide variety of topics pertaining to local affairs, social issues, and scholarly concerns.[117] Elsewhere Haboush suggests that at this point these private academies came to function as something like what Montesquieu referred to as "intermediate bodies" between the state and the people, and in this sense can be seen as displaying aspects of civil society. This is an interesting view, and it needs to be further examined in its proper historical context.[118] One should note, however, that students at private academies did not consciously decide to pursue political engagement rather than quiet scholarship. Rather, they seem to have redefined the notion of scholarship to include participation in political discourse. Thus their seemingly more active participation in political discourse represented less a destruction of the separation of scholarship and politics than a widening of the boundaries of scholarship.

The autonomy and privileges of academies were sought and bestowed on the basis of a notion of separation between scholarship and politics and a belief that academies were moral centers and sites of Neo-Confucian scholarship. During the early stages in the development of private academies, the state and academies seem to have agreed on this conception of the academies. Thus, autonomy and privilege were granted in both the ideological and the practical aspects of academy governance. In the seventeenth and eighteenth centuries as academies increased in number and became more factionalized, they were seen as having transgressed the acceptable boundaries of scholarship. Control and the denial of privileges were sought on the grounds that the academies had deviated from their self-professed roles. Thus, the tug-of-war between autonomy and control was closely tied to each party's presentation of the academies' engagement in scholarship and politics.

# Constructing the Center: The Ritual Controversy and the Search for a New Identity in Seventeenth-Century Korea

## JAHYUN KIM HABOUSH

THE SEVENTEENTH-CENTURY controversy over the mourning ritual for King Hyojong (1619–59, r. 1649–59) is perhaps one of the best-known and most disputed events of later Chosŏn Korea. The issue under discussion was momentous enough: it centered around whether Queen Dowager Chaŭi (1624–88), Hyojong's surviving stepmother, should mourn the deceased king as an eldest son, as a younger son, or as her sovereign.[1] Since a deceased was mourned in accordance with his or her social and familial status, observation of the proper mourning ritual for a monarch was a definitive confirmation of his legitimacy. It is not surprising that the controversy over Hyojong's mourning elicited intense and bitter discussion.

What is strange is that the controversy occurred at all. Indeed, in the cultural grammar of the time, this connoted a challenge to his legitimacy. It was the only instance in the dynasty in which the mourning rituals for a monarch who had reigned successfully were scrutinized and disputed. What is even stranger is that it was Hyojong who was placed under such scrutiny. His birth credentials were above average for Chosŏn kings.[2] He was the second legitimate son of King Injo (1595–1649, r. 1623–49) and Queen Inyŏl (1594–1635) and was appointed heir apparent in 1645 after his older brother Crown Prince Sohyŏn (1612–45) died. He was also universally admired during his ten-year reign. Moreover, his son and heir, King Hyŏnjong (1641–74, r. 1659–74), succeeded him on the throne with no hint of dissent from anyone. And it was in the court of Hyŏnjong that the controversy concerning his father's legitimacy, and by implication his own as well, raged. The issue was debated passionately by an ever-widening circle of politicians and intellectuals, and the controversy had a far-reaching impact on this community. The split was mostly along factional lines, and this controversy can be seen as the catalyst that accentuated the ideological schism between the Sŏin and the Namin, introduced a vitriolic mode of discourse, and ushered in an age of acrimonious and bloody factional strife that was to last for nearly seventy years.

Historians have since viewed the controversy as an event of tremendous symbolic import and proffered a wide variety of interpretations. Still, for several reasons, the meaning of the controversy remains ambiguous. Because the debate was conducted in a language encoded in signifiers whose meanings are not readily accessible to scholars unversed in the classical ritual texts, it tends to appear technical and esoteric. Nor has the way in which the issue has been problematized served to further understanding. Until quite recently, much historical scholarship has been conducted under the rubric of "modernization theory." In that context, such concerns as the symbolism of proper mourning procedures or factional disagreements over them were seen as antithetical to Korean modernity. The prevailing scholarly view of the 1950s and 1960s, for instance, was that the ritual controversy was the epitome of Confucian pedantry and a prime example of the venality of factional strife. An authoritative six-volume history text, *Han'guksa*, characterizes the factionalism as arising from disputes over "such insignificant issues as ritual formalities concerning the length of mourning."[3]

The revisionist scholarship of the past few decades has reassessed the dispute on several fronts. First, there has been an attempt to reevaluate factionalism and to place it in the context of political history. This was one of the issues discussed in my dissertation.[4] In Korea, Yi T'aejin led a movement to divorce factionalism from its negative associations.[5] A 1992 article by Yi Sŏngmu is one of the latest in a series of works devoted to reassessing the ritual controversy from the point of view of the power structure of seventeenth-century

Korea. Yi concludes that the controversy reflects a contest for power among various groups—most significantly, the throne and the bureaucracy—and that its resolution resulted in a tilt toward greater power for the bureaucracy.[6]

A second line of inquiry focuses on the social and political ramifications of the ritual scholarship of the Chosŏn period.[7] Of particular interest are studies of the ideological and scholarly positions of the participants in the controversy, which have transformed them from self-serving power seekers or pedants into statesmen and scholars with beliefs and convictions.[8] One of the more influential studies has been Chŏng Okcha's attempt to site these scholar-officials' positions in the changing intellectual and philosophical trajectory of seventeenth-century Korea. Chŏng begins by observing a particular difference between two representative texts utilized in the controversy—ancient ritual texts such as the *I-li* (Ceremonials and rites) differentiate ritual according to a person's social position, whereas Chu Hsi's *Chia-li* (Family ritual) propagates uniformity of ritual across class boundaries. She then concludes that the Namin, who adhered to the ancient texts, were conservatives, and the Sŏin, who subscribed to Chu Hsi's work or to texts they believed to be consonant with Chu Hsi's, were progressives.

Although Yi Sŏngmu's and Chŏng Okcha's articles suggest new directions, they are limited by the way in which problems are defined. It is not particularly useful to view the ritual controversy as just a power conflict. Obviously, the balance of power between the monarchy and the bureaucracy was recalibrated at this time, but such recalibrations were a constant feature of the Korean polity and continued for the remainder of the Chosŏn dynasty. If the vulnerability of the Korean throne was exposed in the ritual controversy, it also displayed resilience in subsequent periods. From the late seventeenth century until the end of the eighteenth century, the throne reasserted its authority and power. It is far-fetched to say that the ritual controversy represents the beginning of a weakened throne, which Yi sees as the cause for every subsequent evil in Korean history, especially Korea's inability to meet challenges from abroad in the late nineteenth century and the eventual loss of national sovereignty shortly thereafter. This view seeks to find causes for Korea's loss of sovereignty to Japan in 1910 in the events of the seventeenth century. Moreover, a decline in royal power does not necessarily imply a corresponding weakening of the nation. Can one say that the erosion of the power of the crown in England led to a weakened nation? In fact, the Chosŏn dynasty in the seventeenth century should be given credit for its tenacity. Chosŏn Korea was the only polity among the three East Asian countries that did not undergo dynastic or shogunal change, and this despite invasions from these two neighboring countries.

Similarly, one hears echoes of modernization theory in Chŏng Okcha's study in that the "progressive"/"conservative" binary she employs to interpret the intellectual positions of the Sŏin and the Namin is designed to measure their "modernity." The supposed Sŏin preference for uniformity of ritual among classes, on which Chŏng's characterization of their progressiveness is based, was confined to a preference for uniformity between the royal house and the yangban. There is no indication that the Sŏin sought to extend uniformity of ritual to commoners and the lower classes or that their position on uniformity was in any sense consistent.[9]

What is the significance of this celebrated ritual controversy? In recent decades, ritual has become a subject of keen interest in several disciplines, and a large number of theories and approaches have been proposed for studying it. Clifford Geertz, for instance, sees ritual as a symbolic fusion of ethos and worldview. Calling more elaborate and public religious rituals "cultural performances,"[10] Geertz proposes that they are simultaneously the point at which the dispositional and conceptual aspects of religious life converge for the believer and the point at which the interaction between them can most readily be examined by the detached observer.[11] One may dispute whether Confucian rituals were fully religious, but it is difficult to deny that certain grand state rituals of the Confucian monarchy were "cultural performances." The *Kukcho oryeŭi* (Manual for the five categories of state rites) specifies five categories of state rituals in the Chosŏn dynasty, one of which was mourning rituals.[12] Devised in the fifteenth century, these rituals represent the early Chosŏn commitment to being a full-fledged member of the Confucian world while at the same time claiming and attempting to appropriate native traditions.[13]

Existing scholarship on the seventeenth-century ritual controversy cites as reasons for its occurrence such factors as the importance of ritual in Confucian society, the high level of ritual scholarship that emerged from the mid-Chosŏn period, the politicization of rituals, and the sharpening power struggle both among factions and between the monarchy and the bureaucracy.[14] Although all these forces were at work in Hyojong's mourning controversy and constituted the cultural matrix in which the controversy was embedded, they did not produce the event. Many incidents occur at any given moment, but for a particular one to be defined and understood as a historical event requires a number of participants who share a consciousness of a specific historical moment which makes that particular one into a matter of significance.

Controversies about ritual occur at moments when the usual and incremental adjustments to social change that rituals have to make are no longer viewed as sufficient, and the symbolic content of rituals is no longer seen as producing the appropriate meaning either dispositionally or conceptually. Controversies over cultural performances can be described as sites where history intersects with ritual. Controversies occur not only when there is a widespread consciousness of the breakdown of the meaning of symbols but also when there is a felt need and a public will to redefine their meaning. Perhaps we can extend Geertz's notion of cultural performances[15] and see the seventeenth-century ritual controversy as a site where ethos and worldview are being redefined, and their fusion is being renegotiated.

A ritual controversy is usually about a specific ritual; it is the meaning of the symbols of that ritual which is being questioned and redefined. What was the meaning of the symbols involved in the controversy over the mourning rituals for Hyojong? What in the consciousness of the mid-seventeenth-century Chosŏn intellectual community defined and engendered the ritual controversy? I will argue that the mourning controversy represented a discussion of the identity of the Korean monarchy, situated in a much larger discourse of Korean identity. More specifically, it was about a redefinition of the Korean state, its relationship to civilization, and its role in a changed world order. The controversy was engendered by the sense of crisis pervading the mid-seventeenth-century Korean political and intellectual community as it responded to this changed world order.

Korea had been deeply affected by the political and power realignments that had swept the East Asian region for the half century beginning in the 1590s. The physical damage wrought by the Japanese invasions of 1592 and 1597 and the Manchu attacks of 1627 and 1636 was bad enough; even worse was the challenge they posed to the very basis of the Korean episteme of world and self. The Japanese incursions were the first full-fledged invasions from across the Sea of Japan in Korean historical memory, and they overturned fundamental assumptions concerning national security that had been in force for centuries. The ascendancy of the Manchus, resulting in the fall of the Ming and the Manchu conquest of China in 1644, was seen not merely as a change from one dynasty to another but literally as a barbarian conquest of the center of the civilized world. It shattered the premise concerning the world order of which Koreans felt they were a part. It became imperative to reconstruct the epistemological frame in which an imaginary map of self and other could be redrawn.

If we place the ritual controversy within the seventeenth-century Korean search for a new identity, there remains the question of the nature of the identity being sought. Can we see it as national identity? Liah Greenfeld points out that the crisis of identity a society experiences does not necessarily mean that the identity it adopts is "national."[16] National identity or nationalism has been a popular subject of study in the academy in recent years, and there are divergent theories on the subject. I find the notion of unique identity that Greenfeld employs quite useful in conceptualizing the case in point. Whereas she posits that the consciousness of a unique identity of a people is an ingredient of national identity, she rejects the idea that that uniqueness must be necessarily sought in such attributes of ethnicity as a common language or a shared territory. She cites the example of France, in which, she claims, the unique identity of the community concentrated on the "personal attributes of the king or on high, academic, culture."

Greenfeld also cautions against the notion that the consciousness of unique identity necessarily anticipates or leads to the emergence of national identity. Even when it does, these two consciousnesses often do not emerge at the same time. In England and in Russia, they emerged simultaneously, whereas the sense of uniqueness long preceded the sense of national identity in France and the reverse was the case in the United States.[17] If we wish to use Greenfeld's framework, we should consider two sets of questions. First, did the consciousness of a unique identity emerge, or if this consciousness already existed in some form, was it substantially reshaped at this time in Korea? If so, what were its constitutive elements? Second, can we say that the ritual controversy displayed a new consciousness in its discursive practice based on an epistemological transformation? In other words, if there is a new consciousness of the unique identity of the Korean people, is it also an emergent sense of national identity? In this chapter, I discuss the way in which the controversy unfolded, the particular historical moment in which it erupted, and the issues the participants raised and their significations. I also evaluate the question of whether the ritual controversy was a discourse on national identity.

## The Ritual Controversy of 1659–60

The disputes in the ritual controversy of 1659 have been recounted many times, with varying degrees of detail.[18] Here I present only the details necessary for my discussion.[19] The day after King Hyojong died, the Ministry of Rites sent a memo to Hyŏnjong, the heir apparent who was about to succeed his father to the throne, to the effect that the *Manual for the Five Categories of State Rites* made no provision for the kind of mourning the deceased king's surviving stepmother, Queen Dowager Chaŭi, should wear. Since there were different views on the matter, it advised that the ministers of state should be consulted. Hyŏnjong agreed and said that the "two Songs" should play a leading role in the decision.[20] The two Songs were Song Siyŏl (1607–89) and Song Chun'gil (1606–72), who were leaders of the Sŏin. They were students of Kim Changsaeng (1548–1631), the foremost scholar on ritual, and had reputations as authorities on ritual in their own right.

A meeting of the present and past senior ministers of the State Council was convened on that day. Song Siyŏl and Song Chun'gil, who were serving, respectively, as minister of personnel and fourth minister in the State Council, officiated. The ministers proposed that a one-year mourning period be adopted for the queen dowager since this was specified in the *Kyŏngguk taejŏn* (National code) and the *Ta Ming-lü* (Ming legal code) as the length of a mother's mourning for all the primary sons of her husband, irrespective of their birth order. Song Siyŏl and Song Chun'gil concurred. Hyŏnjong approved the plan.

The *Sillok* (Veritable records) informs us, however, that this seemingly easy consensus resulted by prearrangement—private negotiations had been undertaken to relieve the tension that had been rapidly building around this issue. According to the *Sillok*, as soon as Hyojong died, many officials as well as some private scholars had voiced an opinion on the issue of the queen dowager's mourning. Yun Hyu (1617–80), a well-known scholar of the Namin faction, for instance, forwarded his view that the mourning for Hyojong, a monarch who had successfully reigned, should not be based on his filial rank and that the queen dowager should render him a subject's mourning for the ruler, a three-year period in untrimmed mourning (*ch'amch'oe*), the heaviest mourning specified in the *Ceremonials and Rites*.[21] Yun's view was communicated to Prime Minister Chŏng T'aehwa (1602–73), who discussed it with Song Siyŏl. Song rejected this opinion and expressed his own interpretations of the *Ceremonials and Rites*. The *Ceremonials and Rites*, one of the Confucian Classics, had incorporated over the course of time various commentaries by scholars from different periods. In part attempts to explicate the text, these commentaries also contained inconsistencies and ambiguities and lent themselves to different interpretations.

The twenty-ninth chapter of the *Ceremonials and Rites*, for instance, lists cases in which untrimmed mourning attire for three years was required, including a father's mourning for his eldest son, and mourning for one's lord, one's father, or one's husband. A commentary by Chia Kung-yen of the T'ang dynasty on this passage explicates the meaning of "eldest son" (*changja*): "All sons by the legal wife are primary sons (*chŏkcha*). When the eldest son dies, then the second son by the legal wife should be established as the second eldest son (*ch'ajangja*) and designated the eldest son."[22] The text of *Ceremonials and Rites* then asks why a three-year mourning period should be observed for the heir. This is followed by an explanation that it is because both the principle of being the "right substance" (*chŏngch'e*) (i.e., a son) and the transmission (*chŏn*) are of grave importance and that because of these principles a concubine's son (*sŏja*) cannot acquire the status of the eldest son and succeed the ancestral line.

This is followed by Cheng Hsüan's (127–200) comment that because of the importance of these principles, there are four exceptional cases in which the deceased, even though he had become or once had been the heir, is disqualified from receiving a three-year mourning period. Song Siyŏl relied on these four cases to argue for his interpretation. The first case was someone who was of the right substance but who did not retain the heirship—a first son who, because of illness, could not remain the heir. The second was someone who inherited the line but was not the right substance—for example, a grandson through a concubine (*sŏson*). The third was someone of substance but not the right substance—a concubine's son (*sŏja*) who had inherited the line. The fourth was someone who was right but not of substance—a primary grandson who inherited the line.[23]

Unlike Yun Hyu, Song Siyŏl believed that Hyojong should be mourned by his mother strictly according to his filial rank. Moreover, in determining Hyojong's rank, Song applied the most stringent interpretation possible. He is described as having said to Prime Minister Chŏng T'aehwa that Hyojong fit the third and Prince Sohyŏn's son the fourth of the above four cases. That is, Hyojong was of the substance but not the right substance (i.e., a son but not the right son) whereas Sohyŏn's son was right but not of substance (right line but not a son).

Due to the contradictions among the commentaries, the *Ceremonials and Rites* lent itself to two opposite interpretations of Hyojong's filial rank. If one followed Chia Kung-yen, Hyojong was a second primary son who, upon the death of the eldest son, was made the eldest son and inherited the line. If, as Song Siyŏl did, one adopted Cheng Hsüan's commentary, however, Hyojong could be classified as falling under the third of Cheng's exceptional cases—a *sŏja* (i.e., a concubine's son) who inherited the line but, as a son, was disqualified for a three-year mourning. Since his mother had been a primary consort, Hyojong was not a *sŏja*, but Song found a passage in the section of the *Ceremonials and Rites* that speaks of the importance of succession to make him one: "*Sŏja* is the term denoting sons by concubines. Younger sons by a legal wife are younger primary sons (*chungja*), but, in order to distinguish them from the eldest son, they are also called *sŏja* and thus are designated by the same term as sons by concubines."[24] In other words, all sons other than the eldest son are to be called *sŏja* when they are to be distinguished from the eldest son. The passage is obviously intended to stress the special status of the eldest son. Using this passage to make Hyojong into a *sŏja*, Song concluded that Hyojong was not a "right" son. That status belonged to Sohyŏn's son.

Alarmed by the explosive nature of Song Siyŏl's argument, Prime Minister Chŏng is said to have hastily advised him to suppress his observation, especially since one of Sohyŏn's sons was living.[25] Instead, Chŏng argued for the appropriateness of a one-year mourning period, pointing out that the *National Code* specified it as a mother's mourning for all sons[26] and that the Chosŏn court had been observing rituals in accordance with the specifications in the Korean legal code. Noting that the *Ming Legal Code* also specified the same, Song concurred.[27] The one-year mourning was duly adopted as the period for Queen Dowager Chaŭi's mourning for Hyojong.

This decision seems to have left many, especially the Namin, uncomfortable. Yun Hyu, for instance, held that anything less than the heaviest mourning was improper and argued for it on several grounds. The first was the impropriety of evaluating the filial rank of someone who had succeeded to the throne. The second was the importance of rendering the king the three-year period of untrimmed mourning as a sign of respect for his august position. Yun maintained that this was specified in the *Ceremonials and Rites* and cited numerous historical examples to prove his point. The third was the principle of oneness between the succeeding line and the legitimate line. "The legitimate line (*chŏkt'ong*) lies where the succession (*chongt'ong*) has gone." This was what was meant by the principle of "no separation between the legitimate line and the succession." The fourth was the inappropriateness of applying to the royal house the rituals of an ordinary family.

Yun observed that the objection to the proposition that his mother offer the deceased king the heaviest degree of mourning arose from confusing the rituals of the ordinary family with those of the royal house. He stressed that evaluating the ruler's filial rank obscured the supreme importance of the royal succession. Once one became a reigning monarch, he was the right line and the ruler to everyone equally, including his mother. Yun ended the essay with a warning that a miscarriage of ritual or a misapplication of a name would lead to disorder and chaos.[28] He communicated to Hŏ Mok (1595–1682), a respected Namin scholar-official, the importance of correcting the mourning decision. In the third month of 1660, a few months before Queen Dowager Chaŭi's one-year mourning was to come to an end, Hŏ, serving as an inspector at the Censorate, memorialized the throne pointing out the impropriety of the decision of the previous year.

Hŏ Mok based his argument completely on the *Ceremonials and Rites*. Unlike Yun Hyu, a fellow Namin, he agreed with Song that the queen dowager's mourning for Hyojong should be based on his filial rank, but his evaluation of that rank differed from Song's. Quoting Chia Kung-yen's commentary, Hŏ maintained that Hyojong was a primary son who had succeeded his father to the throne and thus, the (second) eldest son. Although he was originally a second son rather than the first, he became the eldest son, thereby inheriting the legitimacy of the throne. Thus, his stepmother should accord him the mourning due an eldest son, a three-year period of wearing trimmed mourning (*chaech'oe*). Hŏ proposed trimmed, rather than untrimmed, mourning, a slightly less heavy mourning, because a son renders his mother a three-year period of trimmed mourning, and a mother should not render a son, even the eldest son, more than he renders her. He requested that, since the rituals of the royal house are of supreme gravity, the queen dowager's mourning be rectified.[29] Hyŏnjong's order that the matter be re-examined immediately embroiled the court in controversy.[30]

Song Chun'gil was the first to respond to Hŏ Mok's challenge. Song strongly defended the decision in favor of a one-year mourning period. It had been made in the belief that the Chosŏn royal family had never observed a three-year period of mourning for a son. Now that Hŏ had suggested that there had been such cases, for example, Queen Chŏnghŭi's (1418–83) mourning for King Yejong (1441–69, r. 1468–69), an inquiry should be made to verify the truth of the statement. Song's assertion bears out in the case of Prince Sohyŏn. Although he was mourned as the eldest son, he was mourned for one year. At that time, Song had argued for a three-year mourning for Prince Sohyŏn as well as for the appointment of Sohyŏn's son as the heir apparent and, for making this suggestion, was dismissed from office.[31]

Afterward Song Chun'gil turned his attention to the *Ceremonials and Rites*, challenging Hŏ Mok's interpretation of the term "eldest son." He seconded Song Siyŏl's position that when younger sons needed to be distinguished from the eldest son, they were called by the same term as a concubine's sons. Song Chun'gil then elaborated on why Hyojong could not be regarded as the second eldest son. A second primary son could be established as the second eldest son only when the original eldest son died very young, leaving no heir of his own, not when he died after reaching adulthood and his parents had already mourned him as the heir. If one were to follow Hŏ's proposal, would the parents have to observe a three-year period of mourning for the third son if the second son were to die, for the fourth son if the third son were to die, and so on? This was why the ritual text emphasized the specialness of the eldest son. In other words, Hyojong was not an eldest son, since his older brother had died as an adult and had left heirs of his own.

Song Chun'gil also disputed a proposition of Yun Hyu which implied that since the succession in the royal house was of utmost importance, the one who succeeded to the throne should be accepted as the heir, and a three-year mourning period should be observed for him regardless of his familial position. By this logic, a three-year period should be the term in cases when a brother or a nephew succeeded. This would be a travesty to proper ritual, which had to be prevented at all costs. Song Chun'gil urged the king to send historians to the archives to examine the *Sillok* to find out which mourning rituals had been observed in similar cases.[32] Historians were subsequently dispatched to the archives to consult the *Sillok* on the mourning rituals that Queen Chǒnghǔi had observed for King Yejong and Queen Munjǒng (1501–65) had observed for King Injong (1515–45, r. 1544–45).[33] This investigation, however, revealed little, since their respective mourning rituals are described only as having been conducted in accordance with precedent.[34]

Several weeks later, Hǒ Mok sent another memorial in which he reiterated his argument in greater detail, complete with a diagram. At the end, he questioned the meaning of the decision of the previous year in favor of a one-year mourning period, which, he maintained, was reserved for a person who succeeded to the line but who was included among the four exceptional cases.[35] In short, Hǒ disputed not only the choice of a one-year mourning period itself but remained unconvinced of the explanation that it had been based on the Korean legal code.

Amid this rapidly spreading controversy, several high ministers of state attempted to avoid being blamed for a wrong decision by pleading a lack of knowledge of ritual matters.[36] Song Siyǒl, however, held fast to his original position. He argued that disregard for the rule that a second eldest son could be established as the eldest son only when the first eldest son died young would violate the principles of "no two right lines" (*muit'ong*) and "not wearing a three-year untrimmed mourning twice [for the same cause]" (*puich'am*). It would not only infringe upon the sanctity of the legitimate succession (*chǒkt'ong*), but it would open the possibility that a father might have to observe a three-year period of untrimmed mourning for successive heirs.

Song Siyŏl did not stop here; he went on to challenge the authority of the commentary that allowed a second primary son to be established as an eldest son. This idea cannot be found either in the original text of the *Ceremonials and Rites* itself, in the additions by Tzu-hsia, or in Cheng Hsüan's commentary. Song declared that Chia Kung-yen's commentary had not been validated by the Ch'eng brothers and Chu Hsi and was thus not authoritative. He also argued against the idea that in the royal house, the successor to the throne should automatically be accorded a three-year mourning period, pointing out that, if this were the case, then this honor would be extended to a successor who was a concubine's son. He concluded by saying that he saw nothing wrong either with basing the mourning decision on the relatively recent *Ming Legal Code*, since the practice of following current rather than ancient ritual codes was a well-established tradition, or with adopting the one-year mourning period based on this code.[37]

Song Siyŏl's open statement that there cannot be two right lines and that the current royal line was not the right one seems to have sent tremors through the scholar-official community. This prompted Yun Sŏndo (1587–1671), a great poet but also a hot-blooded scholar-official of the Namin faction, to accuse Song Siyŏl publicly of challenging royal legitimacy. In highly charged language, Yun laid bare the issue of royal legitimacy, which had been lurking beneath the surface all along. He took Song to task and asked what he meant by attributing the legitimate succession to the dead prince's line when the deceased king (Hyojong) had received the royal succession. "If the late king could not become the legitimate successor even though he, as a second eldest son, obtained his father's decree, received the Mandate of Heaven, and performed the ancestral sacrifices while the legitimate succession lay somewhere else, then was he a false heir apparent (*kaseja*) and was he a regent (*sŏphwangje*)?" What did Song mean by distinguishing between the legitimate succession and the royal succession and separating them into two things? Yun systematically denounced all the main points of Song's argument and lamented that despite the highest respect with which the two Songs had been treated by successive kings, they had been so ungenerous to the late king. He concluded by saying that one could judge the authority and power of the monarchy and estimate how long the dynasty would continue by how his memorial was treated.[38]

As it was, Yun Sŏndo's memorial did not reach Hyŏnjong. It was intercepted by a royal secretary, Kim Suhang (1629–89), a protégé of Song Siyŏl. Accepting assurances that Yun had had evil intentions in writing the memorial, Hyŏnjong ordered his banishment without reading it.[39] This sparked another round of memorials.[40] Song Siyŏl had already left the capital. Song Chun'gil, following his friend, hurriedly retired from office.[41] In the end, Yun Sŏndo's memorial was burned, and he was banished to Samsu county in Hamgyŏng province, which was famous for its unbearable climate.[42]

The one-year mourning period was reaffirmed after repeated conferences and consultations between the king and his officials. Inquiries into precedent provided little assistance, but Hyŏnjong's court based its mourning decision, procedurally at least, on the Korean legal code.[43] The Korean code, which prescribed one year of mourning for all legitimate sons, left the thorny issue of whether Hyojong was given the status of an eldest son unresolved and left the queen dowager's one-year mourning period subject to interpretation. Hyŏnjong accepted the decision, believing that his father was being treated appropriately.

After Yun Sŏndo's memorial, however, it was no longer possible to ignore the all too obvious symbolic meaning pertaining to royal legitimacy that the mourning ritual signified. Feeling that dynastic legitimacy had been called into question, the Namin would not accept a decision that did not definitively affirm that Hyojong was the "right line" and that he had received "legitimate succession." For the next fourteen years they waged a continuous battle to correct the decision. Yun Hyu actively campaigned by writing a number of treatises and letters.[44] Yun dropped any pretense of civility toward the two Songs, whom he denounced as having "discarded the nation" (*kŏguk*). This further deepened the animosity between him and Song Siyŏl. Yun lamented that instead of applying ritual to affirm the uniquely august position of the ruler, the officials were busy evaluating the ruler's family status. He stressed that the ritual of the family was different from the ritual of the state (*kaguk pudongnye*). Yun took exception to the use of the *National Code* or the *Ming Legal Code* on the grounds that the mourning stipulations in them were based on familial relationships and were meant for the ordinary family, not for the royal house. If the decision were to be based on Korean ritual, then the *Manual for the Five Categories of State Rites*, rituals of the state, should be used.[45] In a letter to Hŏ Mok, he pointed out that Hŏ's suggestion that the queen dowager render the late king a three-year period of trimmed mourning would mean applying to the royal house the ritual of the scholar-official family, and thus fail to acknowledge the uniqueness of the sovereign.[46]

Most of the Namin, however, agreed with Hŏ Mok that the decision on Hyojong's mourning should be corrected to reflect his status as the eldest son, thereby affirming that he had become the right line and succeeded legitimately. The movement to rectify Hyojong's mourning rituals acquired such importance that, in 1666, a thousand private scholars from Kyŏngsang province sent a joint memorial to the throne requesting that Queen Dowager Chaŭi's mourning be corrected to clarify the legitimacy of the throne. This lengthy memorial recorded and analyzed in detail all the arguments put forth to that point and all the relevant ritual texts that had been discussed.[47] In rebuttal, the students at the Confucian Academy submitted a joint memorial.[48]

These memorials from students from private academies and the Confucian Academy mark a turning point in political discourse in late Chosŏn Korea. During the sixteenth and seventeenth centuries, increasingly larger circles of scholars and students had begun to participate in public discourse, but until this time, the issues on which they voiced opinions were mostly regional or sectarian in nature, such as requesting or opposing the canonization of specific scholars who had become symbols of specific schools of thought or factions.[49] The issue addressed on this occasion concerned the symbols of the monarchy, irrefutably a question of national significance. These memorials reveal that a perception of the urgency of the mourning controversy reached far beyond the capital elite into the rural intellectual community. They also illustrate that, perhaps spurred by the gravity of the issue, private scholars as well as students at the Confucian Academy were redefining their roles as participants in national discourse and that such channels of communication as memorials were acquiring much wider usage.[50]

The controversy also resulted in defections from the Sŏin. The first was Wŏn Tup'yo (1593–1664), who, as the minister of the right, had participated in the court decision on the mourning ritual in 1660.[51] Another quite prominent one was Kim Suhong (1601–81), a cousin of Kim Suhang and Kim Suhŭng (1626–90) and a member of a leading Sŏin family.[52] The danger of politicization of the issue must have been obvious to all concerned. Later, in 1679, for instance, an anonymous poster charged that Song Siyŏl was planning a rebellion to enthrone a grandson of Prince Sohyŏn.[53] On several occasions, Song apologized for having caused a furor over legitimacy, but he never once flagged in his insistence that Hyojong was not the "right line" and thus had not received the "legitimate succession."[54]

## The Ritual Controversy of 1674

In 1674, Queen Insŏn (1618–74), Hyojong's widow, died. This led to the eruption of a second mourning controversy. Since a wife was mourned according to her husband's status, Queen Dowager Chaŭi's mourning for her daughter-in-law was again based on Hyojong's status. Korean law stipulated a one-year mourning period for the wife of an eldest son and nine months for the wives of remaining sons.[55] Although the Ministry of Rites considered the possibility of a one-year period of mourning, it finally chose nine months. Hyŏnjong accepted this, believing that his mother was being mourned as the wife of an eldest son.[56] By this decision, the Sŏin bureaucracy retroactively and definitively conferred on Hyojong non–eldest son status. This was a position consistent with that of Song Siyŏl.

The 1674 decision, unlike the 1660 decision, could not accommodate ambiguities. Whereas a one-year mourning period was for all sons, a nine-month mourning period was specifically for the wives of younger sons. A nine-month mourning period was stipulated for the wife of the eldest son in the *Ceremonials and Rites*.[57] But since both the 1660 and the 1674 decisions were presumably based on the Korean *National Code*, the officials could not retreat into this mist of ambiguity without acknowledging an explicit inconsistency in the sources. Soon, a memorial arrived from To Sinjing (1604–78), an elderly scholar known for his expert knowledge of ritual matters. To's memorial discussed all the inconsistencies in Queen Dowager Chaŭi's mourning rituals and their significance in terms of the question of Hyojong's legitimacy.[58]

Finally awakened to these implications, Hyŏnjong investigated and emerged outraged and hurt. The monarch's rage finally succeeded in suppressing official resistance. The period of Queen Dowager Chaŭi's mourning for Hyojong's wife was changed to one year.[59] Hyŏnjong began to assert monarchical authority by punish-

ing the Sŏin bureaucrats, but his death only a month after he had reversed the decision left a more effective assertion of royal power to
his only son, Sukchong (r. 1674–1720).[60]

### The Rhetoric and the Symbols of the
### Ritual Controversy

One reason the controversy over the mourning rituals for Hyojong
has confounded modern scholars is the discrepancy between the ap-
pearance and the meaning of the rhetoric of the controversy. Indeed,
the dispute cannot be explained in terms of any of the usual factors
generating royal politics. This was not a succession struggle or a
contest of power between the heirs of Hyojong and those of Prince
Sohyŏn. Nonetheless, there were certain anomalies in the circumstances under which Prince Sohyŏn had died and the line was transferred to Hyojong. In fact, there are intimations that a much larger
political force was at work. Both Crown Prince Sohyŏn and his
younger brother Hyojong, then known as Prince Pongnim, were
taken hostage in 1637 by Ch'ing T'ai-tsung when he invaded Korea.
They spent most of their eight-year captivity in Shenyang, the Manchu capital, until the Manchu court moved to Beijing in 1644. In
1645, the Manchus sent the two Korean princes home. Prince Sohyŏn
was the first to arrive. He returned in the second month of 1645 and
died two months later. Hyojong arrived in the fifth month, a month
after his brother's death, and was appointed heir apparent within
two months of his arrival. Prince Sohyŏn's sudden death so soon
after his return, allegedly of symptoms that resembled poisoning,
led to suspicions of foul play.

A source no less official than the *Sillok* itself enters into a long
chain of speculations on Sohyŏn's death. It implicates Lady Cho,
King Injo's favorite, as the probable culprit in Prince Sohyŏn's murder, but pointedly absolves Injo of any part in or knowledge of
schemes leading to his son's death.[61] This exculpatory attitude toward Injo is not uniformly shared. The modern historian Kim Yongdŏk, for instance, argues that King Injo committed the murder out of
anger and displeasure with his son's pro-Ch'ing stance. Kim pursues
this logic to explain Injo's choice of Prince Pongnim as heir apparent
and his relentless persecution of Prince Sohyŏn's family. Injo never
forgot the humiliation he had suffered when he had to kneel abjectly
before Ch'ing T'ai-tsung. His younger son's fierce anti-Ch'ing senti-

ments, which seem to have developed during his long years of captivity, warmed his father's heart.[62] But despite the obvious differences between King Injo's and Prince Sohyŏn's outlook and the effects these might have had on their relationship, there is also evidence of considerable affection between them,[63] sufficient, in fact, to make intimations of filicide dubious.[64]

Nonetheless, Injo's treatment of Sohyŏn's family and allies was extremely harsh. His persecution of his son's family began soon after the appointment of Hyojong as heir. The four Kang brothers, the brothers of Sohyŏn's wife, were the first to suffer. They were first banished and later tortured to death while being tried for treason.[65] In early 1646, Princess Kang, Sohyŏn's wife, was deprived of her royal title and executed. Subsequently her property was confiscated.[66] In 1647, Sohyŏn's three sons, then age twelve, eight, and four, respectively, were banished. In 1648, the two older ones died.[67] All of this seems far too severe to be interpreted solely as steps to ensure a smooth transfer of the line from the previous heir to the new one. Had this been Injo's aim, he succeeded only too well. Sohyŏn's line was completely stripped of any political influence it might once have possessed. When Hyojong ascended the throne in 1649, he could afford to display royal magnanimity and released from banishment his older brother's surviving son, Sŏkkyŏn, who, isolated and diminished in status, posed no threat to the reigning line of the royal house.[68]

Did the Sŏin's assessment of Hyojong's filial rank in the ritual controversy represent disaffection with Hyojong? As noted above, Song Chun'gil had urged King Injo, after Sohyŏn's death in 1645, to appoint the dead prince's oldest son as heir-apparent.[69] Then when Hyojong died in 1659, the Sŏin made an unflattering assessment of his birth credentials. One might conclude that there had been some strain between the Sŏin and Hyojong. But Hyojong was generally well liked, and his most enthusiastic supporters were the Sŏin. This is hardly surprising—they shared Hyojong's fervent anti-Ch'ing ideology. The Sŏin retained their power during Hyojong's reign and had every reason to believe that they would continue to do so under the new king, Hyojong's son, and indeed they did.

The rapport between Hyojong and the Sŏin is exemplified by the close relationship between the king and Song Siyŏl and Song Chun'gil, the undisputed leaders of the Sŏin. The two Songs, renowned for their scholarship in the Chu Hsi school of orthodoxy, were what was known as *sallim* scholars (literally, "scholars of the mountains and forests"), who, unlike professional officials who entered the bureaucracy by passing the civil service examinations, abjured examinations and official careers and only periodically accepted public posts at royal invitation.[70] Both Songs enjoyed the prestige and high esteem accorded to only a few scholars, and their luster was derived, at least in part, from their independence.[71] Song Siyŏl, the more forceful and influential of the two, for instance, accepted the post of tutor to the young Prince Pongnim in 1635, but after the Chosŏn court capitulated to the Manchus in 1637, he declared it disgraceful to serve in office in such times of humiliation and lived in retirement, refusing all posts. Only Hyojong's staunchly anti-Ch'ing policies and his repeated pleas that they plan together to avenge the humiliation persuaded Song to re-enter the bureaucracy.[72]

In early 1659, a few months before Hyojong died, he granted Song the rare honor of a solitary audience (*toktae*), in violation of Chosŏn custom, which required that all royal audiences with officials be conducted in the presence of historians to record the proceedings.[73] What we know of this tête-à-tête derives from Song Siyŏl's account of it. Song claims that Hyojong expressed great confidence and resolve in his ability to launch an expedition to conquer the Manchus in ten years and requested Song's cooperation.[74] Very few unaccompanied audiences are recorded in Chosŏn history, and these are seen as displaying extraordinary royal trust in the persons to whom they were granted.[75] The view that Song Siyŏl's relationship with Hyojong was one of personal respect and ideological affinity seems to have been prevalent. Upon Hyojong's death, Song was chosen to write his funerary epitaph.[76] Later, after the passions of the ritual controversy had died down, Song Siyŏl was posthumously enshrined in Hyojong's ancestral temple, an honor bestowed upon only a few of the king's most loyal officials.[77] It seems unlikely that the Sŏin's position on Hyojong connoted personal or political disaffection.

What, then, were the issues that were so fiercely contested in the controversy? Phrased in the technical language and rhetoric of the mourning ritual, there were several major points of conflict. The first and most central issue was a new definition of the ruler. This developed in two different contexts. One was the question of how to understand the position of the royal house vis-à-vis the yangban family. The two Songs on the one hand and Hŏ Mok and Yun Hyu on the other disagreed on whether the royal family was to be governed by the same set of ritual rules as the yangban family or by a different set of rules in recognition of its special status. Was the royal family *primus inter pares* or *sui generis*?

This question was related to the complex processes through which the Confucianization of Chosŏn Korean society proceeded. Both the Confucian normative system and Korean native custom influenced this process. The Yi royal family's role in this social transformation was ambiguous. On the one hand, the royal family, especially the king, pioneered and exemplified the rigors of Confucian ritual. For example, in 1517 King Chungjong (r. 1506–44) became the first king to induct his bride as prescribed by Chu Hsi's *Family Ritual*.[78] Afterward this became the norm for weddings in the royal family.[79] This stood in contrast to wedding practices among yangban families, which retained a great deal of indigenous custom.

On the other hand, the royal family did not abide by the rules governing the patrilineal descent group. The patrilineal descent group, which had become the norm for the yangban class by the seventeenth century, incorporated succession through the eldest legitimate son and the marginalization of children by concubines; these were practices new to Korea. As Martina Deuchler shows, however, these practices contained uniquely Korean elements, distinct from contemporary Chinese practice. When the eldest son was incapacitated or had no heir, for instance, the line was not transferred to a younger brother, but continued through an adopted heir of the eldest son.[80] The children of concubines, no matter how illustrious their father's pedigree may have been, were not even considered full-fledged yangban. They were discriminated against in both the public and the private spheres.[81] Despite their Korean elements, these practices were seen as the quintessence of Confucian norms.

With its concerns for bloodline and ability, however, the royal succession did not follow the strict rules of the patrilineal descent group. It remained rather flexible concerning the rules of succession, and even concubines' children were not necessarily excluded.[82] Song Siyŏl's assessment of Hyojong, the most stringent of all possible interpretations, reflected the standards of contemporary yangban families. In contrast, Hŏ Mok reasoned that since Hyojong had been a reigning monarch, he should be accorded the status of successor. In other words, the royal succession was a special case and had to be evaluated by a separate rule.

The second point of disagreement concerning the ruler, which developed between Yun Hyu and the others, was over the separation between the state and the royal house. Should the king always be treated as the head of the state, or should he, in matters concerning his relationship to his family, be treated as a member of a family bound by family rules and ritual? The relationship between the state and the royal house is an extremely intriguing question, but much remains to be done on this topic.[83] During the Chosŏn dynasty, those ritual activities of the ruler that were deemed public were classified as state rituals. Some of the ceremonial activities of the king and his family were also classified as state rituals.[84] The king's ceremonial relationship to his legal mother, for instance, was seen in a public light since two public personages, the king and the queen mother, were involved. Since filiality ranked first among human relationships and since the proper exhibition of it was regarded as the foundation of the social order, royal filiality was in most instances seen as contributing to public order.[85] What is of interest in Yun Hyu's argument is his proposal for a complete separation between the state and the royal house. In this scheme, the king was to be treated as the head of the state even by members of his family, who then became his subjects, and this was to be upheld on all occasions of an even slightly public nature. This is not merely a matter of granting a special status to the royal house; rather, it is one of acknowledging the purely public nature of the state and the sovereign. Here Yun was advancing a new definition of the public and private spheres and a new concept of the relationship between the two spheres.

The more fundamental aspect of this contentious discourse was that it unfolded in an atmosphere of total confusion concerning structures of authority. The participants in the controversy did not agree on the standards by which questions concerning the throne could be evaluated and decided. Not only did they dispute which text and which interpretations should be accepted as authoritative, but their points of departure also seem to have been very different. Although all four of the principal scholars in the controversy cited the *Ceremonials and Rites*, Song Siyŏl accepted only those commentaries approved by Chu Hsi. He disputed Hŏ Mok's argument on the grounds that it was based on Chia Kung-yen's commentary, which had not been validated by Chu Hsi. Song was also willing to concur with the prime minister's suggestion that the decision on

Hyojong's mourning be based on the Korean legal code, because the *Ming Legal Code* stipulated the same observance. Song Siyŏl followed Chu Hsi orthodoxy and the Ming social and legal structures, which he considered consistent with it. In contrast, Hŏ Mok and Yun Hyu argued from a perspective that would enhance the prestige of the Korean ruler. To them, Chu Hsi's failure to validate Chia Kung-yen's commentary was irrelevant, and Yun rejected the *National Code* not because it was Korean but because it was written for the yangban family and was thus inapplicable to the throne.

A related issue, raised in a much more subtle and implicit manner, was the question of the agency for conferral of authority. With the demise of the Ming dynasty, which had functioned as the signatory of the civilized order, an external agency no longer existed. Should, then, a domestic agency be empowered to evaluate and render judgments on royal legitimacy and, if so, who?

## The Demise of the Old Order

The ritual controversy was embedded in the contemporary political and intellectual community's anxiety over the Korean state, which was to a large extent triggered by changes in the international situation in the seventeenth century. In response to the realignments of the power structure in Northeast Asia, Koreans had to redefine the contours of the world order, including their territorial and conceptual mapping of the boundaries between civilization and barbarity, and between self and other. This impinged directly upon the political and cultural identity of the state. While the Ming dynasty reigned in China, the Sino-Korean relation was defined largely in terms of a convergence between the political and the cultural spheres and a harmony between self and the fellow members of the civilized world. Ming China reigned at the center of this civilized world. The Korean relationship with Ming China was presented in terms of a special affinity: both had reclaimed their respective native traditions after a century of Mongol domination, and both subscribed to the Neo-Confucian conception of the world. Koreans regarded the Ming as worthy leaders of the civilized world. True, there was tension between these two neighboring countries of such unequal strength and status—Korea was only one-fortieth the size of China and had to accept its status as a tributary state. The relation was especially tense in the early period. But, as Chosŏn Koreans began to feel more confident of their Confucian culture, they claimed to be the more authentic heirs of Sung Neo-Confucianism and even strongly disapproved of philosophical developments in Ming China.[86]

The potential and, at times, real, conflicts with China in the political sphere, and Koreans' ideological disapproval of Ming scholarship, however, were for the most part subsumed under the rhetoric of a shared commitment to Confucian civilization. The Ming investiture of the Korean king, which was formalized from the reign of the third Chosŏn king, was seen as a signifier of the peaceful relationship between the two countries. Within this framework, Korea maintained a military establishment more to keep order within the country than to expel foreign incursions. Koreans saw their relationship to China as more than a political arrangement; it was a confirmation of their membership in Confucian civilization. This alliance seems to have provided Koreans with a sense of security in the face of a vast array of menacing forces surrounding the civilization of which Korea and China were a part. The main threats were "barbarians" in Manchuria and the northern steppes whom Koreans and Chinese hoped to contain, thereby sustaining peace and security.

This seems to have worked for 200 years. This sense of security, however, began to erode in the last decade of the sixteenth century. The first event that undercut it was the totally unexpected invasion from Japan in the 1590s. It was not that Korea ignored her neighbors across the Sea of Japan. Korean foreign relations were by no means linear. Besides Ming China, Korea also had diplomatic and trade relations with other countries, including Japan and the Ryukyus.[87] Japanese pirates posed a serious problem on Korean shores, as they had in the late Koryŏ and the early Chosŏn period, but until Hideyoshi's invasion Korea had not experienced a massive invasion of inland areas by Japan. Thus, Japan had not figured prominently in the spectrum of national security threats. The Japanese invasion not only took a large toll of lives and had a devastating effect on the economy, but also challenged the long-standing assumption that national defense depended on securing the northern border. Even after peace was restored between the two countries, suspicion and unease remained an undercurrent in Korea's subsequent relations with Japan and a source of insecurity.

The demise of the Ming seems to have created a sense of doom, a sense that the world as they knew it had come to an end and that if they did not wish to be swept away by this whirlwind of disorder, they had to construct a new episteme with which they could understand and conceptualize the changed world order. During the war with Japan, Ming China had sent troops to Korea, thus confirming their mutual commitment against outside threats. This had deepened the Korean sense of kinship with Ming China. Koreans saw the Manchu conquest of Ming China as nothing less than a "barbarian" usurpation of the center of civilization. As far as they were concerned, the world was in shambles. They felt that they had to construct a wholly different notion of their state and their relationship to civilization.

Their response consisted of two closely related components. One was a redrawing of the territorial and conceptual boundaries of civilization and barbarity. Korea no longer conceived of itself as a part of a larger civilized order, but as a lone entity whose survival as a culture required a separation from the larger, "corrupt" order that prevailed externally. The Korean state thus had to be its own center. This task was felt to be urgent and yet complex, because despite the Korean contempt for the "barbarian" Ch'ing, Korea had to remain politically and ritually subservient to it. Korea resisted entering into this relation with the Manchus as long as it could. As part of the Manchus' bid for rule of China, it was important for them to acquire the same symbolic recognition of superior status from their neighbors as the Ming had, and they invaded a recalcitrant Korea to exact the recognition they desired on two occasions, in 1627 and in the winter of 1636–37, the latter of which resulted in a disastrous defeat for Korea.

In 1645, relations between the two countries assumed somewhat normal proportions. Korea performed rituals symbolizing its status as a tributary state of the Ch'ing just as it had done during the Ming dynasty.[88] These rituals, however, signified something completely different—the unbelievable reality of "barbarian" dominance of China, the demise of civilization at its very center, and a disrupted world order.[89] Had Koreans been able to cut themselves off from the "China-centered" world order altogether now that China had become "barbarian," the situation could have been far less complex. As it was, Chosŏn Korea had to accept its tributary status, and, still more onerous, its survival depended on staying in the Ch'ing's good graces.

Cultural accommodation to Manchu ways was never an option. There was an overwhelming sense that Korea was the last bastion of

Confucian civilization and that it should fulfill this mission in the best way possible. In discussing the evolution of French identity, Liah Greenfeld points out a delicate relationship between France's commitment to the Christian Church and its gradual and imperceptible separation from it in the thirteenth century. She claims that the French desire for superiority and autonomy was articulated in the fourteenth century in the assertion that the "French were more Catholic than the Pope."[90]

If the Korean sense of appropriating what is universal as their own seems rather similar to the French nationalization of Catholicism, the Korean sense of mission was far stronger in that they felt they were the only, rather than the most superior, embodiment of the structure of value. The French did not deny the legitimacy of the Vatican, but the Koreans saw the Manchus as illegitimate. Thus, it was not a matter of competition, but one of preservation. This sense of a Korean mission seems to have lasted almost to the close of the dynasty. Thus, in the eighteenth century King Yŏngjo (r. 1724–76) announced that "the Central Plains [China] exude the stenches of barbarians and our Green Hills [Korea] are alone."[91] Indeed, Koreans never really discarded their anti-Manchu stance. Throughout the latter half of the Chosŏn dynasty, they took pride in the fact that, unlike the Chinese, who had been made to adopt the Manchu hairstyle, headdress, and official dress, they had remained truthful to "civilized" habits by perpetuating the Ming hairstyle and Ming dress.[92] These habits, which were seen as the embodiment of civilized behavior, encoded the essence of the civilization they sought to preserve and justified and made urgent their role as the people preserving these norms.

This conscious sense of identity, as a unique people preserving civilized norms, was directly linked to the second component of their construction of an identity—the source of authority for Korean civilization. Ming China had been the leader of Confucian civilization; its disappearance deprived Korea not only of the agent that had validated its membership in the civilized world but also of the structures by which its civilization was valorized. Consequently, Koreans had to construct new structures of authority; this in turn required them to examine the spiritual sources of authority and the corresponding agencies of evaluation. That ritual discourse became the site on which different views on these matters clashed is not surprising. In the cultural matrix of the time, ritual was seen as the manifestation of order as well as a means through which order was preserved and restored.[93] Why did these issues come to the fore at this particular historical moment? Why did they appear so compelling at the time of Hyojong's death in 1659 twenty-two years after King Injo had surrendered to Ch'ing T'ai-tsung and fifteen years after the Ming dynasty had ended?

## Hyojong and the Dream of a Northern Expedition

King Hyojong reigned at a special time in Korean history. He was the first Chosŏn king to come to the throne after the change of dynasties in China in 1644, and he embodied Korea's postwar determination for revenge and longing for the restoration of the old world order. True, his father, King Injo, had performed personal obeisance to Ch'ing T'ai-tsung. This humiliating act was the final episode in the long and slow disintegration of the old order of which he had been a part. Hyojong, on the other hand, had no formal connection with the old order. He was the first Chosŏn king since Chŏngjong (r. 1399–1400), the second ruler, who had not received investiture from the Ming court. He was also the only Chosŏn ruler who spent time as a hostage in a foreign land. In fact, he seems to have felt that the humiliations he had suffered in his eight years of captivity were inscribed on his body, and he expressed a burning desire to retaliate and inflict physical damage on the Ch'ing dynasty. Hyojong is remembered for beginning a serious reorganization of the military.[94] He wanted to restructure and strengthen the Korean army sufficiently so that if the situation proved favorable, Korea might attack the Ch'ing.[95]

To what extent Hyojong's *pukpŏl* (northern expedition) policy was a realistic plan or an ideological posture is difficult to determine. However unrealistic the policy sounds in historical hindsight, Ming loyalists were still active in the south and the west.[96] The Korean court watched their movements intently for any sign of meaningful recovery. The Ming loyalist movements, however, offered scant encouragement. They were driven further and further into peripheral regions,[97] as Hyojong learned to his distress.[98] Moreover, he had to pursue the northern expedition policy with extreme caution. The Manchus were aware of Korean hostility and interfered with internal politics in a high-handed manner. Early in Hyojong's reign, for instance, the Ch'ing court heard of Korean military preparations through a pro-Ch'ing Korean official and forced prime ministers to resign on two occasions.⁹⁹ The official community thus responded fearfully to the king's aspirations for a northern expedition.¹⁰⁰ Still, the intellectual community displayed a nearly uniform commitment to the Chosŏn state, and this seems to have helped safeguard it against the dangers posed by opportunists attempting to ride on Ch'ing coattails. Nothing seems to have dimmed Hyojong's determination. Outwardly he labored to appease the Ch'ing, but he also redoubled his efforts to prepare for attack in the later years of his reign; as noted above, in his famous solitary audience with Song Si-yŏl he is said to have expressed confidence that he would be able to launch the northern expedition and to conquer the Manchus in ten years.¹⁰¹

Hyojong's death, however, signaled the end of the brief period in which Koreans dreamed of a northern expedition and the destruction of the Ch'ing dynasty. It was not that Hyojong's military preparations went completely to waste. The military reorganization that he initiated continued. In a world that was seen as hostile and dangerous, military strength remained a compelling issue, even though it was not successfully resolved.¹⁰² Nor did Koreans publicly accept the termination of their dream of the northern expedition. Indeed, as "Hŏsaeng chŏn" (The biography of Mr. Hŏ) by the famous eighteenth-century scholar of practical learning Pak Chiwŏn (1737–1805) illustrates, their inability to conquer the Ch'ing remained a source of profound humiliation and self-reproach. Korea's aspiration to restore the old world order militarily, however, ended with Hyojong's demise. It was time to mourn its passing and to confront the meaning of the changed order and Korea's role in it. It seems poignant but fitting that it was Hyojong's body, the symbol of the ruined dream, that emerged as the site on which the contestation over the new Korean identity raged. And it was as an abstracted body representing the Yi monarchy that it came under scrutiny.

## The Ritual Controversy and the Korean Intellectual Community

One distinguishing feature of the ritual controversy is that the major proponents of the controversy were ranking *sallim* scholars. The mourning protocol was, of course, implemented by the concerned government agency, but *sallim* scholars set the agenda of the discourse. As mentioned above, Song Siyŏl and Song Chun'gil of the Sŏin faction were *sallim* scholars of great renown. Their Namin counterparts, Hŏ Mok[103] and Yun Hyu, were also *sallim* scholars with resounding reputations for independence and scholarship. In fact, Yun Hyu had yet to accept an official post.[104] *Sallim* scholars often played a significant role as mediators between the government and the larger intellectual community. Their role in the ritual controversy is a representative example.

It is not that politically influential private scholars were new to the Korean intellectual scene. For Confucian scholars, at least in Korea and China, a life devoted to the pursuit of scholarship was a viable alternative to public service. Many had difficulty choosing between the two. Both Chu Hsi of Sung China and Yi T'oegye (Yi Hwang, 1501–70), the seminal scholar of sixteenth-century Korea, were noted for their ambivalence on this issue.[105] In some periods and regions, those who opted for a private life had greater moral prestige than officeholders.[106]

In Korea, when social or political upheavals such as the military coup of the twelfth century or the change of dynasty in the fourteenth century rendered public service inhospitable, scholars often sought refuge in private scholarship. With the proliferation of private academies in the late sixteenth century, however, private scholars emerged as influential members of the intellectual community and as a group constituted a bloc parallel to the scholar-official community. Toward the end of the sixteenth century, the government institutionalized the status of these scholars by devising procedures to invite these scholars to serve in a fixed number of government posts. *Sallim* scholars became an accepted feature of government for the remainder of the dynasty.[107] Thus, the term "*sallim* scholars" came to refer to both those who did not hold posts in the government and those who accepted office, although even in the latter case it was assumed that their tenure in office would be temporary. Placed in a different category from career officials, the *sallim* scholar-officials were given special treatment; this was due in part to a recognition of the resolution required to forgo power and remain a private person. In any event, only a small proportion of the *sallim* scholars received office and then usually only for a brief time.

Sometimes, however, refraining from government service was not just a matter of individual choice but a test of moral integrity. During the seventeenth century, because the Korean court was viewed

as having been tarnished by its capitulation to the Manchus, accepting a government post implied moral compromise, and so the prestige of the *sallim* scholars increased sharply.[108] All four major figures
in the ritual controversy had shied away from government service
and responded to royal invitations only intermittently, claiming that
it was dishonorable to take office in a time of such shame and that
they wished to devote their time to scholarship and the renewal of
order. Their passionate participation in the ritual controversy indicates that they felt the issues under discussion were matters not just
of bureaucratic procedure but of cultural and political significance.
That perception was shared by the entire political and scholarly
community, which extended from the court to the provinces and
participated in the discourse. The positions of these four scholars on
the ritual controversy represented articulate and distinctive points in
a wide spectrum of views held by this community.

### Korea and the Construction of the New Episteme

Despite the pervasive sense that Korea had to construct a new episteme with which to view the world and the self, there was a deep
cleavage over how this should be done. The fundamental divide
among these scholars arose from their different conceptions of national self and of the boundaries between self and other. Those who
conceived of the self as an integrated whole consisting of inseparable
parts related to the other in the totality of its existence, whereas
those who saw the self as a sum of separable parts could relate to a
part of the other. These ideas had direct corollaries concerning conceptions of civilization and the state and the relationship between
them, especially as these applied to the Korean monarchy. From the
beginning, the most profound disagreement between Song Siyŏl and
Song Chun'gil on the one hand and Yun Hyu and Hŏ Mok on the
other concerned the Korean sense of identity and its relation to the
other. The two Songs felt that a "national" entity could be conceived
of in terms of its separate parts, specifically separate cultural and
political entities, and that as a cultural entity Korea was inextricably
linked to a civilization that was defunct in its place of origin, and
that Korea was even, perhaps, the sole remaining embodiment of
that civilization. In other words, they could not conceive of Korea
independently of the larger civilization.

Song Siyŏl's point of departure in considering human civilization was that Chu Hsi's version of Neo-Confucianism was the pinnacle of human achievement. In Chosŏn Korea, where Neo-Confucian scholarship developed largely in the shadow of Chu Hsi, admiration for the Sung philosopher was nothing new.[109] Sixteenth-century Korean scholars, however, allowed themselves enough space to conduct their own search for truth. Yi Yulgok (Yi I, 1536–84), one of the foremost philosophers of that time, openly disagreed with a certain point in Chu.[110] This voice of an independent-minded scholar willing to differ from a towering figure revered by all underscores the confidence of the age in its mastery of the culture of which Chu was the central figure.

Not so with Song Siyŏl. By his time, the very structure that had provided the security and freedom which made disagreement with its central figure a possibility was in disarray. In despair, he struck a fundamentally defensive posture. He attempted to reify Chu Hsi's philosophy into an unchanging, everlasting system of values. Moreover, Song believed not only that an entity could be conceived in terms of separate cultural and political parts, but also that the cultural sphere was superior to the political and indeed that the *raison d'être* of the political sphere was to embody the cultural precepts of its civilization. Thus, he valued the Ming state highly because he viewed it as embodying Confucian civilization. It was, in fact, its last complete manifestation. With the disappearance of the Ming, Korea was left incomplete and orphaned.[111] In order to remain culturally viable, Korea had to adhere faithfully to what Ming China had represented.[112] To Song, the Ming state and Chu Hsi's philosophy represented the institutional and philosophical cornerstones upon which Korea should be valorized.

Song's veneration for Chu Hsi went beyond the commonly held view of Chu as the great synthesizer of the doctrines of the Nature and Principle School (Sŏngnihak) of Neo-Confucianism. To Song, Chu Hsi represented the culmination of truth in whom "the way of Yao and Shun, Confucius and Mencius, is present."[113] He seems to have believed that any deviation from Chu Hsi would constitute a blemish and checked all new ideas against those of Chu Hsi.[114] He emulated and identified with Chu Hsi not only in scholarly matters but also in his personal life.[115] Likewise, he saw any deviation from Ming practice as a departure from the cultural norm. In this sense,

Song saw the Korean mission as one of perpetuating Chu Hsi's scholarship and embodying Ming cultural norms.

On the other hand, Yun and Hŏ regarded Korea as a discrete body whose various parts could not be conceived separately. As such, it had its own autonomous and separate existence apart from its previous membership in the fallen civilization. Yun Hyu and Hŏ Mok searched for a definition of civilization that would allow Korea a distinct and autonomous identity. Rather than remain confined by Sung Neo-Confucian interpretations, they sought inspiration directly from the ideal ages of antiquity, from the era of the sage kings to the Chou period.[116] This allowed them flexibility in considering the Korean case. One idea was that since Korea was directly linked to the wellsprings of civilization, it had no need to be validated by Chu Hsi or Ming civilization. Another was that they could construct a conceptual framework to evaluate specific qualities of the civilizations of the successive historical states. They concluded that later Chinese states, from the Han to the Ming dynasties, fell far short of the ideals of antiquity.[117] This was undertaken not so much to establish the distinct qualities of each historical state as to underscore the notion that civilization was constantly evolving and changing and that none of the historical states should be taken as an inviolate model.

A corollary to this view was the relegation of Chu Hsi to a position of being but one of many scholars. Yun and Hŏ paid homage to Chu Hsi as a great scholar, but they did not subscribe to the view that he was the supreme authority for validating later thought. In this matter, Yun was again more vocal. Hŏ was content to express a preference for the Six Classics (Yukkyŏng) over the Four Books by saying that the high level of writing that Confucius had reached has not truly been understood or equaled in later ages.[118] Although it was expressed indirectly, this was a comparison unfavorable to Chu Hsi.

Yun Hyu, on the other hand, took an iconoclastic approach. He explicitly challenged Chu Hsi's exegetical authority. Using the empirical and philological methods available to him, Yun investigated a number of texts edited by Chu Hsi, then rearranged the *Ta-hsüeh* (Great Learning) and the *Chung-yung* (Doctrine of the Mean). As Martina Deuchler notes in her chapter in this volume, since the Four Books with commentaries by Chu Hsi not only were the cornerstones of Neo-Confucian orthodoxy but also were viewed as sacred by Chosŏn scholars, this certainly was a daring act. Although Yun attempted to justify his rearranging of canonical texts by pointing out that Chu Hsi had done the same, this act earned him the eternal and unremitting enmity of Song Siyŏl. Earlier, Song had admired Yun for his refusal to enter government service,[119] but now he became Yun's most vocal foe. Song termed Yun a "traitor to our [Confucian] culture/way" (*samun/sado chi nanjŏk*) and routinely referred to him as "that enemy Hyu" or "that thief Hyu" (*chŏk Hyu*).[120] Even Hŏ Mok thought that Yun had gone too far by tampering with the texts.[121]

Yun Hyu stressed the inviolability of an individual scholar's quest for truth unrestricted by the theories of previous scholars, however great they may have been.[122] At the same time, he placed an individual's solitary search within the context of humanity's collective knowledge, which constantly evolved and whose benefit was shared by everyone. He maintained that no one person could attain a complete understanding of the universe and, based on what was already known, he wished to investigate further to illuminate the ways of the sage kings, with the sole purpose of sharing his discoveries with others.[123] The objects of his search were the concrete things, institutions, and laws of the classical era, which he held to be models for later ages. Thus although he valued the Classics, it was as "sources for an understanding of the spirit and institutions of the age."[124] The extent to which Yun's views represent a historicist vision, a hermeneutical shift from the Classics to the classical era, "from the *chefs-d'oeuvre* of mankind to the historical interconnection which supports them" in Paul Ricoeur's phrase,[125] has to be further examined. According to John B. Henderson, this transition occurred in China and Europe in the eighteenth and nineteenth centuries.[126] Although a thorough analysis is needed to place Yun in proper perspective, he displayed a rather critical attitude toward tradition. Later, when he finally accepted an official post under King Sukchong, for instance, he suggested to the king that the taboo on using Confucius's given name be dropped and that Chu Hsi's commentaries be discarded.[127]

These scholars also subscribed to different visions of Korea's place in the world and prescribed different strategies for Korea to fulfill that role. Song Siyŏl suggested a defensive approach. Since he held to the view that Korea was inextricably linked to the larger world, he concluded that the restoration of Korea's internal order could not be accomplished without the restoration of order in the larger world. His belief that the function of the state was to serve as a conveyor of culture further convinced him that Korea was duty bound to restore order in the world at large by attacking the barbarian Ch'ing. He invoked nothing less than human emotion and heavenly principle to stress the ethical inexorability of this action.[128]

Having lived through the Manchu invasions, however, Song was aware of their military strength and did not think it possible to conquer them in the near future. Thus, he needed to construct a conceptual framework that would enable Koreans to live with the undesirable reality of Manchu domination of what had been the center of the civilized world and yet still be able to uphold principle. He found his inspiration in the phrase "Respect the Chou and reject / drive out the barbarians" (chon Chu yangijŏk), which he believed to be Chu Hsi's interpretation of the Ch'un-ch'iu (Spring and Autumn Annals). On this basis, he constructed an anti-Ch'ing strategy with which Koreans, "bearing unbearable pain in their hearts," were to "reject the barbarians" resolutely while patiently waiting until Heaven provided them with a suitable opportunity to "drive out the barbarians."[129]

Song briefly entertained the possibility that the transformation from "rejecting" to "driving out" the barbarians might be within his grasp. This was when Song's vocal and unyielding anti-Manchu posture had led King Hyojong to believe that in Song he had found a ministerial partner for his resolute preparations for a northern expedition and to seek his advice. In the famous solitary audience with Hyojong, Song apparently promised to assist the king actively. When he heard the news of Hyojong's sudden death, he seems to have grieved it as a loss of an opportunity to fulfill his cherished dream of "driving out the barbarians."[130] Afterward, Song reverted to the stance of "reject the barbarians." He never again mentioned the northern expedition.[131] In his view, Korea was in a state of suspended animation, forever at loggerheads with the hostile world; its role was mainly to defend and perpetuate the vision of Confucian culture perfected by Chu Hsi with as little change as possible.

Hŏ Mok and Yun Hyu perceived Korea as operating on a much freer trajectory. Consonant with their conception of Korea as a separate and autonomous entity, they believed it capable of perfecting its internal order regardless of any disruption in the larger world. They proceeded from the premise that a nation was composed of inseparable constituents and that the political element was as important a constituent as the cultural element in determining Korean identity. As I discussed above, Yun sought inspiration for Korea in the social order and the system of antiquity. He examined such classical texts as the *Chou-li* (The rites of Chou) and *Li-chi* (The records of ritual) to find a suitable social model for Korea.

Yun Hyu's belief in Korea's intrinsic worth and ability was based on his vision of civilization and history. He stressed an intimate and direct relationship between Heaven and human societies, which possessed the full potential to embody Heaven's will. He brought immediacy to this relationship by reactivating the ancient concept of Lord-on-High (Sangje; Ch. Shang-ti), a personified form of Heaven who responded with joy or anger to the affairs of human society. The quality of a society depended on the extent to which it responded to Heaven's will and realized its potential.[132] Thus, he held that just as he, as a thinking man, was obliged and able to seek and find truth as Chu Hsi had, Korea as an evolving civilization was responsible for examining the entire history of human civilization with a view to choosing which course to follow and was capable of realizing the order and harmony of the classical age. In fact, most of his scholarship was devoted to discovering the philosophical foundation for their realization by analyzing the political and social structures of different ages[133] and to drafting social and political reforms that would bring about this realization in Korea.[134] For example, he wrote a comprehensive plan to reform the government in which he recommended the restoration of many practices of the Chou era.[135]

In Yun's estimation, there was no reason why Korea could not realize the ideals of civilization within its own borders and then spread them to other states. When Yun Hyu finally accepted an official post in 1675, the Ch'ing dynasty seemed threatened by Wu San-kuei's rebellion.[136] He strongly urged the king to launch a northern expedition, but by this time no one thought it a practical idea.[137] Unlike Song Siyŏl's view that the northern expedition was an unrealizable duty, Yun's proposal seems to have been based on an assessment that Korea was adequately equipped with troops and weapons and that disturbances within China offered an opportunity for Korea.[138]

Hŏ Mok also turned to the Classics for inspiration on the contemporary social order. His favorite text was the *Spring and Autumn Annals*. Hŏ paid a great deal of attention to the exterior structure of the social hierarchy. He believed that order depended on maintaining the distinctions among the different classes—the king at the top, then officials and scholars, followed by commoners.[139] This was to be accomplished by rectifying names (*chŏngmyŏng*), the famous recommendation of Confucius, and by observing proper ritual. Charting an independent course for Korea in the future, Hŏ opposed the northern expedition. He believed not only that Korea was unequipped to launch a successful attack but also that the high cost of military preparations and the establishment of a powerful military would invite disorder.[140]

Is there a framework that can accommodate the different visions of these scholars? A nation is often imagined, especially in its earlier stages, in contradistinction to the larger bloc, the civilization or community, in which it is situated. In her discussion of the history of nationalism in England, Liah Greenfeld locates its emergent national consciousness in the break with Rome. She claims that Henry VIII's aim in the Act of Appeals was to imply that "England was a sovereign polity separate from the rest of Christendom" and that this was an "important factor in the shaping of the national identity."[141] Greenfeld also presents medieval France's complicated relationships with the Holy Roman Empire and Rome as indicators of its evolving sense of national identity. The French kings sought to free themselves of external interference from the empire in temporal matters. By the close of the thirteenth century, the legal literature referred to the French king as "the Emperor in his kingdom."[142] The French desire for autonomy was no less strong in spiritual matters. Since France remained Catholic, however, this desire was channeled into becoming the most Christian community, superior even to Rome, rather than into rupture from it, and it led to the sacralization of the French king.[143]

The seventeenth-century Korean scholars' notions of Korea also seem to have depended on their view of Korea in relation to the larger Confucian civilization. Although their constructions were quite complex, we may see the Namin as representing "nationalist" views and the Sŏin a "culturalist" view, measured by their respective points of departure and their conceptual priorities and emphases. Hŏ Mok and Yun Hyu not only imagined a Korean polity independent of and separate from the larger civilization, but also began with the conviction of Korea's inherent uniqueness; other parts of their constructions were made to fit this central point. In contrast, for

Song Siyŏl Korea's specialness lay in its role in the post-Ming world of being the conveyor of Confucian civilization. Consequently, its worth depended on the degree to which it preserved and embodied this civilization.

## The Concept of the Sovereign

The differences in these scholars' conceptions were perhaps most vividly displayed in their notions of the Korean king and his role. All of them placed the ruler at the center of the task of effecting order, but they differed in their views of how this was to be achieved. Song Siyŏl echoed the familiar Neo-Confucian view that the king was the moral foundation of the country, and the rectification of his mind was the origin of national order.[144] Since he felt that Korea was burdened with an urgent task, he regarded cultivation of the royal mind as even more critical. In the two long memorials to Hyojong in 1649 and 1657, he repeatedly stressed that Confucian civilization was in a precarious state in the post-Ming era, that Korea had a pivotal role in perpetuating this civilization, and that it was crucial for the king to cultivate his mind ceaselessly to carry out this awesome task.[145]

Hŏ Mok and Yun Hyu constructed a different notion of the sovereign and the political structures in which he was placed. Hŏ Mok went in the direction of royal absolutism. He equated the state with the person of the sovereign, thus turning the concept of the sovereign into an abstraction. In his view, the king embodied the prestige of the state. Hence, he sought to strengthen the Korean kingship by investing it with the mystical aura of Heaven and presented the Korean king as ruling on Heaven's behalf. In this respect he echoed Yun Hyu, who stressed the intimate relationship between Heaven and human society, but Hŏ elevated the ruler of Korea to the only one who could act on Heaven's behalf. It was through the mediation of the ruler that Heaven and human beings were unified and brought into harmony.[146]

The central role of Heaven in the Confucian concept of kingship had long been established in the notion of the Mandate of Heaven. Hŏ Mok, however, constructed a closer symbolic relationship between Heaven and the ruler. The Korean king was not just ordained by Heaven; he was equated with Heaven: "The ruler regulates [myriad] things in place of Heaven and causes them to find their appointed places."[147] One might describe Hŏ's notion of kingship as a "radical personalization of the political community" and see a certain similarity to the concept of the "Divine King" of seventeenth- and early eighteenth-century France in which the king was the state and "the visible image of God on earth."[148]

Hŏ placed the ruler at the top of a social hierarchy rigidly separated by rank. He maintained that the basic message of the *Spring and Autumn Annals* was nothing more than how to rectify order by "elevating the king and debasing the officials" (*chon'gun pisin*). This was to be done through ritual: "The position of the ruler is truly lofty, and the ritual of the ruler is extremely solemn. . . . The ruler however cannot be lofty by himself but is made lofty through ritual."[149] In addition to ritual, he enumerated music, governance, and the application of law as necessary ingredients for maintaining order.[150] Not surprisingly, Hŏ was averse to any course of action that even remotely suggested a challenge to the authority of the royal house. He objected, for instance, to a proposal to posthumously restore Tanjong (1441–57, r. 1452–55), the boy king who had been deposed by his uncle King Sejo in the early Chosŏn period, on the grounds that this would imply a negative judgment of King Sejo, a pivotal ancestor in the Yi royal line.[151]

Yun Hyu, on the other hand, saw the king as the representative of the state, which was in turn seen as an abstract body consisting of the government and its people. As a way to stress that the two constituents were inseparably linked and interdependent, he evoked a metaphor from *Hsün Tzu*: "The lord is the boat, his subjects the water. It is the water that sustains the boat, and it is the water that capsizes the boat."[152] This was a well-known metaphor, although from the Sung period on the term found in *Hsün Tzu*, *sŏin*, was replaced by *min*. *Sŏin*, which is rendered as "his subjects" in John Knoblock's translation or "the common people" in Burton Watson's,[153] conjures up an image of a group of commoners, whereas *min*, often translated as "the people," is an abstract image of infinite vastness. With *min*, this metaphor of the people as simultaneously a foundation of and a potential threat to the king seems to acquire a much more forceful image.

Although this passage was quoted occasionally in the early Chosŏn,[154] Yun Hyu seems to have been the first to make it the centerpiece of a political ideology. After Yun, this metaphor appeared frequently in political discourse. In the eighteenth century, for instance, monarchs appropriated it to construct an image of a concerned ruler.[155]

In contrast to Song Siyŏl, who emphasized the rectification of the royal mind as the foundation of good government, Yun stressed that statecraft, knowledge, and skills were as essential in governing as navigation was in sailing.[156] Yun proposed a number of revisions in governmental structure and practice. Many of these were quite drastic. He drafted a blueprint for a government in which the king oversaw a much simplified bureaucracy and was in direct contact with the people. Unlike Hŏ Mok, who equated order with maintaining rigid class differences, Yun promoted plans that would open opportunities for greater numbers of people and turn the king into the centripetal figure through whom everyone was connected. Yun recommended the abolition of institutions or procedures that obstructed opportunities for the advancement of commoners or direct contact between the king and the people. He offered two measures to effect this. One was the replacement of the civil service examination with a recommendation system, which he believed would open officialdom to all based on merit and virtue regardless of class or connections.[157] The second was the abolition of the Censorate. From the mid-Chosŏn, the channels of speech (*ŏllo*) of "speaking officials" (*ŏn'gwan*) were a jealously guarded prerogative.[158] Yun believed that the existence of "speaking officials" had the effect of limiting channels of communication, and he proposed that, instead of having "speaking officials," everyone be allowed to voice opinions.[159]

It would be anachronistic to say that Yun Hyu viewed the people as members of a civil society or as holders of sovereignty who dictated their will to the ruler. In his scheme of things, the king had the role of effecting the new order, both internal and external.[160] The king was not only a representative of the state, but also the activator of its ideals. Nonetheless, the people were conceptually transformed from the objects of an idealized benevolent rule into a visible and inseparable constituent of the state; they formed something akin to a partnership with their ruler. Yun did not postulate aristocratic bureaucrats as a separate class; he rejected the idea of their exclusive role. Rather, he saw them as part of the people, those from whom the governing staff should be chosen.

### The Legitimacy of the Korean Throne

Ultimately, the controversy over Hyojong's mourning ritual became a site seething with scholarly passion and political volatility because it focused on the legitimacy of the Korean throne and the agency of its conferral. Song Siyŏl's position, which denied Hyojong the status of being the "right" line, functioned as a catalyst in provoking the controversy. How do we explain Song Siyŏl's seemingly contradictory position on the matter—a professed devotion to King Hyojong conflated with a refusal to grant him the "right" line and "legitimate" succession?

Song Siyŏl's position seems to have been embedded in his belief as a "culturalist." He subscribed to the view that royal legitimacy was constituted by two elements, one defined by political expedience and one by cultural norms. What he was disputing was not the political element but the cultural one. The king's qualifications to rule were not at issue, but his status in terms of an unchanging normative standard was. Song does seem to have felt it imperative to establish that the demands of political expediency were distinct from normative legitimacy based on unchanging principle. He believed that these two had to be evaluated on different bases, that unchanging principle had a superior claim, at least in the realm of theory, and that this claim should be clearly stated. In terms of this binary, Hyojong was an able king, but not an eldest son. Political exigencies, however acute, could not be transformed into absolute norms.

Song also acted on the premise that a scholar-official had a dual identity, as a political self and a cultural self. In the ritual controversy, Song seems to have felt called upon to act as a cultural self. He believed that with the disappearance of the Ming, the Korean throne had lost the agency of external legitimation. For instance, he expressed great anxiety that upon their deaths Chosŏn kings could no longer receive honorary titles (sijŏn) from the Ming court.[161] He seems to have concluded that the scholar-officials, the guardians of Chu Hsi orthodoxy, should fill the vacuum thus created and that this was a sacrosanct duty overriding other considerations. As far as he was concerned, there was no conflict between his loyalty to Hyojong as his ruler and his judgment that Hyojong's birth credentials fell short of the normative standard. In his devotion to Hyojong, he was acting in accordance with the demands of his political self, which valued loyalty to the ruler as a supreme virtue. In judging the king's credentials as an heir, he deferred to the responsibilities of his cultural self, which required scholarly impartiality. Not only did Song divide these selves, but he remained firm in his belief that the concerns of the cultural self should override those of the political self.

At the heart of Song Siyŏl's unyielding insistence lay his strategy for dealing with the larger external world, particularly the question of how one should handle the undesirable reality of Manchu domination of China. If one were to evaluate the legitimacy of the throne by the criteria of political expediency and to automatically acknowledge the legitimacy of its current occupant, then how could one avoid applying the same logic to the Ch'ing dynasty? By this logic, one would have to recognize the legitimacy of the Ch'ing. This was not a possibility for Song Siyŏl. He was ideologically vested in establishing the difference between functional and normative legitimacy and asserting the superior claim of the latter. This was his way of affirming that the Ch'ing dynasty was not legitimate despite its conquest of China and that the world as it was was not the world as it should be.

Conversely, one may describe Hŏ Mok's and Yun Hyu's responses as consistent with their "nationalist" outlook. They found Song's challenge to Hyojong's legitimacy deeply disturbing. Both heartily agreed that the external world was in a state of chaos and corruption, but that was all the more reason for Korea to guard its internal order ever more vigilantly. Since they held to the notion that a country was a single entity in which various elements were parts of a whole, to demean a part was to debase the whole. Hŏ and Yun stressed different points to refute the notion of Hyojong's illegitimacy. Hŏ Mok viewed casting doubt on Hyojong's legitimacy as nothing less than diminishing Korea's prestige and its unique role. He was unwilling to agree that Hyojong's credentials were remiss by any criterion. For him, it was imperative that Hyojong's legitimacy be established by both cultural and political criteria. Yun Hyu, on the other hand, stressed the unacceptability of judging the ruler's legitimacy by one or another set of single criteria, be they cultural or political. Since the state was a supreme body, the legitimacy of its representative should not be discussed in any way that limited the primary and public nature of its position. That was why Yun even parted ways with Hŏ, who insisted that Hyojong had the right credentials as an eldest son. As far as he was concerned, judging Hyo-jong's legitimacy by the cultural norms of the ordinary family was in itself ill-considered and disaster-provoking.

The way Hŏ Mok and Yun Hyu defined their relationship to the sovereign was also determined by their conceptions of self. Neither Hŏ nor Yun denied a Confucian belief in the ministerial duty to assist and admonish the ruler. Having vested the Korean king with the task of creating the new order, they had a much greater stake in his effective performance and virtue. Indeed, Hŏ and Yun were second to none in exhorting their ruler.[162] But they did not believe that their cultural selves could function independently of their political selves. Thus they did not think that scholar-officials had a right to reject or find deficiencies in their ruler's (birth) legitimacy by a cultural norm based on Chu Hsi. This was beyond the bounds of ministerial duty. This was expressed in its most extreme form in Yun Hyu's position that the ruler, once enthroned, should be treated as the head of state by everyone, including the members of his family. Both Hŏ and Yun repeatedly warned against the destructive effects of eroding national prestige by diminishing the ruler.

Although these scholars used the same vocabulary drawn from a shared repository of cultural resources, they used it in different ways. When Song Siyŏl discussed order or legitimacy, he was discussing a cosmic and universal condition and not the condition of any particular state, person, place, or time. For him, legitimacy, that is normative legitimacy, meant a certain cosmic rectitude, a certain propriety in the state of the Confucian cosmos. For Hŏ Mok and Yun Hyu, legitimacy meant the dynastic legitimacy of the Korean ruler, and as a concept it existed independently of the larger cosmos. Thus, whereas Hŏ focused his efforts on structures internal to Korea, Song viewed this effort as secondary to the larger task of establishing universal rectitude. Yun, on the other hand, posited that the internal strength of Korea should be able to rectify the larger world as well.

## Conclusion

The ritual controversy represented a site on which different epistemes of the world and self constructed by seventeenth-century Korean intellectuals clashed. These constructions were prompted by changes in world order and realignments of power in East Asia. The Japanese invasions of the 1590s and the Manchu attacks of 1627 and

1636 left profound scars on the national psyche. The Manchu conquest of China in 1644 represented nothing less than "barbarian" domination of the center of the civilized world, the end of the world as Koreans knew it. Since Koreans could neither accept the new world order, despite the fact that Korea had to maintain a tributary relationship to the Ch'ing, nor change it, they felt compelled to construct a new episteme that would allow them to maintain their identity as a "civilized" people.

These new epistemes were attempts to redraw a conceptual map between self and other. There were two conspicuous features in this process. One was a Korean consciousness of a unique identity—in the face of the "barbarian" domination of the center of the civilized world, Koreans were the only remaining civilized people—and this consciousness emerged as a prominent element in their sense of identity. It appears that this consciousness of a unique identity was shared by the entire scholarly and political community. This was related to another noticeable feature, the domestication of the structures of authority. They no longer looked outside the country to confirm the status of the Korean polity or its culture. Although scholars reassigned the locus of authority—Song Siyŏl, to Korean scholars; Hŏ Mok, to the person of the Korean king; Yun Hyu, to the Korean state—they constructed self-contained structures and domesticated the sources of authority.

The constitutive elements of the epistemes that these scholars constructed, however, differed greatly, based on their different conceptions of self. Song Siyŏl proceeded from the notion of a divided self in his conception of the nation and the individual. Thus, he conceived of Korean identity as consisting of separate cultural and political entities and, consistent with his culturalist view, made the political entity subservient to the cultural entity. Similarly, he attributed dual selves to scholar-officials, a political self and a cultural self; a scholar-official could act as one or the other depending on the demands placed on him at a given moment. Yun Hyu and Hŏ Mok, on the other hand, conceived of a state or an individual as an indivisible and discrete body in which separate parts formed an integrated whole. This notion of an indivisible self also determined their conceptions of the relationship between individual scholars and their ruler.

These scholars redefined the spatial concept of the world as well. The previous assumption that the civilized world consisted of the center, occupied by China, and peripheries was no longer adequate. Song seems to have distinguished the geographical center from the cultural center. He retained the framework of a center and peripheries, but he used it to construct a self-contained world in which Korea functioned as the center of Confucian civilization even though the Manchus dominated the geographical center. Yun Hyu seems to have subscribed to a more complex conception of a world with multiple centers, in which each country constructed its own center. This was, however, employed not to undermine but to support Korea's unique role.

In its subject matter, rhetorical tropes, and scope of participation, the ritual controversy represented a new discursive practice in the intellectual and political community. Its most conspicuous aspect was the new role that scholars assumed as arbiters of the throne. True, historical circumstances warranted a Korean search for a new identity. Nonetheless, it is remarkable that scholars were the ones evaluating and redefining the role and the legitimacy of the monarchy. This was in part due to the fact that the scholar community was becoming increasingly powerful as a social and political force, but in part it seems to have been triggered by a deeply felt sense of national crisis. However one sees it, the incident had grave implications for the redrawing of boundaries between the scholar community and the state. In the intense politicization that followed, both leading scholars in the ritual controversy were executed. Yun Hyu was killed in 1680 for espousing heterodoxy,[163] and Song Siyŏl in 1689 for opposing a royal wish to appoint an infant prince as heir-apparent.[164]

Another aspect that commands attention is the existence of a nationwide political-intellectual community in seventeenth-century Korea. Scholars and officials had channels of communication to express and exchange views among themselves. These included private networks as well as institutional exchanges among academies.[165] This community, something like "a reasoning public,"[166] was bound by a shared commitment to Confucian civilization grounded in veneration for Confucian texts. The members of this community were able to make their views public by sending memorials to the throne, and this mode of communication was utilized with increasing frequency. Hitherto public debate had been confined to sectarian matters. The participation of private scholars and students in the ritual controversy marked the first time that this community engaged en masse in national discourse. This shows not only that this community regarded the ritual controversy as having national import, but also that their perception of their own role in the national discourse was changing.

Can we see the ritual controversy as a discourse of national identity? In the past, because of the dominance of the nation-state both as an eventual destination of polities and as an extensive area of scholarly inquiry, any discussion concerning a nation tends to have been evaluated by the criteria of the nation-state—whether and how an element or an incident could be viewed as a development toward the nation-state. This has been equally true of histories of non-Western nations, which wish to assert their own historical progress toward the nation-state. Not surprisingly, there has been a reaction against this approach. Prasenjit Duara, for instance, cautions against a linear, evolutionary historical vision in which national history is seen as a march toward the nation-state.[167] Both the prevalence of and the resistance against the history of the nation-state seem to have produced among historians of premodern Asia a certain reticence concerning nations predating the modern era. In my view, refraining from discussing the national elements of an event distorts history just as much as perpetually evaluating events in terms of the nation does. With certain events, one can do justice to history only by discussing national elements, but this should be done without constantly measuring them against the nation-state of the enlightenment model.

As soon as one discusses the issue of the national identity of premodern East Asian states, however, one faces a theoretical quagmire. There is no adequate theory available with which to discuss the question. Of the two opposing views, "primordialist" and "modernist,"[168] the modernist views have been far more prevalent. The theories of such influential modernists such as Benedict Anderson and Ernest Gellner are premised on an enlightenment Eurocentric concept of nation.[169] In proposing that the concept of a nation predates modernity and that each country has its own path to nationhood in which sovereignty rests with the people, Liah Greenfeld offers a perspective rather different from the universalist views of Anderson and Gellner, but, of the five nations that she discusses, four are European and the last is the United States of America.[170] E. J. Hobsbawn also criticizes the top-down approach taken by Anderson and Gellner, and proposes that in the case of such historic states with largely homogeneous populations as China, Japan, and Korea, an evolutionary relationship may be established between "proto-nationalism" and modern nationalism.[171] Although this acknowledges that states have their own historical trajectories and hence require different criteria for evaluation, his use of "proto-nationalism" confuses rather than clarifies. Does it lead to a better understanding of the issue to say that Korea was a proto-nation before the modern era? What exactly is a proto-nation? It is obvious that we need alternative approaches to the question.

In our context, this leaves us with the problem of how to discuss whether the ritual controversy was a discourse of national identity. The participants, who eventually included the entire intellectual community, seem to have defined the issue as one involving national identity. Thus, the consciousness of a unique identity among seventeenth-century Korean intellectuals was a consciousness of national identity, but in this form, it was not shared by the people. The ritual controversy, which was a debate over the particular ways in which Korea should enact universal Confucian norms, however, was only part of the manifestation of this consciousness, which also seems to have expressed itself in ethnic nationalism.[172] Koreans paid increasing attention to native myth, history, and territoriality,[173] those elements that Anthony Smith identifies as constituents of ethnic nationalism.[174] The evolving consciousness of Korean national identity is a topic for further inquiry, but it is worth noting the mutual interaction between those elements rooted in universalism and those rooted in nativism.

# Despoilers of the Way – Insulters of the Sages: Controversies over the Classics in Seventeenth-Century Korea

## MARTINA DEUCHLER

THIS CHAPTER EXPLORES the confrontation over interpretation of the Classics between upholders of orthodoxy and those who were seeking their own understanding of the Way. This theme is pursued within the wider question of why the subject of orthodoxy versus heterodoxy emerged with exceptional intensity in the second half of the seventeenth century. What were the historical circumstances that at this particular point in time problematized to such an unprecedented degree the traditional division between the scholar in his role as official and in his role as independent seeker of the Way? What aspects of scholarship were at stake? Why, moreover, did the state interfere in scholarly discourse? Were factional interests alone behind these confrontations? What was the role of King Sukchong (r. 1674–1720) in this power play, and how did he interact with the factions?

In the search for answers to these complex questions, this study focuses on three Confucian scholars who were branded as "despoilers of the Way" and "rebels against the Classics" — Yun Hyu (1617–80), Pak Sedang (1629–1703), and Ch'oe Sŏkchŏng (1648–1715). The cases against them were unique in Chosŏn dynasty history. Never before and never thereafter was "classical scholarship" (*kyŏnghak*) placed at the very heart of conflicting concerns over drawing a clear boundary between orthodoxy and heterodoxy. The nature of what constituted the canon was at stake. An analysis of the accusations against these men and of the ensuing debates inside and outside the government thus not only illuminates the nature of Confucian scholarship in seventeenth-century Korea but also uncovers the degree of its interdependence with government power. Although Yun Hyu's case was a kind of prelude that did not itself lead to a major fracas at court, the cases of Pak Sedang and Ch'oe Sŏkchŏng dragged on over several years and incited some of the most acrimonious court debates of the time.

In Korea, the relationship between the state and scholarship had always been extraordinarily close. Confucian scholarship was conceived as a project that in the first instance had to define the moral framework within which the state could function. The state, thus, depended on Confucian scholars for interpreting the moral judgments of the Classics and translating them into blueprints for political action. On the other hand, the state, with the king at its helm, had to safeguard the Confucian Way as embodied in the canonical literature against challenge or subversion. During the first two centuries of the Chosŏn dynasty, this relationship between state and scholarly community had basically been in a dynamic balance, despite occasional violent conflicts. By the seventeenth century, however, this balance became increasingly threatened by the polarization of political forces in the government and the consequent appropriation of the Way by factional interests.

The politicizing of the Way assumed, moreover, a special configuration because of the new cultural role the Koreans perceived for their country after the fall of the Ming and the rise of the Manchu in China. Although itself deeply humiliated by the Manchu, Korea had survived to become "Eastern Chou" (Tongju) — a position that made Korea responsible for upholding Confucian civilization in the face of barbarian rule in China. It was the degenerate state of Neo-Confucianism, the Koreans believed, that had been chiefly responsible for the Ming's demise. The momentous shift to their country of the responsibility for preserving the Confucian heritage led some Koreans to make a highly idealized version of Neo-Confucianism, with Chu Hsi at its center, the touchstone of this restructured cultural universe. Allegiance to orthodox Sung Confucianism, then, not only signified resistance to Ch'ing China but also manifested a scholar's full participation in a national commitment to the pursuit of "right learning."

All three cases studied in this chapter vividly illustrate how in the name of Confucian orthodoxy deviant views were censured, and political interests pursued. Factional passions never ran as high as during the reign of King Sukchong. An outstanding feature of this conflict is that hermeneutical problems and the extent of a commentator's scholarly freedom were at its very center.

### The Protagonists

Yun Hyu belonged to the Namwŏn Yun, and the scholarly tradition of the family reached back to Cho Kwangjo (1482–1519), under whom his great-great-grandfather had studied. Through marital ties, Yun Hyu's family was connected with some of the most prominent kin groups of the time. From an early age, Yun Hyu showed uncommon promise as a student and created a sensation when, at the age of twenty-two, he presented his first work, the *Sadan ch'ilchŏng insim tosim sŏl* (Discourse on the four beginnings and seven emotions, on the human mind and the moral mind). As his reputation as a scholar grew, he was variously recommended for office, but he always declined to serve and lived mostly in the countryside, true to his vow not to enter government service as long as the shame of the humiliating peace with the Manchu was not removed. He was thus not in office when, in 1659, his contrary opinion in the so-called rites controversy incurred the wrath of Song Siyŏl (1607–89), who had earlier admired Yun Hyu's prodigious scholarship (see the chapter by Haboush in this volume). By that time Yun Hyu had come to be firmly associated with the Namin (Southerners), and Song Siyŏl was the leader of the Sŏin (Westerners). After being defeated by Song, Yun Hyu returned to his studies, and "there was no book under Heaven he did not read." In 1674, he again found himself at odds with Song Siyŏl over ritual matters, but this time his views prevailed, and Song Siyŏl was sent into exile. Only at the age of 59 was he briefly drawn into the government, then dominated by the Namin, but later refused to take up the various appointments offered to him. In 1680, when the Namin lost power to the Sŏin, Yun Hyu was one of the main victims and was forced to take his own life.[1]

After his debut with *Sadan ch'ilch'ŏng insim tosim sŏl* in 1638, Yun Hyu had his first productive period during the next six years when he wrote commentaries on parts of the *Shu-ching* (Book of history) and the *Shih-ching* (Book of odes)[2] and on the *Chou-li* (Rites of Chou). His fascination, however, was clearly with the *Chung-yung* (Doctrine of the mean) and the *Ta-hsüeh* (Great learning). His first work on the *Chung-yung*, the *Chungyong sŏl* (Theories on the *Chung-yung*), was completed in 1644. Between 1667 and the early 1670s, he again was absorbed in annotating these two of the Four Books, and it was in particular his "novel theories" (*sinsŏl*) about the *Chung-yung* that led to an estrangement with Song Siyŏl in the early 1650s and to outright enmity some twenty years later. After admonishing Yun to correct his erroneous views, Song called his incorrigible counterpart "a despoiler of the true Way" (*samun nanjŏk*) and made him a target of severe attacks even after Yun's abrupt death in 1680.[3]

Although their cases were later intimately linked, Yun Hyu seems not to have had personal contact with his younger contemporary, Pak Sedang.[4] A scion of the Pannam Pak, Pak Sedang was connected by marriage as well as by factional affiliation with the Sŏin. His brother-in-law was Nam Kuman (1629–1711), who advanced several times to the high office of chief councilor of state, and became in 1683, when the Sŏin split, one of the leaders of the Soron (Young doctrine). For his attacks on Yun Hyu, Nam was sent into exile by the Namin in 1679. Pak Sedang passed the special *munkwa* examination held on the occasion of King Hyŏnjong's (r. 1659–74) enthronement in 1660[5] and was subsequently appointed to minor posts in the Office of the Censor-General (Saganwŏn) and the Office of the Special Counselors (Hongmungwan). He was not keen on an official career and repeatedly asked to be relieved from office. In 1668, he went to Beijing as a member of the winter solstice mission. Even during the brief years of Namin domination (1674–80), Pak received a few appointments. There is little indication, however, that he ever served for any length of time, even after the comeback of the Sŏin in 1680. On the contrary, he seems to have lived most of his life in "quiet retirement" (*yŏmt'oe*) as a retired scholar (*yain*), and between 1680 and 1693 he authored his main works. His economic circumstances apparently were difficult, for in 1696 he was recommended for government support.[6]

Factional politics and government service were thus not Pak Sedang's main concerns, but he ended his life embroiled in one of the most celebrated factional disputes. In 1702, he agreed to write the epitaph for Yi Kyŏngsŏk (1595–1671), who in 1637 had compiled the inscription for the victory monument that the Manchu demanded King Injo (r. 1623–49) erect at Samjŏndo. Any evocation of those ignominious memories was dangerous enough, but Pak Sedang's text was found by Song Siyŏl's disciples to contain veiled criticism of their late master, who had denounced Yi Kyŏngsŏk as an appeaser. This discovery sparked an intense investigation of Pak Sedang's person and work and led to the condemnation of his *Sabyŏnnok* (Thoughtful elucidations) as a subversive and heterodox piece of scholarship.[7] Pak Sedang was spared exile because of old age and died in 1703 before his case was resolved.[8]

The *Sabyŏnnok*, which gained fame as the focus of the controversy, is preserved in three handwritten copies. It contains Pak Sedang's annotations to the Four Books, to which he later added extensive commentaries on the *Shu-ching* and the *Shih-ching*. The latter remained incomplete. Classical Confucian scholarship, however, was not his sole preoccupation. Although he categorically rejected Buddhism, Pak Sedang studied Taoism and produced copious annotations to the *Tao-te ching* (Classic of the way and its virtue) in the *Sinju Todŏkkyŏng* (New annotations to the *Tao-te ching*), and to the *Chuang-tzu* in the *Namhwagyŏng chuhae* (Annotations to and explanations of the *Chuang-tzu*). He even authored a work on the natural sciences and agricultural techniques, the *Saekkyŏng* (Classic of husbandry), for which he is also regarded as a *Sirhak* (Practical learning) scholar. Although Pak Sedang, thus, commanded a wide range of scholarship, it was the *Sabyŏnnok*, which dealt with the Confucian Classics, that revealed to his contemporaries his dangerous deviations from mainstream Confucianism and made him, after Yun Hyu, the second scholar to be branded by the humiliating title "despoiler of the true Way."[9]

If the Confucian establishment had not been in turmoil over Pak Sedang's case in the early years of the eighteenth century, it is possible that Ch'oe Sŏkchŏng would have escaped the scrutiny of excited prosecutors. One investigation, however, led to the next, and Ch'oe Sŏkchŏng became the highest-ranking official to be indicted because of his scholarship. In 1709, when his case broke, he was chief state councilor and one of King Sukchong's intimates. He was a grandson of Ch'oe Myŏnggil (1586–1647), who had been instrumental in negotiating a peaceful settlement with the Manchu after 1637. Ch'oe

Sŏkchŏng, who had been taught by Nam Kuman, among others, passed the *munkwa* examination in 1671 and subsequently embarked on a distinguished career in government service. As a member of the Soron, he experienced the sharp turnabouts of factional politics, but he managed to stay at the center of power for a remarkably long span of time. Besides being a successful official, Ch'oe Sŏkchŏng pursued scholarly interests and, among other works, compiled a book of annotations to the *Li-chi* (Book of rites), the *Yegi yup'yŏn* (Classifications of the *Li-chi*). Although this work was not the sole cause of his downfall, the controversy around this compilation created that anxious uncertainty at court that could lead to a sudden turn in royal favor against even a trusted official. Ch'oe Sŏkchŏng was dismissed from office, but died in 1715 before the question of whether he should be exiled was resolved. The printing blocks of the *Yegi yup'yŏn*, however, were burned, and the work is no longer extant.[10]

## The Definition of the Orthodox

Ever since the categorical pronouncements by Yi T'oegye (1501–70) that "right learning" was the strict and faithful adherence to Ch'eng-Chu philosophy,[11] Korean Confucians had labored under the commitment of proving themselves worthy followers of the orthodox Way. Any deviation from this path was not only intellectually but also politically dangerous, and conformity was therefore the most prudent course.

Such conservatism was celebrated anew in the second half of the seventeenth century as part of Korean cultural resistance to Manchu rule in China.[12] It was Song Siyŏl who appointed himself guardian of Chu Hsi's philosophical heritage in Korea. As one of his foremost disciples, Kwŏn Sangha (1641–1721), put it in Song's epitaph: Confucius was born during the troubled times at the end of Chou, Chu Hsi in the Southern Sung, and Song Siyŏl at the end of the Ming. If at such critical points in history sages and worthies did not come forth, "the great principles and the great laws" would surely disappear from this earth.[13] For Song, for whom the fall of the Ming had signified the breakdown of Confucian civilization in China, the guardianship of Ch'eng-Chu orthodoxy could no longer be a purely intellectual commitment. It became part and parcel of his political philosophy that connected the preservation of the Ch'eng-Chu legacy with Korea's independence and self-preservation vis-à-vis the

Manchu conquerors of China. Within this new framework, the definition of the orthodox and the pursuit of scholarship acquired a degree of political sensitiveness that demanded constant government
scrutiny and adjudication.

As part of such an awesome intellectual and political tradition,
Song Siyŏl carried the veneration of Chu Hsi even further than
T'oegye and made the great Sung Neo-Confucian the only source of
truth. In Song's definition the Confucian canon comprised more than
the Five Classics and the Four Books. It also included, besides Chu
Hsi's commentaries, the *Chu Tzu ta-ch'üan* (Complete literary works
of Chu Hsi), the *Chu Tzu yü-lei* (Classified conversations of Master
Chu), the *Chin-ssu lu* (Reflections on things at hand), and the *Yi-lo
yüan-yüan lu* (Record of origins from Yi-lo).[14] In short, Song Siyŏl expanded the canon by incorporating Chu Hsi's entire oeuvre in it.
Song's concerns were not with originality. Rather, he saw his principal task as propagating this extended corpus of literature as the final
and definitive stage of the transmission of the Way (*tao-t'ung*) and
aspired to hand it on intact and unspoiled to future generations of
Korean Confucians.

Song Siyŏl was an awe-inspiring figure on the intellectual as well
as on the political scene. He was a tireless and uncompromising ex-
positor of Chu Hsi's thought and ideas and lashed out fiercely
against anyone he perceived as deviating from them. He wrote hundreds of letters to his colleagues and followers and dozens of memorials to the kings he served. In emphatic, at times even aggressive,
terms he stated his opinions, discussed current trends, and above all
warned against those who dared to differ with what he had established as the immutable Confucian truth. His authority as scholar
and teacher was coupled with the prestige of a long and distinguished (even if at times interrupted) government career. He was
the leading figure of the Sŏin and, after the split of 1683, of the Noron (Old doctrine). By marriage he was well connected (even with
some of his later adversaries), and among his supporters were members of the most powerful kin groups of the time. In the second half
of the seventeenth century, Song was unquestionably the dominant
figure of the Confucian establishment, and even after his death in
disgrace in 1689, his ideas continued to have a firm grip on his faction, which was largely made up of his disciples.[15]

It is ironic that Song Siyŏl, who regarded Yi Yulgok (1536–84) as
his intellectual ancestor—the actual link between the two was the

famous ritualist Kim Changsaeng (1548-1631) — would turn out to be such an inflexible and pedantic defender of "right learning," for it was Yi Yulgok who had pleaded for making the Mencian concept of "obtaining truth through one's own efforts" (chadŭk) the touchstone of creative scholarship.[16] Such a personal effort to get at the truth embodied in the Classics did not, in Yulgok's view, lead away from Chu Hsi, but rather constituted an individual contribution to an on-going process of scholarship.

Indeed, Korea did not lack a tradition of textual "dissent" — a tradition that all three protagonists of this chapter cited to justify their own "deviations" from the orthodox path. The scholar-official Yi Ŏnjŏk (1491-1553) was generally identified as the earliest example of a Korean Confucian who boldly came forth with his own version of the Ta-hsüeh, the Taehak changgu poyu (Additional comments [Chu His's] Ta-hsüeh chang-chü). Regretting that the Classics of the sages and the commentaries of the worthies were not without deficiencies and obscurities, Yi Ŏnjŏk felt compelled to go beyond Chu Hsi's textual arrangement and to produce his own reconstruction. Both Yi T'oegye and Yi Yulgok later censured this willful deviation from established norms. This almost cost Yi Ŏnjŏk the greatest Confucian honor, a place in the Munmyo (Shrine of Confucius).[17]

A later "dissenter" was the high official and eminent scholar, Cho Ik (1579-1655), who authored a number of commentaries on the Classics. In the Kyŏngsŏ kondŭkp'yŏn (Annotations on the Classics painfully acquired) and other treatises, Cho Ik wrote frankly that although he was generally following Chu Hsi's lead and did not intend to establish new interpretations (sinŭi), he could not but jot down some notes when he had doubts in his mind and produce his own explications. In his quest for what he called "the reality of meaning" (ŭiri chi sil), he said: "If there are any doubts, one must think [a passage] over and over and investigate it thoroughly and stop only when one comes to a conclusion [i.e., to the real meaning]."[18]

In Song Siyŏl's opinion, these two scholars, as well as those of his contemporaries who followed their example, were guilty of unacceptable "heterodox" deviations (idan) that he had to combat with all his energy — an enterprise that was encapsulated in the often-repeated battlecry "Defend the Way by revering the Classics" (chon'gyŏng wido).

## *The Hermeneutic Process and Scholarly Independence: The Case of Yun Hyu*

All three scholars under consideration here had strong views on the nature of scholarly inquiry and the hermeneutic process. In view of the absolute scholarshly authority ascribed to Chu Hsi, at issue was the crucial question of how much freedom a commentator could assume for himself without arousing suspicion of rejecting Chu Hsi. In the face of Song Siyŏl's attacks for rearranging the *Chung-yung*, Yun Hyu issued the following justification:

In my writings I do not wish to establish points of view different from Chu Hsi's interpretations. All I want to do is to note down problems. In case I had been born in Chu Hsi's time and had become one of his disciples, I would not have wanted simply to follow him blindly and, without seeking an understanding for myself, merely to express my admiration for him. I would certainly have questioned him repeatedly about difficult points and thought about these again and again in the expectation of finally understanding them clearly myself. If, without raising doubtful points and leaving unclear points aside, I had blindly followed him, such devotion and trust would have been fake. Would Chu Hsi have been like this [i.e., have tolerated this]? All I wish to do is to discuss things with my friends in the hope that one day I gradually get [an understanding] for myself (*chadŭk*). Lately, however, Song Siyŏl has rejected [my views] as heresy (*idan*). Song Siyŏl's scholarship never raises any questions, and as to Chu Hsi' interpretations, he foolishly insists that there is no room for discussion. Even if I said that I revered and trusted [Chu Hsi], would this really mean that I had got [a understanding] of my own?[19]

This noteworthy document reveals how a scholar outside Song Siyŏl's circle of disciples viewed the problems besetting classical scholarship in the second half of the seventeenth century. Yun separated the "blind" followers of Chu Hsi from those who tried to come to their own personal understanding of classical wisdom. For the former, the Confucian canon was a closed entity with no room for further exploration and discussion. The latter did not question the authority of Chu Hsi and his contemporaries, but saw them much as themselves: as gropers for the truth who hoped to reach their own understanding (*chasŏl*). In this spirit Yun Hyu is reported to have exclaimed: "How does Chu Hsi alone know the profound meaning of the Classics and their commentaries, and we not?"[20] Or, "How could Chu Hsi know Tzu-ssu's meaning, and I not?"[21]

Yun Hyu characterized his method of reading the Classics and Chu Hsi's commentaries as a repetitive process of recording and editing. Occasional changes he would make only after having an insight of his own or after a discussion with friends or students.[22] He collected his notes in the *Toksŏ'gi* (Reading notes), also known by its alternative title, *Chasŏlchip* (Collection of my own theories). It contained his various revisions of the *Chung-yung* and the *Ta-hsüeh*. In the Preface to the *Chungyong kaeju* (Revised commentary on *Chung-yung*), he wrote:

When I first read the *Chung-yung*, I briefly noted down the main meanings and the sequence of the sentences and phrases that I read in order not to forget them and only in the expectation of discussing them [later]. I read it [*Chung-yung*] again and again over several decades and studied it, and never forgot it in my mind, yet I could not discover great differences [with Chu Hsi's commentaries] and was embarrassed about the lack of progress in my scholarship. . . . Now I have combined into one book what I recorded in my mind and what I have recorded [on paper] at different stages, thinking that I shall get corrections from people who have the Tao. . . . When Chu Hsi annotated all the Classics, he collected all the [previous] theories (*sŏl*), struck a compromise between them, and came up with his own complete theories.

Chu Hsi himself, Yun Hyu noted, was never satisfied with the results of his explorations and continued to search and discuss, and only death stopped him from further amending and correcting his earlier theories. "This I take as my model and intend to make a [similar] effort."[23] Yun Hyu thus consciously put himself within Chu Hsi's own tradition of writing and rewriting the commentaries as a continuous commitment to the Classics. This is also clear from the following passage:

The sages [of antiquity] handed down the Six Classics, and the early Confucians (*sŏnyu*) elucidated their meaning. . . . However, born several thousand years later and discussing them [the Classics] on [the experience of] several thousand years, is it possible that nothing is expected from those [who live] later? . . . When I read the book [i.e., the *Shu-ching*], I took notes as I went along grasping [its meaning] (*sudŭk sup'il*) and what my predecessors have not elucidated, I connected with what I have read and heard, making it the basis for arriving at a correct [understanding].[24]

Yun Hyu laid down his "correct understanding" of the *Chung-yung* in two works, the *Chungyong changgu ch'aje* (Sequence of the Sentences and Phrases of the *Chung-yung*) and the *Chungyong Chuja changgu porok* (Addenda to Master Chu's *Sentences and Phrases of the*

*Chung-yung*).[25] The *Sequence* contains Yun Hyu's new arrangement of the text into ten chapters with twenty-eight subsections (in contrast to Chu Hsi's thirty-three chapters). In the *Addenda*, following Chu Hsi's textual divisions, Yun expanded on the meaning of the text. To Yun Hyu, the *Chung-yung* represented nothing less than the essence of Heaven (*ch'ŏnmyŏng*). In addition to describing the nature of Heaven, the book also explicated "being cautious and apprehensive" as the state of mind by which the superior man served Heaven (*sach'ŏn*). Although Chu Hsi emphasized explaining the Way as an all-encompassing, yet transcendental entity, Yun Hyu seems to have been more concerned with "realizing equilibrium and harmony" (*ch'i chunghwa*)—a state that would prevent the Way from getting lost and enable the myriad things in Heaven and on Earth as well as mankind to recover their true nature. Active reverence of Heaven was thus one of Yun Hyu's central concerns.[26]

This more active interpretation of the Classics' message is also evident in Yun Hyu's analysis of some of the key words in the *Ta-hsüeh*. To him, *kyŏk* (Chin. *ko*) in *kyŏngmul* (Chin. *ko-wu*) did not have the conventional meaning of "investigation of things," given it by Chu Hsi, but rather meant "to communicate with things intuitively through complete sincerity." *Mul* pointed to such actions as "manifesting the clear character" and "renovating the people." In other words, *kyŏngmul* signified spontaneous communication with all things. Moreover, *chi* (*-ji*) in the compound *ch'iji* (Chin. *chih-chih*), "extension of knowledge," had the Mencian flavor of *yangji* (Chin. *liang-chih*) and thus meant grasping things without discursive thinking. Clearly, Yun Hyu distanced himself from Chu Hsi's rationality by postulating individual efforts to create a harmonious moral and human environment.[27]

It was Yun Hyu's daring formulations of individual insights and opinions, conspicuously expressed in his works on the *Chung-yung* and the *Ta-hsüeh*, against which Song Siyŏl objected so strongly. In a celebrated discussion with his Sŏin colleague, Yun Sŏn'gŏ (1610–69), in 1652, Song accused Yun Hyu of devising novel theories and was infuriated at Yun Sŏn'gŏ's suggestion that "[since] meanings and principles (*ŭiri*) are the common property of the world, why should I wish not to let [Yun] Hyu speak his mind?" This remark revealed Yun Sŏn'gŏ's sympathy for Yun Hyu. Thereupon Song branded Yun Hyu as a "despoiler of the true Way" and placed Yun Sŏn'gŏ in the "opposition camp" (*pandang*).[28]

The conflict between Yun Hyu and Song Siyŏl accelerated through the ritual controversies (*yesong*) of 1659 and 1674, but at its core remained their differing views on the value of Chu Hsi's commentaries.[29] Yun Hyu caused a sensation at court when during a royal lecture late in 1674 he suggested to young King Sukchong that it was not absolutely necessary to read Chu Hsi's commentaries on the *Lun-yü* (Analects of Confucius) because they were the stuff "examination Confucians" (*kwayu*) had to labor over.[30] In reaction, Song Siyŏl partisan and royal secretary Kim Manjung (1637–92) exclaimed: "What the sages and worthies meant we cannot have heard! . . . If we do not read the commentaries, how can we find out and comprehend the meaning of the Classics?" In contrast to China, he continued, in Korea Chu Hsi's commentaries had been studied faithfully since the beginning of the dynasty, and there was no reason to abandon them now.[31]

Although Yun Hyu's influence as a "despoiler of the Way" was feared beyond his death—Song Siyŏl was relentless in depicting him as the worst evildoer in the world—it is safe to conclude that what Yun Hyu intended was not to destroy the Four Books but to cast doubt on the notion that Chu Hsi had a monopoly on their interpretation. It was this tendency of demystifying the classical enterprise that led him to propose that the taboo against using Confucius' name (*hwi*) be discarded when lecturing in front of the king. He moreover called for a return to the original texts (*chŏngmun*) because they alone, he insisted, should be the basis of sage learning. He himself compiled a critical version of the *Ta-hsüeh* based on the version found in the *Li-chi* entitled *Taehak kobon pyŏllok* (Special records on the old version of the *Ta-hsüeh*).[32] Why, he asked, was it necessary to refer to the original version? Because after the death of Confucius and his seventy disciples the subtle wording and the general meaning of the classic had become corrupted, but the Ch'eng brothers and Chu Hsi restored the text so that it could shine again in the world. Their interpretations and reconstructions, however, differed from each other. So did the later emendations of people like Wang Po (1197–1274) and the early Korean Confucians. For this reason it was necessary never to tire of "investigating it [the *Ta-hsüeh*] thoroughly and discussing it publicly."[33]

Yun Hyu tried to justify his scholarship by fitting himself into the long tradition of Sung classical expositors like Wang Po who, after Chu Hsi, freely presented new ways of punctuating and reading the classical texts.[34] He therefore denied Chu Hsi the privilege of being revered as the sole infallible commentator on the Classics.

## Pak Sedang's Hermeneutic Enterprise

In his own "Sŏgye ch'osu myop'yo" (Tombstone epitaph for wood-cutter Sŏgye), Pak Sedang wrote autobiographically shortly before his death:

He realized that his talents were weak and insufficient for succeeding in this world. The world moreover was deteriorating daily beyond rescue. Thus, he took leave from office and went into retirement. He settled down outside the East Gate some thirty miles away from the capital in a valley east of Surak mountain. He named the valley Sŏkch'ŏndong and referred to himself as woodcutter Sŏgye. Near water he built a house and did not fence it in. [Instead] he planted peach trees, apricot trees, pear trees, and chestnut trees around it. He cultivated gourds and grew rice, and sold wood for a living. [Even] during the winter months he always went out into the fields and kept company with those who hoed and plowed. At first, he was also at times called to court, but later he no longer answered the frequent summons. He lived [like this] for more than thirty years and then died at the age of over seventy. He is buried some hundred and odd feet behind where he used to live. He once wrote the *T'ongsŏl* to explain the teaching of the *Book of Odes*, the *Book of History*, and the Four Books, and annotated the *Lao-tzu* and the *Chuang-tzu* in order to show their meaning. He took great delight in the words of *Mencius* since he regarded him as independent and nonconformist. [Yet] in the end, he was not willing to surrender himself to him.[35]

This last sentence reveals that woodcutter Sŏgye, while placing himself firmly in the Confucian tradition, strove to maintain a critical mind and was unwilling to enter into easy compromises. It was this critical attitude of mind toward the nature and purpose of scholarship—often strikingly similar to that of Yun Hyu—that eventually embroiled him, despite his life as a rusticated scholar, in the most celebrated Classics controversy of his time.[36]

In the Preface to his *Sabyŏnnok*, dated 1689, Pak Sedang outlined his views on classical literature:

The books of the Six Classics all record the words of the various sages since Yao and Shun. Their principles are delicate, and their meanings complete, their intention deep, and their direction far. Speaking of their delicateness, their wording cannot be altered in the minutest detail, and in their completeness there is not even the smallest mistake. If one wanted to fathom their depth, the bottom could not be reached; and if one wanted to exhaust their distance, the furthest end would not be visible. They indeed are not what the shallow measuring and crude knowledge of biased scholars and shackled Confucians can comprehend. . . . The Commentary says: "If one wants to travel to a distant place, one must start from the nearest point."[37] What does this mean? Is this not whereby we teach unenlightened people so that they will be able to come to an understanding by themselves? If we indeed made the learners of this world grasp this, they would understand that what is meant above by "distant" can be reached from the nearest point.

Pak Sedang pleaded for a step-by-step approach to scholarship, leading from the near to the far, from the coarse to the refined, as the surest method to reach the "utmost of refinement and completeness." He paid tribute to the contribution the Ch'eng brothers and Chu Hsi had made by letting the message of the Six Classics shine again throughout the world. But then he asserted:

As to what the Classics say, their main thrust is one, whereas their branches are numerous. This is what is meant by "one principle, yet one hundred thoughts; same conclusion, yet manifold ways." Therefore, even those with exceptional knowledge and unique understanding, deep insights and subtle attainments, may still be unable to get completely their [i.e., the Classics'] meaning without losing some details. They must therefore wait [with their conclusions until] they have collected widely all the strong points [of others] without losing the smallest good point, and only then nothing crude and partial is left, and nothing shallow or near seeps through. Then, the structure of the refined and complete, the deep and the far, is completely attained.

Pak Sedang concluded this Preface by asserting that his work, the *Sabyŏnnok*, had not originated from a desire on his part to differ from established scholarly norms and put forward his own theories (*sŏl*).[38]

Despite this avowal, however, Pak Sedang was obviously well aware that his critical commentaries were apt to offend the sensibilities of traditionalists. He in fact seems to imply that by providing easy and allegedly complete explanations, the commentaries by Chu Hsi and other Sung Neo-Confucians promoted the "superficiality and crudeness" of his contemporaries' understanding of the Classics. Pak Sedang recognized the Ch'eng-Chu school as no more than an important intermediary stage in the development of Confucianism. After all, Chu Hsi's explanations of how he had arrived at a particular conclusion, Pak Sedang found, were often vague, and thus left it to the brighter sort of scholars to arrive at their own understanding. However, in Pak's judgment, bright scholars were scarce in this world, and the few that existed might not possess sufficient courage to argue against Chu Hsi. The inevitable result was stagnation in scholarship. The dim view Pak Sedang held of contemporary scholarship encouraged him to pursue his own path of inquiry, albeit in silence. As he testified self-consciously, he did not "dare to make noises about it [i.e., his scholarship] to others lest I be accused of craziness and rebelliousness."[39]

### Pak Sedang's Sabyŏnnok

About the origins of the *Sabyŏnnok*, the entry for 1680 of Pak Sedang's *Chronological Biography* provides the following information:

He had already retired and lived in solitude. He consequently put his mind exclusively to studying the Classics. He delved into them for many years and, only after his understanding had become thorough, did he begin to correct mistakes in the sequence of characters and sentences, and to dispute errors in the commentaries and explanations. He wrote it all down and made it into a book he called *T'ongsŏl* (Unified theory) or *Sabyŏnnok*.[40]

The *Sabyŏnnok* deals with all Four Books and two Classics; the following discussion is limited to outlining some of Pak's major interpretations of the *Chung-yung* and the *Ta-hsüeh* that eventually aroused the Confucian establishment against him.

Like many of his predecessors and contemporaries in both Korea and China, Pak Sedang devoted much of his scholarly efforts to the *Chung-yung* and the *Ta-hsüeh*. These two works, Pak Sedang wrote, derived from the version of the *Li-chi* that survived Ch'in Shih-huang-ti's book burning. Consequently they contained many mistakes, only some of which were later corrected by the Ch'eng brothers and Chu Hsi. Errors and uncertainties about the "meaning of words" (*ŏŭi*) thus remained. Pak Sedang devised a hermeneutical method with which he hoped to unlock and restore the original meaning of these books.

Names (*myŏng*; Chin. *ming*) need reality (*sil*; Chin. *shih*), and their referents (*mul*; Chin. *wu*), principle (*i*; Chin. *li*). In their writings, the sages and worthies of ancient times laid down the meanings in respect to names and their referents in order to clarify principle and elucidate reality. Later readers of these writings must first know the names before they can search for their reality; they must first know their referents before they can investigate their principle. Only after knowing the names and their referents will they be able to grasp their meanings.[41]

The reader, in other words, needs a solid comprehension of semantics to understand the concepts and principles contained in words. This, however, was not all. Beyond the meanings of words lay the overall structure, the "arteries and the veins," of a text. The sentences had to be unobstructed, that is, put in proper sequence for the logic of the text to emerge.[42] These methodological insights prompted Pak Sedang not only to investigate key words in the Confucian vocabulary, but also to reorganize the texts.

Like many scholars before him, Pak Sedang wrestled in his commentary on the *Ta-hsüeh* with the meaning of such key terms as *kyŏngmul* (Chin. *ko-wu*) and *ch'iji* (Chin. *chih-chih*). By taking *ch'i* to mean "to search and attain" and *kyŏk* "pattern," or "standard," he reformulated what Chu Hsi had interpreted as "investigation of things" as "to search for a thing's inherent pattern in order to attain it [this pattern] in its standard form." He elaborated: "If there is a thing (*mul*; Chin. *wu*), there must be an inherent pattern (*ch'ik*; Chin. *tse*). Because a thing has such a pattern, one searches for it in the hope of attaining its most correct form (*chŏng*; Chin. *cheng*). Thus, I mean: one wishes to make one's knowledge capable of reaching what is proper in a thing and thus to handle it completely according to its pattern." With this decidedly practical approach to analysis, Pak Sedang rejected as incorrect Chu Hsi's idealistic interpretation of the terms.[43] He insisted on a clear differentiation between "things" (*mul*) and "affairs/actions" (*sa*; Chin. *shih*). " 'The world' and 'the state' are things and not affairs, whereas 'to pacify [the world],' 'to put in order [the state],' and 'to regulate [the family]' are affairs/actions and not things."[44] Such definitions were important to Pak Sedang because, unlike Chu Hsi, he regarded the *Ta-hsüeh* as a beginner's text intended to lead "the learner to use the method of *kyŏngmul* and *ch'iji* in respect to every thing and affair so that with this knowledge he can trace their every pattern." At the end of this process was a full grasp of their reality (*sil*).[45]

Pak Sedang also made a basic change in the structure of the *Ta-hsüeh*. Instead of the "three items" (*samgang*) and "eight steps" (*p'almok*) of Chu Hsi's arrangement, he maintained that in fact there were only two items because "abiding in the highest good" summed up "manifesting the clear character" and "renovating the people." Moreover, none of the "eight steps" matched "abiding in the highest good": the first five steps illustrated "manifesting the clear character" and the remaining three "renovating the people."[46] For Chu Hsi, "manifesting the clear character" was the fundamental action, and "renovating the people" was that action's final goal. In contrast, Pak Sedang interpreted them as of equal importance by classifying both "manifesting" and "renovating" as "affairs/actions" and "clear character" and "people" as "things," thus establishing a dynamic relationship between the two.[47]

Pak Sedang also labored hard and long over the *Chung-yung*, a text he regarded as more profound and enigmatic than the *Ta-hsüeh*. The problems started with the title. He was baffled by Ch'eng I's and Chu Hsi's different interpretations of the character *yong* (Chin. *yung*)—"unchangeable" (Ch'eng I) and "neither one-sided nor extreme" (Chu Hsi)—interpretations that in his view added nothing to the meaning of *chung*, "central." He interpreted *yong* to mean "constant." *Chung-yung* thus meant, he asserted, that "since one wants to achieve what is central in [every] affair, one wishes even more to maintain it [the centrality] constantly without losing it even for a brief moment." In short, Pak Sedang saw as the main message of the *Doctrine of the Mean* not only the attainment of centrality, but above all its active preservation, in the sense that "the Way cannot be separated from us for a moment."[48]

More fundamentally, Pak Sedang disagreed with Chu Hsi's equation of (human) nature (*sŏng*; Chin. *hsing*) with principle (*i*).

Why do I not agree with this? Because it is impossible. If, when speaking of human nature, one calls it principle, and if, when speaking of the Way, one also calls it principle, this makes their contents the same, and no differentiation [between the two] is reached. [In Chu Hsi's commentary on section 1] it is first said of the Way: "If [each human being and thing] complies with the naturalness of its nature, in daily affairs and things there is none who does not follow an appropriate path." Here [in Chu Hsi's commentary on section 2] it is said of the Way that "it is contained in the mind as the nature's virtue." These two theories differ from each other and are not congruous. If the Way were the original substance of the Heavenly principle, then it [chapter 1 of the *Chung-yung*] should have said: "The Way contained in the mind is called [human] nature," and not "to follow nature is called the Way."[49]

Earlier Pak had pointed out that when principle manifests itself in the mind, it becomes (human) nature. "In Heaven, it means principle, whereas in human beings it means human nature." These two terms should not be confused, and therefore the *Chung-yung* spoke of principle, (human) nature, and education. "If these terms are confused, one may well lose the sequence of beginning and end that lies in them [so that] one is unable to understand the meaning of what is said."[50]

Clearly, Pak Sedang intended to separate principle as a metaphysical entity from principle as embodied in human nature. If there were no such differentiation, there would be no need for two different terms.[51] Moreover, preoccupied with terms and their referents, Pak Sedang could not accept that "nature" (sŏng) was supposed to refer to both human beings and things.

[Chu Hsi's] commentary says "nature" pertains to both human beings and things. Now why do I leave things aside and speak only of human beings? Even though things also have a nature, their nature is different from that of human beings. It is not possible to speak [as Chu Hsi has done] of "the virtue of the Five Constants" in connection with things, because this is not the main thrust of the Chung-yung. The commentary says: "Human beings and things—each follows the naturalness of its nature; this is called the Way." Why do I here, too, speak only of human beings? It is because the Chung-yung speaks only of human beings and not of things. The Chung-yung as a book is to educate human beings and not things. Human beings can be educated, things cannot. Human beings are capable of knowing the Way, things cannot.[52]

With such statements Pak Sedang distanced himself considerably from traditional views and presaged the extended debates in the eighteenth century between those who insisted that the nature of human beings differed from that of things and those who recognized no difference between the two.

In sum, Pak Sedang's interpretations tackled not only hermeneutical problems but also fundamental philosophical questions. What he was looking for in the Classics was not a justification of a moral way. Rather, with his independence of mind, he passionately searched for the "reality" hidden behind words. His contemporaries consequently found the approach as well as the direction of his scholarship outside the bounds of orthodoxy.

### The Case Against Pak Sedang

The case against Pak Sedang—its origin, its course, and its resolution—was played out within the factional context of the time. An analysis of this extensively documented case illuminates thought and the relationship between state and scholarship at the turn of the eighteenth century.

The precipitating event was Pak's composition of a tomb inscription in 1702 for Yi Kyŏngsŏk. Although old and reportedly seriously ill, Pak Sedang seems readily to have agreed with the request from Yi's grandson. It provided him with an opportunity to justify Yi Kyŏngsŏk's writing the inscription on the Samjŏndo stele as an inevitable act dictated by the historical circumstances and to express, albeit in veiled form, his disgust for Song Siyŏl, who, even though indebted to Yi, became Yi's severest detractor. More than sixty years after the Manchu humiliation and with both protagonists dead for some time, Pak Sedang's comparison of Yi Kyŏngsŏk to a phoenix and of Song Siyŏl to an owl (believed to be a cunning and false bird) unleashed passions and resentments among Song Siyŏl's followers "like fire." This fire eventually threatened Pak himself and his work.[53]

Although a contemporary witness like Nam Kuman was convinced that Pak Sedang's authorship of Yi Kyŏngsŏk's epitaph alone was responsible for drawing attention to his scholarly works,[54] rumors about Pak Sedang's unorthodox interpretations of the Classics had apparently circulated before he wrote the critical tomb inscription. Although in government circles such rumors were not considered serious enough to warrant investigation, they reportedly disturbed some Confucian scholars.[55] It was thus allegedly out of concern for "this Way" that in spring 1703 the prominent Noron scholar Kim Ch'anghŭp (1653–1722) sent a letter to Yi Tŏksu (1673–1744), one of Pak Sedang's disciples and a student of Kim's as well. Upon hearing the news that Pak Sedang had "destroyed the Classics," Kim wrote, he had been greatly disturbed and searched for words to refute him. Some around him had tried to dissuade him by arguing that compared to Lu Hsiang-shan and Wang Yang-ming, Pak was not worth a discussion, or that because Pak was living in retirement, he should not be attacked. Yet, Kim continued, he was advancing three principal reasons for indicting Pak Sedang: Pak's attack against Chu Hsi was, by extension, an attack against Song Siyŏl; Pak was as bad as Yun Hyu, whom Song Siyŏl had censured as a rebel on account of his alterations of the *Chung-yung*; and Pak must be refuted in order to forestall a flood of divergent opinions. With these dire warnings, Kim Ch'anghŭp inflamed Confucian opinion and initiated the campaign against Pak Sedang, which was to last for almost a decade.[56]

Pak Sedang's works probably were never read outside a small circle of intimates, but rumors about their contents, fanned by Kim Ch'anghŭp's allegations, abounded. Immediately after Kim had sounded the alarm, Hong Kyejŏk (n.d.) and some 180 of his fellow students at the Confucian Academy (Sŏnggyun'gwan) handed in a lengthy memorial. Orthodoxy, they wrote, had reached its climax with Chu Hsi, yet Pak Sedang had not only "insulted the sages and vilified the worthies" by producing, in defiance of Chu Hsi, his own "complete theories" but also disparaged Song Siyŏl on Yi Kyŏng-sŏk's tomb inscription. Pak had not taken Yun Hyu's case as a warning and, on the contrary, followed in his footsteps. It was, moreover, Yun Hyu's faction that had martyred Song Siyŏl, on whom the transmission of the Way in Korea had solely depended. The damage Pak had inflicted on Confucian orthodoxy, the memorialists exclaimed, spread through his disciples who, revering their teacher, transmitted his teachings "in the dark." This was all the more serious because among his disciples were "sons and younger brothers of high officials." "If Pak Sedang were to escape punishment and were left to disseminate his words of rebellion even further, we fear that the ensuing disaster would eventually obstruct the sun and billow up to the sky." The memorialists ended their long and passionately worded submission by making King Sukchong responsible for averting such a disaster and defending the sagely Way. Reminding him of the two ruinous Namin takeovers in 1674 and 1689, they warned that Pak Sedang's case had the potential to become yet another such catastrophe. They urged the immediate confiscation of Pak's commentaries and Yi Kyŏngsŏk's tomb inscription and counseled the king "to throw them into fire and water in order to destroy [the evil] at its roots." King Sukchong, apparently taken by surprise, hastily ordered an investigation.[57]

On the same day, Minister of Rites Kim Chin'gwi (1651–1704)[58] confirmed the memorialists' charges. He reported that Pak Sedang had produced "new theories" (sinsŏl) which conflicted with established wisdom and had altered the sequence of phrases and sentences in the Chung-yung. He recommended that officials of the Office of the Special Counselors be ordered to refute Pak's work paragraph by paragraph. Pak himself should be stripped of rank and office and thrown out of Seoul.[59]

In the face of this massive, state-backed censure of his master, Yi T'an (n.d.), who declared himself a disciple of Pak Sedang, launched a defense. He began on a safe note by expressing unconditional allegiance to Chu Hsi's explanations of the Six Classics, which were in "everybody's mouth" and comparable to "food that cannot be kept away from the mouth for a single day, or to clothing that cannot be kept away from the body for an instant." But because the meanings and principles of the Classics were inexhaustible, doubts could readily arise. It is natural for men, Yi T'an reasoned, to have doubts and to want to clear them up. Therefore, if searching for explanations were equated with destroying the Classics, and taking notes, with insulting earlier sages, would not the teaching of "investigation of things" become irrelevant? Even Ch'eng I and Chu Hsi had encouraged divergent explanations and had in fact differed. Pak Sedang had been living in the countryside for a long time and had simply noted down his private thoughts, eventually producing the *Sabyŏnnok*. Such scholarship, Yi T'an was at pains to point out, had to be judged against the background of historical precedents, and he cited Chang Yu (1587–1638), Cho Ik, Yi T'oegye, Yi Ŏnjŏk, and Kim Changsaeng as illustrious scholars known for their independent interpretations of doubtful passages in the Classics. Had the state ever prohibited the jotting down of private notes? Moreover, Pak Sedang had not been pursuing selfish interests when he wrote the tomb inscription for Yi Kyŏngsŏk. How, Yi T'an asked, could King Sukchong, who had earlier rewarded Pak Sedang, now allow him to be punished like a criminal?[60]

Yi T'an's memorial was seconded by Yi Ingmyŏng (n.d.), another of Pak Sedang's disciples, who accused Hong Kyejŏk and his fellow memorialists of trumping up charges of "destroying the Classics and insulting the sages" against Pak Sedang out of personal resentment. Both Yi T'an and Yi Ingmyŏng were punished for their outspokenness. Under Noron pressure, they were forced to withdraw their memorials; Yi T'an was dismissed from office, and Yi Ingmyŏng was exiled.[61]

When Pak Sedang heard of the royal order that stripped him of rank and office and expelled him from the capital, he awaited the final verdict outside the East Gate. Some ten days after his case had been opened by Hong Kyejŏk's memorial, he was punished with distant exile to Okkwa, a notoriously bad place in a mountainous area of South Chŏlla. Only the intercession of Yi Inyŏp (n.d.), then a subaltern military officer, saved Pak from this ordeal. Admitting that he was incapable of judging the worth of the *Sabyŏnnok*, Yi advanced

Pak Sedang's old age as the main argument for clemency. Moreover, he emphasized the private character of Pak's work and reminded the king that Pak Sedang's son, T'aebo, had lost his life when in 1689 he strongly opposed the expulsion of the king's second wife, Queen Inhyŏn.[62] Surely, the memory of T'aebo's integrity was sufficient to rescue his father now. This plea resulted in the cancellation of the banishment order. After returning to Sŏkch'ŏndong in the fifth month, Pak Sedang died in the eighth month of 1703, at the age of 75.[63]

Even after Pak returned home to await death—a royal favor that was disputed repeatedly—his work remained to be dealt with. Hong Kyejŏk had demanded its destruction as a warning to the world that "Chu Hsi's words cannot be obliterated, and the worthiness of Song Siyŏl cannot be insulted." Although the king ordered the immediate burning of the Sabyŏnnok as well as of the tomb inscription for Yi Kyŏngsŏk, this order could not be immediately executed because the two documents were not available. Yi Chinyang, Yi Kyŏngsŏk's grandson, was stripped of office and subjected to a heavy beating for hesitating to forward a copy of the inscription, and a bold memorialist, Yu Ŏnmyŏng (1666–?), who pleaded for the preservation of the works so that "everyone can read them and recognize the crime of Pak Sedang's errors," was suspected of dubious motives.[64]

While the government authorities waited for the evidence to arrive in the capital, kinsmen of the scholars whom Yi T'an and Yi Ingmyŏng had mentioned in their defense of Pak Sedang protested on behalf of their ancestors. As a representative of the Kwangsan Kim, Third Deputy Commander Kim Chin'gyu (1658–1716), a younger brother of Kim Chin'gwi and a disciple of Song Siyŏl, stood up for his great-great-grandfather, Kim Changsaeng. He angrily pointed out that Kim Changsaeng's Kyŏngsŏ pyŏnŭi (Discussions of doubtful points in the Classics) was completely in line with Chu Hsi's thought and was directly informed by Yi Yulgok's scholarship. It did not in the slightest resemble what Pak Sedang had done. For the Kwangsan Kim, the connection the two Yi had made between Pak Sedang and Kim Changsaeng must have been all the more distressing because the case for the enshrinement of their illustrious kinsman in the Shrine of Confucius was still pending. At the end of his memorial, Kim Chin'gyu requested that Kim Changsaeng's faithful adherence to orthodoxy be attested by a royal edict. The king granted this request without delay.[65] A similar argument was made by Confucian student Yun Yangnae (1673–1751), who asserted in a memorial that note taking while reading the Classics was an integral part of the scholarly process, but that none of the scholars mentioned by Yi T'an and Yi Ingmyŏng had violated the "established arguments of earlier worthies."[66]

Although the urgent question of adherence to orthodoxy had prompted these memorials, tempers ran even higher when the arguments touched on questions of earlier political responsibilities and rekindled old personal enmities. Yi Hasŏng (n.d.), a grandson of Yi Kyŏngsŏk, caused a storm of anger and resentment when he tried to justify his grandfather's role in the composition of the inscription of 1637 and, in great detail, described the tense relationship between Yi Kyŏngsŏk, a Namin, and Song Siyŏl. His audacity in recalling such unhappy memories so long after the events was interpreted as "serving his own selfish desires." Yi Hasŏng's memorial was not accepted, and its author promptly dismissed from his post as a county magistrate.[67]

Throughout the rest of that year, members of the Noron, complaining about the continued circulation of Yi Hasŏng's memorial, issued lengthy statements intended to straighten out what they regarded as Yi Hasŏng's one-sided and distorted account of Song Siyŏl's connection with Yi's grandfather. As the first counselor in the Office of the Special Counselors, Chŏng Ho (1648–1736), who emerged as a particularly outspoken advocate of the Noron viewpoint, asserted, the affair was serious because it was intricately related to "the Way." He ascribed Pak Sedang's avoidance of banishment, and the temporary shelving of the order to burn his works to the support Yi Hasŏng had been able to muster among his many Namin partisans. Referring to a similar case during the reign of King Sŏnjo (r. 1567–1608), Chŏng urged the king to order some eloquent officials to refute Pak Sedang's commentaries paragraph by paragraph and to publicize the refutation throughout the country's public schools in order "to correct the scholars' mores."[68]

Although Chŏng Ho's proposal seems to have found wide support among his Noron colleagues, the task was a delicate and potentially perilous one, and volunteers were not forthcoming. Officials of the Ministry of Rites apparently first approached the "moderate" Soron scholar Yun Chŭng (1629–1714), who, however, did not respond to this summon. After that, a partisan choice presumably became inevitable, and when Kwŏn Sangha, a Noron doyen, declined because of "lack of knowledge and old age," his younger brother, Kwŏn Sangyu (1656–1724), and Yi Kwanmyŏng (1661–1733), a junior official in the Office of the Special Counselors, were chosen for the assignment. Both of them had earlier spoken out against Pak Sedang's "defamation of the grand old man."[69]

### The Refutation of the Sabyŏnnok

The assignment to refute (pyŏnp'a) what was false in Pak Sedang's scholarship and to expose his offenses against "orthodox wisdom" as represented by Chu Hsi was indeed a formidable task. It is clear that neither Kwŏn Sangyu nor Yi Kwanmyŏng felt they had sufficient command of the Classics to counter Pak Sedang authoritatively. Kwŏn Sangyu is reported to have asked the eminent scholar Kim Ch'anghyŏp (1651–1708), a brother of Kim Ch'anghŭp, for help, and the only extant version of the Refutation (Pyŏnp'amun) is found in Kim Ch'anghyŏp's collected works, the Nongamjip.

Kim Ch'anghyŏp limited his examination to the Four Books and, in two separate letters to Kwŏn Sangyu, put down his views on Pak Sedang's "errors." He entitled them Non Sabyŏnnok pyŏn (Discussions of the Sabyŏnnok). Kim used a moderate tone in his argumentation, and because he found Pak Sedang's interpretations at times not "explicit enough to warrant extensive discussion," his statements were generally rather brief.

Kim Ch'anghyŏp censured Pak Sedang for reducing the "three items" in the Ta-hsüeh to two and faulted Pak's scholarship for not finding the appropriate steps for the third item. Kim found Pak Sedang's definition of kyŏngmul, which gave the character kyŏk widely varying meanings, even more faulty. "Pak Sedang accused Chu Hsi of having added the character kung [Chin. ch'iung], 'to investigate,' to kyŏk; yet, his own explanation of kyŏk adds extraneous meanings. His error is rather ridiculous!" Where was the evidence for Pak's view that ko meant "pattern"? Because Pak must have been aware that this gloss did not make sense, he patched his argument up with additional characters. Pak's separation of "things" (mul) and "affairs" (sa) was even more untenable. Kim gave a number of examples in which the two characters were clearly used as a compound and concluded that it was rather stupid of Pak to insist on their separation.[70]

Pak Sedang's interpretations of the characters chung and yong in the Chung-yung left Kim Ch'anghyŏp unimpressed, and he did not think it necessary to comment upon them. He considered the second paragraph, "The Way cannot be separated from us for a moment," far more important and severely reprimanded Pak for his "random attacks" on Chu Hsi. He complained: "His [Pak Sedang's] words here are branching out and are complicated; they are haughty and misleading. It is not easy to get his main points." After he tried to summarize Pak Sedang's interpretations, he concluded that "although Pak Sedang's views are shallow and unsophisticated and therefore laughable, his words are nevertheless rebellious and erroneous, and must for this reason be refuted."

He then pointed out five major errors. The first was Pak Sedang's differentiation of human nature as the embodiment of principle and the Way (*to*) as the vehicle of "things" and "affairs"—a separation that made the Way a human artifact and devoid of Heavenly principle. Second, Pak Sedang did not grasp the true meaning of "to follow our nature" and therefore took *to* as something to walk on. This, however, would place the Way outside the human mind and nature and make it, as far as human beings were concerned, into an unimportant and useless thing. The third error lay in Pak's misunderstanding of the passage "virtuous human nature that inheres in the mind" in Chu Hsi's commentary, which, according to Kim, meant that "the substance of the Way is by nature what it is, without the help of human strength." This error arose because of Pak's distinction between principle and human nature, and his insistence that human beings, by having such nature, cannot separate themselves from it, whether they wish to abandon it or hold forcibly on to it. "If this were so, then even bad guys like Chieh [the last ruler of Hsia] and Chih [a notorious brigand of classical times] would never have strayed from the Heavenly principle, and the cultivation of the Way and the sages' establishment of education would be empty undertakings." How, then, can virtuous nature be different from human nature and principle? Pak Sedang's fourth error was to assume that human beings alone receive the Heavenly imparted nature. Pak's final error was the incorrect reading of Chu Hsi's commentary on the passage about the superior man being cautious and apprehensive.[71]

Among the Four Books Kim Ch'anghyŏp dwelt the longest on the *Chung-yung* (the comments cited above are only a sampling) and the *Mencius* and made only brief comments on Pak's analysis of the *Ta-hsüeh* and the *Analects*. Although he acknowledged that Pak Sedang had faithfully cited Chu Hsi's entire commentaries and discussed them in considerable detail, he found Pak's work "lacking in rigorous argumentation" (t'ongbyŏn). "He [Pak Sedang] did not fully investigate the meanings and the examples of all the commentaries and only looked at one side, thus falsely representing and defaming [Chu Hsi's] discussions in this way."[72] In sum, Kim Ch'anghyŏp censured Pak Sedang for one-sidedness, which had led him away from Chu Hsi into a tangle of erroneous and idiosyncratic views and conceptions. The general tone of his refutation was restrained, and he may therefore not have fulfilled the expectations of Kwŏn Sangyu and Yi Kwanmyŏng, who surely had hoped for critical support from such an eminent scholar of the Classics.

The idea of a refutation of Pak Sedang's Sabyŏnnok was viewed with concern by a junior member of the Office of the Special Counselors, Im Su'gan (1665–1721), who complained—unwisely, as it turned out—about the purely factional context within which Pak's work was scrutinized. "If his false views had led Pak Sedang to go against Chu Hsi, as has been reported in several memorials, his crime of falsehood is unavoidable. However, this [falsehood] did not go beyond what a private person preserved in a wooden box, and men of knowledge, when they see it, will be able to destroy it. It is neither sufficiently [worthy] of being burnt or of being refuted." In earlier times, the Taoists, Im argued, had made fun of Mencius in their books, but never yet had a royal order been given to burn these books; nor had earlier Confucians bothered to refute them, because they did not really harm the sagely Way. The king should therefore rescind his orders, Im pleaded, in order to end the controversy. Sukchong did not take kindly to this suggestion, and a few days later Im thought it wise to retire to the countryside. Left State Councilor Yi Yŏ (1645–1718) found Im's submission, interpreted as support of Pak Sedang, most reprehensible, especially since it came from an official of the Confucian stronghold. Pak's work, Yi Yŏ pressed, had already received too much publicity to allow the king to call off the refutation.[73]

Presumably believing that the Refutation had been submitted officially and the Sabyŏnnok was about to be burned, Ch'oe Ch'angdae (1669–1720) reviewed Pak Sedang's case in a multipage document in a last attempt, it would seem, to vindicate his teacher. It was the fullest and most articulate defense of Pak's scholarship, written by a man—he was Ch'oe Sŏkchŏng's son—who in his early years is said to have spoken out against Chu Hsi "without fear of Heaven" and now expressed his astonishment at a turn of events that he had thought would not be possible "under enlightened rule." The campaign against Pak Sedang, Ch'oe Ch'angdae wrote, originated because of Pak's attack on Song Siyŏl, but now those who had trumped up his case intended to make his scholarship the primary issue and find him guilty of "destroying the Classics and despoiling the worthies." Suspicions were already so strong that it would be difficult to overcome them and change the king's heart. Yet, in the face of such a grave injustice Ch'oe felt that as one of Pak Sedang's former disciples, he could not remain silent.

Ch'oe then launched into a detailed and carefully reasoned discussion of Confucian scholarship in general and Pak Sedang's method of reading the Classics in particular. Whenever he had difficulties with Chu Hsi's commentaries, Pak took notes. Was this destroying the Classics? Or, when he did not readily agree with Chu Hsi's arguments, was this insulting the worthy? Such views could be held only by people unfamiliar with classical scholarship. The Classics, Ch'oe wrote, contain various elements—semantic, doctrinal, psychological, and spiritual—that the sages and worthies used to express themselves. Commentaries have the purpose of refining and clarifying their meaning. Even Confucius' disciples Tseng-tzu and Tzu-lu had encountered difficulties with the classical texts. How much more so those living in later times! With his extraordinary talents and broad scholarship, Chu Hsi had been able to get closer to the original meaning than anyone before him. Yet, he had instructed his disciples not to follow earlier commentaries but to focus solely on the meaning of the original text. Even Chu had admitted that he still had doubts and that there remained unexplored meanings and principles. Consequently, Chu Hsi, Ch'oe insisted, had handed down to later scholars the command to continue searching for the true meaning of the Classics. Classical scholarship, therefore, could not be left to hypocrites who cover up their stagnating scholarship by paying tribute to earlier worthies. "Complete" commentaries, Ch'oe stressed, are an impossibility! Without searching, probing, and investigating, no scholar is able to come to an understanding of his own (*chadŭk*).

Assuming that most of his readers would be unfamiliar with the *Sabyŏnnok*, Ch'oe Ch'angdae quoted long passages from it to show that Pak Sedang had used and evaluated Chu Hsi's commentaries before, reluctantly, making changes of his own. Was this an example of destroying the Classics and insulting the sages? Although Ch'oe expected his readers to deny this emphatically, he nevertheless emphasized Pak Sedang's reverence for Chu Hsi and attributed Pak's occasional contrariness to his stubborn and uncompromising character. But why should an Yi Ŏnjŏk be justified in making changes, and Pak not? According to Ch'oe, the only reasons for singling Pak Sedang out for censure were factional animosity and selfish interest. Confucian scholarship, however, was "the general property of the world."

Toward the end of his long exposition, Ch'oe Ch'angdae raised the important question of who was an acceptable judge of the rights or wrongs of scholarly discourse. Was it the general opinion of Confucians (*yurim kongŭi*), or was it the state? No one could judge Yi Ŏnjŏk during his lifetime, and only later did Yi T'oegye and Yi Yulgok evaluate the merit of his theories. Although they were at times critical, they never insulted him. If they were to come to life again, would they not laugh at those "knowledgeable scholars" who call Pak Sedang names and threaten to destroy his work? Moreover, Pak Sedang was not a salaried official, and in addition he was dead. Was it not an overreaction on the king's part to punish him by stripping him of rank and office? And as for burning the *Sabyŏnnok*, the decision of the various authorities was not unanimous.

Finally, Ch'oe turned to the state of scholarship in Korea. Classical scholarship suffered, he asserted, because everyone was preparing for the examinations and striving for office, and Classics scholars were satisfied with gathering the theories of earlier Confucians. This, Ch'oe declared, was a far cry from true scholarship in the Mencian sense of "obtaining the truth through one's own efforts" (*chadŭk*). He cited Chang Yu's well-known assessment of the diversity of scholarship in China where scholars, pursuing their own lines of thought, often arrived at real breakthroughs (*siltŭk*). In contrast, the Confucian establishment in Korea busied itself with worrying about "so-called Zen adepts, Taoists, and learners of Lu [Hsiang-shan]." Moreover, the case against Pak Sedang intimidated those who wanted to reach their own conclusions, lest they be accused of destroying the Classics and despoiling the sages. With this pessimistic view of the prospects of scholarship in Korea, Ch'oe Ch'angdae entreated the king to tolerate diversity, to stop the order to burn Pak's work, and to reinstate his rank.[74] Ch'oe Ch'angdae's memorial never reached

King Sukchong, however, because in the end Ch'oe decided not to send it.

For almost a year thereafter, Pak Sedang's case seems to have rested as the king waited for the Refutation. In summer 1704, during a royal audience, Yi Kwanmyŏng finally pulled the document from his sleeve and presented it to the king with apologies for the delay. His oral summary must have come as an anticlimax. The *Sabyŏnnok*, Yi Kwanmyŏng reported, although containing words that "contradicted the Classics and violated the Way," did not in fact espouse "supernatural [Taoist?] things" that would mislead the people. Yi found that the work, being entirely based on earlier commentaries, lacked the slightest originality and assured the king that any ordinary scholar only vaguely familiar with the Classics and their commentaries would spot its errors. He recommended that the work be preserved in order to forestall a charge from Pak Sedang's followers that the Refutation had been based on an extract; its destruction would leave no evidence left to prove them wrong. Yi concluded his brief statement with the recommendation that "the work be left intact for the time being so that the people of later generations will clearly understand the perversity of its theories. This may be an appropriate way [to conclude the case]."

Yi Kwanmyŏng's recommendation was seconded by Yi Yŏ, who, after taking a look at the *Sabyŏnnok*, concluded that "its theories are extremely shallow and crude. Indeed it is not worth the bigness of a smile!" It was certainly not heterodox stuff (*idan*) that could harm the Way, and therefore to burn it, Yi thought, would make too big an affair out of the case. This unexpected change of heart clearly bewildered King Sukchong. "At first," he exclaimed, "the order to burn it resulted from the stern intention to reject false theories. Now, however, the high officials and the Confucian officials [of the Office of the Special Counselors] are of the opinion that it should not be burned. This is all right with me!"[75]

It is likely that Yi Kwanmyŏng's oral summary represented only the more conciliatory side of the Refutation, and that the complete version repeated the major accusations against Pak Sedang. Because the official text of the Refutation is no longer extant, this cannot be verified, but this impression is conveyed by the memorial Hong Uhaeng (n.d.) and thirteen other disciples of Pak Sedang handed in a few weeks later. They felt compelled to speak up once more in defense of their dead teacher. The main points Hong submitted followed closely those made earlier by Ch'oe Ch'angdae. The memorial was not accepted, and its author was dismissed from office.[76]

Hong Uhaeng's passionate exposition of the virtues of true Confucian scholarship was not the only reason for the harsh treatment he received, however. He was also accused of showing open disrespect for the "ritual system of the dynasty." Hong's memorial denounced the Censorate and some royal lecturers for, in his view, aggravating Pak Sedang's case by charging him with "having wrecked the rites and ruined the customs." This additional charge had first been brought up by a junior censor in the Office of the Censor-General, Kim Man'gŭn (n.d.), even before the government-ordered refutation had been submitted. Although Kim Man'gŭn's indictment does not seem to have been taken into account by the authors of the Refutation, it indeed further inflamed emotions and had serious consequences for Pak Sedang's descendants.

When Pak Sedang was about to die, he ordered his family not to establish a memorial room (pinso) and present food offerings in the mornings and evenings during the three-year mourning period (samnyŏn sangsik). This violation of the ritual prescribed by Chu Hsi in his Chia-li (Family rituals), Kim Man'gŭn claimed, was further proof of Pak Sedang's "perverse character" and was tantamount to an alteration of the mourning system. "If no stern measures are taken in this affair," Kim warned, "[Pak Sedang's ideas] will be imitated, and the country's institutions will collapse and the people's mores end up corrupted." The news of Pak's ritual deviations shocked the minister of rites, Min Chinhu (1659–1720), and, although he admitted that a son obeying his father's orders could not be accused of a crime, he immediately urged the king to take corrective measures. Yi Yŏ, who had earlier taken a conciliatory stand, counseled that the matter be dismissed, and the king, although disturbed, pointed to the private nature of the decision and was unwilling to authorize Min Chinhu to condemn it as unfilial, but an order was issued declaring the observance of food offerings during the mourning period mandatory. Hong Uhaeng, however, who had tried to justify his teacher's last will by citing "ancient rites" (korye) in the Li-chi and I-li as precedents, was struck off the roster of officials.[77]

Pak Sedang's case rested there, and the official mood seems to have remained unchanged, for early in 1706 Yi T'an complained that

Pak's name was still on the list of criminals, a circumstance that made it impossible for him to continue his official duties. His resignation, however, was not accepted.[78] The turning point in the case occurred later that year when the Soron came to power. During a royal audience, the highest officials, led by Chief Councilor Ch'oe Sŏkchŏng, reviewed the case in detail. Pak Sedang had been found guilty in 1703, Minister of Personnel Yi Inyŏp remarked, but still had not received a royal pardon. His writing of Yi Kyŏngsŏk's tomb inscription and the *Sabyŏnnok*, although apparently faulty, were not matters to be judged by the state. Could he therefore not be taken off the list of criminals? Ch'oe Sŏkchŏng paid tribute to Pak Sedang's scholarship and assured the king that he could not be considered heterodox (*idan*). Ch'oe then called for Pak's rehabilitation. This call was reinforced by the other speakers who, almost without exception, confessed that they had never seen the *Sabyŏnnok*. The majority regarded it as "private notes" that Pak Sedang had not intended for circulation, and therefore had doubts about whether the state had been justified in finding the author guilty. Moreover, the officials argued, Pak Sedang had lived in retirement for close to forty years, and among his disciples there were no "queer characters." General consensus clearly demanded Pak Sedang's rehabilitation, and after reiterating that it had been right to punish Pak Sedang for criticizing Chu Hsi's commentaries, King Sukchong, too, was inclined to close the case by reinstating Pak Sedang as an official.[79]

### The Case of Ch'oe Sŏkchŏng

The factional nature of Pak Sedang's rehabilitation is evident from the eventual climax of the persecution of "heterodox" scholarship — the incrimination of Chief Councilor of State Ch'oe Sŏkchŏng. In February 1709, Yi Kwanmyŏng, by then a royal secretary and earlier one of the authors of the Refutation of the *Sabyŏnnok*, handed in a lengthy memorial in which he made the *Yegi yup'yŏn* the target of his attack against Ch'oe Sŏkchŏng.

Because the *Yegi yup'yŏn* is no longer extant, its nature and contents can principally be gleaned from Ch'oe Sŏkchŏng's two prefaces, which are preserved in his collected works, the *Myŏnggokchip*. From the first, undated preface, written when Ch'oe regarded his work purely "for his own reference," it is clear that Ch'oe subdivided the contents of the *Li-chi* into three major categories: rites of the domestic realm (*karye*); "state rites" (*panggungnye*); and "scholarly rites" (*hangnye*), which comprised the *Ta-hsüeh*, the *Chung-yung*, and further sections on rites, music, learning, and moral behavior. It also included the *Hsiao-ching* (Classic of filial piety). Altogether the *Yup'yŏn* was made up of fifty sections (*p'yŏn*). Ch'oe wrote that he chose this arrangement because Chu Hsi's commentaries and later Ming emendations were too complex and detailed for the beginner to grasp the work's essentials.[80]

When he was director of the Royal House Administration (Tollyŏngbu), Ch'oe wrote the second preface, dated the eleventh month of 1700, in the form of a memorial for the printed edition. A month earlier during a royal lecture, he recalled, King Sukchong had revealed that he had almost finished reading Yi Yulgok's *Sŏnghak chipyo* (Essentials of the learning of the sage), whereupon Ch'oe suggested that the king read the *Ch'un-ch'iu* (Spring and autumn annals) and the *Li-chi*. Because no large-type edition of the *Li-chi* was readily available, Ch'oe proposed that his *Yegi yup'yŏn* be printed, and King Sukchong assented.[81] Ten copies were subsequently submitted to the king for use in the royal lecture. Although he had scrupulously taken Chu Hsi's commentary as his model, Ch'oe wrote, he had "corrected some mistakes and discussed some doubts," and therefore it had taken him more than a decade to finish this work. According to a later, undoubtedly factionally tinted account in the *Sillok*, Ch'oe's editorial efforts were far more substantial than the author admitted. The *Sillok* alleges that Ch'oe made numerous "corrections" and "rearrangements," added here and subtracted there, often substituting his own "theories" for the Ch'eng-Chu commentaries, and even restored the *Ta-hsüeh* and the *Chung-yung* to their original (that is, pre–Chu Hsi) textual sequence.[82]

About nine years elapsed between the printing of the *Yegi yup'yŏn* and Yi Kwanmyŏng's accusatory memorial. In it Yi warned that Ch'oe's compilation differed from Chu Hsi in its treatment of the *Ta-hsüeh* and the *Chung-yung* because Ch'oe Sŏkchŏng's sole intent was to upstage Chu Hsi. If it were given publicity by being read during the royal lectures, the country would not only be misled by "wrong theories" but also be left in doubt about the king's true intentions. Yi then entreated Sukchong to denounce the book by citing an ominous "old saying": "An error in one single character in the text of the Classics spills blood over a thousand miles." Obviously angered, King Sukchong countered that he had already read the entire work and found nothing that would make it comparable to the *Sabyŏnnok*.

He ascribed Yi Kwanmyŏng's assault on Ch'oe Sŏkchŏng to factional strife. "It's an old story—you and your ilk have a strong urge
to satisfy your desire for revenge on high ministers." With these
words the king brushed Yi's request aside, and because of the uproar Yi had caused at court, he was eventually transferred to another
office. A brief postscript to this episode, written by the *Sillok* historians, clearly intended to implicate in this affair, beyond Ch'oe Sŏkchŏng, a wider circle of scholars inside and outside the government.
It enumerated the names of some sixteen living and deceased Soron
personalities—among them such luminaries as Nam Kuman, Pak
Sech'ae (1631–95), Yun Chŭng, Pak Sedang, Chŏng Chedu (1649–
1736)—who, it alleged, had praised the *Yegi yup'yŏn* as "reliably researched and based on evidence." A renewed Noron-Soron confrontation seemed to be in the making.[83]

Pressure on Ch'oe Sŏkchŏng was slowly building. Yi Kwanmyŏng's memorial was seconded by a subaltern of the Office of the
Special Counselors who stated that the widely circulating *Yegi
yup'yŏn* was not comparable to "private notes in a box" and thus
might have an even worse fate. He also pleaded for Yi Kwanmyŏng's exoneration.[84] In answer to these attacks, whose severity,
he felt, went beyond the ordinary, Ch'oe Sŏkchŏng submitted in
self-defense a lengthy memorial. In it he detailed the thinking that
had led him to make some of the changes in the *Ta-hsüeh* and the
*Chung-yung*. Ch'oe was careful to place his own editorial work
within the framework of Yi Yulgok's famous discussion of Yi Ŏnjŏk's offending changes in the *Ta-hsüeh*. Did Yulgok, when he expressed doubts about some of Chu Hsi's textual arrangements, lack
sincerity toward Chu? Was it therefore a punishable act when he,
Ch'oe, drew faithfully from the "various discussions" of former
worthies, while leaving the main text untouched? He had spent
many years on these texts and always endeavored to maintain an
"impartial (*kong*) heart and wide-open eyes." At the end, he asked
the king to accept his resignation. The king, however, sent a special
messenger to his downcast minister reassuring him that "in this
dangerous and frightening world" he had no reason to be anxious.[85]

Nevertheless, a few days later Ch'oe Sŏkchŏng again asked to be
relieved of office, this time on the pretext of illness. The king once
more conveyed royal sympathy to him. Yet, as the king's anxiety
over a fresh factional vendetta grew, Sukchong called in the officials
of the Office of the Special Counselors and expressed his discontent

with the continued evil of factional strife. He clearly accused the Noron of plotting against the chief state councilor.[86] The affair, however, had already spilled beyond the government. Some students at both the preparatory Four Schools and Confucian Academy wanted to submit a communication in support of Yi Kwanmyŏng, yet were dissuaded from doing so by one of their professors, the young Soron sympathizer, Cho T'aeŏk (1675–1728). Those students who had refused to take part in the venture were summarily punished by the school authorities, and their names did not appear on the list of students to whom the king was to lecture personally the next day. Deploring the divisive influence of Yi Kwanmyŏng's false accusations on student attitudes, the king ordered the punishment to be lifted, and the letter submitted jointly. The headmaster of the Academy, Yi Mansŏng (1659–1722), then reminded the king of the close relationship between scholarly discourse (saron) and the state. The Yegi yup'yŏn, he insisted, had poisoned the scholarly atmosphere and excited the Confucians' opinions, and it would not be a good idea for the state to suppress "public discussion" (kongŭi). For their audacity, both the troublesome royal secretary, Yi Kwanmyŏng, and his apologist, Yi Mansŏng, were stripped of office that same day.[87]

This draconian action did not prevent the affair from assuming ever growing proportions, even outside the capital. A Confucian from Yangju, Ch'oe Yut'ae (n.d.), circulated a letter "throughout the eight provinces" in which he scathingly attacked Ch'oe Sŏkchŏng. Ch'oe Yut'ae attributed the false spirit of the time to the corrupting influence the "new classics (sin'gyŏng) of Wang An-shih" had exercised throughout the Four Seas, which had brought forth in Korea a person like Yun Hyu. Song Siyŏl, Ch'oe claimed, had saved the Way, but the Sabyŏnnok again jeopardized it, and now in his Yegi yup'yŏn Ch'oe Sŏkchŏng had set his mind on destroying the Classics and insulting the worthies. Although disparaged as coming from a "country bum and ignoramus," Ch'oe Yut'ae's letter was nevertheless deemed dangerous enough for its author to be exiled to a distant place. A later investigation could not confirm Soron suspicions that Ch'oe Yut'ae had been set up by "big houses" as a decoy for initiating another literati purge.[88]

The trouble, however, could not be halted. On the contrary, the agitation against Ch'oe Sŏkchŏng reached a new level when some hotheaded students of the Four Schools called for the destruction of the Yegi yup'yŏn's printing blocks and all printed copies. This demand was repeated a fortnight later, coupled with the request that the *Yegi yup'yŏn* not be read in the royal lectures. The king, unerring in his support for his chief state councilor, again refused to relieve Ch'oe from office and even ordered him to submit the lecture roster for the *Li-chi*, which was next on his reading list. Increasingly weary, Ch'oe did not dare to comply with this order and only sent in "private suggestions." A few days later, when the king started reading the *Li-chi*, Ch'oe's *Yup'yŏn* was apparently not consulted.[89]

Throughout early summer 1709, memorials from dissenting Confucians poured into the capital from all provinces. The attacks on Ch'oe grew increasingly vicious and connected him directly with such notorious despoilers of the Way as Yun Hyu. With "his small talents and shallow learning," he had dared to destroy the Classics and vilify the sages. The indignation and frustration of the "country Confucians" (*hyangyu*), they complained, was all the more intense because no one in the government seemed to heed their protest, and the king, surrounded by flatterers, kept bestowing favors on Ch'oe. Hinting that the "danger of burning books and burying scholars alive" was never far away, the memorialists provocatively stated that they would gladly endure a purge for Chu Hsi's sake. Despite the fact that the memorials clearly accused him of taking the "wrong" side, Sukchong remained unmoved and ordered that no further memorials from Confucians be accepted. But they kept coming in. In this increasingly tense atmosphere, the censors urged action. They pleaded with the king to destroy the *Yup'yŏn*'s woodblocks and to call in all present and former high ministers, important officials, and major scholars for a great debate on the situation. The king, they implored, could no longer rely on one-sided opinions, but had to seek a general consensus. Sukchong, still unconvinced, considered this not the best method for "securing harmony."[90]

If the king remained unmoved by the increasingly explicit accusations of partiality, Ch'oe Sŏkchŏng felt compelled to confront his accusers and submitted a brief apology, the *Yegi yup'yŏn pyŏnnon* (Discourse on the *Yegi yup'yŏn*), in an attempt to answer his critics point by point. Although the full text does not seem to have been preserved, one of Ch'oe's major points apparently was his apologetic statement that not only Chu Hsi, but he, Ch'oe, too, had spent his whole life on the texts in question—a statement interpreted by his accusers as "debasing a former sage in order to brag about one's own views."[91] The atmosphere had obviously become too heated and volatile for Ch'oe's submission to have a clarifying effect. On the contrary, other Soron, in particular Yun Chŭng, then the right councilor of state, and Pak Sech'ae, then a royal lecturer, were gradually drawn into the imbroglio. Known for his neutrality and sound judgment, Yun Chŭng, when confronted by a questioner, was reported to have unwisely characterized the Ch'oe Sŏkchŏng affair as factional strife, and Pak Sech'ae was suspected of having referred to the *Yup'yŏn* during the royal lectures on the *Li-chi*.[92] The excitement cooled off somewhat during the hot summer when, at the end of the sixth month, Ch'oe Sŏkchŏng's wish to resign from his high position was finally, after "forty letters of resignation and twenty oral pleas," granted by the king.[93]

The respite, however, was only temporary. The moratorium on anti-Ch'oe Sŏkchŏng memorials was broken when Confucians from five provinces again submitted an accusatory memorial, which, however, was not accepted by the Royal Secretariat. But on the same day, Royal Secretary Yi Minyŏng (n.d.) did accept another memorial sent in by hundreds of Confucians on the grounds that "it did not mention the *Yegi yup'yŏn*." The king chided Yi for this rash and naïve action and transferred him to another post. In a royal show of strength, Sukchong reappointed Ch'oe Sŏkchŏng chief state councilor a few days later. Clearly uneasy and anxious about taking up this exalted position again, Ch'oe begged the king to accept his resignation. In the clearest words yet, Sukchong denounced those whom he suspected of having incited the "country Confucians" to hand in memorials. He sharply rebuked Ch'oe for wanting to resign because this "would not only do harm to the matter, but also directly play into their [the plotters'] hands." Admonished to give some thought to this, a meak Ch'oe withdrew.[94]

In the end, in early 1710, a seemingly minor affair precipitated Ch'oe Sŏkchŏng's downfall. Ch'oe was charged with a misdeed in connection with his duties in the Medicinal Office (Yakkuk) and dismissed from his concurrent post of chief superintendent (*tojejo*). A few weeks later, realizing how desperate his position had become, Ch'oe cited illness in his request to be relieved from the state councilorship. The king granted this request, and Ch'oe retired to the countryside. Although Ch'oe was immediately made a minister without portfolio, there were clear signs that Sukchong was undecided about how to deal with what he himself now called the "Ch'oe Sŏkchŏng affair." This turn of events strengthened the courage of the protesters, and a new wave of memorials poured in. More aggressive and acrimonious than ever before, a memorial submitted by two Noron censors, Yi Pangŏn (n.d.) and Yi Kyoak (1653–1728), not only targeted Ch'oe's "small knowledge" with which he had altered the old texts but also accused him of "spreading poison throughout the world, destroying the government, and fanning factional disputes." In his arrogance, and sure of royal support, he did not fear the consequences of the uproar he had caused. It was not too late, however, the memorialists entreated the king, to rectify the situation by dismissing Ch'oe from office. Although Sukchong did not comply with this request immediately, he nevertheless rescinded his order to the Royal Secretariat not to accept memorials from Confucians and explained this change of mind by stating that "after serious rethinking" he no longer considered it proper to suppress the "scholars' spirit." After this, only a little additional pressure was necessary for the events to come to a head. Although he judged Yi Kyoak's arguments "severe," Sukchong finally, in the early spring of 1710, stripped Ch'oe Sŏkchŏng of his patent of office and had him expelled from the capital. This dramatic act was topped two days later with a bonfire in which the printing blocks of the *Yegi yup'yŏn* and all the copies printed with them were reduced to ashes.[95]

Ch'oe Sŏkchŏng's work was destroyed, but the vendetta against his person continued unabated. A quick end of the affair was not in sight, the more so as major posts came to be newly staffed with well-known Noron. Yi Yŏ succeeded Ch'oe Sŏkchŏng as chief state councilor, and Chŏng Ho was appointed chief censor. Both had been Song Siyŏl's disciples. In the early summer, Chŏng Ho attacked Ch'oe Sŏkchŏng in a strongly worded memorial. Chŏng lamented that the Way was in great peril because of a resurgence of heterodox theories and charged that Ch'oe had altered not only Chu Hsi's commentaries, but also the original texts of the sages themselves. Ch'oe, Chŏng asserted, was even worse than Yun Hyu. Linking Ch'oe to Yun Hyu and Pak Sedang, Chŏng urged quick action. If Pak Sedang had been punished severely, Ch'oe's case would not now have arisen. Although the king showed concern, he steadfastly rejected as extreme the request for distant exile.[96] Instead, he later sent Chŏng Ho, adjudged the mastermind behind the renewed uproar, into exile. In contrast, the king repeatedly consoled Yun Chŭng, who had been variously implicated by the troublemakers. After angering the king with his insistence on his fellow officials' innocence,

Yi Yŏ thought it advisable to leave the capital. Ten days later he was relieved of his high office.[97]

Toward the end of 1711, Ch'oe Sŏkchŏng's ban from the capital was lifted, but he preferred to stay in the countryside. Gradually some of his accusers, too, returned to resume office in the capital. The momentum of Ch'oe's persecution was broken, and those memorialists who still had the courage to make their opinions known now pleaded for Song Siyŏl's enshrinement in King Hyojong's ancestral shrine. By the fall of 1713, the factional scene seems to have calmed down sufficiently for King Sukchong to send a messenger to Ch'oe with the assurance that the incident in the Medicinal Office was forgotten and forgiven, and with a call to return to Seoul. Shortly after Ch'oe's reappearance in the capital, a new uproar broke out when some eager Confucians accused him of having slandered Song Siyŏl in his funerary oration (chemun) for Yun Chŭng, who had died in March 1714. Although dismissed by the king as "exaggerated," Ch'oe Sŏkchŏng was haunted by these charges until his death on December 6, 1715.[98]

The chapter on the "despoilers of the Way and insulters of the Sages" was finally closed when in early fall 1722 King Kyŏngjong (r. 1720–24) granted posthumous names to both Pak Sedang and Ch'oe Sŏkchŏng. With this royal gesture, their honor was restored. In addition, Ch'oe Sŏkchŏng was honored as loyal minister by seasonal offerings in King Sukchong's ancestral shrine.[99]

## Conclusions: Manipulated Orthodoxy

The three cases considered in this chapter demonstrate the heavy ideological and political pressures on Classics scholarship in the second half of the seventeenth century. Although the conflict between Yun Hyu and Song Siyŏl had a private character—it was never discussed at court, and Yun Hyu's works were not destroyed—the cases involving Pak Sedang and Ch'oe Sŏkchŏng triggered major controversies at court and in the Confucian community and climaxed in the only book burning during the Chosŏn dynasty. Although Confucian scholarship in Korea had always been linked to politics, in the late seventeenth century, Classics studies were, as never before, manipulated by partisan interests in the name of orthodoxy.

Central to the definition of orthodoxy was the concept of "this Way" (sado)—the Confucian enterprise. After the collapse of the

Ming, its survival had become the responsibility of Korea. This was a political as well as an intellectual commitment that was uniquely shaped by Korea's precarious and insecure position in a greatly changed East Asian world. This undertaking seemed to some Koreans to demand an unequivocal and clear-cut definition of what this Way stood for. Concomitantly, in the process of defining what was "orthodox," sensibilities to "heterodox" aberrations were heightened. Because the Way's concrete manifestation was the Classics, scholarship became the focus of contestation, often summed up in the slogan "defend the Way by revering the Classics" (*chon'gyŏng wido*).

In the second half of the seventeenth century, the pursuit of the Way could not be a "private" (*sa*) affair. On the contrary, scholarship was always exposed to the scrutiny of the "public" (*kong*) domain. But who had the power and authority to define and draw the boundaries between public and private? It was this question that stood at the center of the factional controversies over Classical scholarship. For this reason, the defense of the Way became inextricably linked to factional concerns.

Factionalism was very much about conquering the "public ground" — turning factional interests into a concern of the larger domain of power. The Sŏin and later the Noron, led by Song Siyŏl, saw themselves as the true guarantors of Chu Hsi's heritage, giving their "veneration of the teachers" (*chonsa*)[100] almost mystical dimensions. Thus, when in power, they arrogated to the state the ultimate authority to pass judgment over the contents of scholarship. The Soron took a more moderate stance. Even when dominating the government, they did not think it was up to the state to intervene in scholarly affairs. The Namin, in contrast, believed that the state's sole task was to foster a moral environment in which individuals would be able to realize their human potential. Consequently, the state was not to interfere with the scholars' agenda and curtail their freedom to pursue their own particular paths in search of the truth.

The Noron point of view was supported by such basically conservative institutions as the Office of the Special Counselors and the Confucian Academy, both of which were staffed with officials who paid allegiance to Song Siyŏl. To give their argument added institutional strength, in 1682 the Noron managed to have four Sung Confucians, who had not been so honored in Beijing, enshrined in the Shrine of Confucius in Seoul.[101] The Noron were also able to mobilize for their cause the opinion of the Confucian community at large (*yurim*) — Confucian scholars outside the government whose combined voices could swell, as the circumstances required, to a formidable peak of protest or consent.

These differing interpretations of the state's right to set the scholarly agenda and of its power to decide between orthodox and heterodox, led to the fierce contestation of how the boundary between private and public realms of scholarship should be drawn. For the Sŏin, "private" scholarship was impossible, since any divergent view (*i'gyŏn*) smacked of sectarianism and individualism and novel theories (*sinŭi*) offended against Chu Hsi's immutable wisdom. For this reason, not even Pak Sedang's work, written in solitude, could escape scrutiny; it was by definition a "public" statement. Pak's defenders, on the other hand, insisted on the private nature of his commentaries, which, preserved in a wooden box, had never been intended for a general readership. Although the consequences for anyone bold enough to reduce these issues to purely "factional interests" could be grave, the contest was in the end determined by the political fate of the contesting factions.

The only memorialist who warned that the "learning of the Way" (*tohak*) must not be monopolized by anyone, least of all by one faction, was Ch'oe Ch'angdae. He demanded that the discourse on scholarship (*nonhak*) be returned to where it belonged, namely, the "public discourse of the Confucians" (*yurim kongŭi*). By the term "Confucian forest" (*yurim*), he referred not to Confucian opinion that could be harnessed to political goals but to "independent" scholars who advanced the scholarly debate by their original contributions. For Ch'oe Ch'angdae, "right learning" meant the questioning and re-examining of established standards and norms of scholarship on the basis of fresh insights and deeper understanding of the Neo-Confucian literature. As examples of such independent seekers of the Way, he mentioned Yi Ŏnjŏk, Cho Ik, and Yi Yulgok. Ch'oe deplored that at the end of the seventeenth century their successors in spirit were marginalized and persecuted by the politicized Confucian establishment. Faced with what he viewed as government-sponsored mediocrity, Ch'oe passionately and eloquently argued that the Confucian canon could never be closed, complete, and immutable; that if ever the discourse stopped and "new meanings" (*sinŭi*) ceased to come forth, the canon would turn into a dead letter.

What was the role of King Sukchong in these conflicts? Could he ever stand on "neutral" ground? Factionalism had long been part of Korea's political culture, and it was often officially justified with the argument that because not all opinions could be uniform, the ruler had to tolerate disputes (*sibi*) within officialdom. Such difference of opinion was what fragmented the otherwise homogeneous Korean elite. Suppressing the airing of differences, King Injo had earlier been warned, would put the country at risk.[102] In the second half of the seventeenth century, politics had become even more complicated by Korea's unique cultural mandate. No king liked to be manipulated by factions, but for King Sukchong it seems to have been more difficult than ever before to extricate himself.

The trajectory of the Ch'oe Sŏkchŏng case vividly illustrates the extent to which King Sukchong was a political figure. He was accused of taking sides and, even worse, of interfering with the "public discourse" (*kongŭi*) by stopping the flow of incoming memorials. He, the king, had to keep the "public conscience" (*kongsim*) alive and provide a forum in which the pros and cons (*sibi*) could be aired without hindrance. Instead of presiding over such a public discussion, the king relegated the accusations against Ch'oe Sŏkchŏng to "factional strife" (*tangbŏl*) — a sure indication of the king's disenchantment with the Noron point of view. In a rare defense, Sukchong countered these charges by recollecting that as a youth he often could not persevere in his resolutions and was swayed by the "timely circumstances." "Now, I want to stand firm!" he vowed.[103] But the pressure of "public" opinion proved to be too strong: Sukchong had to dismiss his trusted minister.

Although all three protagonists of this study repeatedly insisted that they neither differed from canonical wisdom nor had anything new or original to say, they were perceived as prime examples of scholars who rebelled against the absolute scholarly standards set by the Confucian establishment. How could such rebelliousness be explained? Their contemporaries looked into their character in search of an explanation. Pak Sedang's critics, for example, pointed to Pak's "perverse" and "obstinate" nature as the source of his biased views. It was not a love for antiquity, some charged, that motivated him to change the ancestral rites, but an obsession with being different. Yun Hyu, too, was suspected of having a deficient character and of "loving the novel and admiring the queer."[104] Although such assessments reveal the helplessness of the assessors rather than the characters of the assessed, Pak Sedang was known as an eccentric and nonconformist. He spent his life as an outsider and was often in conflict even with members of his own faction.[105]

More fundamentally, all three scholars were motivated by that creative impulse of "obtaining the truth through one's own efforts" (*chadŭk*) inherent in the Neo-Confucian tradition. This did not mean to go "willingly" against Chu Hsi—an intellectual misdeed of which Wang Yang-ming had been accused. Rather, it meant, in the spirit of Chu Hsi, to explore what Pak Sedang called the "reality" (*sil*) of things—to go beyond the meaning of words to their referents. Although the term *sil* had already been used by earlier scholars such as Cho Ik, Pak Sedang may have been the first to apply it more systematically to his hermeneutical endeavors.

Few critics ascribed the "deviations" of the three scholars directly to Wang Yang-ming. In view of the ready availability of Wang's works, it is surprising that not more blame was pinned on the Chinese heretic. Wang's works were widely read, as the many references to them in contemporary correspondence testify. To be sure, all three distanced themselves explicitly from the Ming thinker. Ch'oe Sŏkchŏng, who, as the grandson of Ch'oe Myŏnggil, grew up in a family in which Wang Yang-ming must have been a household name, implored his contemporary, Chŏng Chedu, to abstain from his well-known infatuation with Wang, who "seems to make opposition [to Chu Hsi] his affair." By trying to lead his friend back onto firm scholarly ground, Ch'oe revealed his own detailed knowledge of Wang's thought.[106] Wang found few outright adherents like Chŏng, who was equally known as a mainstream Classical scholar. Nevertheless, his influence cannot be completely ruled out. He may have indirectly raised doubts in some minds and given encouragement to probe the canonical texts with a more critical and individualistic, even if not rebellious, spirit.[107]

In a wider perspective, the three protagonists of this essay stood at intellectual crossroads. On the one hand, they still subscribed to the Sung Neo-Confucian agenda of probing into the mind and human nature. This is especially clear in Yun Hyu's case. On the other hand, they were unwilling to endorse the holistic and absolutist views of Chu Hsi–centered Neo-Confucianism and thus anticipated scholarly trends in the eighteenth century. None of the three made a frontal attack on Neo-Confucianism. Rather, they utilized the critical methods used by Sung Neo-Confucians, Chu Hsi included, to produce their own arrangements and interpretations of the texts of the

Classics. If they rebelled, they rebelled against the Noron-led closure of the Confucian canon that suppressed an individual scholar's freedom of research and expression. Chu Hsi himself had never sanctioned the view that the canon was closed. On the contrary, he and later scholars like Wang Po kept alive that crucial intellectual skepticism and scholarly initiative that is characteristic of Sung Neo-Confucianism and necessary for sustaining continued scholarly research.[108] Even if in the course of such inquiries sharp differences with Chu Hsi's interpretations emerged, this was not impiety against Chu Hsi per se. It was the result of pursuing the "meanings and principles" of the ancient texts. Critical scholarship, however, was not tolerated in the particular political atmosphere of late seventeenth-century Korea, and all three scholars suffered the shame of being branded as heterodox—as rebels from within.

What was the legacy of these three rebels to Korean Confucianism? Although this aspect may have been exaggerated in recent scholarship,[109] it is true that Yun Hyu, Pak Sedang, and Ch'oe Sŏkchŏng anticipated scholarly trends that in the eighteenth century came to be known as "evidential research" (*kojŭng*; Chin. *k'ao-cheng*), but their familiarity with contemporary developments in Ch'ing scholarship is uncertain. Pak Sedang was known to have been an early sympathizer of Ch'ing China, but he unfortunately left references neither to his trip to Beijing nor to books he might have received from there.

It is clear, however, that the emphasis of all three on obtaining an understanding of the Classics through one's own efforts presaged Yi Ik's (1681–1763) notion of "genuine experience" (*siltŭk*) as an important tool of classical scholarship. Yun Hyu's call for returning to the original texts of early Confucianism, seconded by Pak Sedang, had already been hailed by Yi Ik's father, Yi Hajin (1628–82), and his son inherited this passion for returning to the roots.[110] Although Yi Ik warned against insulting Chu Hsi, he tried to free himself from the moral straightjacket of orthodox scholarship and to move on, in a new spirit of scholarly inquiry, to textual criticism. He might not have been able to do so with impunity, if such scholars as Yun Hyu, Pak Sedang, and Ch'oe Sŏkchŏng had not, before him, opened the vision of advancing scholarship from an adherence to the "outer forms" (*hyŏngsik*) of conventional wisdom to an exploration of the "inner reality" (*naesil*) of the texts of the Classics.

# Buddhism Under Confucian Domination:
## The Synthetic Vision of Sŏsan Hyujŏng

## ROBERT E. BUSWELL, JR.

BY NO STRETCH OF THE imagination was the Chosŏn dynasty (1392–1910) the best of times for Buddhism in Korea. The intellectual vitality and social influence of the religion had clearly peaked during the preceding Unified Silla (668–935) and Koryŏ (918–1392) dynasties, when Buddhism functioned as a virtual state religion, but Buddhism's traditional place in the national ideology was eclipsed by Neo-Confucianism during the Chosŏn.[1] The growing political influence of Confucian ideologues within the bureaucracy ultimately prompted the Chosŏn court to restrict Buddhist ritual and commercial activities, drastically limiting the religion's political, economic, and social influence.[2] These ideological and political pressures created formidable challenges for the Buddhist church of the age.

But neither was the Chosŏn period the worst of times, a torpid dark age of Korean Buddhism. Buddhist institutions endured despite determined, and at times truculent, polemical attacks from their ideological rivals. Despite the waning of its political power, Buddhism's scholastic traditions remained vibrant. It is as if the monks retreated to the security of their books to sustain themselves during the long decades of suppression. This vitality of Korean Buddhist scholarship contrasts strikingly with the gloom and doom portrayals of the era in the scholarly literature.

And there was one light that shone especially brightly during this challenging time for Buddhism: the monk Hyujŏng (1520–1604), better known in Korea as Sŏsan *taesa*. Hyujŏng is emblematic of those Buddhist leaders during the Chosŏn who sought to respond to Confucian pressures. Although trained initially at the Confucian Academy (Sŏnggyun'gwan), in late adolescence Hyujŏng became a Buddhist monk and rapidly rose to the highest ranks of the Buddhist order of his time. He was one of the most prolific Buddhist writers during the mid-Chosŏn, and his works are representative of the Buddhist response to the growing influence of Neo-Confucianism in Korea. Although much of Hyujŏng's thought derives from the work of his eminent predecessors in Korea, his approach to Buddhist practice and the rapprochement he sought with Confucianism set the agenda for all Buddhist writers during the second half of the Chosŏn dynasty. Hyujŏng's works are also among the best-known products of Chosŏn Buddhism and deserve careful consideration in seeking to understand how Korean Buddhism fared during what was arguably the most critical period in its history.

In this treatment of Hyujŏng, I seek to explore two principal questions. First, how did influential monks like Hyujŏng attempt to respond to the ideological critiques of their religion by rival Confucians? And second, what forms of Buddhist thought and practice did Hyujŏng believe would be most appropriate in the suppressive environment within which Buddhism was now forced to exist? In order to provide some context for my discussion of these questions, I begin by sketching the attitudes of contemporary Confucians toward Buddhism and the manifestations of these attitudes in explicit government policies of suppression. I next treat some of the ways in which Buddhists prior to Hyujŏng responded to these repressive attitudes and policies, using the monk Tŭkt'ong Kihwa (1376–1433) as a representative figure. This background helps to clarify the pedigree of Hyujŏng's thought and to elucidate the contributions he made in forging both an accommodation with Confucianism and a rejuvenated synthesis of Buddhist thought and practice that would come to epitomize Buddhism during the remainder of the Chosŏn dynasty.

## The Chosŏn Suppression of Buddhism

Buddhism and Confucianism had long been in conflict in East Asia. The lines in these polemical arguments were first drawn in China, but we find precise analogues in Korea as well in the anti-Buddhist diatribes of the Chosŏn dynasty. The arguments are virtually the same, except for minor matters of emphasis or nuance and references to the indigenous context, especially the damage Buddhist institutions were claimed to have done to the Koryŏ state.

In China, the growing religious, social, and political influence of Buddhism impinged upon the interests of the Confucians within the government bureaucracy. By at least the fourth century, Confucian ideologues had begun to develop coherent ideological positions to counter the increasing threat that Buddhism posed to governmental control of religion. As Erik Zürcher summarizes, the Confucian literati proffered four distinct arguments against Buddhism. First, the autonomous monastic institutions of Buddhism undermined the political authority and economic prosperity of the state. Second, monastic life was unproductive and did not serve the interests of Chinese society. Third, China was culturally superior to the barbarian foreigners who introduced Buddhism and should not harbor this alien creed. And finally, Buddhism was morally corrupt, because it did not uphold traditional social values, for example, the Chinese emphasis on filial piety.[3]

Because these Confucian attacks threatened the long-term viability of the religion in East Asia, Buddhists quickly rallied to respond to these criticisms with eloquent defenses of their faith. In a cosmopolitan culture like that of China, they asserted, foreign ideas and practices had often proved of immense value; such had been the case with Buddhism. Despite its foreign provenance, Buddhist beliefs and practices were actually in perfect harmony with those of Confucianism and Taoism. Rather than challenging the state, Buddhism in fact served the government's interests by giving its adherents peace of mind and bringing the beneficial influence of the buddhas and bodhisattvas to bear on the fortunes of the state. While a small minority of monks might be venal, their existence did not justify the wholesale condemnation of the religion. Therefore, Buddhist monastic institutions deserved the support of the Chinese state.[4]

In Korea, by late in the Koryŏ dynasty, criticisms of Buddhism were already appearing among the incipient Confucian bureaucratic elite who would engineer Yi Sŏnggye's (1335–1408) assumption of power. Reiterating the utilitarian and moral arguments raised long before in China, these early Korean critics of Buddhism focused on two points: corrupt elements within the order, who were thought to be debasing the true religious objectives of Buddhism; and the financial strain placed on Koryŏ coffers by the court's support of Buddhism. The thrust of this nascent critique appeared in a memorial written in 1352 by the eminent Confucian scholar Yi Saek (1328–96),[5] a Korean who had passed the highest civil service examinations in the Mongol capital and briefly held important positions in the Yüan dynasty administration. Yi Saek was personally sympathetic toward Buddhism and had close contacts with important Sŏn masters of his age;[6] he was not calling for the wholesale rejection of Buddhism, but merely the reform of baser elements in the order and limits on the court's financial commitments to the ecclesia.[7] Although noting the valuable role Buddhism had played in Korea in promoting moral conduct among the people, he nevertheless encouraged the court to establish a licensing system that would force the laicization of monks whose vocations were suspect.

The more vociferous early attacks on Buddhism focused primarily on the economic drain caused by the court's support of lavish construction projects, the monasteries' extensive landholdings and their freedom from taxation, and monks' exemption from corvée labor. In a 1389 memorial, Cho Inok (d. 1396), for example, argued for the expropriation of monastic lands and repeal of the monasteries' tax-free status. Tellingly, however, the perennial Confucian suspicions of celibate monastics appeared as well in his call for the expulsion of monks who did not keep their precepts and his counsel that monks be required to remain in their monasteries, isolated from the laity.[8]

But it was with Chŏng Tojŏn (?1337–98) that the ideological attack on Buddhism as a religion began with a vengeance. In order to effect his vision of a new Confucian state in Korea, Chŏng called for the wholesale rejection of Buddhist tenets and practices: in his view, if the discredited social structures of the Koryŏ were to be reformed, the religious ideology that had supported that society must be corrected as well. His critique entailed a systematic denunciation of Buddhist philosophical beliefs, as a way of exposing Buddhism's inherent flaws and revealing the inappropriateness of the religion within the transfigured society he sought to create. These attacks focused on such basic Buddhist doctrines as karma and transmigration, Buddhism's subjective conceptions of the mind (conceptions that he felt denied the reality of the material world), the antinomian tendencies in Buddhist perspectives on morality, and the antisocial tendencies of the celibate monastic life. Only the court's embracing of orthodox Confucian views (i.e., the views of Chu Hsi) could bring about a truly moral order in society and provide the basis for the new Confucian society that Chŏng and his Confucian-trained colleagues sought to create.[9]

During the early decades of the Chosŏn dynasty, the Yi rulers supported the restrictive programs of their Confucian advisers only halfheartedly, eschewing their doctrinal attacks on Buddhism but acquiescing to the economic and political arguments offered against the power of Buddhist institutions. This ambivalence is apparent, for example, in the policies of Yi Sŏnggye, the founder of the Chosŏn dynasty (known by his posthumous temple name, T'aejo, r. 1392–98). T'aejo noted Yi Saek's patronage of Sŏn Buddhism and held him up as an example of how these two ideologies need not be in conflict.[10] T'aejo appointed Muhak Chach'o (1327–1405) to the position of royal master (wangsa), the highest position in the ecclesiastical hierarchy under the Koryŏ dynasty and the last such appointment to be made during the Chosŏn period. T'aejo also funded some monastery construction projects, including Hŭngch'ŏn-sa, built in memory of his late queen Sindŏk, which became the head monastery of the Sŏn school. His daughter became a Buddhist nun, and he eventually abdicated to retire to a life of Sŏn meditation. But despite T'aejo's personal respect for Buddhism, he still acquiesced in severe restrictions on ordination so as to limit the monastic population and ultimately yielded to bureaucrats' calls for prohibitions on new monasteries.

By the time of T'aejo's son and third Chosŏn ruler, T'aejong (r. 1400–1418), however, polemics against Buddhism began to carry much more weight at court. T'aejong was the first of his family to have received a Confucian education in the old Koryŏ Confucian Academy. The Yi family's hold over power was still somewhat tenuous, and his sympathy toward Confucianism was crucial in winning the bureaucracy's backing. During his reign, not only were the economic power and political influence of Buddhism rigidly circumscribed, but its ritual and religious life was drastically attenuated as well. Soon after T'aejong's accession, all Buddhist rituals were prohibited at court in favor of the Confucian rituals of the Ming dynasty.[11] In 1404, he prohibited Buddhist monasteries from conducting funerals and ordered that all funeral services be carried out according to the Chu Tzu chia-li (Family ritual of Chu Hsi).[12] After successive memorials calling for drastic restrictions on Buddhist activities and expropriation of monastic lands and slaves,

T'aejong finally, between 1405 and 1406, lent his support to a whole-sale suppression of Buddhism. The eleven Buddhist schools active at the inception of the Chosŏn were reduced to seven: the two Sŏn (Meditation) schools of Chogye and Ch'ŏnt'ae (T'ien-t'ai); and the five Kyo (Doctrinal) schools of Hwaŏm (Flower Garland), Chaŭn (Sinitic Yogācāra), Chungsin (an amalgamation of the Pŏpsŏng, or Dharma-nature, school and the Sin'in esoteric school), Ch'ongnam (combining the Ch'ongji Dhāraṇī and Namsan Vinaya schools), and Sihŭng (the obscure "Flourishing Anew" school, usually thought to be a collateral lineage of Ch'ŏnt'ae).[13] All other schools were either disbanded or merged into one of the remaining schools. Only 242 monasteries, divided between these schools, were allowed to continue operating; some 2,000 others were disestablished, and their extensive holdings of lands and slaves expropriated by the state.[14] Severe restrictions on ordination drastically limited the number of monks allowed to remain in the order. Once the last royal master, Chach'o, died in 1405, this position was eliminated, effectively separating the Buddhist hierarchy from the state.

King Sejong (r. 1418–50), despite his own private respect for Buddhism, contributed to the rapid decline in Buddhist institutional fortunes. In 1423, the seven schools of T'aejong's time were amalgamated into two: the Sŏnjong, or Meditation School (combining the Chogye, Ch'ŏnt'ae, and Ch'ongnam schools), and the Kyojong, or Doctrinal School (amalgamating the Hwaŏm, Chan, Chungsin, and Sihŭng schools). This was the first time that Sŏn and Kyo were used in East Asia as names of specific Buddhist denominations.[15] These two schools were allowed only eighteen monasteries each, and all remaining monasteries were disestablished. The Sŏnjong was officially limited to a combined total of 1,970 monks, slaves, and monastic workers, and the Kyojong to 1,800; their landholdings were similarly restricted. Both schools were to be administered from a single monastic headquarters in the capital. Monastic examinations were henceforth to be offered only in Sŏn and Kyo, effectively eliminating independent denominational studies, a policy that inevitably resulted in a radical simplification of the Korean doctrinal system. Buddhist monks resident in the countryside were prohibited from entering Seoul, a restriction that would remain in effect until the Japanese intervention in Korean affairs at the end of the nineteenth century. Buddhists were systematically being excluded from all centers of political power and wider social influence.

Sŏngjong (r. 1468–94) and the despot Yŏnsan'gun (r. 1494–1506) put the final nails in the coffin of Buddhist influence among the elite. Sŏngjong, a fervent advocate of Confucianism, prohibited offerings to monks or Buddhist images, banned the recitation of the Buddha's name (one of the main practices of the Buddhist laity) in the cities, and prohibited the founding of new monasteries or ordination of monks. Yŏnsan'gun disestablished the two remaining monasteries in the capital, the headquarters of the Sŏn and Kyo schools, and abolished the ecclesiastical examination system, crippling the training of new monks and severing the last vestiges of Buddhism's connection to the state. Buddhist monks were now isolated from both state and society. Those few monks able to maintain a vocation were ensconced in a paltry number of mountain monasteries, isolated from the world. By the beginning of the sixteenth century, the Neo-Confucian dominance of Korea was uncontested.

One of the few brief respites from this continued persecution occurred during the reign of King Myŏngjong (r. 1545–67), when the queen-mother Munjŏng (1501–65) (the widow of Chungjong) served as regent to the juvenile king. The queen-mother was a devout Buddhist and supported the efforts of the eminent monk Hŏŭng Pou (1515–65) to revive Buddhism. In 1552 the monastic examinations were reinstituted, for what turned out to be the last time during the Chosŏn dynasty, as a means of recruiting new monks into the order. It was during this fifteen-year lull in the persecution of Buddhism that Hyujŏng passed the examinations and was appointed prelate of both the Sŏn and Kyo schools. But this brief respite in the fortunes of the religion ended tragically in 1565 with the death of its royal protector, Munjŏng, Pou's exile to Cheju Island, and his ensuing assassination by the provincial governor. The following year the monastic examinations were suspended, and ordinations prohibited. Buddhism's official isolation from state and society was complete.

## Buddhist Responses in the Early Chosŏn Period

As the suppression intensified, Buddhist intellectuals sought to mitigate the peril to the religion by seeking an accommodation with the increasingly dominant Neo-Confucian ideologues. Buddhists made no attempt to respond to the economic arguments against Buddhist institutions, a reticence at least partly due to the fact that Buddhists no longer occupied positions of political influence that would have allowed them to memorialize the throne directly in support of their religion. But most of this reticence stems, I believe, from the fact that many monks concurred with these sentiments. There is a long reformist strain in Korean Buddhism that goes at least as far back as the mid-Koryŏ period. Chinul (1158–1210), who anticipated many tendencies that characterize the later Korean tradition of Buddhism, decried the corrupt pursuit of fame and profit among the monks of his age and withdrew from the ecclesiastical hierarchy in order to establish an independent retreat society.[16] The renunciatory tendencies implicit in much of Buddhist thought also blended well with these calls for reform.

Given their tacit support for much of the economic criticism, Buddhist monks usually directed their counterattacks against Confucian ideological critiques. Polemics against Confucianism do occasionally appear in Buddhist literature, but it was far more common for Korean Buddhist apologists, like their brethren in China centuries before, to attempt to show the fundamental harmony between Confucianism and Buddhism, especially their views on morality and ethics.[17] Given Confucianism's ascendancy to state orthodoxy, it would have been unthinkable for the Buddhists to criticize Confucianism directly: an attack on Confucianism would have been an attack on the legitimacy of the state itself, and political suicide. It was entirely appropriate, however, to try to demonstrate why Buddhism was not fundamentally at odds with Confucianism. During the mid-Koryŏ period, Chin'gak Hyesim (1178–1234) had already initiated a Buddhist-Confucian dialogue in Korea similar to that current in Sung dynasty China, a dialogue promoted by such Chinese literati as Chang Shang-ying (1043–1122) and Buddhist monks like Ch'i-sung (1007–72). This ongoing dialogue sought to demonstrate the fundamental unity of Buddhism and Confucianism as two complementary approaches to self-cultivation (a complementarity often extended to Taoism as well). But this long-sought accommodation with Confucianism became much more urgent for Buddhists during the Chosŏn.

Representative of those Buddhists early in the Chosŏn period who sought to respond creatively to the intensifying Confucian invective is Tŭkt'ong Kihwa, usually known in Korea by his funerary name, Hamhŏ. Kihwa was the first monk under the Chosŏn to formulate a feasible Buddhist position in the Buddho-Confucian debate and can serve as a foil against which to look at the contributions of Hyujŏng. Kihwa, like Hyujŏng, entered the Confucian Academy at an early age and was trained in the Confucian Classics. But at the age of twenty, Kihwa realized the impermanence of life following the death of a fellow student and, we are told, decided to become a Buddhist monk. In 1397, he met Chach'o, one of the last royal masters of the Chosŏn dynasty, and received instruction from him. Although principally an adept of Sŏn, Kihwa retained a strong interest in Kyo doctrine, especially the *Yüan-chüeh ching* (Book of consummate enlightenment) and the Perfection of Wisdom (*Prajñāpāramitā*) literature. After his enlightenment in 1404, Kihwa became famous as a lecturer. In 1420, at the age of 44, his renown had spread to the capital, and King Sejong invited Kihwa to stay at Taeja-am on the former palace grounds in Kaesŏng. Kihwa ended up teaching at court for four years. He eventually retired to Pongam-sa, the center of the old Hŭiyang-san school of the Silla Nine Mountains school of Sŏn, where he died in 1433.

Kihwa's career coincided with some of the most virulent anti-Buddhist measures. It was probably during Kihwa's four years in Kaesŏng that he wrote his seminal treatise *Hyŏnjŏngnon* (Treatise on  elucidating orthodoxy), which sought to reconcile the rival beliefs of Buddhism and Confucianism.[18] The treatise, which seems to be addressed to the Confucian ideologues who surrounded him at court, tried to demonstrate that the Buddhist path to sagehood is the equal of that of Confucianism. The greater part of the treatise attempted to answer Confucian criticisms of such fundamental Buddhist beliefs and practices as renunciation of the secular world, the prohibition against killing animals, karmic cause and effect and transmigration, cremation, and finally the seemingly apophatic emphasis in Buddhism on emptiness and extinction.

Kihwa opened his treatise by demonstrating that the seminal message of Buddhism is to realize the basic nature of humanity through the overcoming of obscuring passions. This message he framed in explicitly Confucian terms by paraphrasing a key passage from the *Ta-hsüeh* (Great learning): "I perceive that the directives of the Tripiṭaka are intended to do nothing more than to prompt people to abandon passions and to realize their natures. . . . If we teach people to cultivate [themselves] while relying on this [doctrine], *then their minds can be rectified, their persons cultivated, their families regulated, the nation ordered, and all under heaven appeased*"[19] (italics added). The fundamental harmony between the two traditions is demonstrated by pointing out the parallelisms between basic Buddhist ethical teachings and Confucian moral directives: "What Buddhism calls the five precepts[20] is what Confucianism terms the five constants: not killing is human-heartedness; not stealing is righteousness; sexual abstinence is propriety; abstinence from liquor is wisdom; truthfulness is faith."[21]

But whereas Confucianism uses rewards and punishments as the means to control improper conduct, Buddhism instead seeks to pacify evil through the teaching of cause and effect, which leads to inner calmness of mind, thereby controlling the intentions that prompt action in the first place. "But how, then, can we prompt each and every person to be obedient to the mind? A person who is not obedient to the mind should first be guided through rewards and punishments, which will swiftly make his mind joyous and his obedience sincere. Consequently, in addition to instructing in cause and effect, there is also the admonition on rewards and punishments. That is to say, those who are pliant will accept this [admonition] and those who must be restrained will be forced to submit to it. This, then, is close to Confucianism. For this reason, neither Confucianism nor Buddhism should be abrogated."[22]

At the end of the treatise, after bringing Taoism into the argument, Kihwa concluded by showing how all three teachings coincide with one another in the end:

The words of these three religions arcanely tally with one another, as if they were uttered by a single mouth. If [one wants to know] the relative profundity or shallowness of their practice or the similarities and differences in their religious activities, then you must cleanse thoroughly your mind's maculations and purify completely your eye of wisdom. Only afterward will all the books you have read of the Tripiṭaka, Confucianism, and Taoism be perceived in the activities of your daily life. Then, when faced with birth or death, adversity or boon, you will be able to decide yourself what to do, without waiting for someone else to instruct you [lit. you will nod your head yourself without waiting for instruction]. Why should I force my own assessment on you in order to intimidate you into listening?[23]

Kihwa's ultimate vision, then, is one in which Buddhism supports the ethical norms of the Confucian state by molding the mind to respond without premeditation to those norms. In this way Buddhism could continue as a viable religious force in the Chosŏn dynasty by supporting the new social program of the Neo-Confucians.

### Sŏsan Hyujŏng

Many of the concerns that Kihwa voiced were enunciated by his eminent successor Hyujŏng one century later. But whereas Kihwa's writings often addressed the Confucian ideologues at court, in an active lobbying effort in support of Buddhism, Hyujŏng's audience appears to have been his fellow monks. By Hyujŏng's time, hopes that the Confucians would accede to the accommodative arguments of the Buddhists were all but lost. Hyujŏng instead sought to educate his colleagues in a correct understanding of Buddhism so that they could be informed and dedicated adherents of their religion. Although Buddhism's political and economic power may have weakened, well-trained monks could ensure that Buddhism at least remained an effective religious force in Korea.

Hyujŏng was the pre-eminent monk of the Chosŏn dynasty and the man from whom much of the rest of the subsequent lineage of Chosŏn Buddhism derives.[24] According to his *haengjang* (Account of conduct), Hyujŏng was born in Anju in P'yŏngan province in 1520.[25] His dharma name was Hyujŏng, and his cognomen was Ch'ŏnghŏ, but he is usually known as Sŏsan (West Mountain), because he dwelled for a long time on Myohyang Mountain, in the far northwest of the Korean peninsula. Hyujŏng was born into the Wansan Ch'oe family, when his parents were already in their fifties. Both parents passed away early in his life—his mother when he was eight, his father one year later—leaving Hyujŏng an orphan. Impressed with his talent, the district magistrate, Yi Sajŭng, took Hyujŏng under his wing and sent him to Seoul to study at the Confucian Academy. He took the *chinsa* examination at age fifteen, but failed. Discouraged with his lack of success, he traveled south with several friends on an extended trip to Chiri Mountain. On his travels he began reading Buddhist texts and, inspired, composed a poem: "Returning from drawing water, I suddenly turn my head, / Numberless blue mountains tower amid the white clouds."[26] There, he met the elder monk Sungin (n.d.), who would become his preceptor in 1540. As Hyujŏng's *Account of Conduct* tells us, "he was reading Buddhist texts and reached [a passage that said] 'My mind empty, I pass the examination and become a great man.' He then realized that everything he had studied up to that point was simply useless concepts and thereupon shaved his head [and became a monk]."[27]

From Sungin he learned a full range of Buddhist doctrinal texts and Sŏn materials. Later, through Sungin's introduction, he was able to meet the noted Sŏn master Puyong Yŏnggwan (1485–1571). After being sanctioned (*in'ga*) by Puyong Yŏnggwan, Hyujŏng was traveling through a village when he heard a cock crow at noon. Suddenly awakened, he composed a poem:

> The hair turns white, but not the mind,
> This the ancients divulged.
> Now I hear one sound from the cock,
> And this man's work is finished.[28]

For the next several years, Hyujŏng went on pilgrimage to various mountain monasteries around the Korean peninsula. In 1552 at the age of 32, he was invited to the capital by Pou to take the newly reinstituted monastic examinations. His exam results were so distinguished that in 1554 Pou appointed Hyujŏng prelate of the Kyo school (*Kyojong p'ansa*) and a short time later turned his own post of Sŏn prelate over to Hyujŏng as well. But realizing that he had not become ordained to be an administrator,[29] Hyujŏng resigned his positions in 1557 and left for the Diamond Mountains, to continue his life as a wandering monk. This move proved to be fortuitous, since the Buddhist revival under Pou would come to an abrupt end only seven years later, with Pou himself assassinated.

Hideyoshi's invasion of Korea in 1592 raised Hyujŏng's national profile once again. With the initial successes of the Japanese invasion forces in capturing much of the south and their march beginning toward Seoul in the north, King Sŏnjo (r. 1567–1608) fled the capital for Yongman in Ŭiju in the far north of the Korean peninsula, along the Yalu River. At that point, Kihŏ Yŏnggyu (d. 1592), a disciple of Hyujŏng, led five to six hundred monks in a battle against Japanese forces at the city of Ch'ŏngju, resulting in a major victory for the Koreans. But in the ninth month of 1592, Yŏnggyu was killed together with Cho Hŏn (1544–92), a literatus leading his own guerrilla force, in an attack on Kŭmsan. All the Korean irregulars, some 1,500 men, died.

Sŏnjo, who had become friends with Hyujŏng during the factional strife that began at court early in his reign, asked Hyujŏng for assistance in marshaling forces to quell the invaders. Hyujŏng immediately ordered all monks except the old and infirm to join the ranks fighting the Japanese. At the advanced age of 72, Hyujŏng took charge of organizing monks throughout the country into

monks' militias (ŭisŭnggun), in which some 5,000 monks are estimated to have participated. These militias were in the vanguard of
the counterattack against the Japanese invasion force.

Two of his younger disciples took charge of their own guerrilla operations. Yujŏng (Samyŏng taesa, 1544–1610) organized 700
monks into a guerrilla force at Yujŏm-sa in the Diamond Mountains.
Noemuk Ch'ŏyŏng (n.d) organized 1,000 monks at Chiri Mountain.
Hyujŏng himself, it is said, led 1,500 monks from Pŏphŭng-sa,
where they connected up with the 50,000–man army of the Ming dynasty and participated in the recapture of the cities of P'yŏngyang
and Kaesŏng.[30]

Once the capital was recaptured, Sŏnjo allowed Hyujŏng to retire,
and command of the Buddhist forces passed to Yujŏng and Ch'ŏ-
yŏng. Hyujŏng returned for the last time to his favorite spot, Myohyang Mountain. Six years later, on the twenty-third day of the
prime month, 1604 (February 22, 1604), Hyujŏng realized that he
was about to die and called his disciples to assemble at Wŏnjŏk-am
for a final dharma talk (punhyang sŏlbŏp). As he was finishing his
talk, he picked up his funerary portrait (yŏngjŏng) and wrote his own
epitaph on the back: "Eighty years before, he was I; eighty years
later, I am he." He then wrote letters to his disciples Yujŏng and
Ch'ŏyŏng, who had been unable to attend the talk. Finally, while
sitting in full-lotus position, he passed away. He was 84 years old
and had been a monk for 65 years. After his cremation, his relics
were enshrined in a stupa at Ansim-sa on Myohyang Mountain,
right next to the reliquary of one of the last royal masters of the Koryŏ and early Chosŏn, Naong Hyegŭn (1320–76); one portion of his
bone remnants were enshrined by his disciple Yujŏng to the north of
the Yujŏm-sa in the Diamond Mountains. He is said to have had
over 1,000 disciples, of whom more than 70 were well known.[31]

## Hyujŏng's Reconciliation of Buddhism
## and Confucianism

Much of Hyujŏng's renown among Koreans derives from his role in
organizing the monks' militias that helped turn back the Japanese
invasion. But long before he turned his attention to national survival,
he was intensely involved in the survival of Buddhism. Hyujŏng is
generally acknowledged to be the most important figure during the
Chosŏn dynasty in the effort to revitalize Buddhist doctrine and

practice and put it on the secure footing it needed in order to endure through the remainder of the Chosŏn. If Buddhism was to survive in Korea, younger monks had to be better trained so that they could be informed advocates of their religion. Part of that training meant they would need to understand not only their own tradition but also its intersections with the dominant ideology of their time, Confucianism.

In the preface to Hyujŏng's most famous work, the *Sŏn'ga kwigam* (Speculum on the Sŏn school),[32] a section of his *Samga kwigam* (Speculum on the three schools) that usually circulates independently, Hyujŏng remarked on the motivation that prompted him to write this basic primer on Buddhist doctrine and praxis:

Those who trained in Buddhism in the past never said what the Buddha did not say, and never practiced what the Buddha did not practice. Therefore, what they most treasured were just these precious slips and numinous clauses [of Buddhist sūtras]. But nowadays what those who train in Buddhism transmit and intone are the phrases of the literati; what they solicit and retain are the poems of the literati. They even illustrate the paper with reds and greens, and embellish the bindings with beautiful silks. No matter how many [literati texts] they have, it is never enough. These they consider the greatest of treasures! How different are the treasures of past and present practitioners of Buddhism! Although I am unworthy, I have aspired to the training of the ancients and have treasured the precious leaves and numinous clauses [of Buddhist texts]. However, their phrases are quite prolix; the sea of the canon is wide and vast. There will be few disciples of similar aspiration later who will not have to go to the bother of making their own compilations. Therefore, I chose several hundred of the most important passages from this literature and wrote them down on sheets of paper that I titled *Speculum on the Sŏn School*. Though terse in expression, they are comprehensive in meaning. If, taking these words as your awesome teacher, you study them deeply and understand their subtlety, then in each and every word there would be a living Śākyamuni. Be diligent in this![33]

In a number of brief but seminal works, Hyujŏng revealed the two major concerns that pervaded his writing: why Buddhists should accept an accommodation with Confucianism; and why the bifurcation in the Buddhist church of his time between Sŏn meditation and Kyo doctrine was obsolete and inappropriate. Hyujŏng, like most of the important Buddhist thinkers of the Chosŏn period, was concerned with demonstrating why Buddhism deserved to continue as a viable religious force in Korea. For Hyujŏng this aspiration meant showing how the truths that vivified Buddhism were the same truths that inspired the other religions as well. In his *Chiri-san Ssanggye-sa chungch'ang ki* (Record of the reconstruction of Ssanggye Monastery on Chiri Mountain), dated to spring 1549, three years before he went to the capital to take the monastic examinations, Hyujŏng noted how those who truly understood Confucianism would understand Buddhism, and vice versa. His point was to show that those who unyieldingly clung to either of the two ideologies as sacrosanct were attached to a parochial view that limited them from understanding the full capacities of their minds.

Those who in the past comprehended thoroughly Confucianism and Buddhism and penetrated profoundly to both orthodoxy and heterodoxy abandoned accomplishment and fame and, [content with] one gourd [of water], forgot entirely about their poverty.[34] They stood together with heaven and earth and moved in tandem with the spirits; or else they traveled with perfected men who held no rank or made friends with that which has neither beginning nor end. When they couldn't help it, they at last responded to those [who need assistance], nourishing the myriad things and pacifying all under heaven. With one hand [viz. effortlessly], they were able to lord it over both Yao and Shun. They considered this to be as [easy as] turning over the palm of their hand. They grieved their own griefs and took pleasure in their own pleasures. Why would they take the time to criticize the Confucians and Buddhists, or the Buddhists and Confucians, or to feud with one another or to criticize one another? Our country's Ch'oe Koun [Ch'oe Ch'iwŏn, b. 857] and Chin'gam [Hyeso, 774–850] were such men.[35] Koun was a Confucian; Chin'gam was a Buddhist. Chin'gam established a monastery and first gouged open the eyes of humans and gods. Koun erected a stela and exposed for all to see the marrow of Confucianism and Buddhism. . . . Only after you make Buddhist students be like Chin'gam will they know what makes Confucianism Confucian. Only after you make Confucian students be like Koun will they know what makes Buddhism Buddhist. Therefore, we say that there was none better than Koun at knowing Chin'gam and none better than Chin'gam at understanding Koun. . . .

But a name is just a guest of reality; it is not something to which Koun and Chin'gam clung. They criticized those who spoke well of Confucianism; they criticized those who spoke well of Buddhism; and they criticized those who excelled in arguing that both Confucianism and Buddhism were wrong. Why was this? Because they sought nothing more than reality itself.[36]

Hyujŏng sought to demonstrate the fundamental agreement between Buddhism and Confucianism—and eventually with Taoism as well—by revealing how all creeds and religions were alternative statements of a unitary reality that vivified them all. A statement from Hyujŏng's *Samga kwigam* illustrates his approach.

Confucianism: Although the *Doctrine of the Mean*'s three words—nature, Way, and teaching—may be different terms, these are the same in reality. . . .[37] Although the Way derives from nature, we speak of Way but not of nature. Therefore, people do not realize the original fount of the Way. The Way is elucidated through the teaching, but although we speak of the Way, we do not speak of the teaching. Therefore, people do not realize the dynamic functioning of the Way. Therefore, the one word "Way" subsumes nature and teaching.[38]

Taoism: There is a thing that is consummate; it precedes the creation of heaven and earth. It is utterly great and utterly sublime, utterly vacuous and utterly numinous. Great and vast, detailed and clarified, though probing its corners, you cannot fix its locus; though counting it for eons, you cannot plumb its age. Not knowing what else to call it, I force on it the name "mind." . . . Whether named or nameless, thought or not thought, all derives from it. Therefore it is said, "Mystery of mysteries, it is the gate to all wonders."[39] Its essence is called "the Way." Its function is called "virtuous power." All its functions are generated by the essence, and its essence has no functions that are not sublime. . . . This mind derives from that which has no root and accesses that which has no limit. Although it is real, there is no place where it exists, but it constantly appears through its active functioning. . . . The Way cannot be seen; the Way cannot be heard. Those who know it do not speak of it; those who speak of it do not know it. Moreover, those who speak of it still retain some conception of it. Only those who understand that conception but forget the words can truly speak of it. Therefore you look at it, but it has no form; you hear it, but it has no sound.[40]

Buddhism: There is one thing here that since time immemorial has been bright and numinous, that has never been born and has never died, that can be neither named nor depicted.[41] The Buddha and the patriarchs appearing in the world [were like] waves forming without the wind blowing.[42] But their dharma had many different meanings and their followers had many different capacities, so they could not help but create various kinds of stratagems. They forced [on that one thing] many names, such as mind, or buddha, or sentient being, but you must not produce interpretations while clinging to names. It is right just as it is. But if thoughts are stirred, then it is wrong.[43]

This syncretic approach to the Three Teachings has a long pedigree in East Asian thought, and there was nothing particularly unique in Hyujŏng's treatment of it. He sought to show that a single "way," "consummateness," or "thing" was the source of all the

doctrines of each of these major creeds. That monistic essence revealed itself through its functioning in the world and had to be re-
discovered by looking beyond its various external functions to the
inner essence that vivified them all. Once one had experienced that
essence, all the various concepts used in Confucianism, Taoism, or
Buddhism to explain their systems would be seen as simply provi-
sional descriptions of reality, with no ultimate validity. By realizing
the emptiness of such conceptual depictions—the experience of what
the Buddhists would call enlightenment—the person would no
longer cling to the concepts of his own creed, but would realize that
all three religions offer equally valid descriptions of reality. At that
point, there would no longer be any basis for championing any one
of these creeds over the other two—and thus, no justification for
suppressing Buddhism.

### Hyujŏng's Views on Sŏn and Kyo

Since the middle of the Koryŏ period, Korean Buddhist practice has
been characterized by a remarkable openness among competing approaches to Buddhist thought and praxis. The founder of the indigenous Chogye school of Korean Sŏn, Chinul, was insistent that Kyo
doctrine and Sŏn meditation should function symbiotically in the
spiritual maturation of the Buddhist student. Chinul's approach to
Buddhist training employed Kyo doctrinal study as the foundation
of Sŏn meditation and encouraged, as well, a variety of complementary forms of contemplative practices from the joint cultivation
of concentration and wisdom (chŏnghye ssangsu), based on early
Ch'an writings in China, to complete and sudden faith and understanding (wŏndon sinhae), a form of contemplation emblematic of the
Hwaŏm school of Kyo.

Chinul was also the first Korean monk to teach a new approach to
Buddhist praxis then developing in Sung dynasty China, the technique called kanhwa Sŏn, the "Sŏn of observing the critical phrase."
This type of meditation, which was the hallmark of the Chinese Lin-
chi (Imje) school of Ch'an, used the exchanges (kongan; J. kōan) between Sŏn masters and their disciples as subjects of contemplation,
exploiting the doubt that develops regarding the "critical phrase"
(hwadu) in those exchanges as the driving force in compelling the
mind toward enlightenment. Although Chinul was clearly fasci-
nated by the kanhwa technique, he nevertheless saw it as but one
segment of a more comprehensive regimen of Buddhist training.

Chinul also had no direct contacts with Lin-chi teachers, and thus his interpretations of the *kanhwa* technique were unique and not beholden to the orthopraxy of any one specific school of Chinese Ch'an.

With Chinul's successor Chin'gak Hyesim, however, Korean Buddhist praxis began to coalesce more and more around *kanhwa* Sŏn, to the detriment of the ecumenism advocated by Chinul. Chinul's own system of Buddhism accommodated variant styles of Buddhist thought and practice, including styles indicative of Kyo and diverse schools of Sŏn. But this consolidation around *kanhwa* Sŏn led to the increasing domination of Korean Buddhism by Lin-chi Ch'an perspectives on praxis, with a corresponding de-emphasis on the study of Kyo doctrine.

By the end of the Koryŏ, there is a drastic narrowing of the scope of the Korean Buddhist tradition, with such monks as T'aego Pou (1301–82) promoting a near-exclusive emphasis on *kanhwa* Sŏn as the principal technique of Buddhist praxis. In order to stimulate what he considered to be the atrophied Sŏn school of his day, Pou traveled to Yüan China in 1346 and received transmission from Shih-wu Ching-kung (1272–1352), a teacher in the Yang-ch'i branch of the Lin-chi school of Ch'an, then the predominate school of Chinese Buddhism.[44] The ecumenism that had characterized the indigenous Korean tradition of Buddhism earlier in the Koryŏ was now eclipsed by a more dogmatic form of practice deriving from a single school of Chinese Buddhism.

But once the Korean rulers shifted their allegiance from the Mongol Yüan to the Chinese Ming dynasty, Korean Buddhists began to turn away from these imported Lin-chi forms of practice toward their own indigenous traditions. The figure toward whom most Buddhist intellectuals, including Hyujŏng, looked was Chinul. The ecumenism characteristic of Korean Buddhism during the mid-Koryŏ period, especially the accommodation Chinul urged between Sŏn meditation and Kyo doctrine, was the locus around which was formed the doctrinal edifice that would sustain Korean Buddhism through the remainder of the Chosŏn dynasty.

Hyujŏng was also committed to narrowing the rift between Sŏn and Kyo, which he felt erroneously divided the Buddhist order of his day.[45] In Hyujŏng's view, doctrinal study and meditation complement each other in the training of the Buddhist adept. Two of his works—*Sŏn Kyo sŏk* (Explanation of Sŏn and Kyo) and *Sŏn Kyo kyŏl*

(Secrets of Sŏn and Kyo)—addressed specifically the fundamental unity of purpose melding these two strands of Buddhism. This unity was, however, a theme that was reiterated throughout his writings, from his poems and verses to his best-known work, *Sŏn'ga kwigam*. This work, although intended to be a simple primer on Sŏn thought and practice for Buddhist neophytes, insists on the symbiotic relationship between Kyo and Sŏn.

Hyujŏng, much like Chinul before him, saw Sŏn and Kyo as two necessary subsidiaries in a comprehensive regimen of Buddhist training.[46] As his *Sŏn'ga kwigam* states: "The three places where the World Honored One transmitted the mind is the import of Sŏn. Everything that he said during his lifetime is the approach of Kyo. Therefore it is said, 'Sŏn is the Buddha's mind; Kyo is the Buddha's words.'"[47] His *Sŏn Kyo kyŏl* made the same claim as a way of showing the complementarity of these two variant forms of Buddhism: "Sŏn is the Buddha's mind. Kyo is the Buddha's words. Kyo goes from the verbal to the nonverbal. Sŏn goes from the nonverbal to the nonverbal. In going from the nonverbal to the nonverbal, there is then no one who can describe what that state is. Therefore, we force on it the name 'mind.'"[48] This analysis is quite similar to that Hyujŏng used in his treatment of Buddhism and Confucianism: both Sŏn and Kyo are seen to be two complementary expressions of something still more fundamental—in the case of Buddhism, the "mind" itself.

For Hyujŏng, Kyo, the Buddha's words, was the initial access to Buddhist insight. The doctrines of Buddhism were intended to prepare the neophyte with a correct understanding of the essential nature and various qualities of the mind and the process of meditative development. With this understanding as a foundation, Buddhist adherents were then in an optimal position to abandon Kyo's purely conceptual significance and have a direct personal insight into the religious intent of those doctrines through Sŏn meditative training. As Hyujŏng states in his *Sŏn'ga kwigam*, drawing his terminology from the Chinese Ch'an and Hua-yen syncretist Tsung-mi (780–841) via Chinul: "Students should first, via the verbalized teachings that accord with reality, scrutinize the two concepts of immutability and adaptability. These [two concepts correspond, respectively, to] the nature and characteristics of their own minds, and the two approaches of sudden awakening and gradual cultivation are the inception and consummation of their own training. Subsequently, casting aside doctrinal concepts, they merely take up the one thought that appears before their own minds and contemplate carefully the intent of Sŏn. They then will perforce gain attainment. This is called the living road to liberation."[49]

This position, emblematic of mid-Koryŏ Buddhism, found a new, and highly influential, advocate in Hyujŏng. Although this approach can be traced ultimately to Chinul in Korea, it has a long pedigree in Korean Buddhism. Hyujŏng's immediate inspirations were probably his own Sŏn teacher, Yŏnggwan, and Pyŏksong Chiŏm (1464–1534), both of whom advocated a similar regimen of Sŏn training.

The fundamental difference between Sŏn and Kyo centered on whether their approaches to praxis were primarily *via negativa* or *via positiva*. Sŏn accepted no conceptual descriptions of the nature of practice or enlightenment, whereas Kyo sought to lay out for students the markers they might expect to pass along the path: "Sŏn is that in which there is no start or finish, in which everything is primordially in a single time, autonomous and unobstructed. . . . Kyo is that in which there is both start and finish, and in which there are sequential series of stages involving both cultivation and realization."[50]

In the *Simbŏp yoch'o* (Transcription of the essentials of the mind-dharma), Hyujŏng criticized students who do not realize the complementarity of Kyo and Sŏn and who mistakenly advocate the exclusive practice of one or the other:

The fault of Kyo students: Students of Kyo do not investigate the live word [*hwalgu*, the critical phrase]. In vain they take the learning gained through their intelligence, their mouth, and their ears and show off their brilliance to the world. But their feet do not tread on real ground, and their words and actions contradict one another. Searching here and there among mountains and rivers, they waste in vain gruel and rice, squandering their whole life on the sūtras and śāstras until they finally become the dregs of hell. They will not become lifeboats that save the world.

The fault of Sŏn students: Students of Sŏn become accustomed to cultivating idleness and do not seek out teachers. In the wild-fox cave, they waste their efforts by dozing while they sit. They cannot yet get free from the conditionally arisen events occurring right before their eyes. . . . They only become sprites attached to grasses or hanging from trees. They, too, will not become lifeboats that save the world.[51]

If practice was to advance with a minimum of obstacles, Buddhist students must develop a firm grounding in Kyo before proceeding to Sŏn meditation. Eventually, however, for Buddhist students to succeed in their practice, they must abandon conceptual descriptions of truth for the direct insight into the nature of their minds that can only come through *kanhwa* meditation. For Hyujŏng, Sŏn and Kyo are symbiotically related in the process of *kanhwa* practice, in much the same way that Chinul proposed nearly four centuries earlier.

When one has yet to intuit the live word [*hwalgu,* or "the critical phrase"], one relies on the words of the teachings and then uses the ratiocinations of mind, thought, and consciousness to generate understanding abruptly. The "live word" is that place which the mind, thought, and consciousness cannot reach, where the original mind-king lives; it is like a running beast. The "dead word" is that place which is accessible by mind, thought, and consciousness, where the original mind-king is dead; it is like a running dog. Sŏn and Kyo both arise in a single moment of thought. That place which is accessible by mind, thought, and consciousness, and which belongs to rational cogitation, is Kyo. That place where mind, thought, and consciousness do not reach, and which belongs to meditative contemplation, is Sŏn.[52]

Elsewhere in the *Simbŏp yoch'o,* Hyujŏng provided a succinct statement of his approach to Sŏn practice, a statement that shows how strong the pull of *kanhwa* meditation remains, despite Hyujŏng's conciliatory attitude toward Kyo:

Among the infinite approaches to practice,
Sŏn meditation is supreme.
Over thousands and myriads of lives,
Sit straight in the tathagatas' room.
If you want to understand this matter,
You should examine the patriarchs' checkpoint,
Arouse faith like the great sea,
And establish your will firmly, like a mountain.
During your daily affairs, in all four postures [walking,
        standing, sitting, lying],
Work exhaustively to raise the ball of doubt.
Insipid and tasteless,
The critical phrase will be solitary and singular.
When one realizes the mind has perished and the road
        is eradicated,
A hero's bones should freeze.
When, without doubting, the doubt appears of itself,
That is the point when a person gains dynamism.

Reaching that place,
The flame of birth and death can be extinguished.
If you don't follow these words,
Then you will only gain release in the [nonexistent] year
    of the donkey.
Consistently raise the *kongan*,
Don't float, and also don't sink, . . .
Breaking the ball of doubt regarding the live word,
You will then be called a great hero (*taejangbu*).[53]

Kyo brought one to the threshold of awakening, but only the critical phrase of Sŏn meditation could carry one beyond that threshold into enlightenment:

If one does not produce false thoughts, then perforce there will be the arising of right thought. Furthermore, the first indications that one has reached
the Buddha-land occur through faith. But the secret import of the approach
of Sŏn is then originally without even a single thought; so how then can any
thoughts arise? And since thoughts are originally nonexistent, how is the
stage of faith [the inception of the path to enlightenment] established? If the
stage of faith is not established, then how does the Buddha-land exist? Although [Kyo] speaks of the supreme vehicle, there originally is no supreme
vehicle. How much more so is this the case for the live word investigated by
the practitioners [of Sŏn]! It is like a mass of fire: approach it and you will
burn your face. It has no place where it can be grasped by the teachings of
the buddhas [viz., Kyo]. There is only the great doubt, like fierce flames that
reach into heaven. If suddenly they break the lacquer barrel [of ignorance],
then 100,000 approaches to dharma and infinite sublime meanings will all be
obtained without seeking them.[54]

It is clear from this account that despite the symbiosis Hyujŏng
perceived between meditation and doctrine, Kyo always remained
subordinate to Sŏn in his system. Even in his *Sŏn Kyo sŏk*, one of the
most generous of his works toward Kyo, Hyujŏng still held out Sŏn
as pre-eminent when he compared Kyo to government bureaucrats
and Sŏn to the emperor himself.[55] Kyo, by its very nature of being a
conceptual description of reality, was not up to the task of catalyzing
a direct awakening to that state beyond words. Although not all Sŏn
practitioners may be able to attain enlightenment instantly, they
were assured that eventually their training would succeed: "All
those who train in the intent of Sŏn must try instantly to break
through the live word of the patriarchs. But even though they have

yet to awaken, they are sure to attain enlightenment in either three days, or five days, or seven days, or at least a single lifetime."[56] This same assurance was not given to students of Kyo.

Kyo was therefore a necessary, but still insufficient, step on the path to true enlightenment, a step that only came as the conceptual understanding engendered through Kyo was transcended: "All the buddhas [viz., Kyo] explain the bow; all the patriarchs [viz., Sŏn] explain the bowstring. The unobstructed dharma of the Kyo school then returns to the one taste. Sweeping away the traces of this one taste then reveals the one mind of the Sŏn school."[57] And again: "What we call [Sŏn's] separate transmission outside the teachings is not something that can be realized through learning or knowledge. Only after you have probed the extinction of the mind's road (simno) can you know this."[58]

As an expedient description of truth, Kyo did, however, appeal to the needs of people in the present degenerate age of Buddhism, in which few practitioners had the talent necessary to make use of the shortcut of kanhwa Sŏn:

The previous buddhas and previous patriarchs have sung together the song of the separate transmission outside the teachings. Can this be realized through rational thought or deliberation? This is what we mean when we refer to a mosquito atop an iron ox. Now, during this degenerate age, there are many people of inferior capacity who do not have the capacity for this separate transmission. Therefore, they only value the [Hwaŏm] approach of consummate subitism and therewith give rise to perception and learning, faith and understanding, along the road of principle, the road of meaning, the road of the mind, and the road of words. They do not value the shortcut approach [of kanhwa Sŏn], which breaks the lacquer barrel and which has no road of principle, no road of meaning, no road of mind, no road of words, no taste, and no groping.[59]

The only hope for reconciling this division between Sŏn and Kyo lay in training a new generation of Buddhist students who would be able to experience the enlightenment that transcends all dichotomies, even religious ones.

The fundamental distinction between Sŏn and Kyo derived not so much from their inherent differences in approach as from the misconceptions of students of Buddhism about those approaches. Sŏn, incorrectly understood, has all the conceptual problems inherent in Kyo, whereas a person with true insight into Kyo would realize that all concepts were indicative of the experience of Sŏn enlightenment:

"If a person loses it when he speaks [lit. in his mouth], then the subtle smiles he has when [the Buddha Śākyamuni] held up the flower [the transmission of the enlightened mind in Sŏn] are just traces of Kyo. But if he obtains it in his mind, then the coarse words and petty talk of the mundane world are all the intent of Sŏn's separate transmission outside the teachings."[60] For someone with consummate insight, the perceived distinction between Sŏn and Kyo would be seen as contrived and intrinsically erroneous.

### *Hyujŏng's Legacy in Chosŏn Buddhism*

An impartial appraisal of Hyujŏng's work would find little that is startlingly original. Many of his perspectives on Buddhist thought derive from the insights of Chinul, some four centuries before, and his reactions to Confucianism are heavily indebted to the approaches of earlier Chosŏn dynasty Buddhists like Kihwa. Perhaps it is not unfitting to call Hyujŏng a transmitter, not an innovator. Unlike the heavily Lin-chi orientation of much of late Koryŏ Buddhism, Hyujŏng's work is deeply beholden to the earlier Korean vision of a synthesis between meditation and doctrine.

This more ecumenical style of Korean Buddhism had been eclipsed during the late Koryŏ by the increasingly dominant *kanhwa* Sŏn approach, which reduced all of Buddhist training to contemplation on the critical phrase (*hwadu*) of the *kongan*, or Sŏn case. Many of the distinctively Korean features of the Buddhist tradition that had developed during the mid-Koryŏ — especially its eclecticism in matters of doctrine and praxis — vanished from the religion during the late fourteenth century, eclipsed by this rigorously sectarian form of Lin-chi Ch'an (Imje Sŏn), the dominant school of Chinese Buddhism during the Yüan dynasty. Hyujŏng still remained devoted to the *kanhwa* technique and identified himself principally as a Sŏn adept. Even so, he retained a strong interest in doctrine and followed the mid-Koryŏ lead in attempting to reconcile the two strands of the Buddhist church. While maintaining an emphasis on *kanhwa* Sŏn, Hyujŏng sought to re-create a place for the study of Kyo doctrine in a comprehensive schema of Buddhist thought and practice. In the religious approach that Hyujŏng advocated, the *kanhwa* Sŏn that so dominated the late Koryŏ was supplemented by the accommodating attitude toward Kyo emblematic of mid-Koryŏ Buddhism.

But why did Hyujŏng promote such an accommodation? He may

have felt that without both rigorous doctrinal understanding and diligent Sŏn training, there would be little hope for Buddhists to maintain their own tradition against the persistent pressures from rival Confucians. By looking back to the putative golden age of Korean Buddhism during the mid-Koryŏ, Hyujŏng seemingly hoped to restore the past glory of an effective, and uniquely Korean, approach to Buddhist thought and praxis. This restoration could only come through unifying the efforts of all Buddhists, adherents of Sŏn and Kyo alike, in the common welfare of their religion. This concern may account for why even a text entitled *Speculum on the Sŏn School*, despite being heavily beholden to the *kanhwa* Sŏn of the Lin-chi school of Ch'an, would still pay so much attention to correct understanding of the Kyo doctrine. It is a quintessentially Korean presentation of Sŏn and a paradigm for Korean Buddhism throughout much of the rest of the Chosŏn dynasty.

Hyujŏng's pliant stance toward Kyo, however, does not mean that his works resolved all tensions between advocates of Sŏn and Kyo in Korean Buddhism. Indeed, most attempts to reconcile Sŏn and Kyo throughout Korean history came from monks whose affinities clearly resided with Sŏn. The attempted assimilation of these two branches of Buddhism was typically one-sided, with the independent identity of Kyo lying in the balance. This concern remained, even with someone as sympathetic to Kyo as Hyujŏng. The postface to Hyujŏng's *Sŏn Kyo sŏk* notes, for example, that three disciples of Hyujŏng distributed this text to Sŏn meditation and Kyo lecture halls throughout the country, where it immediately sparked intense controversy. These discussions prompted some fifty students of both Sŏn and Kyo to gather before Hyujŏng to debate the relative merits of the two traditions. Although no winner was declared in the debate, it is telling of Hyujŏng's ultimate sympathies that, in the transcript at least, the Sŏn advocates clearly have the upper hand throughout. Hyujŏng himself ordered that some of the highlights from the exchanges be recorded and used as the postface to his text.[61]

But, thanks to the efforts of Buddhists like Hyujŏng, Kyo was eventually restored once again to nearly equal footing with Sŏn within the Korean Buddhist tradition. Hyujŏng's renewed recognition of the place of Kyo within Korean Buddhist practice led to a resurgence in doctrinal study during the late Chosŏn. Two generations after Hyujŏng, so many renowned and respected specialists in scripture and doctrine appear in Hyujŏng's lineage—monks like P'ungdan Ŭisim (1592–1665) and Wŏlchŏ Toan (1638–1715)—that some scholars have gone so far as to assert that Kyo learning, rather than Sŏn meditation, had by then become the principal focus of the Korean Buddhist tradition.[62] The increasing emphasis on scholarship within the Korean tradition also catalyzed new advancements in the scholarly study of Sŏn texts. Emblematic of these more analytical accounts of Sŏn is Paekp'a Kŭnsŏng's (1767–1852) *Sŏnmun sugyŏng* (Hand mirror of the Sŏn school), whose treatment of various types of Sŏn, though departing markedly from Hyujŏng, would be further explored in later Sŏn writings at the end of Chosŏn.[63]

Despite a plethora of extant materials, Korean Buddhism after Hyujŏng remains one of the most underresearched areas in Korean Buddhist studies and deserves much more attention than it has so far gleaned from scholars. But, what we can say with confidence is that the efflorescence of both Kyo and Sŏn late in the Chosŏn dynasty derives from the sixteenth- and seventeenth-century efforts of Hyujŏng, first, to forge an accommodation with Confucianism and, second, to synthesize anew Sŏn practice and Kyo learning into the Korean Buddhist tradition.

# Popular Religion in a Confucianized Society

## BOUDEWIJN WALRAVEN

*How could the Office of the Inspector-General*
*offer up sacrifices to a nameless ghost?!*
—Ŏ Hyoch'ŏm

BY THEIR VERY NATURE, the elite in any society casts a disapproving eye at the religious beliefs and practices of those they regard as social inferiors. The common people, for their part, often wish to emulate those of superior status but find the ways of the elite uncongenial and unsuited to their needs. The inevitable result is tension. In Chosŏn Korea (1392–1910), where Confucianism, Buddhism, and popular beliefs coexisted, the tension between popular and elite beliefs was particularly strong, much stronger than it had been in the preceding Koryŏ period (918–1392) when Confucianism had not yet turned against Buddhism. During the Koryŏ, Buddhism enjoyed the favor of the court, and aristocrats and government officials did not spurn the aid of the *mudang, the professional shamans*. In the Chosŏn period, Confucian scholar-officials looked with contempt on most manifestations of popular religion and seriously attempted to reduce its influence. They were particularly hostile toward the wildly dancing mudang, who claimed to be in direct communication with the gods and the spirits of the dead. The socially despised mudang, who were generally illiterate and female, came to be the perfect antithesis of the respected, highly educated Confucian literati with their carefully restrained and dignified demeanor. As representatives of popular religion, the mudang occupy a central place in the relationship between elite and popular beliefs in late Chosŏn society.[1]

Although the thinking of the elite and the common people differed considerably, a certain measure of accommodation was necessary to maintain a viable society. Elite and popular beliefs functioned within a social context, and as long as certain conditions were met, social actors felt no need to exploit the potential for conflict. The elite generally insisted on maintaining "correct" principles derived from a worldview essential to the legitimation of their dominance. But they could afford to condone or ignore heterodox beliefs and practices that did not challenge their position.

The history of popular religion in the Chosŏn period cannot be studied without taking into account the growing influence of Confucianism. The Confucian transformation of Korea that started in the late fourteenth century was not simply a change in state ideology. Confucianism modified many areas of life, including the relationship between elite and popular culture, and continued to transform ever wider areas of society, even after it had altered major state institutions and yangban society during the first two centuries of the dynasty. The Confucianization of Korea may be seen as a civilizing process that first affected a relatively small literate elite and led to efforts by this elite to establish and maintain political control over a basically uneducated mass.[2] From a different perspective, one may say that the elite withdrew from certain forms of culture (which then became truly popular culture),[3] using their distinctive "civilization" to justify their claim to social privilege.[4]

The elite, however, did not merely manipulate ideas to their own advantage; they internalized the values they preached. The civilizing process changed the personality of those affected by it, resulting in increased self-control and new, more refined sensibilities and new canons of taste. Consequently, their efforts to further civilization had as much ideological as political and social aspects and involved social psychology as well as codes of behavior. With time, the new civilization of Confucianism was eventually accepted, at least in part, by other segments of society in a process that had political implications and reflected the growing influence of the elite worldview on other social groups.[5] In other words, the coin of the "cultural capital" of the yangban elite gained wider circulation.[6]

The most succinct and eloquent demonstration that the Confucianization of Korea was a civilizing process in the sense outlined above (and not merely the acceptance of certain philosophical tenets and social institutions) is the description of the ideal product of Confucianization in Pak Chiwŏn's (1737–1805) story *Yangban chŏn* (The tale of a yangban): a Confucian gentleman devotes himself to studying the Classics and emulating the sages, bears hunger and cold stoically, does not eat raw onions, never throws dishes or beats his wife when he is angry, controls himself at all times, whether talking, eating, smoking, bathing, or walking, and, when ill, does not call a mudang. A contemporary handbook of yangban etiquette shows that the enumeration of the do's and don't's of a civilized man in this satirical story is not exaggerated.[7]

Korea's Confucianization had notable consequences for the mudang and their activities. However much elite scholars disapproved, mudang rituals did not disappear, but they were progressively relegated to the category of popular, unofficial, or private religion. The Chosŏn state identified completely with Confucianism, and official reliance on mudang consequently diminished. Complaints by literati about the mudang and the patronage they received in high quarters continued, however, right to the end of the Chŏson period. This raises doubts about the effectiveness of the campaigns against them. Nevertheless, the changes in the relationship between Confucianism and popular religion are quite clear when differences in social status and geographical region and between the public and the private spheres are taken into account within a historical framework. Confucian ideals, whether by official pressure or on their own merit, were most thoroughly assimilated by the elite in the capital and by yangban men in general, whose claims to public office were dependent on their study of the Confucian classics, and in the spheres of life that were considered public rather than private. In contrast, mudang rituals (even though they changed with the times) continued to flourish and were even tolerated by the government among the lower orders of society, in regions outside the capital, and, perhaps most important, in the inner, private quarters of families of all classes where women lived.

This chapter treats two aspects of the relationship between elite and popular beliefs: their differences, from which tension arose; and their interactions, which allowed the two segments of society to function as parts of one entity. Together, and often in complementary ways, Confucianism and popular religion shaped the behavior of Chosŏn period Koreans.

Following an examination of Neo-Confucian thought in relation to popular ways of thinking, I survey public and private rituals as practiced over the course of the Chosŏn period. Women played an important role in popular religion and acted as intermediaries between elite and popular beliefs. For this reason, I devote particular attention to their ritual activities and needs in order to draw attention to certain spheres of life in which Confucian rituals were felt to be insufficient and certain rituals attempted to bridge the gap between Confucianism and popular belief and served the needs of both the elite and the commoners. Finally, I discuss the ways in which Confucianization affected the rituals of the mudang.

Unfortunately, the source materials for this study are extremely one-sided and consist almost entirely of writings by members of the elite, with their extreme bias against mudang. To compensate for this, it is necessary to make judicious use of later sources, for example, works of the late nineteenth century, when new media and changed circumstances allowed the expression of different points of view, and of the results of twentieth-century fieldwork. Without the latter, certain important aspects of shaman rituals, such as their extraordinary potential for dramatic psychological catharsis or their attraction as occasions for escaping the burdensome routines of daily life, would not be understood.

## Neo-Confucian Thinking and Popular Religion

What prompted the Neo-Confucian yangban literati to reject certain forms of popular religion, in particular, the rituals of the mudang? Was it a logical consequence of their philosophy and, if so, of which aspects? Can, for instance, Confucian opposition to mudang rituals be explained simply as disbelief in the existence of invisible beings with whom the mudang entered into contact? Or, is it possible to explain the tension between Neo-Confucianism and popular religion by examining only abstract concepts and ideas without taking into account the concrete, social setting in which they operated?

Long before the emergence of Neo-Confucianism in Sung China, Confucian thinking tended to discount a literal interpretation of the ritual of feeding the ancestral spirits and to attach more value to its social and psychological functions.[8] In Neo-Confucian cosmology, no distinction between natural and supernatural, or divine, phenomena is made.[9] Everything in the universe is "natural"; that is, it is subject to the same law, the one principle (*i*; Chin. *li*), which manifests itself in material force (*ki*; Chin. *ch'i*). All phenomena appear and disappear through the condensation and dispersion of *ki*. There are no mysterious, capricious gods, creators, or transcendent rulers of our world outside this system. Moreover, there is no eternal soul, because a person's *ki* eventually disperses after death.

This intellectualist view of the universe was in conflict with religious belief in a continued spiritual existence after death. It was used, for example, in polemics against the Buddhist doctrine of reincarnation. Even in Neo-Confucianism, however, a spiritual, incorporeal part of a person could survive for a while after death, especially if it had no descendants to offer it worship or if the person had died prematurely or in tragic circumstances.

Kwŏn Kŭn (1352–1409), a major figure in early Korean Neo-Confucianism, for example, was responsible for the institutionalization of sacrifices to restless spirits (*yŏgwi*), whose accumulated resentments were supposed to cause epidemics.[10] The spirits of particularly forceful personalities were not supposed to disappear immediately after death and were thought to retain the power to manifest themselves in the world of the living. The eighteenth-century scholar Yi Chunghwan (1690–?) gave two examples. The spirit of the Koryŏ loyalist Chŏng Mongju (1337–92) appeared to protest the decision of a king of the Yi royal house, which had been responsible for his death, to grant him official rank posthumously in the Chosŏn bureaucracy.[11] And for three centuries after his death, the spirit of General Ch'oe Yŏng (1316–88), a hot-blooded warrior, regularly returned to satisfy his sexual appetites with the maidens serving in his shrine. (Ch'oe Yŏng is still worshipped as an important deity by the mudang.)[12]

The scholar Yi Ik (1681–1763) recognized that this world consists only of *ki*, but he allowed for the possibility that *ki* coagulates in such a way as to create spirits (*kwisin*). This, he thought, could happen in two ways. Whereas a normal person's *ki* dissolves after death, exceptional persons of great virtue and spiritual power might retain a presence in this world even after their demise. Yi Ik also considered it possible that the veneration of spirits would bring about a coagulation of *ki*. This could happen, he explained, in response to prayers from people who worshipped spirits without a proper pedigree at unlicensed shrines.[13] Spirits could, in other words, be created or sustained by faith. Yi Ik's recognition of spirits did not predispose him to leniency toward the mudang, however. He repeatedly emphasized that spirits could not be trusted and played tricks on the ignorant and foolish who were inclined to worship them. Spirits might pose, for instance, as prominent figures from ancient history, like the mother of the Silla general Kim Yusin (595–673) (who was worshipped in a local shrine). But how, asked Yi Ik, could a spirit exist for thousands of years? No one who understood the great principle of the universe (that all phenomena are but temporary manifestations of *ki*) would be deceived by such beings.[14]

Yi Ik was not alone in these opinions. Chŏng Yagyong (1762–1836) opined that the removal of heterodox shrines and mudang would deprive the *kwisin* of their base and thus put an end to their importunities.[15] The *Ch'oe saengwŏn chŏn* (The tale of Licentiate Ch'oe) written by Yi Ok, a contemporary of Chŏng,[16] argues that a belief in spirits leads to spirit manifestations, with disastrous consequences. A man, who came to believe in spirits after a mischievous neighbor threw stones at his house, was vexed from then on by strange occurrences, and within a few months his wife died. Another man, who moved into a haunted house, forbade the members of his household to react to spirit manifestations, and very soon he was left in peace. The story also asserts that no advantages are gained by employing mudang.

Because of this tale, Yi Ok has been called a nonbeliever or atheist,[17] but no reading of the story can support such a conclusion. He rejected spirit worship and mudang, but he did believe in spirits, as did nearly everyone else. Most believed in the existence of an incor-poreal part of humans, qualified though it may have been, as part of the normal order of the universe. No Neo-Confucian scholar would have categorically dismissed the reality of the invisible beings the shamans served. Contrary to what one might expect, the denial of a distinction between natural and supernatural did not lead Confucians to doubt the existence of supernatural phenomena, since no fundamental conceptual barrier divided the world of human beings from that of the spirits.

Neo-Confucianism undoubtedly contained elements that might  estrange its adherents from the popular view of spirits, particularly with regard to their importance to human beings, but it did not encourage a complete denial of their existence. Moreover, the question of Neo-Confucian beliefs about spirits is of limited, mainly philosophical, importance. The assumed existence of spirits served as the basis for rituals that created a social reality which was meaningful to the participants, regardless of individual views about the proceedings. For this reason, different opinions about the nature of the beings addressed in rituals could peacefully coexist. This made it less probable that the more sophisticated, nonliteral, interpretations would lead Confucians away from a view of spirits similar to that found in popular religion.[18] Because the reality of the spirits never became a point of contention, and the rhetoric and the outward forms of ritual (such as the opening of doors for the ancestral spirits and the use of spirit tablets with little holes to allow the spirits to enter and to leave) encouraged a literal interpretation, the majority of the ritual participants were probably inclined to believe that the spirits of ancestors did appear when sacrificial rites (*chesa*) were performed for them.[19]

The sophisticated Neo-Confucian view of spirits as propounded by thinkers like Kwŏn Kŭn does not, however, suffice to explain the rejection of the beliefs and practices of the mudang. Why did scholars like Yi Ik so deeply mistrust the spirits of popular religion? Are there other aspects of Neo-Confucianism that explain the elite's strong opposition to the activities of shamans? The cosmology of Neo-Confucianism does contain elements that might provide a basis to harmonize Confucianism and popular religion. Other elements, however, could lead to conflict.

In the Neo-Confucian vision, the great principle of the universe links human beings to all other phenomena in the cosmos. The structure of the human world corresponds to that of nature and other cosmic phenomena (the four cardinal virtues of humans, for instance, correspond to the four seasons). This idea was philosophically elaborated in a highly sophisticated way and cannot be equated with a simple microcosm-macrocosm scheme.[20] Nevertheless, it is a concept that lends itself to accommodation with simpler forms of belief. Such accommodation was helped by the fact that Confucian concepts, sophisticated as they might be in their full philosophical elaboration, were expressed at times in simple terms hardly different from popular beliefs. A Confucian tract for women expresses the idea of cosmic unity very concretely: "[The human] head follows the form of heaven; it is round and carries heaven above. One's feet follow the form of the earth; they are square and step on the earth. Two eyes, corresponding to the sun and moon, shine with brightness. Corresponding to the Five Peaks of China, the face has five peaks [forehead, nose, chin, and the two cheekbones]; corresponding to the four seasons, four limbs sprout from the body; corresponding to the five primary substances, there are five fingers and five toes on each [hand and foot]."[21] The popular view of the universe is less systematized, less ordered, but basically it is similar: the world in which humankind live and the world of spirits and gods operate according to the same principles, and there is no great transcendental divide between the two. In both the Confucian and the popular visions, human fortune and misfortune are linked to the invisible other sphere.

It becomes easier to understand why tension arose between Confucianism and popular religion when the Confucian view of state and society and its practical implications are examined. Rulers ruled, directly or indirectly, by the grace of Heaven. The divine and secular hierarchies were interlinked or were even two branches of one and the same system, and thus the Confucian government laid claim to religious as well as political authority.[22] Everyone with responsibility for governing from the king to the local magistrate occasionally acted as an officiant in sacrificial rituals commensurate with his status. The worship of gods outside the official hierarchy or the worship of recognized deities by the wrong officiant was seen as a potential threat to the social order. The mudang posed a serious problem in this respect, because the very essence of their mission was to enter into direct communication with the gods and spirits who, in the course of shamanic rituals, descended into their bodies. From this the mudang derived their authority independent of governmental approval.[23] Even if possessed by officially recognized deities (though often they were not), mudang nevertheless operated outside the proper hierarchical relationships. Sources from both the early and the late Chosŏn period indicate that mudang frequently claimed to be possessed by the spirits of personalities respected by the elite, such as deceased generals and ministers of state.[24] In the eyes of the elite, this was an inexcusable attempt by the lowly mudang to arrogate to themselves the authority of their social superiors.[25]

Chosŏn Confucians were slightly more tolerant of certain other representatives of popular religion, such as blind exorcists (*p'ansu, sogyŏng,* or *changnim*). These male ritual specialists chanted scriptures in Buddho-Taoist style and specialized in healing by catching malignant, disease-causing spirits.[26] The spirit world they dealt with did not differ significantly from that of the mudang; and they were employed for the same purposes, but because they were not possessed by deities who lent them a special, and potentially dangerous, authority, they posed less of a threat to the social hierarchy. Moreover, their style of performing was seen as more "civilized."

In the great scheme of the universe as defined by Confucianism, virtue was of supreme importance. If things were as they ought to be, the greatest virtue belonged to the ruler, who derived his authority from it; thanks to his virtue, his rule would be blessed.[27] The spiritual power (*yŏng*) of the virtuous king would affect the gods (*sin*), so that they would protect his people. Due to this protective power, it was explained, officials and exiles sent to the distant island of Cheju never drowned on the way.[28] Conversely, natural calamities were warnings from Heaven that government ought to be improved.[29] Thus, the well-being of the people as a whole depended on the moral caliber of the monarch. Smaller units of society, such as families or kin groups, similarly depended on the virtue of their members. Collections of moralistic sayings from the Classics such as the *Myŏngsim pogam* (Precious mirror for enlightening the heart) gave the unambiguous message that happiness was the reward for good behavior and that evil deeds would eventually bring misfortune. This kind of semipopular literature was widely read and may be regarded as summarizing generally accepted morality.[30] To try to influence one's fortune by employing outsiders such as the mudang instead of relying on one's own moral power was a reprehensible manipulation, an attempt to obtain personal profit without personally contributing to the common weal through the practice of virtue.

On first sight, certain forms of state ritual seem to contradict the notion that blessings should be obtained by practicing virtue. At times of crisis such as droughts, foreign invasions, or epidemics, Confucian officials would perform sacrifices to invisible powers in rituals in which the notion of receiving blessings through virtue seems to have been secondary. Such official sacrifices resembled mudang rituals, which at times were also performed to combat drought and other natural calamities. Here, the potential for a reconciliation between popular and official religion was greatest. The question remains, however, whether officials offered these sacrifices in the expectation of divine help or because they were regarded as useful in soothing the feelings of the population. A definitive answer is hard to give.[31] The notion of virtue was not entirely absent in the invocations used during these rituals, however, and the display of sincerity (*sŏng*) in their performance might in itself have been considered a form of virtue.[32]

The vision of a strictly hierarchical social system embedded in the universe did not appeal to everyone. It was persuasive only to those who through education and social career had obtained a wider perspective beyond household or local community — the male members of the yangban elite. They alone identified fully with this public order in which "immoral worship" (*ŭmsa*) had no place. When their private aspirations were thwarted, however — when they failed the examinations or advancement in office did not materialize — even they were tempted to resort to prayers through mudang.[33]

Adherence to Confucian norms was not a matter of philosophical persuasion or intellectual conviction alone. Confucian scholarship and behavior were the symbolic capital used by the yangban to hold on to their dominant position or achieve prominence within their own circles.[34] Consequently, reliance on mudang was taboo for men who laid claim to yangban status, whatever their private opinion concerning mudang. Public association with shamans would have jeopardized their position. Song Siyŏl (1607–89), one of the most famous Confucians of the second half of the Chosŏn period, in instructions written for his daughter, gravely warned her not to allow mudang rituals to be performed at home, since this would inevitably lead to the loss of yangban status.[35] The seventeenth and eighteenth centuries were times of intense status competition. The number of official positions was much smaller than the number of yangban aspirants, and for many members of the elite it was necessary to maintain social status by means other than officeholding. The rejection of certain manifestations of popular religion seems to have become more than a matter of personal inclination.

Thus, the refusal of the yangban to participate in certain forms of worship was not merely a consequence of their philosophical convictions. It also depended on social factors, for example, taste, which, as Pierre Bourdieu has reminded us, differs according to social class and serves to demarcate social distinctions.[36] This is illustrated by a late eighteenth-century anecdote about a group of yangban who went to pay their respects to three deities enshrined in a mountain fortress. Their visit indicates that they had no fundamental objections against the veneration of these gods. They withdrew in disgust, however, when they saw that the three crude cast-iron images flanked two garishly adorned female statues with red-painted lips and powdered faces. These female statues not only offended Confucian ideas of propriety but also shocked the gentlemen's aesthetic sensibilities.[37]

The elements in Neo-Confucianism that led to a rejection of the mudang and many aspects of popular religion concerned, above all, practical matters: the ordering of society, the maintenance of a proper social hierarchy, and the ritual duties of different categories of persons. In social reality, Neo-Confucianism served to distinguish and legitimize the yangban elite, who found the form and circumstances of mudang rituals, with their lack of sobriety, the free mingling of the sexes, and extravagant expenses, to run counter to Confucian social values.[38] In more general terms, such as the belief in the existence of invisible beings and ideas of the relationship between humankind and the cosmos, elite philosophy and popular religion contained points of similarity. Consequently, there was a continuum between two opposite poles: on the one side, the highly sophisticated, learned Confucian scholar who regarded moral cultivation as a primary duty and did not take the act of sacrifice as a literal feeding of spirits, and on the other side, the totally uneducated fisherman for whom the sacrifices to the gods were an attempt to avert calamities and obtain material benefits.[39] The middle ground between the two extremes was open to negotiation. Different social groups occupied particular positions along this continuum, elite yangban at one end, country yangban somewhere toward the middle, farmers and fishermen near the other end, but shifts were possible. Nor did individuals occupy the same position at all times; they, too, could adapt their position to specific circumstances.[40]

This continuum was not a matter of theory or concepts alone, but also of ritual practice. Whatever Confucians thought of spirits, they made sacrifices to their ancestors, to local guardian spirits, and to abandoned ghosts, all of whom were worshipped in mudang rituals as well. Of course, they may have done so with mental reservations, with an inner detachment, and without being inclined to regard the offerings of food and drink literally as the feeding of invisible beings. The possibility of a more literal interpretation, however, and thus a rapprochement with popular religion, did always exist. In the eyes of the less sophisticated, Confucian sacrifices would be a vindication of the rightness of sacrifices per se.[41] Apparent contradictions in the religious history of Chosŏn Korea, such as the persistence of mudang rituals in the households of the yangban who professed to abhor them, seem less blatant when they are considered with this notion of a continuum in mind.[42]

### Mudang and the Public Realm

The history of the relationship between the state and shamans in the earliest periods is obscure because of a scarcity of materials.[43] For the Koryŏ dynasty, records reveal the existence of mudang who in many ways seem to have performed rituals similar to those found in later periods. Although the government occasionally followed the mudang's advice,[44] the shamans were of low social status, and already in this period there is evidence of tension between shamans and the elite. Examples are the disdainful attitude toward an old mudang expressed in a poem by Yi Kyubo (1168–1241), the irreverent testing of divine powers by Ham Yuil (1106–85), a law forbidding mudang to live in the capital, and a prohibition against granting them land.[45]

During the Chosŏn dynasty, the government made concerted attempts to bring all forms of worship under control and to suppress those forms considered undesirable.[46] Buddhism, Taoism, and mudang rituals became targets for criticism and repressive legislation by Neo-Confucian officials.[47] In contrast to Koryŏ precedents, the measures taken in the early Chosŏn were more systematic and comprehensive in scope and aimed at creating a well-regulated, standardized system of worship. The government established new categories of deities to be venerated and reviewed currently worshipped deities to decide if they should be incorporated into one of these new categories.[48] The form of worship, the physical representation, and the titles of those admitted to the select group of officially recognized deities were made to conform to uniform standards. In general, images of the gods had to be replaced by wooden tablets (of the right kind of wood). This depersonalization was part of an attempt to eliminate veneration of the wives, concubines, and daughters of deities. Once the selection was made, the government does not seem to have allowed additions to accommodate (and bring under control) popularly worshipped deities.[49]

These restructuring measures resulted in the creation of an official pantheon quite distinct from the gods of popular religion. Although there remained some ambiguous cases involving local tutelary spirits and the gods of mountains and rivers, the government tried to discourage "private" worship of officially recognized deities. This was connected with what may be called the "status" aspect of ritual.

Much care was taken to define which gods should be worshipped by what category of person. The hierarchy of deities was made to correspond to the social hierarchy, and the right and responsibility to officiate at the great majority of sacrifices were granted to those who exercised power, such as the king, ministers, magistrates, and eldest sons. Even when different categories of people performed the same type of sacrifice, distinctions were made. In Confucian-style ancestor worship, for example, high officials were allowed to worship more generations of ancestors than were low-ranking officials.[50] Non-officeholders were expected to worship only one generation of ancestors and the village god at the village shrine (isa).

As a means of bringing the mudang under control, they were registered and put under the supervision of a government agency in charge of the sick.[51] A tax was levied on the registered mudang. This may originally have been intended as a repressive measure, but it came to be fiercely criticized by the literati, who alleged that officials refused to eradicate illegal cults for fear that this would reduce their revenues.[52] Nevertheless, the tax was still levied in the late nineteenth century (ironically, the legal code specified that the proceeds of the mudang tax were to be used to pay for the caps of officials of the highest rank, the symbols of their dignity).[53]

Inevitably, the attempt to change long-standing practices and ancient beliefs met with resistance, and many laws and regulations did not immediately have the desired effect. Nevertheless, shamans were gradually eliminated from public rituals and the center of public life, the capital. The ban on mudang in the capital, which had already been in force (at least nominally) in the Koryŏ period, was repeated in the early Chosŏn. In the beginning, this measure seems hardly to have been enforced at all.[54] One important exception was made: to the chagrin of certain officials, a small number of mudang, the most prominent of whom was a "royal mudang" (kungmu), were exempted from the ban.[55] These mudang seem to have been well remunerated by their patrons, for the 1485 Kyŏngguk taejŏn (National code) stipulated that the members of the highest category had to make contributions to the tribute sent to the Ming three times higher than those required from "rich inhabitants" of Seoul and Kaesŏng.[56] It is not clear when the position of kungmu disappeared, but after 1613 they are no longer mentioned in the Veritable Records (Sillok).[57] The ban against mudang residing in the capital was regularly repeated in later legal codes.[58] At least some mudang seem to have been permitted to remain until the late eighteenth century; in 1777, however, all mudang were sent to live south of the Han River. In consequence, Seoul could no longer collect the tax on mudang.[59] The formal exclusion of the mudang from the center of power was complete. Still there is ample evidence, including repeated bans, that they continued to enter the capital to serve their patrons, the women of elite households, with private rituals.

Near the end of the dynasty, shamans were still frequenting the royal palaces. Two of these were so politically influential that, through their female patrons, they could influence appointments to the bureaucracy. It is said that "provincial governors and local magistrates came out of their sleeves in great numbers."[60] Contemporary lists of items used for rituals and of their costs, kept in the Palace Library (Changsŏgak), record expenditures of considerable sums of money on mudang rituals, which were performed under the supervision of ladies-in-waiting at the royal court.[61]

Powerful as they may have been informally, in public rituals of the central government the mudang had lost their role. Prayers for rain seem to be the state-sponsored ritual in which mudang participated longest. In an agrarian society such as Chosŏn Korea, droughts meant crop failures and famines. Famines, in turn, gave rise to epidemics among the weakened population. Such disasters had to be averted at all costs. Mudang prayers for rain were commissioned by the central government until the first half of the seventeenth century. Possibly the last instance of mudang participation in official rain rituals dates to 1638, when the Ministry of Rites stated explicitly that shamans should no longer be employed in these rituals.[62] Further evidence for the diminished role of the mudang is provided by King Yŏngjo's (r. 1724–76) order in 1745 to delete the rain rituals of mudang and blind exorcists (which, he said, had been abolished long ago) from the *T'aesang chi*, the handbook of the Office of Rites (T'aesangsi). Thereafter, mudang disappear from the official histories in connection with centrally sponsored state rituals, although rain prayers continued to be performed in purely Confucian form until the end of the dynasty.[63]

At lower administrative levels, the mudang apparently continued to perform rituals for rain until the end of the nineteenth century,[64] but it is not clear if they did so in an official capacity. There is some indication, however, that the mudang were also excluded from the official rain rituals at the lower levels. Writing about the correct form of rituals to be performed by local magistrates, Chŏng Yagyong lists a number of heterodox methods of praying for rain practiced in the early nineteenth century.[65] He does not mention the use of mudang among them. It is not entirely clear whether this means that no mudang were used or whether he did not even want to discuss mudang, because he was fiercely opposed to shamanic ritual. But the description of rain prayers in the countryside and in the capital by Charles Dallet in his *Histoire de l'église de Corée*, which was based on information from contemporary missionaries active in Korea, does not mention mudang either.[66]

Materials from the early twentieth century confirm the impression that mudang had, at best, a limited role in official rainmaking rites in the countryside. After 1910, county magistrates, assisted by local worthies, in many instances continued to perform some of the traditional sacrifices. They apparently adhered quite faithfully to the old rituals.[67] This is not to say, however, that they practiced purely Confucian forms of rain prayers; some of the rituals were those that Chŏng Yagyong had condemned a century earlier and had been forbidden by law before that.[68]

Mudang took part in the proceedings in a minority of cases. In only four out of nineteen localities were shamans involved.[69] In Ch'angwŏn (South Kyŏngsang province), the ritual was performed by the magistrate (*kunsu*), representatives of the local elite, mudang, and blind exorcists. In that order, they took turns in one and the same ritual.[70] In Sŏnsan (North Kyŏngsang) and Sinch'ŏn (Hwanghae), men prayed in the mountains while mudang assisted in a ritual performed around a dragon made of mud in the town.[71] In these three instances, both officials and mudang prayed for rain but kept a certain distance, either performing different parts of the same ritual or acting in completely different ceremonies.[72]

If mudang played only a limited part in the rain prayers, what about the rituals for local guardian deities, the *sŏnghwang*? Both Western and Korean authors label these local gods as shamanic.[73] If this is true, which remains to be seen, this means that a firm link existed between the cults of the mudang and the government, because quite early in the dynasty each magistrate was obliged to worship the *sŏnghwang* (Chin. *ch'eng-huang*)[74] of the locality he administered.[75] But retrievable data[76] lead to quite a different conclusion. As the dynasty progressed, the distance between the mudang and the official *sŏnghwang* cult seems to have grown progressively greater.

Certain facts do point to the presence of popular elements in the *sŏnghwang* cult. A review of the places where *sŏnghwang* were worshipped, as recorded in local gazetteers, shows the greatest possible variation in the location of their altars, in contrast to those for the Gods of Soil and Grain (*sajiktan*, always to the west of the magistracy) and for abandoned ghosts (*yŏdan*, to the north of the magistracy). Local popular traditions concerning numinous places may thus have been accommodated in the official worship of the *sŏnghwang*. Frequently, in conformity with the ancient Korean belief in mountain gods as local protectors, the *sŏnghwang* shrines (*sŏnghwang-sa*) were located on mountains. Local communities also kept their own traditions with regard to the identity of their protective gods. The *sŏnghwang* of Koksŏng in Chŏlla province, for instance, was said to be the spirit of a native of that locality—the Koryŏ general and meritorious subject Sin Sunggyŏm (?–927).[77] Attacks by sixteenth-century central government officials against irregular rituals involving mudang at local *sŏnghwang* shrines seem to confirm the unofficial character of these cults. Some even proposed that these shrines be destroyed altogether.[78] One critic speaks of the fervor among numerous worshippers during the festival of the *sŏnghwang* of Kŭmsŏngsan near Naju. (The popular worship of that deity was already a matter of concern during the Koryŏ dynasty because it was regarded as a threat to public order and social propriety.)[79] In this period, a strong popular element in the worship of the local *sŏnghwang* is undeniable. When the entire Chosŏn period, particularly its second half, is considered, however, the *sŏnghwang* cult appears in a different light. It is less a rich mixture of popular religion and official worship than an instance of growing state control.

The *sŏnghwang* cult first appeared in Korea in the reign of King Munjong of Koryŏ (r. 1046–83),[80] but centuries after that, in the earliest years of the Chosŏn period, no nationwide network seems to have existed. In a review of existing cults, which should not be considered exhaustive, made during the reign of King Sejong (r. 1418–50), only three *sŏnghwang* were mentioned among many deities of other kinds.[81] The presence of a *sŏnghwang* shrine in every locality where a magistrate resided resulted from a central government attempt to establish an orderly system of ritual. This effort included the establishment of local altars for abandoned spirits (*yŏgwi*) to provide a Confucian remedy for the danger of epidemics that they could cause.[82] In fact, *sŏnghwang* and *yŏje*, the ritual for abandoned spirits, were closely connected. Although the codes specified that the rites at *sŏnghwang* shrines were held in spring and autumn,[83] local *sŏnghwang* altars appear in the ritual codes as well as in most other writings in the context of the *yŏje* ritual. The ritual statutes apportioned the task of assembling the spirits for *yŏje* to the *sŏnghwang*, the invisible counterpart of the local magistrate, who was worshipped together with the *yŏgwi*. But three days before a *yŏje* ritual, the *sŏnghwang* received sacrifices at his own altar, in which the magistrate informed him of the task awaiting him. The detailed instructions for this sacrifice did not include the use of mudang. The decision to institute the *yŏje* ritual was taken in 1401, but it took some time before it was regularly performed everywhere. Likewise, the creation of a network of officially approved *sŏnghwang* altars took time.[84]

The *sŏnghwang* cult to which officials objected during the reign of King Chungjong (r. 1506–44) was the old, popular cult, not the cult propagated by the government, which was closely related to *yŏje*. During the first half of the sixteenth century, when the Confucianization of Korea made great strides, the clamor against customs viewed as reprehensible was loudest. In the years that followed, the tendency was to eliminate popular elements from the *sŏnghwang* cult, at least to dissociate the official cult from irregular practices. The worship of images, still current in some places, also came under attack; for example, in sixteenth-century Chŏnju (home to one of the more prominent old *sŏnghwang* cults), the god's image was destroyed by the provincial governor.[85]

Two centuries later the situation had changed considerably. Attacks against the local (popular) *sŏnghwang* are no longer found in the *Sillok*. Concern was voiced that magistrates did not always perform the sacrifices themselves,[86] but not that they erred by making concessions to popular religion by, for example, employing mudang. In sum, an official *sŏnghwang* cult had come into being that, in spite of some minor lapses,[87] was clearly distinguished from popular practices.[88]

This is not to say that the popular worship of the *sŏnghwang* ceased altogether. At the same shrines used by the magistrate to offer sacrifices, people might, in contravention of official policies, come to pray for themselves and perhaps even hire mudang for this purpose. But there was no fusion of official and popular cults. The government made no concessions on the issue of local guardian deities; this contrasts with the situation in China, where the government recognized the personal character of the local gods by, for example, offering special sacrifices on their birthday.[89] Nor could mudang challenge government control of the shrines, as the Taoist clergy could in China. An early-twentieth-century observer accurately characterized the Korean state of affairs when he noted that the mudang were wont to perform their rituals *alongside* local shrines.[90]

There continued to be places where gods who were not part of the official hierarchy were worshipped. The early Chosŏn reformers' wish to institute a system of village shrines (*isa*) in communities below the county level so that villagers might worship in approved fashion was never implemented except in a few isolated instances.[91] Most village communities kept their own forms of worship of tutelary spirits. In many places, the population and the mudang continued to worship guardian deities that dwelled in old trees, in simple shrines, or in heaps of stones. The fact that some of these gods were called *sŏnghwang* (usually pronounced *sŏnang*) is confusing, but it does not mean that they were officially recognized. The *sŏnang* was like the *sŏnghwang*, from whom he had borrowed the name, a *deus loci*, but his cult was definitely irregular (*ŭmsa*).[92]

Confronted with forms of worship outside the official system, not all magistrates followed the same course. Some tried to end them.[93] The most striking example during the second half of the Chosŏn period is the "civilization campaign" conducted by the governor of Cheju Island, Yi Hyŏngsang (?-1733), who had 129 shamanistic shrines and two Buddhist temples burned down.[94] The extreme character of this campaign probably was provoked by the fact that Cheju Island was an outlying region and was still relatively unaffected by mainland culture. Occasionally gazetteers indicate that literati considered preferences for mudang rituals a sign of backwardness, expected among unpolished rustics in isolated places.[95] Elsewhere, mudang seemed to have lost ground, making it easier to ignore them, as some magistrates did. When irregular cults were not too glaring, government officials often preferred to accommodate them in some way.[96] We may conclude, however, that they generally took care to maintain a suitable distance between the official cult and the local customs they tolerated and that accommodation did not mean that mudang were allowed to take part in rituals beside the king's representatives. This may be inferred from extant descriptions of local customs, which give an idea of the forms this accommodation took.

In Kosŏng, a town in Kangwŏn, the magistrate would worship a local deity on the first and fifteenth of each month, customary dates for Confucian sacrifices. This was not irregular in itself, but the representation of the god in the shrine was. It was a mask made of silk, which was taken out of the shrine on the twentieth day of the twelfth month, when a townsman wearing the mask would become possessed by the god. Dancing all the while, the "god" then visited government offices and went around the town giving everyone his blessing.[97] Here an ordinary citizen took the role usually reserved for the mudang, who are not mentioned in the account.

In another town, Ch'ŏngan in North Ch'ungch'ŏng, in the third month the head clerk of the magistrate's office led a group of local inhabitants to a big tree on a mountain where a god called Kuksa (National Teacher) resided and escorted him and his spouse to the town. The divine couple would be installed in the yamen and entertained with food, drink, and music. For this purpose mudang were employed. In all the offices of the county's administration, sacrifices would be made to the god.[98] The unorthodox nature of this cult is obvious from the dwelling place of the deity and from his marital status. It was probably allowed because the cult was important to the government clerks (as may be inferred from the separate sacrifices in different offices).

In Kangnŭng in Kangwŏn, according to an old gazetteer,[99] the sŏnghwang was worshipped in spring and autumn as elsewhere. Apart from that, there was a form of worship the author designated as "peculiar." On the fifth day of the fourth month, one of the most prominent clerks, with the help of mudang, would bring a god, also called Kuksa, down from his shrine on the Taegwan Pass and escort him into the town, while people in great numbers watched along the road. In the town, the government slaves came out to welcome the god, who would be enshrined in the sŏnghwangdang, where he stayed for a month. His sojourn in the town ended with a big festival on the fifth of the fifth month.[100]

In the last two cases, the role of government clerks (hyangni) merits attention. In certain ways these servants of the magistrate held an intermediate position in society. Since they were in daily contact with the elite and were literate, they could absorb elite values. Yet their subordinate place in the system stood in the way of complete identification with the culture of their superiors. The ambiguity of their position is reflected in their ritual practices. On the one hand, from the late eighteenth century on, some of them followed the example of the yangban and established shrines for ancestors who had distinguished themselves by a display of Confucian virtues.[101] On the other hand, they favored "irregular" cults such as that of Pugŭn, a deity worshipped everywhere in yamen offices, in spite of attempts at suppression.[102] As other sources confirm, government clerks were often involved in the worship of local deities.[103] Even though magistrates allowed this, they do not seem to have been directly involved in the more irregular forms of worship. In fact, they may have used the clerks to their own advantage. The clerks' participation allowed magistrates to remain unsullied by improper practices, while signifying interest in official quarters in rituals important to the population because disaster was believed to strike if they were left unperformed.[104]

According to recently recorded oral tradition, mudang attached to the magistrate's office in the provinces were used to welcome a new magistrate, to celebrate the homecoming of scholars who had passed the government examinations, and to participate in village festivals.[105] Here their public functions should not be interpreted as public recognition of their importance as religious specialists. It is likely that the shamans were called on not so much as magico-religious specialists but as entertainers who created a festive atmosphere with their singing and dancing. The same may have been true for the assistance of the mudang in the celebrations of a Confucian scholar's triumph. The simple ritual they performed on such occasions (*hongp'ae kosa*) can be understood as a traditional benediction to add to the festivity of the proceedings. That mudang were valued (and tolerated) as entertainers emerges also from a late nineteenth-century source that depicts the king and the queen leaning against a pillar enjoying the performances of mudang and artists of all kinds.[106]

Other public rituals in which mudang participated were festivals for the guardian deities (*sansin, tongsin, sŏnangsin,* etc.) of villages in which the government sponsored no prescribed rituals of its own. (For this reason one might question if they should be called public, even though they were for the benefit of a community.) Such festivals permitted greater freedom for popular religion, and the role of the shaman seems to have been more important. By the end of the Chosŏn period, however, it is clear that the mudang generally helped celebrate only some of these festivals. From the abundant materials on village festivals collected in the first half of the twentieth century, the conclusion may be drawn that by the late nineteenth century important parts of most rituals for local guardian deities were performed not by mudang but by male members of the community, who conducted sacrifices in Confucian style complete with ritual invocations in Chinese.[107] This Confucian style was not always matched by a corresponding Confucian content, however. For deities represented in purely anthropomorphic form, who often had (equally venerated) wives and daughters, the mundane expectations of the ritual performance as well as the lack of an ethical component might have been repulsive to strict Neo-Confucians.[108] Yet, the adoption of a Confucian style signified a clear break with the tradition of popular religion embodied in mudang rituals and shows that progressive Confucianization and the corresponding diminishing of the role of popular religion were not entirely dependent on pressures exerted by the government. Local leaders voluntarily opted for a style of worship that, in their eyes, was more civilized and conferred more social prestige.

The status aspect of the various rituals also helps to explain the distance that was always maintained between Confucian officials and shamans—a distance brought about by differing concepts of ritual as well as by the disparity of their standing in terms of political power and social prestige. Apparent contradictions in the relationship between provincial officials and mudang are resolved when this aspect is taken into consideration. At first sight it is strange that the yangban were so scornful of shamans when, according to a critical newspaper article, as late as 1901 mudang were attached to every local government office.[109] We cannot ascertain the feelings of all officials about mudang rituals and cannot be sure that they were completely skeptical concerning the powers of the mudang. After all, on the conceptual level one can find similarities between Confucian and shamanistic rituals, and it is not impossible that in their way of thinking some yangban were closer to the shamans than they would have liked to admit, publicly or even to themselves.[110] One cannot exclude the possibility that certain magistrates expected that the prayers of the mudang would further their careers, as the newspaper account suggested. Socially, however, the distinction between Confucian and mudang rituals was quite clear. Confucianism was firmly associated with authority and higher social status. Certain shamanic activities were allowed by those in power, but only for groups with a lower social position: government clerks, commoners, or women. By rejecting shamanic rituals for themselves and tolerating them for others, they did, in effect, assert their own superiority.

### Private Rituals

In the early Chosŏn period, mudang still performed public rituals alongside government officials. They were also employed in private rituals for *yangban* families. Yangban would entrust the spirits of their parents or grandparents to the divine protection (*wiho*) of mudang shrines. Since this ran counter to the new policy that encouraged all yangban to worship their ancestors in purely Confucian style, the practice was strongly attacked.[111] Despite initial reluctance to adopt customs alien to Korean tradition, Neo-Confucian reformers were successful in the end. Before the middle of the Chosŏn period, yangban took pride in worshipping their ancestors correctly in their own ancestral shrines (*sadang*).

The pressure exerted from above to effect reforms in an area of life normally considered "private" draws attention to the fact that cross-culturally the distinction between public and private is not without complication. In fact, the family in Chosŏn Korea did not belong entirely to the private sphere. In particular, as Don Baker discusses in his chapter in this volume, ancestor worship was public in the sense that it was considered the backbone of the social order, so much so that in later years the government undertook immediate punitive action when early Korean Catholics decided to destroy ancestral tablets.

Ancestor worship in its public aspect was above all a matter that concerned men, since public life ("outside") was the exclusive preserve of men. The place for women was "inside," the home. It was the women, for whom only a secondary, supporting role in the Confucian ancestor rituals was reserved,[112] who organized mudang rituals for the deceased even after Confucian ancestor worship had been well established. When King Hyojong (r. 1650–59) died in 1659, a mudang ritual was held at the behest of his wife; during the rite the late king spoke through the mouth of a mudang.[113] Although this ritual, because of its scale and, above all, because of the "public" character of the deceased, led to a harsh official reaction, such rituals generally took place without interference if performed inconspicuously in the inner quarters. The men of the family might disapprove (Was it not undignified for the spirit of a respected ancestor to appear and speak through the mouth of a low-class woman?), but many nevertheless preferred to stay away and feigned ignorance of the proceedings.[114]

The nature of women's and men's dealings with the ancestors was quite different. Whereas Confucian-style *chesa* performed by the men was intended as a decorous demonstration of respect for beloved and benevolent ancestors, the mudang employed by the women tried in their rituals to solve more practical problems—guiding the spirit of the deceased to the world of the dead and preventing the survivors from being harmed by spirits with a lingering grudge. The confrontations between the spirits of the dead and their surviving female relatives, with the mudang as mediator, could lead to great outbursts of emotion. This was no doubt another reason why upper-class men, who were trained to restrain their behavior, did not feel comfortable with such rituals.

In addition to acting as psychopomps and pacifiers of disgruntled spirits, the mudang performed the important "private" task of healing. Disease was thought to be inflicted by resentful or angry gods and spirits or was attributed to invisible, noxious influences that could be resolved or exorcised through shamanic ritual. From the beginning of the dynasty, different rituals were used against epidemics; initially these were Buddhist or Taoist, and only later was the Confucian ritual for abandoned ghosts (*yŏje*) adopted.[115] The only officially regulated contribution the mudang made to public health was as helpers assigned to the government agencies caring for the sick. Because their role in this regard is unclear, I confine this discussion to a review of their private rituals for health.

Although recognizing that illness could be caused by spirits, Confucians objected to curative mudang rituals for various reasons. They believed they were simply not effective, because the mudang did not have the right kind of power over the invisible forces that caused disease. King Yŏngjo was among those who expressed disbelief in the capacities of the mudang as healers.[116] Another objection was that one should not try to manipulate, by prayers or rituals, the will of Heaven. Fate (*myŏng*) had to be accepted as decreed by Heaven, a fate that might be changed by the practice of virtue but by nothing else. Prayers for recovery from illness were to be found in the Classics, but these were offered up by the sages in a spirit of obedience to the will of Heaven; for ordinary people, prayer was not the right way to cope with illness.[117] Some Confucians protested against mudang rituals because shamans often held the spirits of deceased relatives responsible for disease. From a Confucian point of view, this was wicked and an expression of disrespect.[118]

As we saw above, around 1800, when Pak Chiwŏn wrote his tales, to ask a mudang for help when ill was thought incompatible with the status of a yangban. Yangban women, however, were not deterred by this. The author of a contemporary etiquette book for yangban deplored numerous needless deaths because women, when there was an illness in the family, rejected the benefits of medicine or doctors and had rituals performed; to make things worse, they also observed certain taboos that were deleterious to health.[119] If women did heed the admonitions not to employ mudang to cure illness, they might call a blind exorcist or themselves go to pray in the mountains or near a river. This also met with criticism. Song Siyŏl regarded both practices as undesirable, but he did not reject them so absolutely as he did the employment of mudang; if the in-laws of his daughter favored such practices, he told her, she should not object.[120] It is significant that Song apparently expected his daughter to be confronted with such practices. However much Confucians might deplore them, they were common in the women's quarters of yangban houses.

The relationship between women and private rituals by mudang is so close that it deserves further examination. By the second half of the Chosŏn period, elite men had almost completely turned away from mudang even for private rituals, whereas the women of their households continued to rely on them despite Confucian pressure. This calls for an explanation, especially given the influence Confucianism exerted in the long term on men of even relatively low status, as can be deduced from the widely observed Confucianization of village rituals.

In principle, Confucian teachings were for all members of society, including women. Confucians recognized women's crucial roles in securing the well-being of the family. "A family's ruin or success depends on the women," a didactic poem said.[121] Accordingly, it was important to educate women properly and to instruct them in Confucian values. Women who excelled in Confucian virtues were publicly honored by the government. To shield women from evil influences, contacts with shamans were frowned on, and visits of yangban women to mudang were forbidden.[122] Books instructing women in proper behavior warned against reliance on mudang:

Tseng Tzu said that there is nothing children cannot do when their parents are ill, but you should not make use of Buddhism or male and female shamans. If from the days of old one could have profited from Buddhism or shamans, would not the saints of the past and the great sages have made use of them? It is not just that there is no profit in it, it will even do harm.[123]

Or,

Ignorant of the fact that ghosts are treacherous and malicious and have proved to be unreliable, women are led astray by grotesque mudang, deceiving their superiors within the household and squandering their property.[124]

The same message was given in long poems (*kasa*) widely distributed in yangban households of the eighteenth and nineteenth centuries. One such poem contrasts a well-behaved, modest, and frugal, that is, a truly "civilized" (i.e., Confucianized), woman to a sloppy, gossiping shrew, completely illiterate and totally lacking in self-control. The first achieves happiness through her own efforts; the second hopes to find it through rituals and prayers. "How would even spirits help / If one's heart is like this?!"[125]

Confucian propaganda of this kind was certainly not without effect. The scholar-official Yu Hŭich'un (1513–77), for instance, praised his wife who refused to call a mudang when she was ill and paid no heed to her daughters' urging.[126] But Confucian campaigning against shamanism was only partly successful—even the ladies of the court continued to patronize mudang. Women were generally less exposed to Confucian thinking, were not directly involved with the institutions of the Confucian state, and had less invested in Confucianism. Few yangban women had a formal education beyond learning to read and write the Korean alphabet. Nor did women have the experience of working in a hierarchical bureaucracy, which would have made much more convincing the Confucian concept of worship, with its equally bureaucratic hierarchy of deities who were to be addressed only by those who, because of their place in society, had the authority to do so.

Elite men were usually content to acquiesce in women's lack of education. Since the separation of social roles was a fundamental aspect of Confucianism,[127] behavior and thinking that would have been unacceptable in yangban men were far less objectionable in women. A woman might be forgiven for consulting a mudang as long as it was done out of devotion to her superiors and her family and without public loss of face. Tolerance was even easier for a woman of low status. An instructive anecdote has it that an old female slave, afraid that her master would run into trouble because of his recklessness, went to a mudang to pray that he might change his behavior. People who heard this story laughed, but also praised the slave for her loyalty (a Confucian virtue, after all).[128] At the other end of the social scale was the example of Myŏngsŏng wanghu, the mother of King Sukchong (r. 1674–1720). Who would have dared to blame her when, following the instructions of a mudang, she bathed every day in a cold stream to prepare herself for prayers that her son might recover from his illness and consequently died of these rigors?[129] The mudang, however, was punished. In contrast, a shamanic ritual performed by order of the queen dowager in 1624 was criticized for exerting a corrupting influence on the still youthful crown prince.[130]

Male acquiescence to mudang rituals in the women's quarters may also be explained from the point of view of status maintenance. To maintain elite status, it was vital to adhere punctiliously to Confucian standards. What women did within the seclusion of the home, however, was of lesser concern. Women thus could continue to perform rituals for the benefit of the entire family. They had, moreover, reasons of their own to favor popular forms of religion over Confucian rituals. Women found it comforting to perform rituals that concerned the most important aspects of their lives—giving birth to and raising children. The position of a woman within a family depended foremost on her ability to produce a male heir. Children determined her status within the household and were the main object of her affections. Confucianism, however, had no remedies for the anxieties caused by childlessness, children's illnesses, and child rearing. From a woman's point of view, Confucian rituals focused on the wrong end of the family—ancestors rather than children. Even though the proper performance of ancestor worship was thought to ensure the prosperity of descendants, it cannot have satisfied the emotional needs of women.

Women were more directly affected by childlessness than men. Although to remain without a son was condemned as a lack of filial piety, a man had options to remedy the situation not available to women. If a wife did not conceive (which was considered to be her fault, not her husband's), a man could divorce her[131] or adopt an heir. When children were ill, the husband might be worried, but he would generally suffer less than did his wife, who was much more involved with the children not just because child rearing was her daily task but also because marriages were patrilocal and a woman, cut-off from her natal family and surrounded by strangers, would direct most of her affections to her offspring. Only her children really belonged to her, and to them she consequently devoted most of her love and care.[132]

Women's prayers, although in principle condemned, were in practice often condoned. A prominent Confucian such as Song Siyŏl did not encourage such prayers (he considered them useless), but he thought they could be tolerated if this contributed to social harmony within the family. Even King Chŏngjo (b. 1752, r. 1776–1800) once related without disapproval or embarrassment that the queen-mother Chŏngsŏng, (1692–1757; his grandfather Yŏngjo's first wife) prayed to Heaven for an heir to the throne (i.e., a son to the crown prince).[133] Noting that he himself had been born exactly one cycle of sixty years after the queen-mother, he remarked that this did not seem to be a coincidence, suggesting the possibility that he regarded such prayers as effective.

Elite men objected far less strongly to solitary prayers than they did to mudang rituals, but women derived much greater emotional support from rituals specifically devoted to deities promoting child-birth, such as Samsin. These dramatic rituals not only furnished a framework for prayers, but they could also, in a dramatically convincing form, offer assurances of good fortune. Women understandably found it difficult to do without them. The nineteenth-century Tongguk sesigi (Annual events of Korea) describes an endless stream of women that gathered from the third day of the third month until the eighth day of the fourth month in Chinch'ŏn in North Chŏlla at the temples of the Dragon King and Samsin to pray with mudang for offspring.[134]

Childlessness was not the only problem addressed by mudang on behalf of women. They could, and still can, be counted on for songs asking for an abundance of milk for breast-feeding mothers,[135] for exorcisms to cure children's diseases,[136] and for rituals to cure naughtiness and unruly behavior.[137] The importance of the mudang's role as a protectress of children is expressed in the words of the mother of Ch'unhyang, Korea's most famous fictional heroine: "When I raised that brat, my only child, my only daughter, without a father, so frequent were all kinds of ailments when she was small that [it was as if] the doctor and our mudang had come to live with us."[138] In real life, the weak health of the son of Queen Min (1851–95) prompted her to commission prayers and rituals on an unprecedented scale.[139]

Children could be given special protection against illness and bad health by fictitious sales to or adoptions by the gods of the mudang. Through a direct, pseudo-genealogical link, divine strength could be transmitted to these "grandchildren" of the gods. The two favorite mudang of Queen Min were said to have many such adoptive sons, no doubt from prominent families.[140] This form of adoption is predicated on a concept of the family as an organic unity in which strength may flow from ancestors to descendants, a concept Confucians wholeheartedly accepted.

Women's tendencies to seek the help of mudang may have been fostered, unintentionally, by the Confucian attitude toward spirits (*kwisin*). Tracts, such as the one quoted above, strongly condemned *reliance* on spirits but used *belief* in them to promote discipline. "If in your heart you say, 'How cruel is my fate, how terrible are my parents-in-law,' and allow this mood to go on for a while, the Sun and the Moon will shine on it [and expose you], the spirits will show their dislike, and calamities will befall you."[141] If a woman eats something by herself [without sharing], "the spirits who sit next to her will glare at her, and fortune that was to come her way will depart [again]."[142]

These tracts also encouraged a literal interpretation of Confucian ancestor worship. Although women could not participate directly, they had the important task of preparing the food with great regard for cleanliness and with "sincerity": "If one acts in this way, the soul (*sillyŏng*) will partake of the food, and the descendants will be happy. . . . How could one worship one's ancestors without sincerity, lacking in cleanliness? If one acts in such a way that the soul does not partake of the food, calamities will befall the descendants."[143] These fragments present the act of sacrifice and the benefits for the living as directly related, as they are in a mudang ritual.

If women continued to rely on mudang, they did not totally reject Confucian values, especially those directly related to the family. The most outstanding female paragons of Confucian virtue were exhibited in compilations commissioned by the government to encourage such values. In works such as the *Samgang haengsil to* (The virtues of the Three Bonds, illustrated) and the *Oryun haengsil to* (The virtues of the Five Human Relationships, illustrated), women who killed themselves rather than allow their virtue to be compromised, who fed ailing parents-in-law with their own flesh, and who dutifully mourned them and their husbands after death were held up for emulation. Ironically, while being exemplary Confucian wives and daughters-in-law, they may well have been patrons of mudang, considering the scale of mudang activities even in elite households. Nor is this illogical, since the aims of their rituals were not contrary to Confucian values. Inasmuch as they offered comfort to women, they made it a little easier for them to fulfill their arduous domestic tasks.

Shamanic rituals offered opportunities both for enjoyment and for catharsis and the unleashing of pent-up feelings. They also contributed to the integration of women into their husbands' families by providing occasions when all the women, among themselves, could engage in religious ritual. When a young bride entered a strange household, a special ritual was held to pray that the bride might pass the difficult first years "gently" (kopke) and without conflict.[144] Noxious influences responsible for marital discord could be chased away with a salp'uri ritual.[145] Because a woman's affection for her offspring was the most important emotional tie linking her to her affines, rituals through which motherly concern was expressed and anxiety allayed could be instrumental in promoting identification with the husband's family. The stronger the bond between a woman and her children, the stronger her bond with her husband's family.

Women, in short, did not have to be in a state of inner rebellion against their husbands to have recourse to mudang ritual. On the contrary, some of the feelings that prompted such behavior were warmly applauded by even the staunchest Confucians. This, in turn, made it easier for men to tolerate shamanic activities at home.

### In-Between Rituals

Mudang rituals could provide remedies for those needs left unsatisfied by Confucianism. When, however, recourse to mudang was thought unacceptable or undesirable, alternative forms of private ritual were performed. These are hard to classify because they contain elements of both popular religion and Confucianism. Three examples will demonstrate the ways the gap between popular religion and elite ritual could be bridged.

Mudang can provide treatment akin to psychotherapy by explaining feelings of depression as due to the intervention of spirits or noxious influences and by performing a symbolic action to remove the causes.[146] Confucian ritual cannot fulfill such a therapeutic function. What, then, did a member of the elite who believed in the existence of spirits do when he attributed his psychological malaise to an invisible being? The following case is recorded in the *Sillok*. In 1822, a former official who felt himself oppressed by a spirit made an altar together with some friends and sacrificed to the spirit in Confucian style.[147] The spirit declared (the manner is not recorded, but possibly the man himself was possessed) that he was a general of the late Koryŏ period. He demanded food and drink and behaved, according to the censor-general who reported this, in a thoroughly improper manner. Though approached in Confucian style, the spirit was obviously shamanic in character. The pantheon of the mudang contains many such spirit generals. A sacrifice to such a spirit naturally offended the guardians of orthodoxy. Above all, it was thought outrageous that the ritual invocation mentioned some of the greatest sages of Korean Confucian history. This incident may be taken as evidence that under particular circumstances certain members of the elite were unable to do without elements of popular religion, even though the yangban as a class had effectively distanced itself from the mudang.

A second example of mixed ritual seems to have caused less controversy, perhaps because it was related to the world of women. When four royal palaces were abandoned in 1908, it was reported that there were shrines dedicated to the spirits of unmarried princesses within their compounds.[148] These princesses, having no descendants, could not receive Confucian ancestor worship, but mudang would perform rituals for their spirits.[149] Mudang interpret the term "ancestors" (*chosang*) to mean all deceased relatives, both patrilineal and matrilineal, even children.[150] In this case, however, the princesses were permanently enshrined, and judging from the names of the rites, *ch'arye* (performed in the daytime on feast days) and *hyangsa* (performed at night on the anniversary of the day someone had died), they received proper Confucian-style ancestor worship.[151]

These sacrifices for unmarried princesses may have resulted from feelings of piety and affection, but the Confucian as well as popular idea that spirits without descendants could be dangerous was almost certainly involved. Confucianism prescribed the *yŏje* ritual to deal with this problem, but this ritual treated the spirits as an anonymous group without individuality.[152] It was designed neither to express piety for deceased relatives nor to offer solace when specific afflictions were attributed to the vengefulness of their spirits.[153] Whichever way they are interpreted, the sacrifices for the princesses draw attention to the lacuna left by the overwhelming emphasis Confucianism placed on the patrilineage.

Rituals performed by women included the *ant'aek* and *kosa* ceremonies for household gods, for which they often called a mudang.[154] The gods worshipped on these occasions belonged to the shamanic pantheon. Surprisingly, there is evidence from the early twentieth century for the existence of a similar ritual in a Confucianized style with, at times, a shade of Taoism, which was performed after a house had been repaired or when a family moved to another house. The officiants often were men reading invocations in Chinese.[155] This was not part of the standard Confucian family ritual and reflects concepts behind shamanic ritual. Mudang regarded as potentially dangerous any building activities in and around the house and the transfer of objects from outside the house to within.[156] Such rituals filled a gap in Confucianism, namely, the omission of rituals for the concrete, physical household (men, women, children, servants, and even cattle), in contrast to the family as part of the time-transcending lineage, and for the house itself, which as a structure literally enveloped the household and was metaphorically identified with it.[157]

### One Act, Two Meanings

Where two different ways of thinking coexist, the same fact may be interpreted or perceived in two different ways. Even though this situation is a potential source of conflict, it may also offer opportunities for accommodation, provided that the difference in interpretation is ignored by those concerned.

The authorities of Chosŏn Korea publicly honored women of exceptionally virtuous conduct by Confucian standards by permitting the erection of special gates or commemorative stelae. Many women so honored were "chaste women" (*yŏllyŏ*) who, faced with defilement or slander, killed themselves rather than suffer dishonor. The act could, however, be seen in a completely different way. These paragons of virtue were also potential sources of danger, because the force of their resentment made their spirits stay near the living after death. Female spirits with lingering grudges were especially feared in popular religion, and similar notions could be found among the elite.[158] The zeal with which village heads and local authorities recommended such women for public honors may in many cases have been due to fear rather than to respect. To bestow honors on them could be a way to placate their spirits, as Murayama Chijun reported in the 1920s.[159]

There is also earlier evidence for this. An incident of 1739 shows a connection between the fear of wrathful female spirits and the rewarding of exemplary behavior by women, and not just in the eyes of the villagers.[160] A widow who resisted the incestuous advances of a nephew was killed by him. After the crime was discovered, the culprit escaped. The county was subsequently afflicted by a severe drought, which was attributed to the woman's resentment. The county magistrate offered a sacrifice at her grave, whereupon there was a downpour of rain. Apparently this ad hoc ritual did not please an official of the Inspectorate. He recommended that renewed efforts be made to apprehend the criminal and that the woman be suitably honored as a *yŏllyŏ*.

Certain forms of worship practiced under government auspices may be similarly explained. The worship at special altars of soldiers who died in battle (*minch'ungdan*) is also open to a double interpretation. On the one hand, the ritual rewarded and promoted the civic virtue of loyalty. On the other hand, it was intended to appease resentful spirits. Worship at the *minch'ungdan* occasionally was a countermeasure against raging epidemics (for which restless spirits, *yŏgwi*, were held responsible).[161]

In the *yŏje*, which were sacrifices for the category of restless spirits in general, the official and popular interpretations nearly converged. The government acknowledged that the grudges of restless spirits could cause disease and that therein lay the immediate reason for worshipping them. Yet in the official view, the *yŏje* was more than the feeding of hungry ghosts; it was also a demonstration of the monarch's benevolent desire to alleviate the sufferings of his poor subjects and thus, in a sense, a justification of his authority.[162]

Modern fieldwork by Griffin Dix furnishes another example of the coexistence of a popular and elite interpretation of one and the same act.[163] Some informants interpreted the custom of putting rice into the mouth of the deceased with the words "This is one hundred bales, a thousand bales, ten thousand bales," as an expression of the descendants' hopes that through the protection of the dead person they might receive great wealth; others viewed it as symbolic nourishment for the spirit.[164] The first interpretation is, of course, the popular one, the second that of the Confucian elite. There is no reason to doubt that these conflicting explanations of one part of the funerary ritual also existed in the Chosŏn period.

## Developments Within Mudang Rituals

In "two-tiered" cultures like Korea, where elite culture and popular culture are clearly separate, the temptation is to pay attention chiefly to historical change within the well-documented culture of the upper class, while assuming that the culture of the lower classes remained more or less the same throughout the ages. This assumption has rightly been criticized.[165] It is all the more important to trace changes within popular religion, since they are relevant for the interaction of popular and elite culture. One factor promoting the complementary coexistence of the two was the adaptability of the popular tradition, which was mainly oral and not bound to a standard of orthodoxy laid down in scripture. Proceeding from certain basic premises, such as the assumptions that the invisible world of gods and spirits directly influences the life of man and that it is possible to communicate with that world, popular religion changed and, adapting itself to new circumstances, survived. Such changes within popular religion during the Chosŏn period are traced here mainly on the basis of twentieth-century research materials, since earlier sources are fragmentary and highly biased.

Valuable in this respect are the *muga*, the songs of the mudang, not because they are, as is sometimes assumed, mere survivals from a far distant past but because they change and thus *record* change.[166] One example of the influence of Confucianism on the *muga* and the mudang is a dialogue in which the word sincerity, *chŏngsŏng*, plays a key role. The concept of sincerity has a long pedigree in Confucianism, dating to Mencius, the *Doctrine of the Mean* and the *Great Learning*, and it received particular emphasis in Neo-Confucianism.[167] At some point during the Chosŏn dynasty, popular religion seems to have borrowed the term *chŏngsŏng*, and *chŏngsŏng ŭl tŭrida*, "to offer sincerity," became a synonym for "to sacrifice." Both in Confucianism and in popular religion, sincerity became a requisite for the performance of ritual and was deemed essential to its success.

The passage from a twentieth-century shaman song translated below not only shows an awareness on the part of the mudang of certain Confucian objections to popular practices but also illustrates how the term *chŏngsŏng* could function as a "password," which made it possible to slip from one frame of discourse into another. It provides the means to reconcile a popular practice with the Confucian point of view. The song is about a king and a queen without an heir. When the queen broaches this topic, the king says that it is apparently his fate (*myŏng*) to remain childless, a typical Confucian reaction when rituals to obtain blessings are proposed. His wife, however, does not agree:

"We have not been able to have descendants because our *chŏngsŏng* has been insufficient. Let's try to get descendants by offering up prayers to famous mountains and great rivers."

Then the king replied: "Wicked thoughts! If one could have descendants by making sacrifices (*chŏngsŏng tŭryŏ*), would anyone in this world be without them . . . ."

When he spoke thus, his wife respectfully said: "It is not like that. Not everybody is capable of showing sincerity. To show sincerity (*chŏngsŏng tŭrigi*) is even more difficult than having descendants. If my sincerity is exceptional, there is nothing in this world I cannot do. 'If one's sincerity (*chŏngsŏng*) is exceptional, [such] perfect sincerity (*chisŏng*) moves Heaven,' they say; it is out of the question that we will fail."[168]

The king has no reply to this and grants permission.

This fragment is interesting not only because of its familiarity with Confucian objections to popular religion, but also because of the two ways in which *chŏngsŏng tŭrida* is employed. The king uses it disapprovingly in its popular meaning of "bringing sacrifices," whereas the queen in her rejoinder shifts to the original, literal meaning: "to offer one's sincerity," thus lifting her argument to a higher level to overcome Confucian resistance. Not surprisingly, in a mudang song, the popular point of view wins out.

In many passages, the *muga* show an at least superficial acceptance of Confucian values. "Who will make ancestral sacrifices for us," laments a childless king.[169] Prayers for offspring are primarily prayers for sons, the only ones who, according to Confucian custom, can perpetuate ancestor worship.[170] When they are born, the gods are asked for help to ensure that they will display Confucian virtues and be loyal servants to the country and filial sons to their parents.[171] In the shaman song of the Abandoned Princess (Pari kongju), the souls that go to the (Buddhist) Western Paradise are filial children, loyal subjects, and affectionate siblings.[172] This song, including its main theme of filial piety, probably has Buddhist origins,[173] but its audiences would have taken it simply as an affirmation of a Confucian virtue. Such Confucian elements in the *muga* suggest that during the Chosŏn period those who followed popular religious tradition respected Confucianism as a dominant moral orthodoxy.[174] Mudang did not become Confucians, but they could not escape a certain degree of Confucianization.

The prestige of Confucianism is also evident in other *muga*. One lists as books the Buddha Sakyamuni supposedly read in his youth: *The Thousand Characters, Boys' Studies, A Primer for the Young and Foolish, The Book of Songs, The Book of History*, the *Analects*, the *Mencius*, and *The Book of Changes*.[175] Another *muga* reproduces the Confucian theory of the origin of Heaven and Earth and the Ten Thousand Beings, as the operation of the Great Ultimate in material force and the ensuing transformations of *yin* and *yang* and the Five Agents.[176]

It is not only the *muga* that furnish evidence that shamans adapted themselves to Confucian values. In the second half of the Chosŏn period, mudang and their husbands (*mubu*), who provided the musical accompaniment for shamanic rituals, were organized in regional associations. These associations provided mutual help, set rules to limit competition, and represented their members in dealings with the government. A number of documents pertaining to these organizations have been preserved.[177] These documents, nearly all written in Chinese (with occasionally some clerk's writing, *idu*), show that with one exception these organizations were run by men who patterned their behavior on Confucian models. Following a custom that prevailed in government offices, they rendered worship to their "teachers" (*sŏnsaeng*), who were their predecessors or organizational "ancestors," twice a year.[178] One document asks the authorities to reward a *mubu* who demonstrated exemplary filial piety, mustering well-known topoi from Confucian works such as *Oryun haengsil to*: the miraculous procurement of out-of-season food craved by a parent, feeding a parent with one's own blood to cure illness, and the faithful observance of the three-year mourning period.[179]

As this document illustrates, Confucian forms of worship had become the accepted norm for men even if they were from a mudang milieu, and shamanic ritual had been relegated to the sphere of women (and to that of men without aspirations to "civilized" behavior, those who were at a great physical or social distance from the sources of Confucian culture).[180] The *mubu*, who also were frequently employed as musicians by local magistrates, were in a good position to absorb elements of yangban culture even though their social status was very low. In fact, it is likely that numerous elements of yangban culture such as *sijo* found their way into the songs of the mudang through the *mubu*.[181] The incorporation of these elements was facilitated by the continued reliance of upper-class women on the mudang. In its present form, shamanism, especially as practiced in Seoul, undoubtedly owes much to the patronage of wealthy aristocratic ladies. The constant changing of elaborate and costly costumes to symbolize the descent of different deities into the mudang, typical for Seoul, would be unthinkable if the mudang had to rely entirely on peasants living at subsistence level.

The detailed classification and ranking of shamans according to the spirits that descend into them (probably confined to mudang from the capital) seems to have been a phenomenon dependent on lavish support from wealthy patrons.[182] Such a specialization is possible only when rituals are performed on a large scale. Moreover, the idea of classifying shamans in a hierarchy may have been reinforced by the example of the bureaucracy of the royal court.

### Conclusions

The Neo-Confucian officials of the early Chosŏn period who did not assign the social and the divine to fundamentally different categories did not exclude religious ritual from their reforms. They propagated forms of ritual that, together with corresponding symbols and values, became an essential part of their culture and justified their dominance. The reformers thus initiated a process that between 1400 and 1900 greatly affected popular religion. To a large extent, the changes in popular religion were a consequence of the progress of Confucianization, which manifested itself on many levels and affected even those who could not understand the subtle intricacies of Neo-Confucian philosophy. The aim of the early reformers was to replace forms of worship they disapprove of with impeccable Confucian rituals. Although this aim was never fully realized, the relationship between elite and popular beliefs changed over the centuries. Elite beliefs came to be identified exclusively with Confucianism. Whereas during the Koryŏ period Buddhism enjoyed great prestige and officials were occasionally inclined to give credit to the claims of the mudang, in the Chosŏn period adherence to Buddhism and, to an even higher degree, contacts with shamans became incompatible with elite status.

In Korea, Confucian orthodoxy seems to have been of greater relative importance to the political elite in defining their own social identity than in neighboring countries. Consequently, unorthodox ideas and beliefs and popular rituals were kept at a greater distance. In China, there was greater latitude for elite scholars to pursue alternative lines of thought.[183] The condemnation of Buddhism in China by orthodox Confucians does not seem to have affected elite behavior as much as it did in Korea.[184] The Chinese government, though no less intent than its Korean counterpart on bringing rituals under control, appears to have been more willing to recognize and accommodate cults of popular origin, even if they continued to attract popular interest. An example of this is the cult of the sea goddess Ma Tsu, who, first recognized during the Sung, was repeatedly honored by the government and in 1737 received the title "Empress of Heaven" (T'ien Hou) from the Ch'ien-lung emperor.[185] Korean history has no comparable example of a widely popular deity honored by the government in this way.

The fact that social status and Confucianism were so closely related in Korea may explain in part why the tension between elite thinking and popular religion appears to have been stronger there than in China and Japan. In Japan, Neo-Confucianism became important at a rather late date but never to such a degree that the entire ruling class identified with it. It was not from the outset the legitimating ideology of the new Tokugawa shogunate, and even when promoted by the shoguns, it never monopolized government support. Moreover, there was no examination system that imposed acceptance of its tenets on all who aspired to office. And almost as soon as it started to gain influence, it was vigorously challenged by thinkers with quite different ideas.[186] Thus, the religious and philosophical preferences of the elite retained a much greater diversity than they did in Korea. Quite a few *bushi* studied Neo-Confucianism and many more were influenced by it, but it never became a major part of their social identity.

In Korea, after Confucianism had transformed the institutions of the elite, Confucian values began to filter down to other layers of society. In turn, the lower strata cited their acceptance of these values (proof that they were "civilized") to justify claims to social distinction, even if only within their own local communities. By the end of the dynasty, Confucian civilization had affected the behavior of much of the population. In fact, most men had been Confucianized to a certain degree. Often this meant that they also accepted Confucianized forms of ritual, although men of low status or with particularly dangerous jobs, such as fishermen, continued to rely on mudang rituals for reassurance. The Confucianization of men resulted in Confucianism increasingly becoming a marker of another social distinction, this time not of status but of gender. Popular religion, mudang rituals, prayers to mountains, and visits to Buddhist temples came to be associated with women. This association was already in existence at the beginning of the Chosŏn period, if not earlier, but became stronger as more and more men withdrew from popular religion.

The result of this is still visible in present-day Korea: women are the majority of participants in practically all religious activities. Although Confucianism cannot be said to have been completely irreligious, it did discourage many forms of religious behavior, such as prayers for happiness. As a consequence, many Korean men came to feel that religion, especially in its more devotional forms, was something better left to their wives.[187]

Thus, Korean shamanic rituals came to be performed predominantly by women. It is impossible to know the exact proportion of male to female shamans during the Koryŏ dynasty, but developments during the Chosŏn period undoubtedly made a career as a shaman less attractive and more difficult for men. In the eighteenth century, Yi Ik noted that there had been male shamans in the past, but that they had been replaced by women, who could more easily enter the inner quarters.[188] Apparently in his time the situation was similar to that prevailing at present—relatively few male shamans, who often exhibit behavior different from the normal role patterns of their sex.[189] Perhaps there were even fewer male shamans than today, since social norms at that time strongly condemned contacts between women and men who were not close relatives. One consequence of the "feminization" of shaman rituals, as regards both patrons and shamans, was that Korean female shamans participated in a wider range of activities than their counterparts in China, who had to leave the performance of rituals for major gods to men.[190]

The relegation of mudang rituals to specific areas within society substantially diminished the subversive potential inherent in shamanic possession. Mudang could threaten the hierarchy of authority

by entering into direct communication with the spirits, but as long as
this happened in a context that was from the government's point of
view marginal, it did not seriously threaten public order.

What the gods said through the mouths of mudang generally did
not pose a challenge to authority because it was part of the discourse
of the separate, private world of women and seldom touched the
public realm of men.[191] There are, to be sure, a few examples of shamans who aroused concern because they were implicated in religious activities with rebellious potential,[192] but these mudang operated outside their usual spheres of action. They were quickly and
sternly dealt with and never constituted a real danger to the government. If mudang did exert political influence, it was through the
(sometimes not inconsiderable) power elite women had over men.
They used their influence not to undermine the system but to obtain
benefits from it, for instance, to secure official posts for male relatives and relations.[193] There seems to be some evidence of this from
the late nineteenth century, when Queen Min and her relatives were
at the height of their power.[194]

The fact that men, even in rural communities, largely adopted
Confucianized rituals also had political implications. This signaled
their acceptance of the culture of the ruling elite and, by extension,
of its right to rule. The adoption of a Confucian style by villagers
may be regarded as symbolic of their identification with the state.

Confucians were unrelenting in their criticism of popular religious practice, but they never managed to eliminate popular religion
completely. Perhaps this was to their own advantage. The continued
activities of mudang did not necessarily weaken Confucianism. Because shamans served the needs of women, helping them to cope
with their roles as wives and mothers and providing them with
emotional relief and entertainment, the mudang supported women
in the fulfillment of their tasks within the family. The mudang
thereby strengthened the family, the foundation of society in Confucian thinking. Present-day Korean "familism," often regarded as a
Confucian heritage, owes as much to shamanism as it does to Confucianism. Just as a good Confucian wife supports her husband from
behind the scenes, so might the rituals in the women's quarters support Confucianism in an unseen manner.

# A Different Thread: Orthodoxy, Heterodoxy, and Catholicism in a Confucian World

## DON BAKER

TASAN CHŎNG YAGYONG (1762–1836), a prolific author and a pre-eminent philosopher of the second half of the Chosŏn dynasty, once explained in two brief essays what precisely made "heterodoxy" heterodox. "Generally speaking, any school of thought that focuses exclusively on one specific maxim as its guiding precept will be heterodox."[1] Tasan saw danger in any excessively narrow approach to moral cultivation, the chief concern of Korean Neo-Confucianism. He recognized that people differ and that a specific formula which works for one person or one group may not work as well for others.

In Tasan's opinion, Wang Yang-ming's (1472–1529) famous injunction to "follow your own innate knowledge of the good" worked for Wang, since he had been endowed with a superior moral character. He could trust his own innate sense of right and wrong. His followers, however, did not have the same innate moral compass. When they looked within for guidance, they mistook what felt good for what was good. Wang's precept lulled his followers into complacency and kept them from seeking the external guidance they needed in order to live moral lives. It is the effect Wang's teachings had on his followers, not any moral flaws in Wang himself, that convinced Tasan the Wang Yang-ming school was dangerous and therefore heterodox.[2]

For Tasan, ideas in isolation were neither orthodox nor heterodox. All else being equal, it was the effect those ideas had on behavior that determined their acceptability or unacceptability. Such moral pragmatism was not unique in the Confucian world. As one scholar has noted, as far back as the Warring States period in China, when Confucianism was first formulated, the ethical import of an assertion was a primary factor in evaluating it: "What were important to the Chinese philosophers, where questions of truth and falsity were not, were the behavioral implications of the statement or belief in question. In other words, the Chinese asked: What kind of behavior is likely to occur if a person adheres to this belief? Can the statement be interpreted to imply that men should act in a certain way?"[3] Mo Tzu (fifth century B.C.E.), who was condemned as heterodox for his doctrine of universal love but respected for his theories of knowledge, provided an explicit formulation of this practical approach to knowledge. "A theory must be judged by three tests. What are these three tests of a theory? Its origin, its validity, and its applicability. . . . And how do we judge its applicability? We judge it by observing whether, when the theory is put into practice in the administration, it brings benefit to the state and the people."[4]

This pragmatic dimension to concepts of acceptability and orthodoxy continued to influence Confucian thinking in China and Korea until the modern era. A recent collection of studies devoted to the question of orthodoxy in late imperial China[5] concludes that in China during the last centuries of the premodern era, religious pluralism prevailed alongside moral orthodoxy. In other words, Confucian China included a number of religious groups with varying beliefs about the nature of the supernatural realm and humanity's relationship to it. The Chinese state, with its staunchly Confucian bureaucracy, imposed on all religious communities a moral orthodoxy of Confucian ethical and ritual standards and obligations. Chinese were free, however, to hold a variety of religious beliefs as long as they remained loyal to the state and filial to their parents and did not appropriate the rituals that the state used to legitimize its own authority and preserve social order and harmony. Only those religious organizations that seemed to threaten the state by denying its legitimacy or threatened society by encouraging members to act contrary to accepted moral norms came under attack by the state.[6] A similar religious pluralism coexisting alongside moral orthodoxy can be seen in the latter half of the Chosŏn dynasty in Korea.

The religious community in Korea was not as diverse as that in China. Nonetheless, there were many practicing Buddhists and shamans on the peninsula. As the chapters in this volume by Robert E. Buswell, Jr., and Boudewijn Walraven reveal, they were tolerated by Korea's Confucian government. Neither Buddhists nor shamans and their clients were persecuted by government officials solely for what they believed. Although their beliefs were denigrated by the ruling elite as superstitious and irrational, as long as they did not challenge the fundamental moral code of Neo-Confucian Korea, they were permitted their heterodox (*idan*) views.

Confucius (551–479 B.C.E.) had warned that, "The study of strange doctrines is harmful indeed!"[7] The word Confucius used in denouncing strange doctrines is *idan* (Chin. *i-tuan*), literally "a different thread."[8] Twenty-three centuries later Tasan and other Koreans borrowed the term to label ideas and practices, such as Buddhism, that did not follow the way laid down by the sages of ancient China and thus threatened to unravel the common thread of Confucian morality from which the moral order was woven.[9]

Confucius spoke in vague generalities when he condemned threats to his teachings in the sixth century B.C.E. In eighteenth- and nineteenth-century Korea, his followers were more specific in their denunciations. Mencius in the fourth century B.C.E. had taught them to reject the ideas of Yang Chu and Mo Tzu. Chu Hsi, in the twelfth century, had condemned Buddhism and Taoism. T'oegye Yi Hwang (1501–70), whom some considered the Korean Chu Hsi, convinced Koreans to add the teachings of Wang Yang-ming to that list of unacceptable teachings. And many of T'oegye's followers in the eighteenth century wanted to add Catholicism to this list of heterodox schools of thought.

Catholicism had entered Korea in the seventeenth century by means of books written by Jesuit missionaries in China and brought back by visitors to Beijing. Although no Koreans were converted to Catholicism by these books until the last quarter of the eighteenth century, the ideas the Catholic priests espoused in them were debated and denounced as *idan* as early as 1724.[10] Sin Hudam (1702–61) and An Chŏngbok (1712–91), both staunch Neo-Confucians, insisted that Catholic teachings hindered the promotion of morality and therefore should be condemned as heterodox.

*new beliefs have to be debated, articulated
defended by followers
within the orthodox confine*

Those few Korean Confucians who began converting to Catholicism in 1784 defended their new beliefs with the argument that Catholicism was most definitely not strange or heterodox but was instead completely orthodox.[11] The ensuing debate over the orthodoxy or heterodoxy of Catholicism became, at the same time, a debate over the meaning of the terms *orthodoxy* and *heterodoxy* and their range and reference.

The debate over Catholicism arose among those members of Korea's Neo-Confucian community who had inherited T'oegye's philosophical and ethical orientation, particularly those who relied on the interpretation of T'oegye's teachings by Sŏngho Yi Ik (1681–1763). This branch of Korean Neo-Confucians, which included Sin Hudam, An Chŏngbok, and Chŏng Yagyong, relied, in descending order of importance, on four defining criteria for orthodoxy in evaluating statements whose validity was not easily empirically apparent.

First of all, orthodoxy, that is, correct ideas, had to be accompanied by orthopraxis, correct behavior, to merit recognition as true orthodoxy. Only those ideas, assertions, and claims—whether psychological, philological, philosophical, ontological, or ethical—that encouraged proper behavior, or at least did not discourage such behavior, could be accepted as truly orthodox. The traditional Confucian values of loyalty, filial piety, and selfless dedication to the common good were the touchstones, forming the court before which all ideas had to plead for acceptability. This pragmatic approach derives from T'oegye's vision of truth as primarily a guide to proper behavior.[12] As Sŏngho explained, what difference did it make whether people were "orthodox" or not if they did not do what they were supposed to do?[13] An Chŏngbok made a similar point, writing to a friend in 1783 urging him not to rely on verbal arguments alone in deciding what to believe but instead to test the practical applicability of ideas in order to determine their acceptability.[14]

Equally critical was a grounding in a plausible reading of the Confucian canon. As JaHyun Kim Haboush and Martina Deuchler discuss in their chapters in this volume, there was some dispute over how much weight was to be assigned to Sung dynasty commentaries relative to the original Confucian Classics on which they were commenting. By the late eighteenth century, there were some in Korea as well as in China who questioned whether those Classics had to be approached only through later commentaries or whether they could be approached directly.[15] Nevertheless, there was broad agreement that

Confucian tradition, grounded in the Classics, provided a standard against which ideas, assertions, and claims could be evaluated. As An Chŏngbok stated, "Anything that is not Confucian is heterodox."[16] Just as both Catholics and Protestants, although they have argued over whether the Bible should be interpreted by the individual reader or through the medium of centuries of Christian tradition, have agreed on the primacy of the Bible's words, so, too, Korean Neo-Confucians accepted the recorded words of Confucius and Mencius as definitive. Supporting this canonical criterion for orthodoxy, another Sŏngho disciple, Hwang Tŏkkil (?–1767), wrote that true Confucians would not say or do anything the great men of old would not have said or done. "We illuminate the great Confucian Way in order to block the selfishness of individuality, and we promote orthodoxy (*chŏnghak*) in order to expose noncanonical theories."[17]

These first two criteria were interrelated. The behavior that orthodoxy promoted was deemed proper because it was ordained by the Classics. And the moral message of the Classics was respected and protected because the Classics taught men the proper way to behave. Consequently, any statements, any doctrines, that undermined fidelity to the Confucian moral code enshrined in the Classics were *idan*, heterodoxy.

In addition to the textual and behavioral evidence for orthodoxy, Koreans also expected ideas claiming orthodox status to appear in Chinese dress. Those that had not originated in China at least had to have undergone some measure of sinicization. Moreover, Korean Confucians determined to remain orthodox adopted only those ideas and practices that had previously been declared acceptable by respected Confucian scholars in China. A Chinese stamp of approval was not in itself sufficient grounds for acceptance, however, as the Korean rejection of Wang Yang-ming attests. Nevertheless, Sŏngho and like-minded Confucians in eighteenth-century Korea would not even grant ideas a hearing unless they came bearing Chinese credentials. As An Chŏngbok argued in a letter to a disciple who was flirting with Catholicism, "I have heard of China transforming barbarians, but I have never heard of barbarians transforming China."[18] Sin Hudam echoed that rejection of Catholicism as Western and therefore inferior to Confucianism. "The various states of Europe are nothing but barbarian tribes on the fringes of civilization. Europeans have no basis for claiming for themselves or their civilization the same respect that China and Chinese receive."[19]

This third criterion is related to the fourth. To win a positive hearing, ideas should not only be sinicized but also well-aged. Novel ideas were automatically suspect. The only way new ideas could win a hearing was to disguise themselves in old clothing. All else being equal, the older the better. That is why some Koreans were intrigued by the arguments of Matteo Ricci (1552–1610) and other Jesuit missionaries in China that Catholic teachings were more faithful to the earliest Confucian texts than were the later commentaries of the Sung.[20] However, that patina of age, like a Chinese pedigree, was a necessary but not a sufficient condition for acceptance as orthodoxy. After all, the heterodox teachings of Buddhism, Mo Tzu, and Yang Chu could also claim a long history. An Chŏngbok wrote Ch'ŏnhak ko (An examination of Catholicism) to show that although many of the ideas and practices Catholics espoused resembled ideas and practices mentioned in Chinese records from centuries past, those ideas and practices had been rejected back then and so should be rejected again by his contemporaries.[21]

These last two criteria of historical and cultural coloring usually came into play only after the first two principles of ethical and canonical compatibility had been applied. In eighteenth- and early nineteenth-century Korea, the two questions Neo-Confucians asked most often in testing ideas to determine whether they were orthodox or heterodox, whether they followed or threatened the thread of Confucian tradition, were: Did those ideas encourage or discourage proper behavior? Did they contradict or support the moral message of the Confucian Classics?

This practical Korean approach to distinguishing orthodoxy and heterodoxy, acceptability and nonacceptability, was quite similar to the Chinese approach. Likewise, it was quite different from the traditional Western approach, which Jesuit missionaries brought from Europe to China and, via their writings, to Korea. European Catholics emphasized belief, a tradition with roots in the first centuries of the Christian church, when church authorities determined who was a true Christian and who was a heretic on the basis of adherence to the interpretations of the institutional church.[22] Obedience to church doctrinal authority was the touchstone and has remained so into the modern era, as can be seen in the seventeenth-century condemnation of Galileo by church authorities.[23]

The Roman Catholic stress on doctrinal purity as the prime criterion for orthodoxy contrasts sharply with the emphasis Korean Neo-

Confucians placed on the behavioral implications of claims to orthodoxy. A Confucian state such as Chosŏn Korea normally felt no need to compel rigid adherence to specific formulations of Confucian teachings. There were no Confucian inquisitions uncovering secret heretics who deviated from Neo-Confucian doctrinal tenets, neither in China nor in Korea. Scholars could freely debate contentious issues such as the relationship between *li* and *ki* to the Four Fonts and the Seven Feelings or the exact meaning of the phrase "the investigation of things" in the revered Classic, the *Great Learning*. Only when the political authority of the state or the rituals and ethics that were the core of Confucian practice were challenged did the government feel compelled to intervene in intellectual disputes.

The Jesuit missionaries who came to China in the seventeenth and eighteenth centuries consequently entered a world that generally tolerated private deviation from orthodox thinking but condemned such nonconformity if it went beyond the realm of ideas into organized public action that challenged the authority of the state. Just as in eighteenth-century Korea, what a person believed in the privacy of his own heart was of little concern to the Confucian state. What a person did with others was not. Buddhism, for example, was *idan*, yet Buddhists were not punished merely for believing in Buddhism or frequenting temples. However, when they met secretly with other Buddhists at night and prepared to welcome the coming of the Maitreya, whom they believed would replace the emperor, they violated the laws of the state and risked official censure and punishment.[24] The Chinese state had learned from experience that secretive Buddhist sects could turn rebellious and had to be controlled.

Similarly, Chinese governments chastised those who violated regulations governing ritual or disobeyed the moral rules governing human relationships, since ritual and social morality were the glue holding Confucian society together. Confucian officials acted vigorously to protect the social order. They showed less concern for how closely the thinking of the masses mirrored the orthodox interpretations of Confucian philosophy.[25] Challenges to accepted ethical norms were prohibited, although disagreement on minor philosophical or doctrinal issues was permitted as long as that disagreement remained within the boundaries delineated by orthodox morality. Religious pluralism was tolerated, as long as moral and ritual orthodoxy was maintained.[26]

When Catholic converts first appeared in Korea at the end of the eighteenth century, they hoped that such Chinese precedents for doctrinal latitude would allow them to prove to their staunchly Neo-Confucian government that although some of their ideas were new and different, they should not be condemned as heterodox and evil, since their religion and behavior were consistent with and supportive of classical Confucian ethical principles.

## Precedents for Judgment

In evaluating Catholicism, Korean Neo-Confucians in the eighteenth century did rely on precedents from Chinese tradition, supplemented with some from their own past as well. Those who declared Catholicism *idan* invariably directly or indirectly likened it to one or more of the teachings condemned as ethically dangerous in the past, just as those who had converted from Neo-Confucianism to Catholicism argued that Catholicism resembled Confucianism much more closely than it resembled any of the traditionally *idan* schools of thought.

For example, the frequent anti-Catholic charge that European religion lacked proper respect for rulers and parents echoed Mencius's complaints against Yang Chu and Mo Tzu.[27] Yang Chu taught that one should think of oneself first, that self-interest should be paramount. Mencius argued that such selfishness was a denial of the just claim of a ruler to loyalty and obedience. Mo Tzu went to the opposite extreme, in Mencius's view. By advocating that human beings should love everyone equally, Mo Tzu denied the special claim parents have on the hearts of their offspring. Mencius concluded that to refuse to acknowledge special obligations to rulers and to parents was to show oneself more beast than human.[28] Catholic converts in Korea had to argue, both in their actions before arrest and in their answers when interrogated after they were arrested, that they, unlike Yang Chu and Mo Tzu, did recognize the importance of loyalty and filial piety.

Another accusation revived from the past to be used against Catholics was that they, like Buddhists and the Taoists before them, destroyed the moral bonds that made a human community possible.[29] Catholic converts in Korea, in order to support their claim to orthodox status, were forced to show that despite their belief that two of the three major enemies of virtue were the flesh and the world, they were not like the Buddhists and the Taoists and did not reject either the bodies their parents had given them or the world in which human relationships were realized.[30]

One prominent theme in early Chosŏn Neo-Confucian attacks on Buddhism was that Buddhists frightened people with talk of heaven and hell. Hope of illusionary future rewards or fear of imaginary future punishments turned people's attention away from the real world. Another frequent accusation was that the Buddhist mode of self-cultivation, because of its stress on individual enlightenment, encouraged selfish withdrawal from society.[31] Both themes reappeared in the eighteenth century when many Neo-Confucians in Korea saw Catholicism as bearing a dangerous resemblance to the Buddhism their forerunners had condemned. This raised additional barriers for Catholics to cross on the road to recognition as adherents of orthodoxy.[32]

Although Koreans relied heavily on Chinese precedents in distinguishing the orthodox from the heterodox, they did not limit themselves to pious repetitions of Chinese judgments. They had enough confidence in their own command of Confucian principles to decide for themselves if doctrines that even the Chinese tolerated fit Korean Neo-Confucian criteria of orthodoxy. Not only did mainstream Korean Confucian scholars in the eighteenth century not accept any school of thought the Chinese Confucian tradition condemned, but many went further and branded as *idan* some ideas the Chinese had found acceptable.

For example, Sŏngho and Sin Hudam, among others, mistakenly believed that Catholicism was flourishing in China, since European priests served as official astronomers in Beijing and many Jesuit books available in Korea contained laudatory prefaces by Chinese Confucian officials. This presumed cachet of Chinese approval was not enough to sway Confucian scholars such as Sin and Yi Hŏngyŏng (1719–91), who felt that Koreans should proudly proclaim their rejection of Catholicism so that all the world would know that in Korea, at least, there were still scholars who held fast to the legacy of Mencius and Chu Hsi and had not been deluded by evil doctrines.[33]

This eighteenth-century rejection of Catholicism was not the first time Korean thinkers had differed from their fellow Neo-Confucians in China. Three centuries earlier, T'oegye had condemned the teachings of Wang Yang-ming, which were popular in China at that time. T'oegye was particularly disturbed by Wang's assertion that principle resided complete within our own minds and therefore there was no need to engage in the exhaustive study of principles in external things and events that Chu Hsi had demanded.

As T'oegye saw it, Wang's stress on truth within, on innate knowledge of the good, was dangerously one-sided and self-centered. T'oegye wrote that unless subjective insights into principle were confirmed with objective principles in the external world, the original impartial mind that alone makes people truly human would be lost. He cautioned that if Koreans followed Wang Yang-ming's advice, they would turn inward, as the Zen Buddhists do, rather than reaching outward with their moral strength, as good Confucians should do.[34] Wang's ideas were therefore heterodox, morally dangerous, and had to be condemned alongside those of Mo Tzu, Yang Chu, Buddha, and Lao Tzu.[35]

T'oegye's writings were a major influence on Korean Neo-Confucian thought for the rest of the Chosŏn dynasty. Wang Yang-ming never enjoyed the respectability in Korea that he had in China. Moreover, T'oegye's distrust of the body and its instincts and emotions, expressed through his rejection of Wang's overreliance on innate knowledge of the good, stimulated an ascetic and morally pessimistic strand in Korean Neo-Confucianism. T'oegye's separation of i (Chin. li) and the Four Beginnings of virtue from ki (Chin. ch'i) and the Seven Emotions further reinforced this declining confidence in both the trustworthiness of human emotions and the efficacy of human efforts. That tendency toward rigid self-denial and moral frustration became particularly strong in the eighteenth century among the Namin, the political faction to which Sŏngho and his disciples belonged.[36]

The first Korean converts to Catholicism, as well as its first critics, were Namin. Both converts and critics were motivated by a common desire to overcome the moral frailty of the human mind. The critics, because of their recognition of the strength of selfish desires, reacted strongly against Catholic teachings, which seemed, in their view, to encourage self-centered and therefore immoral attitudes and behavior. The converts, on the other hand, were convinced that faith in the Catholic god provided a way to overcome the selfishness that was so often the cause of ethical lapses.

Many Namin in the eighteenth century grew increasingly frustrated with the gap between their intention to live moral lives and their inability to act consistently and think morally.[37] More and more, they found themselves drawn to a pair of terms Chu Hsi had used to highlight the essential difference between right and wrong. Chu Hsi had written, "All affairs have only one of two fonts: the right one is the impartiality (*kung*; Korean *kong*) of heavenly principle, and the wrong one is the selfishness (*szu*; Korean *sa*) of desires."[38] Both Catholics and anti-Catholics drew on this dichotomy either to condone or to condemn ideas and practices.

For them, the degree to which an idea represented *kong*, selflessness, or *sa*, selfishness, determined whether that idea was orthodox or *idan*. An assertion that appeared to represent concern for personal benefit without regard for the needs of society as a whole was immoral and therefore unacceptable. A contrary assertion that placed the needs of the community above those of the individual was moral and therefore orthodox. The anti-Catholic An Chŏngbok stated this principle as clearly as anyone. "The difference between the basic approaches of Confucianism and Catholicism is the difference between selflessness (*kong*) and selfishness (*sa*)."[39] For An, of course, Catholicism represented selfishness, a point made clear in the closing paragraph of a lengthy essay criticizing Catholicism. "Catholic doctrines and practices are all manifestations of individual selfishness. There is no comparison with the purely selfless stance of our Confucianism."[40]

*Kong* means much more than the English translation "selflessness" indicates. In English, selflessness implies a willingness to sacrifice one's own interests for the good of others, as well as a lack of excessive longing for the rewards power, prestige, and money can bring an individual. In Neo-Confucianism, *kong* meant all this and more. *Kong* implied not just deference to the needs of others but identification with others. One infused with the spirit of *kong* knows that a person exists as part of a much larger whole and therefore thinks and acts morally and correctly only when he or she thinks and acts as a member of society rather than as an isolated individual. Such a person is believed to be not only unselfish but also impartial. By identifying with the surrounding world, the person can react to and judge people and events as they are in themselves, not just as they relate to personal self-interest.

*Sa* also means more than its English counterpart indicates. Someone dominated by *sa* not only puts personal interests first, greedily pursuing personal profit at the expense of others, but also turns inward, away from the external world, and thus denies an important part of the self. Self-centered thoughts and actions isolate one from the social and material environment that surrounds and shapes an individual. A person with a mind distorted by sa is exposed by personal biases, by an incomplete understanding of how everything, including the self, relates to everything else. Unable to fully comprehend that which is going on in the surrounding environment and unwilling to recognize personal responsibilities to the larger community, such a person fails to properly develop the social vision that would permit his or her development into a truly human and truly moral being.[41] According to Sin Hudam, this distorted vision lay behind heterodoxy. "There are thousands of deviant doctrines (*idan*), all different, yet all flow from the common spring of selfishness."[42] Sin supported this judgment by citing Chu Hsi, who had warned his followers to distinguish thoughts that originated in our true human nature and were therefore free of the distortions of selfishness and could be trusted from those that were generated by our bodies and were therefore corrupted by considerations of individual self-interest and to be viewed with caution.[43]

If this description of *kong* and *sa* is correct, selfishness in eighteenth- and early nineteenth-century Korea was both an ethical and a cognitive flaw.[44] Ideas rooted in selfishness were seen as both immoral and irrational. Conversely, selflessness was both an ethical and a cognitive value. Ideas generated by and supportive of an unselfish and impartial perspective were seen as moral, rational, and correct. Such was the eighteenth-century Korean Neo-Confucian judgment of *idan* and orthodoxy, a view that dominated the intellectual world in which the first Korean Catholics appeared.

### Sŏngho, Tasan, and the Broadening of Horizons

This was a perspective shared by Sŏngho, the philosophical father of many of the first Korean Confucians to take Catholicism seriously. Sŏngho was a staunch follower of T'oegye's approach to Neo-Confucian thought and practice. He carried T'oegye's mistrust of *ki* and *sa* even further than T'oegye had and taught what can only be called a form of Confucian asceticism. Sŏngho's deep suspicion of the body and its temptations led him to advocate severe restraint in the exercise of even those normal human desires for food and sex necessary to the survival of the human race. For example, he encouraged husbands and wives to sleep in separate rooms in order to make it easier for men to resist the pull of the flesh. He also suggested that men eat less than one full bowl of rice at every meal so that they will become accustomed to leaving physical desires less than completely satisfied.[45]

Although he was a committed Neo-Confucian, Sŏngho was open to advice on self-discipline from heterodox schools. He once compared Buddhist monks favorably to Confucian scholars because of their compassion, their respect for their teachers, and their self-control and said that Confucians would do well to imitate some Buddhist ascetic practices.[46] Moreover, he was impressed by some Catholic advice on cultivating virtue. He read *Ch'i k'e* (Seven victories) by Diego de Pantoja (1571–1618), a missionary tract extolling the seven cardinal virtues of humility, charity, patience, compassion, temperance, diligence, and self-restraint and commented afterward that the book surpassed all Confucian writings in its use of similes to elucidate the relationship between vice and virtue. Sŏngho wrote, "This book will be a great help in our effort to restore proper behavior." However, he added: "It is surprising, though, to find talk of god and spirits mixed up in this otherwise fine work. If we excise all such nonessential bits of grit and copy only the parts in it that are worthwhile, then we can treat it as orthodox Confucianism."[47]

In rejecting the theological distractions introduced by the Jesuit author, Sŏngho displayed the stance he also exhibited toward Buddhism. He was willing to borrow techniques for cultivating virtue from any source, but he would brook no challenges to the Confucian idea that the ultimate aim was always moral discipline. His guiding philosophy was an ethical pragmatism rooted in Confucian respect for loyalty, filial piety, and other expressions of selflessness.[48]

When Catholic books offered techniques for overcoming selfish tendencies, he approached them with an open mind. If their ideas worked, he would use them. However, he found their talk of god more of a hindrance than a help, since it turned one away from the problems of this world and focused attention on an illusionary supernatural realm instead. In a comment on the *T'ien-chu shih-i* (The true meaning of the Lord of Heaven), the catechism by Matteo Ricci, Sŏngho warned, "Their Lord of Heaven is the same as the *Sangje* of we Confucians, but the way they respect, serve, fear, and trust god is just like the way the Buddhists treat Śākyamuni."[49]

The ambiguity Sŏngho displayed toward Catholicism and his willingness to see both good and bad points in Catholic beliefs and practices produced both anti-Catholic and pro-Catholic disciples. Sin

Hudam, An Chŏngbok, and Yi Hŏn'gyŏng, for example, wrote detailed critiques of Catholic doctrine and practice.[50] However, Tasan Chŏng Yagyong was even more willing than Sŏngho to entertain ideas and suggestions from heterodox sources. Tasan never met Sŏngho, but he was a member of the same faction of Korean Neo-Confucianism, the Namin, which was guided in its thinking by the writings of T'oegye and Sŏngho. Tasan, too, made Confucian virtues the unassailable foundation upon which he erected a moral and political philosophy with bricks taken from both orthodox and heterodox sources. As he made clear in his commentary on the passage from the *Analects* that dealt with orthodoxy, heterodox schools should not be ignored or condemned out of hand. They must not be the primary focus of attention, but they could be mined for practical techniques to pursue Confucian aims. Of course, they should never be allowed to encroach on fundamental Confucian assumptions about human nature and morality.[51] Confucians must remain Confucians.

Unlike Sŏngho, Tasan saw some ethical advantages to belief in god. Such a belief, he thought, was necessary to inspire men to overcome their natural selfish tendencies, do good, and avoid evil. That may be because he, even more than Sŏngho, was acutely conscious of human moral weakness. Tasan took to heart T'oegye's "Diagram of the *Admonition for Mindfulness Studio*" (*Kyŏngjaejam-do*). In that diagram, T'oegye borrowed Chu Hsi's *Admonition for Mindfulness Studio* (*Ching-chai-chen*) to explain the importance of always keeping a calm and focused mind, as though in the presence of the Lord on High. He counseled constant caution and care, without a moment's relaxation of vigilance, for the consequences of even the slightest slip were awesome: "Falter for a single moment and selfish desire will burst forth in full force. Make the slightest mistake, and heaven and earth will be turned upside down, destroying the basic moral principles governing society and bringing about the collapse of civilization."[52]

Although attention to this admonition was not new, the seriousness and literalness with which Tasan and a few of his relatives and friends took that admonition was. Previous generations of Neo-Confucians had tended to treat such demands for constant vigilance against the slightest slip into selfishness as the ultimate goal toward which all should strive, but the small band of Sŏngho's disciples read the admonition as a demand to be met perfectly every day. Just as few Christians, outside pacifist sects such as the Quakers, have tried to implement Christ's command to love one's enemies, few Neo-Confucians had truly expected to immediately gain total mastery over the distractions of the mind and the selfish desires of the body. Tasan was an impatient exception. He expected that Neo-Confucianism would provide him with all the tools needed to achieve instant moral perfection.

Such stringent moral expectations created feelings of guilt in those unable to remain constantly calm, unperturbed, and filled with nothing but selfless thoughts twenty-four hours a day. Tasan recalled a conversation with his older brother, Chŏng Yakchŏn (1758–1816), in which Yakchŏn told him, "I have a lot to repent. Everyday I remind myself of all that I have done wrong." Tasan commented that his brother's remark caused him to reflect on human frailty and that he had come to realize that his earlier optimism was unwarranted. He noted that individuals, no matter how wise or diligent, are unable to achieve perfection, since they are not just disembodied minds but possess bodies filled with passion and carnal urges. Even the sages of ancient China were not perfect. If they had been perfect, they would not have been human. But, Tasan went on, humanity can turn this evil into good. Just as manure can be used to fertilize rice fields, regret and contrition can serve to fertilize minds. If humans constantly remind themselves of serious mistakes they have made in the past, even mistakes they no longer commit, then that feeling of remorse can stimulate them to reform. Repentance can build virtue from sin.[53]

Tasan's recognition of inherent human weakness, of guilt as an inescapable yet useful feature of the human condition, contradicts one of the fundamental assumptions of Confucian ethics: that human beings are inherently perfectible. Frustration at repeated failures to conform to the Neo-Confucian vision of rectitude led to guilt. That guilt led to disillusionment with one of the cornerstones of Neo-Confucian thought. Conventional Neo-Confucian moralists presumed that all have within themselves the potential for sagehood, the ability to form a trinity with heaven and earth. Tasan asked if everyone can be a sage, why is not everyone a sage? Especially, he asked himself, why was he, who tried so hard to eliminate self-centered biases and follow moral principles, unable to go through even a single day without straying at least once in thought or action? The guilt Tasan felt at his inability to live up to the high standards of self-denial and self-discipline that Sŏngho set for himself and his followers prepared Tasan to respond favorably to Catholic writings, which claimed to identify a source of moral strength in the personal deity found in the earliest Confucian Classics.[54]

In Tasan's view, living virtuously required more effort than Chu Hsi and the other Neo-Confucians, who maintained a theory of inherent virtue, had realized. Tasan rejected the mainstream position that when the mind is in a state of nonarousal (that is, when the mind is not responding to external stimulation with feelings of pleasure, anger, sorrow, or joy), it need only be kept calm, unmoving, and focused inward with serious concentration. He charged that such quietism was nothing more than Zen Buddhist doctrine disguised in Confucian language. Rather than trying to clear the mind of thought and feelings, a person should instead maintain a constant sense of awe and apprehension, remaining ever aware how difficult it was to be consistent in the pursuit of virtue and how easy it was to fail.[55]

Awe and apprehension combined in Tasan to produce an attitude of kyŏng (Chin. ching). Kyŏng is a major Neo-Confucian concept, variously rendered into English as "earnestness," "seriousness," "mindfulness," "composure," "attentiveness," and "prudence."[56] Kyŏng refers to an internal state of complete control over the mind in which thoughts are not allowed to wander or feelings to stir and total attention is directed toward one thing. As one prominent Western scholar of Chinese Neo-Confucianism has noted, "Often this one thing represented the unity of all things in principle."[57] In the oldest Confucian Classics, those written before the Han dynasty, however, kyŏng is best translated as "reverence" and refers to one's outward attitude toward others or toward heaven. Tasan emphasized that original meaning of kyŏng. He called for humans to reinforce a stance of cautious apprehension of their own moral frailty through a feeling of reverence for Sangje, the god of the Confucian Classics.

Tasan's introduction of god at this point was not, on the surface, a radical departure from Neo-Confucianism. As noted above, in *Admonition for Mindfulness Studio*, Chu Hsi had advised his disciples to cultivate a calm and focused mind as though they were always in the presence of Sangje. Chu Hsi placed the presence of god in the hypothetical because, to him, god did not exist as a person but was simply another name for the impersonal *i*, the normative pattern that gave order to the universe.[58] T'oegye, although he too talked of god, supported Chu Hsi's gloss of this personal term as a figurative reference for an impersonal moral force.[59] Tasan, however, repudiated that interpretation, pointing out that, in the earliest Confucian texts, the terms for god clearly referred to an intelligent personality governing the universe.[60]

Tasan had noticed a significant contradiction in Neo-Confucian thought and practice. Confucianism was built on social morality, with ethics defined in terms of a person's relationship to his fellow humans. People were considered virtuous only if they displayed the proper attitudes and behavior toward superiors and inferiors, parents and children, older and younger siblings, and spouses and friends. Yet, Neo-Confucianism also demanded that people maintain an attitude of *kyŏng*, and *kyŏng* could most easily be cultivated by withdrawing from the distractions of the external world of people and objects. Although *kyŏng* was intended to be a means to an end, the necessary mental preparation for moral action, Tasan feared that for some it had become an end in itself. Those who achieved inner peace often, like the Buddhists, hesitated to risk that pleasant state in encounters with the real world. He believed that the danger of such a lapse into quietism could be lessened by replacing the abstract metaphysical terminology of Sung Neo-Confucianism with the concrete anthropomorphic language of the Classics.

As Tasan saw it, the Neo-Confucian vision of *kyŏng* as primarily a composed and concentrated state of mind undermined the link between internal moral attitudes and external ethical behavior which was the mark of earlier Confucian morality. Tasan sought to revive that link by reversing the Neo-Confucian orientation and reclaiming an external object of reverence from the original Confucian tradition. Just as people should show respect for their elders, loyalty to their superiors, and filial piety to their parents, they should display respect and reverence for god so that they would always remain in a proper moral frame of mind even when no one else was around. Always and everywhere, morality for Tasan involved a relationship with another.[61] He rejected the Neo-Confucian concern for disinterested attentiveness and substituted reverence for god.

Tasan reasoned that only if humans were conscious that god watched their every move and knew their every thought would they be able to maintain constant attention to propriety. Abstract, impersonal *i* had no power to instill righteous fear into human hearts. But awe of god's unlimited vision would keep people from relaxing their guard against selfish desire for even a single moment. Individuals could be persistent and consistent in watching over themselves, even when alone, only if they were aware that god, too, was watching them.[62]

The ever-watchful god in which Tasan believed was not the Christian god, however. He was instead a Confucian god, the personification of the Confucian virtues of selflessness (kong), benevolence, and righteousness.[63] Tasan called god the ruler of the cosmos, not its creator. His god combined the objectivity of impartiality and selflessness with the intentionality of a personal deity. As objective subjectivity, Sangje implanted and managed the pattern (i) that provided order in the universe, providing a personal grounding for an ethics of personal relationships. In Tasan's Confucian universe, however, the physical material making up that universe appears to have had no beginning in time and needed no creator. Nor did his god appear directly to impart revelation. Tasan wrote that we learned the will of god by listening to our own conscience.[64]

Furthermore, Tasan said nothing of god passing judgment on the souls of the dead and passing out rewards and punishments for the deeds of this life. In fact, Tasan said little about god's nature or activities, except that god was to be held in awe as the intelligent governor of the normative pattern that directed the universe. Tasan did not bother with the detailed description of the divine attributes that occupied so much of the attention of Catholic theologians. His god was solely a moral force. That was what made him a Confucian god.[65]

Tasan may have been stimulated to look for a personal deity in the Confucian Classics by his reading of Matteo Ricci's T'ien-chu shih-i.[66] However, as the personification of that fundamental Confucian virtue of selflessness, Tasan's Sangje was different from Ricci's Deus.[67] As objective subjectivity, Sangje remained within the bounds of Confucian orthodoxy, a supporter rather than a subverter of Confucian morality. Despite the arguments of some scholars that Tasan was a closet Catholic in the last decades of his life when he was writing his theistic commentaries on the Classics, Tasan showed until the end that he placed Confucian values, and the rituals that enshrined them, above any theological assertions.[68] He recognized the merits of the Catholic argument that people should honor Sangje, but he felt that Catholics did not pay sufficient attention to the need to honor their parents and their rulers. Just as Wang Yang-ming had led people astray with his overly narrow prescription to follow innate knowledge of the good, so, too, the theocentric Catholic approach to ethical obligations posed a threat to Confucian values and praxis.

Although Korean Catholics knew from 1790 on that Catholic doctrine forbade the performance of traditional Confucian memorial services for ancestors, Tasan wrote volumes on the proper performance of such rituals and left strict instructions for his descendants to perform those rituals properly.[69] That, in addition to the lack of uniquely Christian characteristics in the god he describes in his commentaries, shows that Tasan believed in a god who undergirded rather than undermined orthodox Confucian morality and ritual. Using the late Chosŏn dynasty Confucian yardsticks of moral pragmatism and canonical conformity, in which ethical dictates determined what could be accepted as true more than abstract truth determined what was deemed moral, we can see that Tasan was a Confucian theist, but a Confucian nonetheless.

### Paul Yun: Martyr for the New Orthodoxy

The same cannot be said for his cousin, Yun Chich'ung (1759–91). Yun was one of the first Koreans converted to Catholicism after Tasan's brother-in-law, Yi Sŭnghun (1756–1801), returned from Beijing in 1784 as the newly baptized Peter Lee and began preaching his new faith to friends and relatives. In 1790, when another Korean returned from a trip to China with a message from the French priests in Beijing that Catholic law forbade the standard Confucian ancestor service, the stage was set for a confrontation between Confucianism and Catholicism.

In spring 1791, Paul Yun Chich'ung's mother died. He and his Catholic cousin, James Kwŏn Sangyŏn (?–1791), decided that they would follow all the customary Confucian mourning rituals except the rites involving the ancestral tablets. Going beyond the instructions from Bishop Gouvea in Beijing, they not only did not make a tablet for Yun's mother but also burned all the ancestral tablets in their possession and buried the ashes. Given the central role of the tablets in the mourning ceremonies, their absence could not go unnoticed by relatives who came to Chinsan county in Chŏlla province to join Yun in mourning the loss of his mother.[70] Rumors soon spread of Yun and Kwŏn's violation of the regulations governing Confucian mourning ritual, and they were arrested by the magistrate of Chinsan county. In Yun Chich'ung's account of his interrogation by Magistrate Sin Sawŏn and Governor Chŏng Minsi, the depth of this Catholic challenge to mainstream Neo-Confucian conceptions of orthodoxy and orthopraxis is readily apparent.

Yun attempted to justify his destruction of the ancestral tablets by using logic and reason to show the absurdity of the memorial service. Yun's defense, adopted from the Catholic insistence on the irrational and superstitious character of Confucian ritual, clashed with the Confucian concern for the symbolic and ethical significance of the rite. Yun's account shows Yun and his interrogators talking past each other rather than to each other. Yun kept insisting that his actions were in accordance with what he believed to be true. His interrogators kept insisting that Yun admit the immorality of his actions and the teachings of his Catholic books. Yun could not understand how actions that offended logic and reason could be moral. Neither the magistrate nor the governor could understand how considerations of logical truth or falsity could be allowed to affect a person's performance of his social obligations.[71]

When he converted to Catholicism, Yun shifted from the pragmatic orientation of Neo-Confucianism, in which the purpose, the moral import, of a ritual determined how that ritual was interpreted, to the doctrinal orientation of Catholicism, which imposed a literal interpretation on both ritual objects and ritual behavior. In other words, Yun had moved to a stress on the beliefs that a ritual implied, whereas his Neo-Confucian interrogators held on to the primacy of the ritual itself and its ethical-behavioral implications.

Yun argued that it was an affront to the dignity owed his father and mother to treat pieces of wood, the ancestral tablets, as though they held parental souls. He noted that the fourth commandment ordered Catholics to honor their fathers and mothers. If one's parents were actually present in those wooden ancestral tablets, then Catholics would be obligated to show respect for the tablets. But those tablets were made of wood. "They have no flesh and blood relationship with me. They did not give me life nor educate me. . . . How can I dare to treat these man-made pieces of wood as though they were actually my mother and father?"[72] Yun argued further that it was foolish to place food and drink before a block of wood, even if a soul were present in it. Yun pointed out that the soul was not a material object and could get no nourishment from material goods, no matter how delicious the wine or nutritious the meat.

Furthermore, even the most filial son did not try to serve his parents food and drink when they were asleep. "If people cannot eat while they sleep, how much more foolish is it to offer food to our parents when they are dead? How can anyone who is sincere in his filial piety try to honor his parents with such an absurd practice?"[73]

This Catholic Korean even dared to challenge the fundamental assumption of Confucian morality, which made loyalty and filial piety the absolutes from which all other values and virtues were derived. He denied that those two virtues were complete and axiomatic in themselves but instead argued that "the basis of loyalty to the ruler is the laws of god, and the basis of filial piety toward one's parents is also the laws of god."[74] This was a radical contradiction of the core of Confucian thought. Rather than accepting the virtues of filial piety and loyalty as the standards by which all else was to be judged, Yun claimed that filial piety and loyalty were themselves only conditional obligations, binding on humans only because god, the source of all value, has so willed.[75] His Confucian interrogators could not imagine ethical behavior flowing from such an assumption.

Paul Yun was well aware that his stance differed dangerously from the behavioral orientation of his Korean Confucian contemporaries, who placed concern for what should be done ahead of concern for what should be believed. When told to provide a short summary of Catholic teachings, he presented them in as strongly a Confucian light as possible. Rather than explaining his belief in the divinity of Jesus Christ and his power to redeem men from their sins, Yun simply stated, "What we practice can be reduced to the ten commandments and the seven virtues."[76] In order to persuade his Confucian interrogators that Catholicism was more orthodox than heterodox, Yun reduced Catholicism to its moral commands and defined it essentially as a collection of guidelines for ethical behavior, guidelines for the most part identical to those of Confucianism, though they were generated by a non-Confucian god.

His interrogators and jailers were not fooled. Yun's claim to be a true Confucian at heart was dismissed.[77] From Magistrate Sin on up, his jailors and judges recognized that Catholicism was more than Confucian morality cloaked in Western theological rhetoric. Yun's actions, even more than his beliefs, sealed his fate. As Governor Chŏng pointed out to him, King Chŏngjo (r. 1776–1800) had ordered the destruction of all Catholic books in 1788.[78] By reading books the king himself had condemned, Yun had displayed disloyalty. But that was a minor mistake compared to the more grievous error of acting on the precepts taught in those forbidden writings. When Yun refused to perform proper mourning ritual and chose to destroy his family's ancestral tablets instead, he lowered himself to the level of beasts and brought upon himself the most severe of punishments.[79]

The language of the many memorials demanding the death penalty for Yun and Kwŏn further supports the conclusion that it was what they did and did not do, more than what they did and did not believe, which provoked the animosity of so many of Korea's Neo-Confucian scholars, both in and out of the government. The most common charge against them was not merely that they held heterodox ideas but that they had acted contrary to fundamental moral principles, "wounding morality and perverting righteousness" (sangnyun p'aeŭi).[80] When King Chŏngjo agreed to order their execution, the charge on which he based his decision was that they had behaved immorally, not that they held uncanonical beliefs. It was their destruction of ancestral tablets in accordance with their Catholic faith, more than their Catholic faith itself, that provided the grounds for their beheading.[81]

If Yun had merely entertained Catholic ideas while continuing to follow Confucian rules of morality and ritual, he might have escaped with no more than a severe warning for dabbling in heterodoxy.[82] However, he was not content merely to believe in Catholicism. He was determined to practice it as well. Yun's redefinition of orthodoxy, grounding it in belief in god's existence and obedience to god's will rather than in the ethical principles (i) that governed Confucian behavior and ritual, allowed Catholic theological doctrine to dictate his behavior. His Catholic conception of orthodoxy thus became the framework for a challenge to the very foundations of Neo-Confucian morality. This could not be overlooked. By rejecting the traditional subordination of religion to morality, Yun brought on his own death sentence. He moved beyond idan, which could be tolerated, into the much more dangerous realm of sahak (perverse teachings), which could not.[83] On December 8, 1791, Paul Yun and James Kwŏn were martyred for their fidelity to their new Catholic faith. Yun's belief that religious truths determined morality and his denial that Confucian moral presuppositions determined what could and could not be believed cost him his life.[84]

### Defining the New Orthodoxy

This fatal shift in not just the content but also in the very definition and conception of orthodoxy was probably introduced into Korea by Christian missionary publications written by Jesuit priests in China. Ricci's *T'ien-chu shih-i* was particularly influential in converting Korean Confucians to the Catholic way of thinking.

In this basic introduction to the fundamentals of Catholic doctrine, Ricci, although claiming that Catholicism was the fulfillment, not a rejection, of pristine Confucianism, subtly attempted to shift the ground on which the debate over orthodoxy would take place. Ricci ignored the important Confucian criterion of moral pragmatism and offered instead the standard for orthodoxy that prevailed in the Europe of his day. Ricci argued that one had to know what something was before one could decide how to relate to it; this contrasted sharply with the Korean Neo-Confucian notion that relationships determine what something is. In practical terms, Ricci taught that a person had to decide whether god really existed and precisely what sort of god he was before that person could decide what moral principles to follow. Orthodoxy, including orthodox behavior, had to be based on correct beliefs, particularly belief in the true god.[85]

In eighteenth-century Neo-Confucian Korea, however, with its emphasis on orthopraxis, people had to know how to behave toward their fellow human beings before they could decide how to behave toward, and what to believe about, any possible supernatural entities. The promotion of proper and appropriate behavior by human beings toward other human beings was supposed to be the ultimate goal of all Neo-Confucian endeavors. Any belief in spirits, gods, or ghosts had to be subordinated to that fundamental aim.

Many Koreans, including Confucian scholars, believed that there were spirits powerful enough to both afflict disease and other forms of trouble on those who displeased them and reward with good fortune those who pleased them. However, no orthodox Korean Neo-Confucian believed that there were spirits powerful enough to challenge the basic Confucian moral code. In fact, what pleased most spirits more than anything else was action that conformed to that moral code. That is what spirits rewarded, just as they were also believed to punish those who were disloyal, unfilial, or otherwise acted in non-Confucian ways. In this Neo-Confucian universe, spirits were supposed to encourage adherence to Confucian values rather than generate opposing moral commands of their own. Any spirit alleged to act otherwise would be quickly condemned as a false and evil spirit meriting condemnation and repudiation.

This is a crucial point of incompatibility between the Catholic and the Neo-Confucian assumptions about what religion is and what role it should play. To Catholics, religion meant belief in one god who generated moral commands and then enforced them. In contrast, religion in Neo-Confucian Korea often represented belief in a multitude of gods, who, if they cared about morality at all, merely enforced moral codes that society already accepted as emanating from i, the cosmic normative pattern. Catholicism, which refused this subordinate role, thus clashed with both the Confucian definition of religion as well as with the Confucian expectation of the role religion should play in society.

Catholicism not only denied that religion was subordinate to morality, it reversed that relationship and made morality dependent on religion. God, not society, the state, or tradition, determined what was moral and what was not. As Thomas Aquinas (1224–74), the Chu Hsi of late medieval Catholicism, definitively explained, "Morality is based primarily on god's wisdom. It is his wisdom that establishes creatures in their proper relationship with each other and with him; and it is precisely in that relationship that the essence of a creature's moral goodness consists."[86] If anything, it was society that should follow religion's pronouncements, rather than religion that should merely reflect and support society. This difference between Neo-Confucian and Catholic views of the role of religion in society made the practical implications of the disagreement between Catholics and Confucians over the nature of orthodoxy potentially explosive, since it allowed Catholics to claim an orthodoxy independent of society, a subversive notion in the Neo-Confucian universe.

One reason Catholics and Neo-Confucians disagreed on the relationship between religion and morality is that they did not use the same religious or philosophical language. Even in translation into classical Chinese, conceptual gaps yawned wide. The key Neo-Confucian concept of i is a good example.

I was morality itself, the cosmic network of appropriate interrelationships, the universal moral pattern of selfless harmonious interaction. It was i, through its universalizing tendency, that held the universe together. Orthodoxy, to Neo-Confucians, by definition was that which conformed to *i*. Yet Ricci dismissed *i* as nothing more than a parasitical abstraction of no moral significance. Ricci and the Catholic converts who followed him misunderstood *i* to mean static principle rather than dynamic pattern.

Ricci argued vigorously that *i* could not be the active organizing force in the universe that Chu Hsi said it was. According to Ricci, *i*, which he interpreted as an abstract rational principle defining what something was and how it should function, could not itself be an object or entity. *I* could exist only in conjunction with some concrete object. In Thomistic terminology, a principle was an attribute, a secondary characteristic of an entity, rather than a substance, the core entity itself. Before the universe began, there were no principles, since before individual objects existed, their attributes could not exist. Only when god created the universe did principles appear. God, not *i*, was the creator and organizer of the universe.[87]

In addition, a defining principle was unconscious and incapable of self-movement or volition. Therefore, it could not have created on its own the world, which contains the conscious and moral mind of the individual. "A principle cannot give other things what it itself does not have. The true source of all things must have a mind capable of conscious knowledge and able to make moral decisions."[88] This insistence on treating Neo-Confucian references to *i* as references to some thing, either a substantial entity or a characteristic of an entity, rather than to a pattern or network that was more function than substance, meant that Ricci misunderstood one of the defining concepts of Neo-Confucian thought and therefore misunderstood what Neo-Confucians meant by orthodoxy.[89]

*I* as pattern was far from the dead abstraction Ricci believed it to be. When Ricci derided *i* as a subordinate property, an attribute or accident incapable of creative activity, he was thinking of *i* as comparable to the white color on a white horse. The horse may be truly white, yet he would still be a horse if he were brown instead. Therefore in no way could whiteness be conceived as essential to the horse's existence nor could whiteness be credited somehow with any part in the production of horses.[90] However, when Neo-Confucians talked of *i*, they talked, not of properties or attributes, but of functional relationships. A frequently used example was the normative pattern that governed the behavior of a subject toward his superior and of the ruler toward his subject or that which regulated the duties of a son toward his father and the obligations of a father toward his son. As understood by Neo-Confucians, *i* determined more what someone should do rather than what he looked like.

Therefore, when Korean converts to Catholicism, such as Paul Yun, deprived *i* of its central formative role in the Confucian universe and put god in its place, they did more than simply change the philosophical and ethical doctrines to which they had subscribed. In Neo-Confucian eyes, they had abandoned morality itself. All the arguments Catholics in Korea presented to make belief in god the core of their new definition of orthodoxy failed to convince those to whom orthodoxy was inseparable from orthopraxis (adherence to Confucian morality). Among those joining Paul Yun in making that Catholic argument, which fell on mostly deaf ears, was Yun's cousin, and Tasan's brother, Augustine Chŏng Yakchong (1760–1801).

Chŏng Yakchong was one of three Chŏng brothers active in the Korean Catholic community in its formative years. His younger brother, Tasan, and his older brother, Chŏng Yakchŏn, soon retreated back within the walls of Confucian orthodoxy when the martyrdom of Paul Yun made it clear to them that Catholicism and Neo-Confucianism were not as compatible as they had thought.[91] Both condemned Catholicism as an evil heterodoxy when they were arrested and interrogated in the anti-Catholic persecution of 1801. Yakchong, on the other hand, became more, not less, fervent under persecution and was a major figure in keeping Catholicism alive on the peninsula between the execution of Paul Yun in 1791 and the great persecution of 1801.

When Augustine Chŏng faced his persecutors in 1801, he boldly defended his beliefs as the true orthodoxy, telling his interrogators: "Do you think I would follow these teachings if I thought they were evil, heterodox doctrines? I follow Catholic teachings because I know that they are the most fair and impartial (*kong*), the most correct and orthodox (*chŏng*), and the most genuine and true."[92] He went on to explain that god is both the supreme ruler and the paramount parent of the cosmos and any teachings which did not include respect for god were an offense against both heaven and earth.

Before his arrest on February 11, 1801, and his execution on April 8 of that same year, Chŏng Yakchong wrote an introduction to the principal doctrines of Catholicism in *han'gŭl*.[93] That book, the *Chugyo yoji* (Essentials of the lord's teachings), survived his martyrdom to become the basic catechism of the Korean Catholic church for another century and beyond.[94] It is a perfect example of how the new model of orthodoxy-doctrine provided the basis for moral principles rather than vice versa.

The catechism opens with logical arguments for god's existence, not with exhortations to the cultivation of virtue.[95] Even the trinitarian doctrine of three persons in one god is introduced early in the text, long before the ethical implications of the assertion of god's existence are addressed.[96] The first moral principle Yakchong specifically mentions is the need to worship the one true god and the related sin of worshipping false gods.[97] Worship of the true god is thus given clear priority over loyalty to political rulers or filial piety to parents, a sharp break with Korean tradition. The other nine commandments are given only a glancing mention, showing how moral principles have retreated into the background of this theological conception of orthodoxy. As a result of this subordination of morality to theology, Yakchong was condemned not for being a doctrinal heretic but for moral perversion and accused of promoting *sahak* and undermining the ethical foundations of society.[98]

Conspicuously absent from this introduction to Catholic doctrines are traces of the traditional Confucian education Yakchong received during his youth. That may be because he was writing for the already converted, the less educated members of the infant Korean Catholic community who were not steeped in the Confucian Classics or the Neo-Confucian interpretation of the Classics. Or, it may be because his catechism was not so much the product of his own independent thinking as it was his translation into Korean of what he had read in Jesuit missionary publications from China and what he had learned from conversations with Chou Wen-mo (1752–1801), the Chinese priest who ministered to the Korean Church from 1794 until his martyrdom in 1801 and who had worked closely with Augustine over those six years.[99] Therefore, Yakchong's catechism is framed entirely within the imported Catholic paradigm of orthodoxy.

His son, Paul Chŏng Hasang (1795–1839), did not receive the standard Confucian education his father had received, since his father had been executed and his uncles scattered into exile when he was only five years old. Nevertheless, Hasang shows a greater sensitivity to how Korea's Neo-Confucian ruling elite evaluated moral, philosophical, and religious claims than Yakchong had. Knowing that he would be arrested someday for inheriting his father's central role within Korea's nascent Catholic community, Hasang prepared a defense of his Catholic faith to present to the Korean court.[100] That defense, entitled *Sang Chaesang sŏ* (A letter to the State Council), shows Hasang trying to justify his advocacy of a new orthodoxy by appealing to the standards of the old orthodoxy.[101] In a little under 3,700 Chinese characters, Paul Chŏng argued that the Chosŏn dynasty was laboring under a misapprehension when it condemned Western religion as heretical, immoral, and subversive.

Hasang began his defense by reminding the State Council that before a doctrine could be condemned, it must be tested against the dual standards of righteousness and rationality. Only those doctrines ascertained to be contrary to righteousness and rationality (*i*) could be condemned. On those grounds, Catholicism should not be condemned. First, it did not offend righteousness. It could do no harm to Confucianism and could not threaten the social order, since it was nothing more than the way everyone from the emperor down to the common man should behave in everyday life.[102] "Does Catholicism harm the family? Does it harm the state? Look at what Catholics do, study their behavior, and you will see what kind of people we are and what kind of teachings we follow. Catholics are not rebels. Catholics are not thieves. Catholics do not engage in lewd activities or murder."[103] He also pointed out that Korea already tolerated Buddhists, shamans, geomancers, and fortunetellers; why could it not tolerate Catholics as well, especially since Catholic teachings, and Catholics themselves, were much more rational and much less of a threat to society and morality than were those superstitious practices and those who practiced them?[104]

Unlike his father, Hasang did consider the Ten Commandments important enough to discuss in his explanation of the foundations of his faith. He listed all ten and then pointed out that only the first three deal directly with human relationships with god and the other seven enjoin humans to interact properly with their fellow humans.[105] Whereas the last seven are similar to the precepts of Neo-Confucians, the first three add a dimension, Hasang argued, that makes Catholicism even more supportive of righteousness and rationality than Neo-Confucianism is.

His argument is based on Catholic usage of the term *i*. He used that term more in the Riccian sense of rational principle than in the mainstream Neo-Confucian sense of moral pattern. His exploitation of the ambiguity of the term, however, allowed him to advance logical arguments for the existence of god that then led him to conclude that since god exists as the creator and sustainer of all in the universe, including humanity, people should display filial piety toward their Father in heaven, just as *i* requires that they display filial piety toward their parents on earth.[106]

Hasang knew that basing his arguments on *i*, whether in the Neo-Confucian sense of normative pattern or the Catholic sense of abstract principle, would probably not in itself be sufficient to convince his persecutors that Catholicism was not heterodox. He therefore appealed to the other standards Neo-Confucians used in evaluating claims, assertions, and ideas of moral and philosophical import.

He knew that Neo-Confucians expected acceptable ideas to be based on language found in the Confucian canon. Although Rome had ordered Catholic missionaries in China to cease equating the Catholic god with Sangje, the god of the Confucian Classics, Hasang sidestepped those orders to argue that early Confucians did make specific references to a supreme being. He went on to argue that Catholicism has its own classics as well, classics even more complete and error free than the Confucian Classics.[107] Therefore, on the basis of both canonical conformity, as well as ethical implications, Catholicism should at least be tolerated by Confucians, if not recognized as the superior way.

The arguments that the ancient Confucian Classics recognize god's existence and that Catholic records are even older and more complete allowed Hasang to argue from the Classics that Catholicism was acceptable according to two less critical standards of evaluation as well. Not only did god appear in the first Chinese texts, but Christianity itself had a long history in China. Moreover, at a time when Korea was persecuting Catholics, China not only did not outlaw Catholicism but even permitted Catholics from abroad to enter China and live there. Therefore, Catholicism not only had a Chinese seal of approval but also had the patina of respectable old age.[108]

Ultimately, however, Hasang argued that the issue of whether Catholicism is to be considered orthodox and worthy of support or heterodox and deserving of suppression is resolved by one basic question: Do Catholic teachings run counter to morality and encourage people to act in unacceptable ways? Do Catholics act properly or not?[109] His answer is a straightforward claim for the acceptability and orthodoxy of his religious beliefs. Rather than being the evil heterodoxy Korean government officials were claiming it was, Catholicism instead was "most holy and sagely, the most fair and impartial (*kong*), the most correct and orthodox (*chŏng*), the most genuine and true, the most perfect and complete, and the most singular and unique of all teachings."[110]

Paul Chŏng was no more successful in convincing Korean Confucian officials that Catholicism was harmless and orthodox than his father Yakchong or his father's cousin, Yun Chich'ung, had been. Instead, he joined them in martyrdom, suffering execution at Sŏsomun on September 22, 1839, for giving priority to Catholic doctrine over Confucian morality, and for being faithful to the new definition of orthodoxy that it entailed. Despite his attempt to disguise his Catholicism in Confucian colors, Hasang was condemned as a villain devoid of moral principles who had betrayed both his nation and his cultural heritage.[111]

## Belief, Behavior, and the Catholic-Confucian Divide

When Yun Chich'ung, Chŏng Yakchong, Chŏng Hasang, and their fellow Catholic pioneers converted to Catholicism and provoked this deadly confrontation with Neo-Confucianism, they inadvertently opened a window into the world of eighteenth-century Korean Neo-Confucian concepts and values. When Korean Neo-Confucians debated among themselves such issues as the relationship between *i* and *ki*, or even the orthodoxy or heterodoxy of Wang Yang-ming's writings, most of their shared assumptions remained implicit. There was no need to state explicitly what all parties already thought or believed.

However, when Korean Neo-Confucians encountered Catholicism in the eighteenth century, they confronted an alien intellectual world. Catholicism was a product of a comprehensive worldview, a Weltanschauung, radically different from that which underlay Neo-Confucianism.[112] The questions Catholics raised, the answers Catholics expected, and more important, the way those questions and answers were formulated and evaluated, presupposed a conceptual and axiological framework even more foreign to the Neo-Confucian stance toward the world than those assumed by Buddhism and shamanism. Forced to justify and defend their values and beliefs against such an alien challenge, Korean Neo-Confucians in the eighteenth century unveiled the tacit assumptions supporting those beliefs and values. Under attack, the implicit became explicit. Thrown into sharp relief by comparison with opposing preconceptions from the West, the hidden premises of mainstream Korean intellectual life in the eighteenth century were uncovered.

Two concepts highlighted in greater clarity by this clash of opposing worldviews are orthodoxy and heterodoxy. The arguments both for and against Catholicism put forward by Koreans in the late 1700s and the early 1800s suggest that it is risky to rely only on Western concepts of heterodoxy (doctrinal deviation) or orthodoxy (doctrinal acceptability) in analyzing that dispute. For those attacking Catholics and Catholicism, heterodoxy, *idan*, covered a much broader range than simply doctrinal differences. In the moralistic perspective of the Namin, doctrinal claims could not be fully examined and evaluated outside their behavioral context. The ethical implications of ideas, as much as the ideas themselves, provided the criteria for distinguishing heterodoxy from orthodoxy.

The converts to Catholicism offered an alternative definition, privileging belief over practice. They argued that they could not justifiably be labeled heterodox since their beliefs were sound and any deviation from traditional Confucian moral practice was an unavoidable consequence of those true beliefs. That argument assumed a concept of orthodoxy that placed greater emphasis on doctrinal correctness than Korean Neo-Confucians, particularly the Namin, were usually willing to grant. Although both the early Korean Catholics and their Neo-Confucian opponents agreed that correct ideas and proper behavior were important, they disagreed sharply over which was more important. Traditionally, Neo-Confucians in Korea had accepted only those beliefs that were compatible with their moral principles. Catholics reversed that, accepting instead only those moral principles that were compatible with their beliefs. That reversal presented a radical challenge to previous definitions of heterodoxy and orthodoxy.

A term for orthodoxy that appears throughout the debate over Catholicism is *chŏnghak*, "orthodox learning." When used by Catholics, *chŏnghak* usually means "correct ideas," but when that same word is wielded by Neo-Confucians as a weapon against Catholics, it has a much broader range. In the classical Chinese language of Neo-Confucianism, *chŏng* functions more like an adverb than an adjective, giving it a more dynamic reference than the static term "orthodox" normally indicates in Catholic writing. *Chŏnghak* in Neo-Confucian arguments refers as much to appropriate or accepted behavior as it does to appropriate or accepted ideas. Thus, by the

Namin definition, Catholics could never be considered orthodox, even if their heterodox beliefs were ignored, since they did not behave properly.

Conversely, if Catholics had behaved properly and conformed to Confucian codes of behavior, although they still would have been considered heterodox, it is unlikely they would have encountered such fatal hostility. *Idan* that merely proposed unusual interpretations of the Classics or approaches to self-cultivation were condemned but seldom persecuted. However, when heterodoxy became perverse teachings (*sahak*), when it moved beyond questioning accepted ideas to reject orthodox ritual and ethical precepts, then the Confucian scholars and the Confucian state felt compelled to attack it and its followers. The difference between *idan* and *sahak* was merely a matter of degree. All *sahak* fell under the heading of *idan*, although not all *idan* were *sahak*. The difference between heterodoxy, which was tolerated, and perverse doctrines, which were persecuted, lay less in greater divergence from the accepted readings of the Neo-Confucian canon than in the behavioral implications of that divergence.

*Reference Matter*

# Notes

## Introduction

1. See, e.g., JaHyun Kim Haboush, *A Heritage of Kings: One Man's Monarchy in the Confucian World* (New York: Columbia University Press, 1988); and James B. Palais, *Confucian Statecraft and Korean Institutions: Yu Hyŏngwŏn and the Late Chosŏn Dynasty* (Seattle: University of Washington Press, 1996).

2. See Martina Deuchler, *The Confucian Transformation of Korea – A Study of Society and Ideology* (Cambridge: Harvard University, Council on East Asian Studies, 1992).

3. See the various articles in Wm. Theodore de Bary and JaHyun Kim Haboush, eds., *The Rise of Neo-Confucianism in Korea* (New York: Columbia University Press, 1985).

4. Michael C. Kalton, *To Become a Sage: The Ten Diagrams on Sage Learning by Yi T'oegye* (New York: Columbia University Press, 1989).

5. Young-chan Ro, *The Korean Neo-Confucianism of Yi Yulgok* (Albany: State University of New York Press, 1989).

6. For details, see Martina Deuchler, "Self-cultivation for the Governance of Men: The Beginnings of Neo-Confucian Orthodoxy in Yi Korea," *Asiatische Studien* 34, no. 2 (1980): 9–39. The five Korean scholars were Cho Kwangjo, Yi Ŏnjŏk, Kim Koengp'il, Chŏng Yŏch'ang, and Yi Hwang.

7. See Benjamin Elman, *From Philosophy to Philology: Intellectual and Social Aspects of Change in Late Imperial China* (Cambridge: Harvard University, Council on East Asian Studies, 1990).

8. See Kai-wing Chow, *The Rise of Confucian Ritualism in Late Imperial China: Ethics, Classics, and Lineage Discourse* (Stanford: Stanford University Press, 1994).

9. Yi T'aejin, ed., *Chosŏn sidae chŏngch'isa ŭi chaejomyŏng* (Seoul: Pŏmjosa, 1985).

10. For a discussion of religious pluralism in China, see Kwang-Ching Liu, ed., *Orthodoxy in Late Imperial China* (Berkeley: University of California Press, 1990), p. 14.

11. For studies of the Buddhism of the early Chosŏn period, see various papers in Lewis R. Lancaster and Chai-shim Yu, eds., *Buddhism in the Early Chosŏn* (Berkeley: University of California, Institute of East Asian Studies, 1996).

12. A large number of studies on academies in China have appeared in recent years. See, e.g., various articles in Wm. Theodore de Bary and John W. Chaffee, eds., *Neo-Confucian Education: The Formative Stage* (Berkeley: University of California Press, 1989); and in Benjamin Elman and Alexander Woodside, eds., *Education and Society in Late Imperial China, 1600–1900* (Berkeley: University of California Press, 1994).

13. Alexander Woodside, "The Divorce Between the Political Center and Educational Creativity in Late Imperial China," in Elman and Woodside, eds., *Education and Society in Late Imperial China*, pp. 458–93.

14. Ellen G. Neskar, "The Cult of Worthies: A Study of Shrines Honoring Local Confucian Worthies in the Sung Dynasty (960–1279)" (Ph.D. diss., Columbia University, 1993), pp. 79–93.

15. Robert Hymes, "Academies and the Local Community," in de Bary and Chaffee, eds., *Neo-Confucian Education*, pp. 446–50.

16. For previous scholarship on the ritual controversies, see Miura Kunio, "Orthodoxy and Heterodoxy in Seventeenth-Century Korea: Song Siyŏl and Yun Hyu," in de Bary and Haboush, eds., *The Rise of Neo-Confucianism in Korea*, pp. 411–44; and Mark Setton, "Factional Politics and Philosophical Development in the Late Chosŏn," *Journal of Korean Studies* 8 (1992): 47–63.

17. See JaHyun Kim Haboush, "Rescoring the Universal in a Korean Mode: Eighteenth-Century Korean Culture," in Hongnam Kim, ed., *Korean Arts of the Eighteenth Century: Splendor and Simplicity* (New York: Asia Society Galleries, 1993), pp. 23–33.

## Yŏng-ho Ch'oe, *Private Academies and the State*

1. Yu Hongnyŏl, *Han'guk sahoe sasang sa non'go* (Seoul: Ilchogak, 1990), pp. 59–92.

2. Yi T'aejin, "Sarim kwa sŏwŏn," in Kuksa p'yŏnch'an wiwŏnhoe, ed., *Han'guksa* (Seoul, 1978), 12: 127.

3. Chŏng Manjo, "Chosŏn sŏwŏn ŭi sŏngnip kwajŏng," *Han'guk saron* 8 (1980): 26–35. See also idem, *Chosŏn sidae sŏwŏn yŏn'gu* (Seoul: Chimmundang, 1997).

4. Chu Sebung, *Munŭng chapko*, 7: 23a, in *Han'guk munjip ch'onggan* 27 (Seoul: Minjok munhwa ch'ujinhoe, 1988).

5. Ibid., 7: 23.

6. Ibid., 8: 2b.

7. *Myŏngjong sillok* 10: 6a–b. See also *Sosu sŏwŏn tŭngnok* (Seoul: Chōsen-shi henshūkai, 1937), 15a.

8. *Chŭngbo munhŏn pigo* (Seoul: Tongguk munhwasa, 1964), 210: 1a.

9. *Myŏngjong sillok*, 10: 6a–b.

10. Ibid.

11. *Yŏrŭp wŏnu sajŏk*, 2: 533.

12. *Sŏnjo sillok*, 65: 20a.

13. Ibid., 65: 27a.

14. *Myŏngjong sillok*, 10: 6b.

15. Wing-tsit Chan, "Chu Hsi and the Academies," in Wm. Theodore de Bary and John W. Chafee, eds., *Neo-Confucian Education: The Formative Stage* (Berkeley: University of California Press, 1989), p. 398.

16. Ibid., p. 397.

17. Michael Kalton remarks that "in T'oegye's view the great value of these rules is that they express the essence of all learning, on whatever level, in terms of its fundamental content and methodology" (Michael Kalton, trans. and ed., *To Become A Sage: The Ten Diagrams on Sage Learning by Yi T'oegye* [New York: Columbia University Press, 1988], p. 107).

18. Warren W. Smith, Jr., "The Rise of the *Sŏwŏn*: Literary Academies in Sixteenth Century Korea" (Ph.D. diss., University of California, Berkeley, 1971), p. 133.

19. Yi T'oegye played an important role in founding the Isan Academy in 1554 at Yŏngju in Kyŏngsang province and composed the twelve-article rules for it. The rules of the Sŏak Academy are also similar to those of the Isan, the first five articles of the two academies' regulations being almost the same. Founded in 1561 at Kyŏngju, the Sŏak Academy also had a close association with Yi Hwang from the beginning. Yi Yulgok founded the Ŭnbyŏng Study Hall (*chŏngsa*) in 1578 at Haeju, which was later renamed the Sohyŏn Academy. He wrote the rules for this academy (*Ŭnbyŏng chŏngsa hakkyu*), which consisted of 22 articles. Yulgok also composed the rules for Munhoe Academy, which was founded at Haeju in 1549 to enshrine Ch'oe Ch'ung (984–1068), a great Confucian of the Koryŏ dynasty.

20. Yu Hongnyŏl, *Han'guk sahoe sasang sa non'go*, pp. 105–6.

21. Yi I, *Yulgok chŏnsŏ* (Seoul: Sŏnggyungwan taehakkyo, 1958), 15: 49a.

22. Ibid., 15: 43b.

23. Kim Wŏnhaeng (1702–72), *Miho chŏnjip* (reprinted—Seoul: Yŏgang ch'ulp'ansa, 1986), 14: 29a.

24. *Musŏng sŏwŏn wŏnji* (Chŏngŭp: Musŏng Sŏwŏn, 1936), p. 143; reprinted in *Sŏwŏnji ch'ongsŏ* (Seoul: Minjok munhwasa, 1987), vol. 9.

25. Ibid., 65: 6b.

26. *Namgye Pak Sech'ae munjip*, 52: 12b–13a.

27. For the full text, see Yi Hwang, *Chŭngbo T'oegye chŏnsŏ*, 41: 51a–52b.

28. For the rules of the Sŏak Academy, see Yu Hongnyŏl, *Han'guk sahoe sasang sa non'go*, p. 106.

29. For the curriculum of the public schools, see Yi Sŏngmu, " The Influence of Neo-Confucianism on Education and the Civil Service Examination System in Fourteenth- and Fifteenth-Century Korea," in Wm. Theodore de Bary and JaHyun Kim Haboush, eds., *The Rise of Neo-Confucianism in Korea* (New York: Columbia University Press, 1985), pp. 141–42.

30. *Yulgok chŏnsŏ*, 15: 45a.

31. Ibid., 27: 8b–9b.

32. JaHyun Kim Haboush, "The Education of the Yi Crown Prince: A Study in Confucian Pedagogy," in de Bary and Haboush, eds., *The Rise of Neo-Confucianism in Korea*, p. 193.

33. Pak emphasized the core curriculum of the Four Books, the Five Classics, the *Elementary Learning*, and the *Family Ritual*. After the completion of the study of these works, he suggested further study of other Classics, histories, and the writings of Chu Hsi and the two Ch'eng brothers (see *Namgye Pak Sech'ae munjip*, 65: 61b).

34. Kim's curriculum started with the *Elementary Learning*, to be followed in order by the *Great Learning*, the *Analects*, the *Mencius*, the *Doctrine of the Mean*, the *Heart Classic*, *Reflections on Things at Hand*, and then by the study of other Classics. When the student had completed this cycle, he was to start from the beginning again (see *Miho chŏnjip*, 14: 20b).

35. *Miho chŏnjip*, 14: 31; *Musŏng sŏwŏn wŏnji*, p. 144.

36. Yi Ch'unhŭi, *Yijo sŏwŏn mun'go mongnok* (Seoul: Kukhoe tosŏgwan, 1969), pp. 22–24.

37. For a full text of the Sŏksil Academy's regulations, see *Miho chŏnjip*, 14: 29a–32b; for the Munhoe Academy, see *Namgye Pak Sech'ae munjip*, 65: 6a–10b.

38. See *Miho sŏnsaeng kangŭi*, in *Miho chŏnjip*, pp. 607–24.

39. See *Namgye Pak Sech'ae munjip*, 65: 23a–26a.

40. For instance, Kim Wŏnhaeng's work includes eight such responses to students at six different academies, such as the Sohyŏn Academy and the Hwayang Academy. Pak Sech'ae likewise responded in writing to students at four different academies (see *Miho chŏnjip*, 8: 37a–42a; *Namgye Pak Sech'ae munjip*, 35: 36b–40b).

41. *Yulgok chŏnsŏ*, 15: 45a.

42. *Miho chŏnjip*, 14: 31b; *Musŏng sŏwŏn wŏnjip*, p. 144.

43. This is found in the rules for Munhoe Academy; see *Namgye Pak Sech'ae munjip*, 65: 10a.

44. Yu Hyŏngwŏn, *Pan'gye surok* (Seoul: Tongguk munhwasa, 1958), 9: 40b.

45. *Miho chŏnjip*, 14: 31b–31a; *Musŏng sŏwŏn wŏnji*, p. 145.

46. *Namgye Pak sech'ae munjip*, 65: 9b.

47. *Myŏngjong sillok*, 10: 6a–10a.

48. *Sŏwŏn tŭngnok* (Seoul: Minch'ang munhwasa, 1990), p. 524 (Sukchong 18/4/3).

49. Chŏng Manjo, "17–18 segi sŏwŏn wŏnu e taehan siron," *Han'guk saron* 2 (1975): 263. The annual average is based on my calculation.

50. Ibid., p. 265.

51. For the full text of the memorial, see *Hyojong sillok*, 18: 54b–55a.

52. Ibid., 18: 55a–b.

53. Ibid., 19: 2a–3b.

54. Ibid., 19: 3b–4a and 22a–b.

55. *Sŏwŏn tŭngnok*, p. 181 (Sukchong 1/9/28).

56. Yi Chesin (1536–84) observed that "there is a vast difference in esteem and honor" (Yi Chesin, *Ch'ŏnggang sŏnsaeng huch'ŏn soeŏ*, in *Taedong yasŭng* [Seoul: Kosŏ kanhaenghoe, 1911], p. 188).

57. Both Pak Sech'ae and Yu Sangun (1636–1707) were explicit on the different qualities of these two institutions. For Pak's praise of the relative merit of private academies, see *Namgye Pak Sech'ae munjip*, 52: 10b–11a and *Sŏwŏn tŭngnok*, p. 577 (Sukchong 20/10/6). For Yu's similar assessment, see *Sŏwŏn tŭngnok*, p. 700 (Sukchong 25/7/15).

58. Ch'oe Yŏng-ho, "Yuhak, haksaeng, kyosaeng ko," *Yŏksa hakpo* 101 (1984). See also *Han'guk kunjesa* (Seoul: Yukkun ponbu, 1968), 1: 48.

59. *Sŏwŏn tŭngnok*, p. 23 (Injo 22/8/28).

60. Ibid., p. 183 (Sukchong 1/9/28).

61. Ibid., p. 381 (Sukchong 11/5/22).

62. *Sŭngjŏngwŏn ilgi* (Seoul: Kuksa p'yŏnch'an wiwŏnhoe, 1969), 23: 562d (Sukchong 33/8/30).

63. *Sŏwŏn tŭngnok*, p. 181 (Sukchong 1/9/28).

64. *Yŏngjo sillok*, 47: 38a.

65. *Chŏngjo sillok*, 38: 26b.

66. *Sŏwŏn tŭngnok*, pp. 700–701 (Sukchong 25/7/15).

67. *Chŭngbo munhŏn pigo*, 210: 15b.

68. *Sŏwŏn tŭngnok*, p. 868 (Sukchong 43/11/19).

69. For a good discussion on the difference between *sŏwŏn* and *sau*, see Chŏng Manjo, "17–18 segi ŭi sŏwŏn sau e taehan siron," *Han'guk saron* 2 (1975): 215–22.

70. *Injo sillok*, 45: 41a.

71. *Sŏwŏn tŭngnok*, p. 710 (Sukchong 26/10/12).

72. Chŏng Manjo, "17–18 segi ŭi sŏwŏn sau," pp. 232–55.

73. *Yŏrŭp wŏnu sajŏk*, 2: 115–17. See also Chŏng Manjo, "17–18 segi ŭi sŏwŏn sau," pp. 235–36.

74. *Chodurok* (Miryang section), n.p.; and *Chŭngbo munhŏn pigo*, 213: 9b. Also see *Chōsen jimmei jisho* (Seoul: Chōsen sōtokufu, 1937), p. 1521; and *Han'guk minjok munhwa taebaekkwa sajŏn* (Sŏngnam, Kyŏnggido: Han'guk chŏngsin munhwa yŏn'guwŏn, 1990), 8: 837 and 11: 276.

75. *Yŏrŭp wŏnu sajŏk*, 2: 115–17.

76. Yi Suhwan, "Chosŏn sidae sŏwŏn ŭi injŏk kusŏng kwa kyŏngjaejŏk

kiban" (Ph.D. diss., Yŏngnam University, 1990), pp. 42–43; Yi Suhwan, "Sŏwŏn ŭi chŏngch'i sahoesajŏk koch'al," *Kyonam sahak* 1 (1985): 25–28.

77. *Hyŏnjong sillok*, 8: 10a–13a.

78. *Hwayang chi* (n.d.) 2: 36a–48b; *Sŏwŏn tŭngnok*, pp. 639–44 (Sukchong 21/12/16) and pp. 650–51 (Sukchong 22/9/6). Hwayang Academy went on to become one of the most powerful and feared institutions in late Chosŏn, both politically and economically. Its regular requests for monetary contributions were received with fear as the "black warrant of Hwayangdong" (*Hwayangdong mukp'ae*), and at least on one occasion a person who failed to respond favorably was threatened with castration. See Pak Chehyŏng, *Kŭnse Chosŏn chŏnggam* (Tokyo, 1886), reproduced in *Chōsen gakuhō* 59 (1971): 37b–38a; and Ch'oe Sŭnghŭi, *Han'guk komunsŏ yŏn'gu* (Seoul, 1981), pp. 422–24.

79. *Myŏngjong sillok*, 16: 63b–64a; *Yŏrŭp wŏnu sajok*, 2: 555–56.

80. *Hyŏnjong sillok*, 7: 25a.

81. *Yŏrŭp wŏnu sajok*, 2: 287–88.

82. *Ch'unghyŏn sŏwŏn chi*, pp. 79–89 (in *Sŏwŏn chi ch'ongsŏ*, vol. 9).

83. *Sŏwŏn tŭngnok*, p. 203 (Sukchong 2/5/11).

84. Ibid., pp. 25–26 (Injo 23/2/19).

85. For a good study of this, see Chŏng Manjo, "Yŏngjo 14-nyŏn ŭi Andong Kim Sanghŏn Sŏwŏn kŏllip sibi—t'angp'yŏngha No-Soron punjaeng ŭi iltan," *Han'gukhak yŏn'gu*, 1 (1982).

86. For a good discussion on the factional politics, see JaHyun Kim Haboush, *A Heritage of Kings: One Man's Monarchy in the Confucian World* (New York: Columbia University Press, 1988), chap. 4; and Yi Ŭnsun, *Chosŏn hugi tangjaengsa yŏn'gu* (Seoul: Ilchogak, 1988).

87. *Sŭngjŏngwŏn ilgi*, 41: 948a (Yŏngjo 9/1/13).

88. *Yŏngjo sillok*, 47: 28b–30b. *Sŭngjŏngwŏn ilgi*, 48: 133 (Yŏngjo 14/6/20).

89. *Chodurok*, 2: 52–56.

90. *Sŭngjŏngwŏn ilgi*, 48: 133a (Yŏngjo 14/6/20).

91. For a good discussion of *t'angp'yŏng*, see Haboush, *Heritage*, pp. 142–65.

92. *Sŭngjŏngwŏn ilgi*, 48: 147b (Yŏngjo 14/6/23).

93. Ibid., 48: 148a.

94. Ibid.

95. Recent studies by some South Korean scholars have called attention to the rising tension surrounding the power of local offices in the late Chosŏn dynasty. See Kim In'gŏl, "Chosŏn hugi ŭi hyanggwŏn ŭi ch'ui wa chibaech'ŭng tonghyang," *Han'guk munhwa*, 2 (1981): 167–251; and Chŏng Manjo, "Yŏngjo 14-nyŏn Andong Kim Sanghŏn sŏwŏn kŏllip sibi."

96. *Sŭngjŏngwŏn ilgi*, 48: 211b (Yŏngjo 14/7/16).

97. Ibid., 48: 231b (Yŏngjo 14/7/22).

98. Ibid., 48: 149b (Yŏngjo 14/6/23).

99. Chŏng Manjo, "17–18 segi ŭi sŏwŏn sau," p. 276.

100. Yi Yŏngch'un, "Song Siyŏl," *Han'guk minjok munhwa taebaekkwa sajŏn* (Sŏngnam, Kyŏnggido: Han'guk chŏngsin munhwa yŏn'guwŏn, 1990), 13: 22.

101. *Sukchong sillok*, 26: 42b.

102. Ibid., 27: 39a–b.

103. *Sŏwŏn tŭngnok*, pp. 646–47 (Sukchong 21/12/16).

104. *Chodurok*, p. 32.

105. *Kyŏngjong sillok*, 11: 18b, 22a–b, 25a–26b; *Kyŏngjong sujŏng sillok*, 4: 6a–9a.

106. See Haboush, *Heritage*, chap. 4; and Yi Ŭnsun, *Chosŏn hugi tangjaengsa*.

107. *Yŏngjo sillok*, 3: 14b, 18a–b.

108. *Sŏwŏn tŭngnok*, pp. 1020–21 (Yŏngjo 1/1/14).

109. Yi Suhwan, "Chosŏn sidae sŏwŏn ŭi injŏk kusŏng," pp. 86–87.

110. Ibid., pp. 69–92.

111. *Miho chŏnjip*, 14: 20b.

112. *Musŏng sŏwŏn wŏnji*, p. 28.

113. Ibid., p. 141.

114. Yi Ch'unhŭi, *Yijo sŏwŏn mun'go*, pp. 23–24.

115. JaHyun Kim Haboush, "Academies and Civil Society in Chosŏn Korea," in Leon Vandermeersch, ed., *La société civile face à l'état* (Paris: École française d'Extrême-Orient, 1994), pp. 386–87.

116. *Hyŏnjong sillok*, 12: 4b–20a.

117. Haboush, "Academies and Civil Society," p. 387; Chŏng Tonmok, *Han'guk sŏwŏn kyoyuk chedo* (Taegu: Yŏngnam taehakkyo, 1979), pp. 131–35.

118. Haboush, "Academies and Civil Society," pp. 388–89.

## JaHyun Kim Haboush, *The Ritual Controversy and the Search for a New Identity*

1. During the Chosŏn dynasty, a stepmother mourned her husband's legitimate children as though they were her own.

2. Despite the Yi house's nodding acknowledgment of the ideal of primogeniture, it yielded more often than not to the practical necessity of designating a competent heir, and the majority of Yi kings were not first-born sons. Of the twenty-seven Yi kings, at most ten were first sons and not by terribly strict definitions at that.

3. *Han'guksa*, 7 vols. (6 vols. and a reference volume), ed. Chindan hakhoe (Seoul: Ŭryu munhwasa, 1959–63), 4: 27.

4. JaHyun Kim Haboush, "A Heritage of Kings: One Man's Monarchy in the Confucian World" (Ph D. diss., Columbia University, 1978).

5. Yi T'aejin, "Tangjaeng ŭl ŏttŏk'e pol kŏsin'ga?" in idem, ed., *Chosŏn sidae chŏngch'isa ŭi chaejomyŏng* (Seoul: Pŏmjosa, 1985), pp. 13–25. Takeshi

Hara suggests that Haboush's research stimulated the movement to break free of the "factionalist" historical interpretation in Korea in the 1990s; see Takeshi Hara, "Kankoku kokushi gakkai ni okeru Richō ōken kenkyū no genzai," *Discussion Paper Series* J-38 (June 1994): 2–3.

6. Yi Sŏngmu, "Sipch'il segi ŭi yeron kwa tangjaeng," in idem et al., *Chosŏn hugi tangjaeng ŭi chonghapchŏk yŏn'gu* (Sŏngnamsi, Kyŏnggido: Han'guk chŏngsin munhwa yŏn'guwŏn, 1992), pp. 80–82.

7. It was not until the late 1970s and early 1980s that serious studies of ritual began to appear in appreciable numbers. One of them was Yu Chŏng-dong's "Yeron ŭi chehakp'a wa kŭ nonjaeng," in Han'guk ch'ŏrhakhoe, ed., *Han'guk ch'ŏrhak yŏn'gu*, vol. 2 (Seoul: Tongmyŏngsa, 1978). In the 1990s, a number of interesting studies of ritual appeared, including Chi Tuhwan, "Chosŏn chŏn'gi kukka ŭirye yŏn'gu — Chujahak suyong kwajŏng kwa kwallyŏn hayŏ" (Ph.D. diss., Seoul National University, 1990); Chŏng Ok-cha, "Sipch'il segi chŏn'ban yesŏ ŭi sŏngnip kwajŏng — Kim Changsaeng ŭl chungsim ŭro," *Han'guk munhwa* 11 (1990): 407–48; and Ko Yŏngjin, "Chosŏn chunggi yesŏl kwa yesŏ" (Ph.D. diss., Seoul National University, 1992).

8. Some studies focus on a single participant. There are a number of articles on Song Siyŏl, Hŏ Mok, and Yun Hyu. For Song Siyŏl, representative articles include Ch'oe Ch'anggye, "Uamhak ŭi minjoksajŏk chaejŏngnip," *Paekche yŏn'gu chip* 10 (1979): 193–215; Kim Chunsŏk, "Sipch'il segi chŏngt'ong Chujahakp'a ŭi chŏngch'i sahoe ron," *Tongbang hakchi* 67 (Sept. 1990): 87–196; Son Munho, "Song Siyŏl ŭi chŏngch'i sasang yŏn'gu," *Hosŏ munhwa nonch'ong* 4 (1989): 33–47; Yi Yŏngch'un, "Uam Song Siyŏl ŭi chonju sasang," *Ch'ŏnggye sahak* 2: (1985) 129–64. For Hŏ Mok, see Chŏng Okcha, "Misu Hŏ Mok yŏn'gu," *Han'guk saron* 5 (Oct. 1979): 197–232; Han Yŏngu, "Hŏ Mok ŭi kohak kwa yŏksa insik," *Han'guk hakpo* 40 (Autumn 1985): 44–87; Kim Chunsŏk, "Hŏ Mok ŭi yeaknon kwa kunjugwan," *Tongbang hakchi* 54–56 (June 1987): 245–75; and Kim Kilhwan, "Hŏ Mok ŭi hangmun kwa sasang," *Han'guk hakpo* 18 (Spring 1980): 24–45. On Yun Hyu, see Han Ugŭn, "Paekho Yun Hyu yŏn'gu," 3 pts., *Yŏksa hakpo* 15 (Sept. 1961): 1–29, 16 (Dec. 1961): 63–107, 19 (Dec. 1962): 91–120; and Yu Yŏnghŭi, "Paekho Yun Hyu sasang yŏn'gu" (Ph. D. diss., Koryŏ taehakkyo, 1993).

9. Several decades earlier, in a debate concerning whether to confer posthumous royal titles on Injo's parents, the main opponent to the measure was Kim Changsaeng, a Sŏin renowned for his ritual scholarship and the teacher of Song Siyŏl. Although Kim, as his student Song would later be, was against granting exceptions to the occupant of the throne that would strengthen the royal line, his argument, unlike Song's, was based on the primacy of the public over the private in the royal succession as well as the distinctiveness of succession laws, which separate the royal family from ordinary families. Ko Yŏngjin ("Chosŏn chunggi yesŏl," pp. 189–91) rightly notes the consistent positions taken by Kim Changsaeng and his disciples, pointing out that on both occasions they argued from the position of the

primacy of lineage rules. Ko, however, does not take into account Kim's rhetorical construction. Kim's argument falls so closely within the rhetorical tradition of ritual controversies, such as the one in the fifteenth-century Ming Chinese court, that the meaning of his position requires an analysis of his rhetoric in terms of contemporary discourse.

10. Geertz borrows the term from M. Singer, "The Cultural Pattern of Indian Civilization," *Far Eastern Quarterly* 15 (1955): 23–26.

11. Clifford Geertz, *The Interpretation of Cultures* (New York: Basic Books, 1973), p. 113.

12. The five categories were auspicious or sacrifical rituals, mourning rituals, diplomatic rituals, military rituals, and wedding rituals. See *Kukcho oryeŭi*, 5 vols. (Seoul: Pŏpchech'ŏ, 1981).

13. *Kukcho oryeŭi* was completed in 1474. See Yi Pŏmjik, "*Kukcho oryeŭi* ŭi sŏngnip kwajŏng e taehan il koch'al," *Yŏksa hakpo* 122 (June 1989): 1–27.

14. See the works cited in notes 6, 7, and 8 to this chapter.

15. Geertz (*Interpretation*, p. 112) sees cultural performances as sites where the interaction between ethos and worldview takes place.

16. Liah Greenfeld, *Nationalism: Five Roads to Modernity* (Cambridge: Harvard University Press, 1992), pp. 16–17.

17. Ibid., pp. 12–14.

18. Chi Tuhwan, "Chosŏn hugi yesong," *Pudae sahak* 11 (1987): 77–125; Kang Sangun, "Yesong kwa No-So pundang," *Asea hakpo* 5 (1968): 88–117; Yi Sŏngmu, "Sipch'il segi yeron," pp. 9–82; Yi Yŏngch'un, "Cheilch'a yesong kwa Yun Sŏndo ŭi yeron," *Ch'ŏnggye sahak* 6 (1989): 107–56.

19. My account is based on standard historical records such as the *Sillok* and the collected writings of the participants in question.

20. *Hyŏnjong sillok* (hereafter *HS*), in *Chosŏn wangjo sillok*, 1: 1a–b.

21. *HS*, 1: 1b.

22. Juan Yuan, ed., *I-li chu-su* in *Shih-san-ching chu-su* (Taipei: Kai-ming shu-chü, 1959), p. 1100c.

23. Ibid., 1100c–1101a.

24. Ibid., 1101a.

25. Sohyŏn's youngest son, Sŏkkyŏn, was living.

26. *Kyŏngguk taejŏn*, 2 vols. (Seoul: Pŏpchech'ŏ, 1962), 1: 237.

27. *HS*, 1: 1b–2a.

28. Yun Hyu, "Chŏnnye saŭi" in *Paekho chŏnsŏ* (hereafter *PC*), 3 vols. (Taegu: Kyŏngbuk taehakkyo ch'ulp'anbu, 1974), 2: 1045–51.

29. Hŏ Mok, *Kugyŏk Misu kiŏn*, 6 vols. (Seoul: Minjok munhwa ch'ujinhoe, 1979), 3: 24–26.

30. *HS*, 2: 10b–11b.

31. *Injo sillok*, 46: 29a–30a, 34b–36a.

32. *HS*, 2: 14b–15b; Song Chun'gil, *Tongch'un sŏnsaeng munjip*, 4 vols. (Seoul: Kyŏngin munhwasa, 1987), 3: 22b–24b.

33. Yejong was King Sejo's (1417–68, r. 1455–68) second son and was appointed heir apparent after his older brother, the previous heir apparent, died in his twentieth year. Queen Chŏnghŭi was his mother. Yejong's familial position was the same as that of Hyojong (*HS*, 2: 15b–16a). Injong was Chungjong's (1488–1544, r. 1506–44) first son, and Queen Munjŏng was his stepmother.

34. *HS*, 2: 24b–25a. The records of mourning procedures for Yejong say only that in every respect they followed exactly the precedent of the previous reign (*Sŏngjong sillok* in *Chosŏn wangjo sillok*, 1: 3). This would refer to the mourning procedures for Sejo, but Sejo was not survived by his mother. Thus the extremely detailed records of mourning procedures for Sejo do not include his mother's mourning for him (*Yejong sillok* in *Chosŏn wangjo sillok*, 1: 4b–5b).

35. *HS*, 2: 21a–23b; Hŏ Mok, *Kiŏn*, 3: 26–27.

36. *HS*, 2: 25a.

37. *HS*, 2: 25a–27b; Song Siyŏl, *Songja taejŏn* (hereafter *ST*), 8 vols. (Seoul: Pŏgyong munhwasa, 1985), *ST*, 26: 1b–7b (1: 546–49).

38. *HS*, 2: 27b–31b; Yi Yŏngch'un, "Cheilch'a yesong," pp. 107–56.

39. *HS*, 2: 31b–32a.

40. Kwŏn Si (1604–72), a well-known scholar and an affine of Song Siyŏl, defended Yun Sŏndo (*HS*, 2: 38a–b), whereas the Censorate demanded his interrogation (*HS*, 2: 34a–b).

41. *HS*, 2: 32a.

42. *HS*, 2: 39a, 43a.

43. *HS*, 2: 35a–b, 37a–38a.

44. In addition to memorials and letters, Yun Hyu wrote sixteen essays in defense of his position on the mourning controversy; see *PC*, 2: 1045–80.

45. *PC*, pp. 1045–56.

46. *PC*, pp. 1057–58.

47. *HS*, 12: 4b–20a.

48. *HS*, 12: 22a–26a.

49. Chŏng Tonmok, *Han'guk sŏwŏn kyoyuk chedo yŏn'gu* (Taegu: Yŏngnam taehakkyo ch'ulp'anbu, 1979), pp. 60–120. Also see Yŏng-ho Ch'oe's chapter in this volume.

50. JaHyun Kim Haboush, "Academies and Civil Society in Chosŏn Korea," in Léon Vandermeersch, ed., *La société civile face à l'état* (Paris: École Française d'Extrême-Orient, 1994), p. 387.

51. Although Wŏn at first went along with a one-year mourning period, he apparently changed his mind, and almost immediately after the decision had been made, he unsuccessfully attempted to reopen the case. In a memorial, he said that in the ruling house, the succession was of utmost importance; thus the rituals and rules governing the succession should be different from those of scholar-official families. The heir who succeeded to the throne automatically became the legitimate line, even if he had been a secondary

son by a concubine. As a way of showing that Wŏn's memorial echoed Yun Hyu's letter to Hŏ Mok, the *Sillok* duly recorded Yun's letter; see *HS*, 2: 44a–45b.

52. *HS*, 11: 39b–46a.

53. *Sukchong sillok*, 8: 12a–b, 30a–b.

54. E.g., see Song's memorials in *ST*, 10: 7a–12b; and 11: 1a–9a, 17a–b.

55. *Kyŏngguk taejŏn*, 1: 237.

56. *HS*, 22: 7a–b.

57. Juan Yuan, *I-li chu-su*, 32: 1114b, 33: 1118c.

58. *HS*, 22: 24b–26a.

59. *HS*, 22: 33b–35a.

60. Haboush, "A Heritage of Kings," pp. 56–58; Yi Yŏngch'un, "Pokche yesong kwa chŏngguk hwan'guk—Che ich'a yesong ŭl chungsim ŭro," *Kuksagwan nonch'ong* 22 (1991): 219–60.

61. An entry in the *Sillok* for the twenty-seventh day of the sixth month, a dozen days after Prince Sohyŏn's funeral, discusses the curious circumstances of the prince's death. The symptoms suggested murder. Earlier, King Injo had been unhappy to learn that Prince Sohyŏn was briskly conducting commercial transactions during his captivity in China, and a certain Lady Cho was brazenly hostile to the prince and his wife and ceaselessly impugned them to the king. See *Injo sillok*, 46: 48b.

62. Kim Yongdŏk, "Sohyŏn seja yŏn'gu," *Sahak yŏn'gu* 18 (Sept. 1964): 433–89.

63. Their exchanges of poems during Prince Sohyŏn's years in China are full of longing for each other, and these sentiments seem genuine; see Yi Ugyŏng, *Han'guk ŭi ilgi munhak* (Seoul: Chipmundang, 1995), pp. 65–66.

64. Kim's article was written at the time when modernization theory was in vogue. It laments the death of Prince Sohyŏn, who was interested in Western science and Catholicism (to which he had been exposed through the Jesuit missionaries whom he met in Beijing), as a missed opportunity for Korea to modernize early and adopt Western science.

65. *Injo sillok*, 46: 67a; 47: 7a–b, 47: 22b.

66. Ibid., 47: 1b–2a, 26a–27a, 40b–41a.

67. Ibid., 49: 38a, 51b.

68. Sŏkkyŏn was released from banishment in 1650, but he was restored to his princely rank only in 1659 at the same time his older brothers were also posthumously restored to their previous ranks (*Hyojong sillok*, 3: 7b, 21: 22b–23b).

69. Song Chun'gil was relieved of his post for sending this memorial (*Injo sillok*, 46: 34b–36a).

70. *Sallim* designated those scholars who publicly renounced the civil service examination and officialdom. They were a part of the Confucian scholarly community (*sarim* or *yurim*), but were distinguished by their stance on public service. Their prestige grew from the late sixteenth century and

peaked during the seventeenth century. In 1646, King Injo agreed to reserve several posts in the Crown Prince Tutorial Office for *sallim* scholars. See U Insu, "Sipch'il segi sallim ŭi chinch'ul kwa kinŭng," *Yŏksa kyoyuk nonjip* 5 (1983): 143–77.

71. Song Siyŏl passed first on the preliminary examination in 1633, but he did not take the *munkwa*, the final examination. Song Chun'gil also took the preliminary examination in 1624, but did not take the *munkwa*.

72. For Song Siyŏl's life and career, see *Yŏnbo* in *Songja taejŏn purok, kwŏn* 1–12. *ST*, 7: 12–276.

73. The *Sillok* records the earlier part of this audience, which was carried out in the presence of historians. Then the king ordered them to leave. At this point the *Sillok* pointedly says that since the historians were not present, no one knew what was discussed; see *Hyojong sillok*, 21: 14b–15b.

74. Song Siyŏl, *Toktae sŏrhwa*, ms. (Kyujanggak, 1659).

75. I could find only one other "solitary audience" in the *Sillok*. The other was between King Sukchong and Yi Imyŏng in 1717, and it created a furor (*Sukchong sillok*, 60: 22a–b).

76. Song Siyŏl, "Yŏngnŭng chimun," in *ST*, 181: 1a–23a.

77. Song Siyŏl is listed among six ministers; see Kim Sundong, ed., *Han'guk kosa taejŏn* (Seoul: Hoesangsa, 1965), p. 541

78. Patricia Buckley Ebrey, *Chu Hsi's Family Ritual* (Princeton: Princeton University Press, 1991), pp. 54–61.

79. Martina Deuchler, *The Confucian Transformation of Korea: A Study of Society and Ideology* (Cambridge: Harvard University, Council on East Asian Studies, 1992), pp. 249–51.

80. Ibid., pp. 129–78, 223–30.

81. They were excluded from the regular bureaucracy and could not become heirs to their fathers; see Martina Deuchler, "Heaven Does Not Discriminate," *Journal of Korean Studies* 6 (1988–89): 121–63.

82. Hahm Pyong-choon, "The Rule of Royal Succession During the Yi Dynasty," in idem, *The Korean Political Tradition and Law* (Seoul: Royal Asiatic Society Korea Branch, 1967), pp. 85–107.

83. One of the most interesting works on this question in China is Howard Wechsler's *Offerings of Jade and Silk* (New Haven: Yale University Press, 1985). Wechsler maintains that a growing divergence appeared between state rituals and imperial family rituals in the early T'ang, and that state rituals began to receive greater attention.

84. *Kukcho oryeŭi*, for instance, includes the life cycle rituals of the king and the heir apparent, the weddings of royal children, and the king's ceremonial behavior to those who had any claim to public status. On *karye* and *hyungnye*, see *Kukcho oryeŭi, kwŏn* 3–5, 7–8.

85. Confucian rulers saw rich possibilities for acquiring moral authority through displays of filiality; see Harold Kahn, "The Politics of Filiality: Justi-

fication for Imperial Action in Eighteenth-century China," *Journal of Asian Studies* 26, no. 2 (Feb. 1967): 197–203.

86. Many Korean Confucians felt that they were more faithful to authentic Confucianism than Chinese scholars, many of whom had embraced Wang Yang-ming's philosophy; see Martina Deuchler, "Reject the False and Uphold the Straight: Attitudes Toward Heterodox Thought in Early Yi Korea," in Wm. Theodore de Bary and JaHyun Kim Haboush, eds., *The Rise of Neo-Confucianism in Korea* (New York: Columbia University Press, 1985), pp. 399–404.

87. On Korean-Ryukyuan relations, see Kenneth R. Robinson, "Korean-Ryukyuan Interactions in the Inner Sea, 1389–1636," forthcoming.

88. For details, see *T'ongmun'gwan chi* (Tokyo: Kankoku chinsho kankōkai, 1907).

89. The Chosŏn court routinely referred to Ch'ing envoys as "barbarian messengers *(hoch'a)*," and King Sukchong referred to the K'ang-hsi Emperor as "that northerner *(pugin)*"; see *Sukchong sillok*, 17: 30.

90. Greenfeld, *Nationalism*, pp. 94–95.

91. *Yŏngjo sillok*, 69: 25a; JaHyun Kim Haboush, *A Heritage of Kings: One Man's Monarchy in the Confucian World* (New York: Columbia University Press, 1988), p. 41.

92. Haboush, *A Heritage of Kings*, p. 77.

93. On various scholars' stress on ritual as a key to establishing order, see Song Siyŏl, "Kichuk pongsa," in *ST*, 5: 1a–33a; Hŏ Mok, "Ch'unch'u chaei pal," in *Kiŏn*, 2: 179 *(kwŏn 62)*; Yun Hyu, "Non pokche so," in *PC*, pp. 240–45.

94. Yi T'aejin, *Chosŏn hugi ŭi chŏngch'i wa kunyŏngje pyŏnch'ŏn* (Seoul: Han'guk yŏn'guwŏn, 1985), pp. 154–73.

95. Yi Kyŏngch'an, "Chosŏn Hyojongjo ŭi pukpŏl undong," *Ch'ŏnggye sahak* 5 (1988): 177–259.

96. For a thorough account of the movements, see Lynn A. Struve, *The Southern Ming, 1644–1662* (New Haven: Yale University Press, 1984).

97. The court of Yung-li, the last claimant to the Ming throne, was driven into the aboriginal territory of extreme southwestern Kwangsi by the winter of 1651 and stayed there for four years. By 1659, it was driven into Burma. In 1662, Yung-li was captured and was executed. Another branch of the movement led by a loyalist, Cheng Ch'eng-kung, also came to an end in Taiwan in 1662. See ibid., pp. 151–94.

98. For examples of the Korean court's awareness of the Ming loyalist movements, see *Hyojong sillok*, 12: 7a–b, 23a–b; 13: 1b; 14: 3b–5a, 37b–38a; and 19: 31a–32b.

99. Prime Ministers Yi Kyŏngsŏk (1595–1671) and Yi Kyŏngyŏ (1585–1657) had to resign (ibid., 3: 12b–21b, 5: 30b–6: 1a).

100. Yi Kyŏngch'an, "Chosŏn Hyojongjo," pp. 220–27.

101. According to Song Siyŏl's account, Hyojong expressed confidence in his ability to accomplish this task because he thought, based on his eight

years as a hostage, that he knew Manchu vulnerabilities; he also felt that the Manchus were losing their military spirit. He then asked for Song's active cooperation. See Song Siyŏl, *Toktae sŏrhwa.*

102. Yi T'aejin, *Kunyŏngje,* pp. 174–97.

103. On Hŏ Mok's life, see Chŏng Okcha, "Hŏ Mok Misu yŏn'gu," *Han'guk sahak* 5 (Oct. 1979): 199–204.

104. For the many posts Yun Hyu was appointed to and refused, see Han Ugŭn, "Paekho Yun Hyu yŏn'gu," pt. 1, *Yŏksa hakpo* 15: 6–15.

105. For Chu Hsi, see Conrad Schirokauer, "Chu Hsi's Political Career," in Arthur F. Wright and Denis Twitchett, eds., *Confucian Personalities* (Stanford: Stanford University Press, 1962), pp. 162–88. For Yi T'oegye, see Yun Sasun, *T'oegye ch'ŏrhak ŭi yŏn'gu* (Seoul: Koryŏ taehakkyo ch'ulp'anbu, 1980), pp. 6–20.

106. For such a predeliction in the late Ming, see Willard Peterson, *Bitter Gourd* (New Haven: Yale University Press, 1979).

107. For a list of *sallim* scholars who received official appointments from the late sixteenth to the early eighteenth centuries, see U Insu, "Sipch'il segi sallim ŭi chich'ul kwa kinŭng," pp. 161–62.

108. U Insu, "Sipch'il segi sallim ŭi seryŏk kiban kwa chŏngch'ijŏk kinŭng" (Ph.D. diss., Kyŏngbuk University, 1992), pp. 12–13.

109. As is well known, Chosŏn Koreans disapproved of the popularity of Wang Yang-ming in Ming China and remained faithful to Chu Hsi.

110. Yi I, *Yulgok chŏnsŏ* (Seoul: Sŏnggyun'gwan taehakkyo tonga yŏn'guwŏn, 1961), 10: 12b.

111. See the many letters he wrote to Pak Sech'ae in *ST,* 65: 1a–49b.

112. Song Siyŏl, "Kich'uk pongsa," in *ST,* 5: 1a–33a.

113. Song Siyŏl, "Chŏngyu pongsa," in *ST,* 5: 56a.

114. Unfortunately, Song's philosophical precepts did not exactly agree with those of Chu on several major points (i.e., *li* and *ch'i*). Deeply disturbed by this discrepancy, he undertook a painstaking examination of Chu's exposition hoping to demonstrate that Chu's teachings had been misrepresented by his compiler. See "Chuja onnon tongi ko," in *ST,* 130: 14a–26a.

115. Miura Kunio, "Orthodoxy and Heterodoxy in Seventeenth-Century Korea: Song Siyŏl and Yun Hyu," in de Bary and Haboush, eds., *The Rise of Neo-Confucianism in Korea,* pp. 419–21.

116. For a discussion of the "back to the origins" movement in seventeenth-century China, see Benjamin A. Elman, *From Philosophy to Philology: Intellectual and Social Aspects of Change in Late Imperial China* (Cambridge: Harvard University Press, Council on East Asian Studies, 1984), p. 61.

117. Hŏ Mok, "Tap Pak Togil non munhaksasŏ," *Kiŏn,* 1: 62–65, 2: 202–4; Yun Hyu, "Manp'il" (*sang, chung, ha*), in *PC,* 2: 1097–176, esp. pp. 1153, 1172–73.

118. Hŏ Mok, "Tap Pak Togil non munhaksasŏ," *Kiŏn,* 1: 62–65, 2: 202–4; Chŏng Okcha, "Misu Hŏ Mok yŏn'gu," pp. 226–28.

119. Yu Yŏnghŭi, "Paekho Yun Hyu," p. 14.

120. Song Siyŏl, "Ugi," in *ST*, 132: 1a–10b, esp. 2b, 9b.

121. Hŏ Mok, "Tap *Yojŏn, Hongbŏm, Chungyong* kojŏng chi silsŏ," *Kiŏn*, 1: 56–59.

122. Yun Hyu, "Chuja changgu porok," in *PC*, p. 1461.

123. Yun Hyu, "Toksŏgi sŏ," in *PC*, pp. 997–98.

124. For a discussion of the shift from the Classics to the classical era, see John B. Henderson, *Scripture, Canon, and Commentary* (Princeton: Princeton University Press, 1991), pp. 214–15.

125. Paul Ricoeur, "The Task of Hermeneutics," in idem, *Paul Ricoeur, Hermeneutics, and the Human Sciences: Essays on Language, Action, and Interpretation*, ed. and trans. John B. Thompson (Cambridge: Cambridge University Press, 1985), p. 48.

126. Henderson, *Scripture*, 214.

127. *Sukchong sillok*, 2: 34b–35a, 4: 12a–b.

128. For representative writings by Song on this topic, see "Samhaksa chŏn," in *ST*, 213: 1a–25b; and Kim Chunsŏk, "Sipch'il segi chŏngt'ong Chuja hakp'a," pp. 92–93.

129. Yi Yŏngch'un, "Uam Song Siyŏl," pp. 141–47.

130. See Song's letter to Ch'ŏng Yang (?–1668): "Yŏ Chŏng Ansuk" (dated the fifteenth of the fifth month, 1659), in *ST*, 35: 15a–16a.

131. Yi Yŏngch'un, "Uam Song Siyŏl," p. 155.

132. Yun Hyu, "Sangŏn," in *PC*, pp. 507–13; "Kyŏngin illok," in *PC*, pp. 1333–84, esp. p. 1346. For Yun's views of Heaven, see Miura, "Song Siyŏl and Yun Hyu," pp. 427–33.

133. For his many treatises on them, see Yun Hyu "Manp'il," in *PC*, pp. 1097–76.

134. Yu Yŏnghŭi, "Paekho Yun Hyu," pp. 97–170.

135. Yun Hyu wrote this for King Sukchong. For the reform plans, see Yun Hyu, "Konggo chikchang tosŏl," in *PC*, pp. 1177–271. Also Yu Yŏnghŭi, "Paekho Yun Hyu," pp. 154–63.

136. John Will, Jr., "Maritime China from Wang Chih to Shih Lang," in Jonathan Spence and John Will, Jr., eds., *From Ming to Ch'ing* (New Haven: Yale University Press, 1979), pp. 230–31.

137. When, in 1678, the news arrived that the situation was favorable to Wu, Yun Hyu brought up the issue again but nothing came of it; see Han Ugŭn, "Paekho Yun Hyu" pt. 3, *Yŏksa hakpo* 19: 114–17.

138. Hong Chongp'il argues that Yun Hyu's proposal for a northern expedition was purely ideological and unaccompanied by any practical preparations; see his "Sambŏllan ŭl chŏnhuhan Hyŏnjong Sukchongnyŏn'gan ŭi pukpŏllon," *Sahak yŏn'gu* 27 (June 1977): 85–105. Yu Yŏnghŭi ("Paekho Yun Hyu," pp. 177–79) argues that it was based on a practical assessment as well as ideology. My reading coincides with Yu's.

139. Hŏ Mok, "Chasŏ-i," *Kiŏn,* 3: 67–68. Chŏng Okcha, "Misu Hŏ Mok yŏngu," pp. 213–15.

140. Chŏng Okcha, "Misu Hŏ Mok yŏngu," pp. 205–13.

141. Greenfeld, *Nationalism,* pp. 51–52.

142. Marie-Madeleine Martin, *The Making of France* (London: Eyre and Spoffiswode, 1951), pp. 88, 100–101; quoted in Greenfeld, *Nationalism,* p. 94.

143. Greenfeld, *Nationalism,* pp. 91–95.

144. For a discussion of Neo-Confucian views on this, see JaHyun Kim Haboush, "The Education of the Yi Crown Prince," in de Bary and Haboush, eds., *The Rise of Neo-Confucianism,* pp. 161–76.

145. See Song Siyŏl, "Kich'uk pongsa" and "Chŏngyu pongsa"; also Kim Chunsŏk, "Sipch'il segi chŏngt'ong Chujahakp'a," p. 129.

146. Hŏ Mok, "*Ch'unch'u chaei pal,*" in *Kiŏn,* 2: 207.

147. Ibid.

148. Greenfeld, *Nationalism,* pp. 112, 158.

149. Hŏ Mok, "Chasŏ-i," in *Kiŏn,* 3: 60; "Iye chin'gye ch'a" in *Kiŏn,* 3: 141; Kim Chunsŏk, "Hŏ Mok ŭi yeaknon kwa kunjugwan," pp. 256–73.

150. Hŏ Mok, "*Ch'unch'u chaei pal,*" in *Kiŏn,* 2: 207.

151. Chŏng Okcha, "Misu Hŏ Mok yŏngu," p. 218.

152. John Knoblock, *Xunzi: A Translation and Study of the Complete Works,* 3 vols. (Stanford: Stanford University Press, 1988–94), 2: 97. Harvard-Yenching Concordance, no. 22, p. 26.

153. The same passage in Watson's translation is as follows: "The ruler is the boat and the common people are the water. It is the water that bears the boat up, and the water that capsizes it"; see Burton Watson, *Hsün Tzu: Basic Writings* (New York: Columbia University Press, 1963), p. 37.

154. I.e., Cho Sik, "Minam pu," in *Nammyŏng chip,* 1: 2a–3a (*Yijo ch'oyŏp myŏnghyŏn sŏnjip,* Seoul: Sŏnggyun'gwan taehakkyo, 1959). I am indebted to the anonymous reviewer of the manuscript for the Harvard University Asia Center for this citation.

155. See Yŏngjo's pronouncement (Haboush, *A Heritage of Kings,* pp. 109–10).

156. Yun Hyu, "Ŏje chusutosŏlhu sosik," in *PC,* pp. 1007–9.

157. Yun Hyu, "Chin sohoe so" in *PC,* pp. 238–39, 268–69; Yu Yŏnghŭi, "Paekho Yun Hyu," pp. 158–60.

158. Concerning the increasingly powerful role of "speaking officials," see JaHyun Kim Haboush, "The Censorial Voice in Choson Korea: A Tradition of Institutionalized Dissent," *Han-kuo hsüeh-bao,* 12 (1993): 11–19.

159. Yun Hyu, "Manp'il," *sang,* p. 1104, *chung,* pp. 1120–23; Yu Yŏnghŭi, "Paekho Yun Hyu," pp. 160–61.

160. Yun Hyu, "Ungjisŏ," in *PC,* pp. 191–97; Yu Yŏnghŭi, "Paekho Yun Hyu," pp. 150–77.

161. Song Siyŏl, "Kich'uk pongsa," in *ST*, 5: 31a.

162. See Hŏ's (*Kiŏn*, 3: 9–24, 123–46) and Yun's (*PC*, pp. 318–598) various memorials to the throne.

163. This was the first recorded execution for heterodoxy in Chosŏn history. For details, see Martina Deuchler's chapter in this volume.

164. Song Siyŏl's memorial expressed disapproval indirectly by praising a Ming emperor's discretion and wisdom in delaying a decision on the heir-apparent. Sukchong termed it contempt for the throne. See *Sukchong sillok*, 20: 7b–9a.

165. Haboush, "Academies and Civil Society," p. 387.

166. This is a term coined by Jürgen Harbermas; see "The Public Sphere," *New German Critique* 1, no. 3 (Fall 1974): 50.

167. Prasenjit Duara, *Rescuing History from the Nation* (Chicago: University of Chicago, 1995).

168. Anthony D. Smith, *The Ethnic Origins of Nations* (Oxford: Blackwell, 1986), pp. 6–13.

169. Benedict Anderson, *Imagined Communities*. Rev. ed. (London: Verso, 1991); Ernest Gellner, *Nations and Nationalism* (Ithaca: Cornell University Press, 1983).

170. Greenfeld, *Nationalism*, pp. 29–484.

171. E. J. Hobsbawn, *Nations and Nationalism Since 1780: Programme, Myth, Reality* (Cambridge: Cambridge University Press, 1990), pp. 46, 66, 137.

172. See JaHyun Kim Haboush, "Rescoring the Universal in a Korean Mode: Eighteenth-Century Korean Culture," in Hongnam Kim, ed, *Korean Arts of the Eighteenth Century: Splendor and Simplicity* (New York: Asia Society Galleries, 1993), pp. 23–33.

173. For Korean interest in their ancestral land expressed in cartography, see Gari Ledyard, "Cartography in Korea," in J. B. Harley and David Woodward, eds., *The History of Cartography* (Chicago: University of Chicago Press, 1994), vol. 2, book 2, pp. 235–345.

174. Smith, *The Ethnic Origins of Nations*, pp. 129–208.

## Martina Deuchler, *Controversies over the Classics*

1. For biographical data on Yun Hyu, see Han U'gŭn, "Paekho Yun Hyu yŏn'gu," pt. I, *Yŏksa hakpo* 15 (Sept. 1961): 1–15. See also the extensive biographical account (*haengjang*) in *Paekho chŏnsŏ* (reprinted – Taegu: Kyŏngbuk taehakkyo ch'ulp'anbu, 1973), 3: appendixes 2–4. Two recent works on Yun Hyu are Yu Yŏnghŭi, "Paekho Yun Hyu sasang yŏn'gu" (Ph.D diss., Koryŏ taehakkyo, 1993); and Yun Sasun, "Paekho Yun Hyu ŭi kyŏngsegwan kwa kŭndae chŏngsin," *Yuhak yŏn'gu* 1 (1993): 203–12. Whereas Yu Yŏnghŭi analyzes Yun Hyu's philosophical contribution, Professor Yun deals with

Yun's views on contemporary matters such as military preparedness, institutional reform, and economic issues.

2. For a discussion of Yun Hyu's commentaries on the *Shu-ching* and *Shih-ching*, see Yu Yŏnghŭi, "Paekho Yun Hyu sasang yŏn'gu," pp. 23–34.

3. For a chronological list of Yun Hyu's works, see Han U'gŭn, "Paekho Yun Hyu yŏn'gu," pt. I, p. 15. Some of Yun's works, such as the *Chungyong Taehak husŏl* (Later theories on the *Chung-yung* and the *Ta-hsüeh*) seem to be lost. In *Chosŏn yugyo yŏnwŏn* (Sources of Confucianism of the Chosŏn period) (reprinted—Seoul: Asea munhwasa, 1973), p. 94, Chang Chiyŏn mentions some additional works whose whereabouts, however, are unknown. See Yu Yŏnghŭi, "Paekho Yun Hyu sasang yŏn'gu," p. 22.

4. There was apparently no exchange of letters between the two.

5. *Hyŏnjong sillok* (Seoul: Kuksa p'yŏnch'an wiwŏnhoe, 1955–63), 3: 50b.

6. Between 1662 and 1700 the *Sillok* lists dozens of appointments at short intervals, but according to the *Yŏnbo* (Chronological biography), in 1668, at the age of 40, Pak Sedang retired to his country seat at Sŏkch'ŏndong and remained there, except for a trip to Beijing. His highest positions were departmental head (*p'ansŏ*) and inspector-general (*taesahŏn*). See his *Sŏgye chŏnsŏ* (Reprint—Seoul: T'aehaksa, 1979), 1: 440ff. It would be meaningless to list all the *Sillok* entries here.

7. Although there were strong demands for the destruction of the *Sabyŏnnok*, the work was fortunately not burned, as I wrongly stated in "Reject the False and Uphold the Straight: Attitudes Toward Heterodox Thought in Early Yi Korea," in Wm. Theodore de Bary and JaHyun Kim Haboush, eds., *The Rise of Neo-Confucianism in Korea* (New York: Columbia University Press, 1985), pp. 403–4.

8. For an extensive biography of Pak Sedang, see Yun Sasun, "Pak Sedang ŭi sirhak sasang e kwanhan yŏn'gu," in idem, *Han'guk yuhak non'gu* (Seoul: Hyŏnamsa, 1980), pp. 195–207. Two recent works on Pak Sedang are Yun Sŏkhwan, "Sŏgye ch'ŏrhak ŭi pan-Chujahakchŏk sabyŏn kujo wa sidaesŏng" (M.A. thesis, Koryŏ taehakkyo, 1989); and Yi Hŭijae, "Pak Sedang sasang yŏn'gu" (Ph.D. diss., Wŏn'gwang taehakkyo, 1994).

9. For a discussion of the *Sŏgye chŏnsŏ*, see Yun Sasun, "*Sŏgye chŏnjip*," in idem, *Han'guk yuhak non'gu*, pp. 386–94.

10. Ch'oe Sŏkchŏng's biography deserves more extensive investigation. For a brief summary, see *Han'guk inmyŏng taesajŏn* (Seoul: Sin'gu munhwasa, 1967), pp. 943–44. His collected works are known as the *Myŏnggokchip*.

11. For a discussion of Yi T'oegye's definition of "right learning," see Martina Deuchler, "Reject the False and Uphold the Straight," pp. 384–86.

12. For a discussion of the revival of the Ch'eng-Chu school in early Ch'ing China, see Kai-wing Chow, *The Rise of Confucian Ritualism in Late Imperial China: Ethics, Classics, and Lineage Discourse* (Stanford: Stanford University Press, 1994), p. 53.

13. *Songja taejŏn* (reprinted—Seoul: Han'guk samun hakhoe, 1971), 7: 312 (*purok* 13: 1a–b).

14. Ibid., 5: 50–51 (138: 20b–21a). For a discussion of Song Siyŏl's attitudes toward Chu Hsi, see Miura Kunio, "Orthodoxy and Heterodoxy in Seventeenth-Century Korea: Song Siyŏl and Yun Hyu," in de Bary and Haboush, *The Rise of Neo-Confucianism in Korea*, pp. 416–21.

15. As yet, no definitive biography of Song Siyŏl exists. For details, see the extensive *Chronological Biography*, in *Songja taejŏn*, 7: 44–311. Kang Chujin has studied the marriage relations between Song Siyŏl and leading figures in opposite factions; see his *Yijo tangjaengsa yŏn'gu* (Seoul: Sŏul taehakkyo ch'ulp'anbu, 1971), pp. 127–36.

16. For a brief discussion of Yi Yulgok's views on independent efforts of scholarship, see Martina Deuchler, "Reject the False and Uphold the Straight," pp. 392–95.

17. For a brief discussion of Yi Ŏnjŏk's case, see Martina Deuchler, "Self-Cultivation for the Governance of Men: The Beginning of Neo-Confucian Orthodoxy in Yi Korea," *Asiatische Studien* 34, no. 2 (1980): 28–9, 31.

18. Ch'oe Sŏkchŏng, *Myŏnggokchip* (reprint), 20: 19b; *Kyegamnok*, A IV, 25a–26a.

19. *Tohak yŏllyu sok* (On the origins of the learning of the Way, cont.), as quoted in Yi Pyŏngdo, *Han'guk yuhaksa* (Seoul: Asea munhwasa, 1987), p. 332 n6. The *Kyegamnok* (Records of the years 1703 [*kyemi*] and 1704 [*kapsin*]) contains the records pertaining to Pak Sedang's case and is preserved in a handwritten version in two volumes in the Kyujanggak Archives, Seoul National University. This version was used for this study. "A" means vol. 1, and "B" vol. 2. Another copy in a different handwriting is appended to Pak Sedang, *Sŏgye chŏnsŏ*, vol. 2.

20. Song Siyŏl in a letter to Yun Chŭng in 1684; see *Songja taejŏn*, 7: 259–60 (*yŏnbo* 10: 8b–9a).

21. *Sukchong sillok*, 6: 57a. Tzu-ssu, Confucius' grandson, was believed to have been the author of the *Chung-yung*. Similar questions were asked half a century later by the young Tai Chen (1724–77). See Ann-ping Chin and Mansfield Freeman, trans., *Tai Chen on Mencius: Explorations in Words and Meaning* (New Haven: Yale University Press, 1990), p. 1.

22. Yun Hyu, *Paekho chŏnsŏ*, 3: 1891.

23. Ibid., 2: 1447.

24. *Tok Sangsŏ* (On reading the *Book of History*), in ibid., 3: 1641.

25. The two works are contained in Yun Hyu, *Paekho chŏnsŏ*, 3: 1447–61, 1461–1500. The preface of the Addenda is dated 1668.

26. For an analysis of Yun Hyu's version of the *Chung-yung*, see Yu Yŏnghŭi, "Paekho Yun Hyu sasang yŏn'gu," pp. 36–44. Also see Miura Kunio, "Orthodoxy and Heterodoxy," pp. 427–33.

27. Yun Hyu's interpretations of the *Ta-hsüeh* are principally found in his

*Taehak kobon pyŏllok* (Separate record on the old version of the *Ta-hsüeh*), in *Paekho chŏnsŏ*, 3: 1501–14.

28. Song Siyŏl, *Songja taejŏn*, 7: 59–60.

29. This is not to say that Chu Hsi did not play a role in the rites disputes. The *Chu Tzu chia-li* (Family rituals of Master Chu) was the most important ritual handbook in Korea. Yet, his Rules were challenged by such older authorities as the *I-li* (Book of ceremonies and rites) and the *Li-chi* (Book of rites).

30. *Sukchong sillok*, 2: 14a.

31. Ibid., 4: 13a–b.

32. It is contained in Yun Hyu, *Paekho chŏnsŏ*, 3: 1501–14.

33. "Taehak chŏnp'yŏn taeji ansŏl," in ibid., 3: 1524; *Sukchong sillok*, 4: 13a–b. See also Han U'gŭn, "Paekho Yun Hyu yŏn'gu," pt. I, pp. 20–21; and Miura Kunio, "Orthodoxy and Heterodoxy," pp. 427–38.

34. For a discussion of the Sung exegetical tradition, see Kai-wing Chow, *Rise of Confucian Ritualism in Late Imperial China*, pp. 167–68.

35. Pak Sedang, *Sŏgye chŏnsŏ*, 1: 295–96 (14: 28b–29b).

36. Pak Sedang as a man and thinker deserves a monograph-length study. The most detailed analysis of his thought hitherto is that by Yun Sasun in his "Pak Sedang ŭi sirhak sasang e kwanhan yŏn'gu." For an earlier study of Pak Sedang, see Yi Pyŏngdo, "Pak Sŏgye wa pan-Chujahakjŏk sasang," *Taedong munhwa yŏn'gu* 3 (Dec. 1966): 1–18. This article provided the basis for the chapter on Pak Sedang in Yi Pyŏngdo's *Han'guk yuhaksa*, pp. 337–50. See also Yun Sŏkhwan, "Sŏgye chŏrhak ŭi pan-Chujahakjŏk sabyŏn kujo wa sidaesŏng."

37. *Chung-yung*, 15: 8b. Wing-tsit Chan, *A Source Book in Chinese Philosophy* (Princeton: Princeton University Press, 1963), p. 102.

38. Pak Sedang, *Sŏgye chŏnsŏ*, 2: 2.

39. Ibid., 1: 26, 31.

40. Ibid., 1: 448 (22: 18a–b). Pak Sedang did not explain how he came to choose the title *Sabyŏnnok* for his work. He may have known of the *Ssu-pien lu* of his Chinese contemporary Lu Shih-i (1611–72). According to his disciple Yi T'an, *sabyŏn* was a contraction of *sinsa myŏngbyŏn* (to think carefully and to distinguish clearly). The meaning of *T'ongsŏl* was explained as "one theory is going through [the whole work]"; see *Kyegamnok*, A IV, 23b.

41. Pak Sedang, *Sabyŏnnok, Chungyong*, 1a–b, in *Sŏgye chŏnsŏ*, vol. 2.

42. Pak Sedang, *Sŏgye chŏnsŏ*, vol. 1, 22: 21a; and vol. 2, *Sabyŏnnok, Taehak*, 24a–b, 37a–b.

43. Yi Hŭijae ("Pak Sedang sasang yŏn'gu," pp. 56–58) points out that Pak Sedang's interpretation of *kyŏk* is close to the meaning Wang Yang-ming gave to *ko*, "to correct," that is, to correct what is wrong in one's mind. Pak Sedang, however, never referred to Wang Yang-ming's most fundamental notion of intuitive knowledge.

44. Pak Sedang, *Sabyŏnnok, Taehak*, 3b–4a.

45. Ibid., 4b.

46. Ibid., 1a–b. Pak Sedang agreed with Chu Hsi's reading of "renovating" instead of "loving" the people.

47. Yun Sasun, "Pak Sedang ŭi sirhak sasang e kwanhan yŏn'gu," p. 262.

48. Pak Sedang, *Sabyŏnnok, Chungyong*, 1b–2a.

49. Ibid., 4b–5a.

50. Ibid., 3a.

51. Pak Sedang' s differentiation of Heavenly principle and human nature is close to that postulated earlier by Chu Hsi's disciple, Ch'en Ch'un (1159–1223), who devoted a special treatise to explaining and distinguishing the meanings of these terms. As to "human nature is principle," he asked why two terms were used, if the two are really the same. His answer: "'Principle' refers generally to the common principle of the cosmos and man. 'Human nature' is the principle within ourselves." See John B. Henderson, *Scripture, Canon, and Commentary: A Comparison of Confucian and Western Exegesis* (Princeton: Princeton University Press, 1991), pp. 165–66.

52. Pak Sedang, *Sabyŏnnok, Chungyong*, 3a–b.

53. Pak Sedang, *Sŏgye chŏnsŏ*, vol. 1, *purok*, 22: 27a–b. For a detailed description of Yi Kyŏngsŏk's career and an analysis of Pak Sedang's tomb inscription, see Yi Ŭnsun, *Chosŏn hugi tangjaengsa yŏn'gu* (Seoul: Ilchogak, 1988), pp. 139–71.

54. Nam Kuman, *Yakch'ŏnjip*, 29: 43b–44a.

55. *Sukchong sillok, po'gwŏl chŏngo*, 34B: 1a; 38A: 40b.

56. *Kyegamnok*, A I, 1a–10b; *Sukchong sillok*, 38A: 38b–40b.

57. *Kyegamnok*, A II, 13b–21a; *Sukchong sillok*, 38A: 35b–37b.

58. Kim Chin'gwi's sister was Sukchong's first wife, but died in 1680 at the age of twenty without having given birth to a son.

59. *Kyegamnok*, A III, 21b–22a; *Sukchong sillok*, 38A: 37b–40b.

60. *Kyegamnok*, A IV, 22a–30b; *Sukchong sillok*, 38A: 43b–45a.

61. *Kyegamnok*, A V, 44b; VII, 33a–44a; IX, 46a–47b; *Sukchong sillok*, 38A: 44b–45a, 45b–46a.

62. For the circumstances that led to Pak T'aebo's death, see Chŏng Sŏkchong, "Sukchong tae kapsul hwan'guk kwa chŏngbyŏn ch'amyŏ kyech'ŭng punsŏk," in Yi T'aejin, ed., *Chosŏn sidae chŏngch'i ŭi chaejomyŏng* (Seoul: Pŏmjosa, 1985), pp. 136–40.

63. *Kyegamnok*, A X, 47b–48b; *Sukchong sillok*, 38A: 46a–b; *Sŏgye chŏnsŏ*, vol. 1, *purok*, 22: 27b–30a. The Chronological Biography, written by Yi T'an, suggests that Kim Chin'gwi was behind the choice of such a harsh place as Okkwa.

64. *Kyegamnok*, A XII, 53b–54a, 54b; *Sukchong sillok*, 38A: 48b–49b, 50b–51a.

65. *Kyegamnok*, A XIII, 55a–59a; *Sukchong sillok*, 38A: 49b–50a.

66. *Kyegamnok*, A XIV, 59a–66b; *Sukchong sillok*, 38A: 54a–b.

67. *Kyegamnok,* A XV, 66b–83a; *Sukchong sillok,* 38A: 54b–56b, 57a–b, and 38B: 5b. Similar memorials in defense of their grandfathers' roles in 1637 were submitted by Yi Yŏ for Yi Sik (1584–1647), and by Chang Chinhwan (n.d.) for Chang Yu. See *Kyegamnok,* A XVI and XVII, 83a–86b, 86b–89b.

68. *Kyegamnok,* A XVIII, 89b–94a.

69. Ibid., XIX, 94b–98b; *Sukchong sillok,* 38B: 2b–3b, 15b–16a; Kwŏn Sangha, *Hansujae sŏnsaengjip,* 3: 15a–b.

70. Kim Ch'anghyŏp, *Nongamjip* (reprint), 15: 1a, 5a–7a, 23a–25a.

71. Ibid., 15: 7a–13b, 25a–32b.

72. Ibid., 15: 6b, 14a, 23a.

73. *Kyegamnok,* A XXIII, 130b–132b; *Sukchong sillok,* 38B: 22a–23a, 24a, 34a–b.

74. *Kyegamnok,* A XXIV, 132b–152a; Ch'oe Ch'angdae, *Kollyunjip,* 8: 1a–20a; Yi Ŭihyŏn, *T'ogokchip,* vol. 14, 28: 10a–11a.

75. *Sukchong sillok,* 40: 1a–2b.

76. *Kyegamnok,* B III, 5b–30a; *Sukchong sillok,* 40: 8a–10b.

77. *Kyegamnok,* B I and II, 1b–5b, V, 31a–33b, VII, 34b–35a; *Sukchong sillok,* 38A: 46b, 39: 58b–60b, 66a–67b. Kim Manch'ae, Kim Chin'gwi, and Kim Chin'gyu, who were descendants of Kim Changsaeng, handed in a memorial in which they protested Hong Uhaeng's allegation that Pak Sedang's action could be justified on the basis of Kim Changsaeng's preference for ancient rites. See *Kyegamnok,* B VIII, 35a–42b. Later, in 1710, at the instigation of Censor-General Chŏng Ho, Pak Sedang's third son, T'aehan, was imprisoned for disobeying the court order and for his failure to perform proper ancestral rites. See *Kyegamnok,* B XI–XIV, 51a–60b; *Sukchong sillok,* 48: 19a–20b, 30a–31b.

78. *Sukchong sillok,* 43: 3b.

79. *Kyegamnok,* B IX, 43b–47a; *Sukchong sillok,* 44: 4a; *Sukchong sillok,* po'gwŏl chŏngo, 44B: 1b–2a.

80. *Myŏnggokchip,* 7: 29b–31a.

81. Pak Sech'ae's *Ch'unch'u pojŏn* (Annotations to the *Ch'un-ch'iu*) was printed at the same time.

82. *Myŏnggokchip,* 8: 2a–3a; *Sukchong sillok,* 34: 2: 11b, 47: 5a–b.

83. *Sukchong sillok,* 47: 3b–5b.

84. Ibid., 47: 6a–b.

85. *Myŏnggokchip,* 20: 11a–14b; *Sukchong sillok,* 47: 6b–7a.

86. *Sukchong sillok,* 47: 7b–8a, 9a.

87. Ibid., 47: 11a–12b.

88. Ibid., 47: 15b–17a, 18a, 18b–19a, 24b.

89. Ibid., 47: 17a, 19a, 19b, 20a, 21b.

90. Ibid., 47. 24b–26b, 26b–27a, 27b.

91. Ibid., 47: 27b–28b, 28b–29a; *Myŏnggokchip,* 20: 27a–29a.

92. *Sukchong sillok,* 47: 29a–b.

93. Ibid., 47: 33a.

94. Ibid., 47: 46b, 47b, 48a.

95. Ibid., 48: 8b, 11b, 11b–12a, 12a–b, 12b–13a.

96. *Kyegamnok*, B X, 47b–51a, XI, 51a–53a; *Sukchong sillok*, 48: 18b–20b; Chŏng Ho, *Changam sŏnsaengjip*, 6: 1a–7a, 9: 5a–b.

97. *Sukchong sillok*, 48: 20b–21a, 21a–b, 23b–24a, 39b, 49: 1b–3b, 4a–b, 5a–b, 6a.

98. Ibid., 50A: 1b, 54: 22b, 23a, 33b, 55: 1bff, 56: 24b; *Myŏnggokchip*, 10: 43a–44b.

99. *Kyegamnok*, B XXIV, 86a; *Kyŏngjong sillok*, 9: 7b, 9b–10b. Later there were several requests to remove Ch'oe Sŏkchŏng from Sukchong's shrine, but King Yŏngjo rejected them all. *Yŏngjo sillok*, 8: 21b–23a, 9: 31b.

100. *Sukchong sillok*, 38B: 6a.

101. For a discussion of the changes in the Munmyo in 1682, see Chŏng Okcha, *Chosŏn hugi munhwa undongsa* (Seoul: Ilchogak, 1990), pp. 11–15. The three Sung scholars were Yang Shih (1053–1135), who was a disciple of the two Ch'eng brothers, Yang's disciple Lo Ts'ung-yen (1072–1135), and Li Tung (1088–1158), who was Lo's disciple and Chu Hsi's teacher. Chu Hsi's principal disciple and son-in-law, Huang Kan (1152–1221), was subsequently added to the list.

102. For a discussion of factionalism at the beginning of the seventeenth century, see O Such'ang, "Injo tae chŏngch'i seryŏk ŭi tonghyang," *Han'guk saron* 13 (1985): 66–74.

103. *Sukchong sillok*, 49: 2a.

104. Han U'gŭn, "Paekho Yun Hyu yŏn'gu," pt. I, p. 25.

105. Yun Sasun, "Pak Sedang ŭi sirhak sasang e kwanhan yŏn'gu," p. 207.

106. See Ch'oe Sŏkchŏng's letter to Chŏng Chedu (dated 1692) in *Myŏnggokchip*, 13: 59a–60b.

107. Yun Sasun ("Pak Sedang ŭi sirhak sasang e kwanhan yŏn'gu," pp. 250–53) has recently suggested that Pak Sedang's thought was also influenced by his Taoist studies. Pak Sedang, the Taoist scholar, has not yet been fully studied, and this connection cannot be taken into consideration here.

108. Kai-wing Chow has made these points clear in his *Rise of Confucian Ritualism in Late Imperial China*, pp. 129–35, 167–68.

109. See Mark Setton, "Factional Politics and Philosophical Development in the Late Chosŏn," *Journal of Korean Studies* 8 (1992): 37–80.

110. For a discussion of Yi Ik's Classical scholarship, see Han U'gŭn, *Sŏngho Yi Ik yŏn'gu* (Seoul: Sŏul taehakkyo ch'ulp'anbu, 1980), pp. 28–36.

## Robert E. Buswell, Jr., *Buddhism Under Confucian Domination*

I am especially grateful to Professor W. J. Boot of the University of Leiden, the respondent to the conference paper from which this article derives, for his extremely careful and detailed reading of that earlier draft and for his many valuable suggestions for revision. I have also benefited from the astute comments and queries of JaHyun Kim Haboush and Martina Deuchler, the two editors of the volume.

1. For background on the socioeconomic and ideological role of Buddhism in traditional Korea, see An Kyehyŏn, *Han'guk Pulgyosa yŏn'gu* (Seoul: Tonghwa ch'ulp'ansa, 1986), esp. pp. 289–94. I have surveyed briefly the place of Buddhist monasteries in Korean society in my book, *The Korean Approach to Zen: The Collected Works of Chinul* (Honolulu: University of Hawaii Press, 1983), pp. 17–21, and in the paperback abridgment of that book, *Tracing Back the Radiance: Chinul's Korean Way of Zen*, Classics in East Asian Buddhism, no. 2 (Honolulu: University of Hawaii Press, for the Kuroda Institute, A Kuroda Institute Book, 1991), pp. 17–21.

2. For surveys of the restrictions on Buddhism during the Chosŏn period, see An Kyehyŏn, *Han'guk Pulgyosa yŏn'gu*, pp. 288–89; U Chŏngsang and Kim Yŏngt'ae, *Han'guk Pulgyosa* (Seoul: Sinhŭng ch'ulp'ansa, 1976), pp. 134–38; Yi Kiyŏng, *Han'guk ŭi Pulgyo* (Seoul: Sejong Taewang kinyŏm saŏphoe, 1974), pp. 159–62; and Kamata Shigeo, *Chōsen Bukkyōshi* (Tokyo: Tokyo University Press, 1987), pp. 202–13. The most thorough, even if at times supercilious, coverage of Chosŏn Buddhism remains Takahashi Tōru, *Richō Bukkyō* (1929; reprinted—Tokyo: Kokusho kankōkai, 1973). My account is indebted to these, and other, sources.

3. For a masterful discussion of these four anticlerical arguments, as well as the Buddhist response, see Erik Zürcher, *The Buddhist Conquest of China: The Spread and Adaptation of Buddhism in Early Medieval China* (Leiden: E. J. Brill, 1959), 1: 254–85.

4. Ibid.

5. For his biography, see *Koryŏ-sa*, ed. Chŏng Inji (1396–1478) et al., photolithographic reprint (Seoul: Asea Munhwasa, 1983), 115: 1a–28a.

6. For Yi Saek's contacts with Buddhism, see An Kyehyŏn, "Yi Saek ŭi Pulgyo kwan," in idem, *Pulgyo sahak nonjŏk* (Seoul, 1965), pp. 99–127.

7. See discussion of this memorial in Chai-sik Chung, "Chŏng Tojŏn: 'Architect' of Yi Dynasty Government and Ideology," in Wm. Theodore de Bary and JaHyun Kim Haboush, eds., *The Rise of Neo-Confucianism in Korea* (New York: Columbia University Press, 1985), p. 75; and John Isaac Goulde, "Anti-Buddhist Polemic in Fourteenth and Fifteenth Century Korea: The Emergence of Confucian Exclusivism," (Ph.D. diss., Harvard University, 1985), pp. 177–79. Goulde's dissertation is helpful in understanding the wider East Asian contexts of the Buddhist persecution during the Chosŏn.

8. See the memorial in *Koryŏ-sa*, 111: 34b–35a; noted and discussed in Goulde, "Anti-Buddhist Polemic," p. 186.

9. For Chŏng's role in initiating the anti-Buddhist policies of the Chosŏn, see Chai-sik Chung, "Chŏng Tojŏn," pp. 75–80.

10. "Once he [T'aejo] went to a monastery to make offerings to the Buddha. He then said, 'Yi Saek is one of the great Confucians of his generation.

Yet even he revered the Buddha!'" *T'aejo sillok* in Kuksa p'yŏnch'an wiwŏn-hoe, ed., *Chosŏn wangjo sillok* (Seoul: T'amgudang, 1982), 2: 16a15, 2: 20b15–21a2. See also discussion in Goulde, "Anti-Buddhist Polemic," pp. 214–15.

11. *T'aejong sillok*, 1: 3a–4b; cited in Goulde, "Anti-Buddhist Polemic," p. 223.

12. *T'aejong sillok*, 10: 7a; cited in Goulde, "Anti-Buddhist Polemic," p. 226.

13. For these seven schools, see Kim Yŏngsu, "Ogyo yangjong e tae-haya," *Chindan hakpo* 8 (1937): 74–101; cited in Hee-sung Keel, *Chinul: The Founder of the Korean Sŏn Tradition*. Berkeley Buddhist Studies Series, no. 6 (Berkeley, Calif.: Center for South and Southeast Asian Studies, 1984), pp. 164–65 n9.

14. Yi Sangbaek estimates that some 2,000 monasteries and 17,000 acres of land were expropriated by the government, with some 10,000 monastery slaves turned over to the army; see "Yu-Pul yanggyo kodae ŭi kiyŏn e tae-han il yŏn'gu," in idem, *Han'guk munhwasa yŏn'gu non'go* (1947; reprinted — Seoul: Ŭryu Munhwasa, 1954), pp. 120–21; cited in Goulde, "Anti-Buddhist Polemic," pp. 229–30.

15. An important point made by Keel, *Chinul*, p. 165. Before this time the term *Sŏnjong* (*Ch'an-tsung*) had been simply a generic name for a number of variant lineages of teachers that derived their lines from Bodhidharma, the putative founder of Ch'an, and not a specific sectarian designation; see Theodore Griffith Foulk, "The 'Ch'an School' and Its Place in the Buddhist Monastic Tradition" (Ph.D. diss., University of Michigan, 1987).

16. See his *Kwŏn su Chŏnghye kyŏlsa mun*, which I translated in *The Korean Approach to Zen*, pp. 97ff; and the discussion in the introduction to that book, pp. 21–22.

17. One of the earliest, and most explicit, attempts at such Buddho-Confucian accommodation appears in the Chinese *T'i-wei Po-li ching*, a Bud-dhist apocryphon, written ca. 462–64, which seeks to show the parallelisms between fundamental concepts of Confucian and Buddhist ethics. See Pelliot MS #3732, in *Tun-huang pao-tsang* (Taipei: Hsin-wen-feng, n.d.), 130: 284b; Makita Tairyō, *Gikyō kenkyū* (Kyoko: Jinbun kagaku kenkyūsho, 1976), p. 193. For a detailed study and exhaustively annotated translation of this im-portant text, see Kyoko Tokuno, "Byways in Chinese Buddhism: The *Book of Trapuṣa* and Indigenous Scriptures" (Ph.D. diss., University of California, Berkeley, 1993).

18. *Han'guk Pulgyo chŏnsŏ*, ed. Han'guk Pulgyo chŏnsŏ p'yŏnch'an wi-wŏnhoe (Seoul: Tongguk University Press, 1986), 7: 217–25 (hereafter cited as *HPC*, followed by volume, page, register, and line number, where rele-vant).

19. *Hyŏnjŏngnon*, *HPC*, 7: 217a21–b1, b9–11. The second sentence para-phrases *Ta-hsüeh* 1: 4, James Legge, *The Chinese Classics*, 1: 357: "The ancients who wished to illustrate illustrious virtue throughout the kingdom, first

ordered well their own States. Wishing to order well their States, they first regulated their families. Wishing to regulate their families, they first cultivated their persons. Wishing to cultivate their persons, they first rectified their hearts."

20. Following the Wŏn'gi-sa edition; *HPC*, 7: 217, collation note 15.

21. *Hyŏnjŏngnon, HPC*, 7: 217b24–c2. The pedigree of such equations in sinitic Buddhism is long; similar statements can be found in the fifth-century apocryphon *T'i-wei Po-li ching*; see note 17 to this chapter; and Tokuno, "Byways in Chinese Buddhism."

22. *Hyŏnjŏngnon, HPC*, 7: 218a12–18.

23. Ibid., 7: 225b8–13.

24. Virtually all Korean monks from the seventeenth century on belonged to the lineage of Hyujŏng or the collateral line of his dharma-brother Puhyu Sŏnsu (1534–1615), fellow disciples of the Sŏn master Puyong Yŏnggwan (1485–1571).

25. *HPC*, 7: 735a–c; a brief account of his life based on this text appears in Yi Nŭnghwa, *Chosŏn Pulgyo t'ongsa* (1918; reprinted—Seoul: Poryŏn'gak, 1979), 2: 336–37. The number of Korean works on Hyujŏng is voluminous. The most exhaustive study to date is Kim Yŏngt'ae, *Sŏsan taesa ŭi saengae wa sasang* (Seoul: Pag'yŏngsa, 1975). For a thorough treatment of Hyujŏng's thought, see Song Ch'ŏn'ŭn, "Hyujŏng ŭi sasang," in Sungsan Pak Kilchin paksa hwagap kinyŏm saŏphoe, ed., *Han'guk Pulgyo sasangsa: Sungsan Pak Kilchin paksa hwagap kinyŏm* (History of Korean Buddhist Thought, presented in commemoration of the sixtieth birthday of Sungsan, Dr. Pak Kilchin) (Iri: Wŏn Pulgyo sasang yŏn'guwŏn, 1975), pp. 831–77. In English, see also U Chong-sang, "High Priest Hyujong: Unity of Zen and Doctrinal Buddhism," *Korea Journal* 2 (Feb. 1973): 22–27. Studies on Hyujŏng's best-known work, *Sŏn'ga kwigam*, are listed below in note 32 to this chapter.

26. *Saguk Ilto taesŏnsa Ch'ŏnghŏdang pimyŏng*, in Chōsen sōtokufu, ed., *Chōsen kinseki sōran* (Keijō [Seoul]: Chōsen sōtokufu, 1919), 2: 853, line 9ff; the full inscription appears at ibid., pp. 852–55. See also Yi Nŭnghwa, *Chosŏn Pulgyo t'ongsa*, 1: 470, line 6.

27. *HPC*, 7: 735a15–18. The first line is a paraphrase of the enlightenment verse of P'ang Yün (740–808), the famous Layman P'ang; see *P'ang chü-shih yü-lu* 2, *Hsü-tsang ching* [*HTC*], 120: 39a.

28. *Ch'ŏnghŏdang pimyŏng*, in Yi Nŭng-hwa, *Chosŏn Pulgyo t'ongsa*, 1: 470, line 9; Yi Nŭnghwa, *Chosŏn Pulgyo t'ongsa*, 2: 336, line 7.

29. Hyujŏng is quoted as saying, "How could this be part of my original resolve to go forth into homelessness?" *Haengjang*, in *Ch'ŏnghŏdang chip*, appendix, *HPC*, 7: 735a19.

30. For a brief survey of these monks' militias, see U Chŏngsang and Kim Yŏngt'ae, *Han'guk Pulgyo sa*, pp. 141–42.

31. For the events surrounding Hyujŏng's death, see *Ch'ŏnghŏdang pimyŏng*, 2: 854; and Yi Nŭnghwa, *Chosŏn Pulgyo t'ongsa*, 1: 471 and 2: 337.

32. A comprehensive study of this text has been made by Sin Pŏbin, *Sŏsan taesa ŭi Sŏn'ga kwigam yŏn'gu* (Seoul: Sin'giwŏnsa, 1983). For a brief overview of the text, see Henrik H. Sorensen, "On the *Songa Kugam* [sic] by Sosan Taesa," *Proceedings of the 9th Annual Conference of the Association for Korean Studies in Europe* (Chantilly, France: Association for Korean Studies in Europe, 1985), pp. 276–86. For the many different recensions of this important Chosŏn dynasty Buddhist text, see U Chŏngsang, "Sŏn'ga kwigam ŭi kanhaeng yup'o ko," *Pulgyo hakpo* 14 (1977): 161–72. Portions of the text were translated by Rebecca Bernen, "Sŏsan Taesa and His *Handbook for Zen Students*" (B.A. thesis, Harvard University, 1978), a remarkable translation by any scholarly standard, but especially for an undergraduate. An idiosyncratic translation, which misses many of the Buddhist nuances of Hyujŏng's writing, is O'Hyun Park, *Essentials of Zen Buddhism (Chanjia Guijian by Tuiyin)* (Lakemont, Ga.: CSA Press, 1985).

33. *Samga kwigam, HPC,* 7: 625b.

34. "One gourd" (*ip'yo*) is an allusion to Confucius's praise in the *Analects* of his disciple Yen Hui's joy amid adversity. See *Lun-yü* 6: 9 (Legge 1: 188); noted also in *Mencius* 4B: 29: 2 (Legge 2: 335): "'Admirable indeed was the virtue of Hui! With a single bamboo dish of rice, a single gourd dish of drink, and living in his mean narrow lane, while others could not have endured the distress, he did not allow his joy to be affected by it. Admirable indeed was the virtue of Hui!'"

35. For Hyeso's stela inscription, see Yi Nŭnghwa, *Chosŏn Pulgyo t'ongsa,* 1: 105–12; no such reference appears in his stele, however.

36. *Chiri-san Ssanggye-sa chungch'ang ki,* in *Chŏnghŏdang chip, kwŏn* 5, *HPC,* 7: 705c2–12, 706b3–6, 10–13.

37. See *Chung-yung* 1: 1 (Legge, 1: 383): "What Heaven has conferred is called The Nature; an accordance with this nature is called The Path of Duty; the regulation of this path is called Instruction."

38. *Samga kwigam* 1, *HPC,* 7: 616a.

39. *Lao-tzu* 1.

40. *Samga kwigam* 2, *HPC* 7: 617c4–7, 10–14; 618b21–23; 618c7–9.

41. Hyujŏng seems to be alluding here to the preface to Kihwa's *Kŭmganggyŏng ogahae* (Five masters' commentaries to the *Diamond Sutra*); *HPC,* 7: 10a–b; and see Bernen, "Sŏsan Taesa," p. 132 n3.

42. Alluding to the forty-first case of the *Wu-men kuan, Taishō shinshū daizōkyō* (Revised tripiṭaka compiled during the Taishō Era), ed. Takakusu Junjirō and Watanabe Kaikyoku (Tokyo: Daizōkyōkai, 1924–35), no. 2005, 48: 298a20 (*T* 2005: 48: 298a20).

43. *Samga kwigam* 3, *HPC,* 7: 619a.

44. See Kwŏn Kijung, "Koryŏ hugi ŭi Sŏn sasang yŏn'gu," (Ph.D. diss., Tongguk University, 1986), pp. 163–67.

45. For Hyujŏng's views of Sŏn and Kyo, see Chŏng Hakkwŏn, "Kankoku Richō jidai Seikyō taishi no Zen-Kyō kan," in Sekiguchi Shindai,

ed., *Bukkyō no jissen genri* (Tokyo: Sankibō Busshorin, 1977), pp. 447–65; and Hee-Sung Keel, "Words and Wordlessness: Hyujong's Approach to Buddhism," *Korean Culture* 9, no. 3 (Fall 1988): 24–37.

46. For Chinul's influence on Hyujŏng, see Keel, *Chinul*, pp. 167–74.

47. *Sŏn'ga kwigam*, HPC, 7: 635b9. The three places where the Buddha transmitted the mind, according to Sŏn lore: the stūpa at Bahuputraka (Many Offspring), where he shared his seat with the elder Mahākāśyapa; Mount Gṛdhrakūṭa (Vulture Peak), where he held up the flower for all his assembly to see; and between the twin sāla trees after his death, where he exposed his feet three times through his coffin while Mahākāśyapa was circumambulating. All refer to Sŏn stories of the transmission of the dharma to his eventual successor, Mahākāśyapa. The quote is taken from Chinul's preface to his *Hwaŏmnon chŏryo* (Excerpts from the exposition of the *Flower Garland Sutra*), HPC, 4: 768a6–8; translated in Buswell, *The Korean Approach to Zen*, p. 25. Chinul gets the idea himself from Tsung-mi's *Preface to the Fountainhead of Ch'an* collection: "The sūtras [viz., Kyo] are the Buddha's words. Sŏn is the Buddha's mind" (*Ch'an-yüan chu-ch'üan chi tou-hsü* 1, T 2015.48: 400b10–11).

48. *Sŏn Kyo kyŏl*, HPC, 7: 657b5–9.

49. *Sŏn'ga kwigam*, HPC, 7: 636b2–6.

50. *Simbŏp yoch'o*, HPC, 7: 649b5–10.

51. Ibid., 648b5–15.

52. Ibid., 649a19–b2.

53. "Song of Sŏn," in ibid., 650c–651a.

54. *Sŏn Kyo sŏk*, HPC, 7: 655b22–c6.

55. Ibid., 656b7–9; noted in Keel, "Words and Wordlessness," p. 27.

56. *Simbŏp yoch'o*, HPC, 7: 649a11–14.

57. *Sŏn Kyo sŏk*, HPC, 7: 655a12–14. A close parallel to this passage appears in Hyujŏng's *Sŏn'ga kwigam* (HPC, 7: 636b18–20): "All the buddhas explain the bow; all the patriarchs explain the bowstring. The buddhas explained the unobstructed dharma, which then returned to the one taste. Sweeping away the traces of this one taste then revealed the one mind to which the patriarchs pointed."

58. *Sŏn Kyo kyŏl*, HPC, 7: 657c8–10.

59. Ibid., 658a3–9.

60. *Sŏn'ga kwigam*, HPC, 7: 635b24–c2.

61. *Sŏn Kyo sŏk*, HPC, 7: 656c–657a.

62. A point made by U Chŏngsang and Kim Yŏngt'ae (*Han'guk Pulgyosa*, p. 158).

63. *Sŏnmun sugyŏng*, HPC, 10: 514–527. For studies of this text, see, among other works, Nukariya Kaiten, *Chōsen Zenkyōshi*, trans. Chŏng Hogyŏng as *Chosŏn Sŏn'gyo sa* (1930; reprinted—Seoul: Poryŏn'gak, 1978), pp. 632–67; and Han Kidu, *Han'guk Sŏn sasang yŏn'gu* (Seoul: Ilchisa, 1991), pp. 546–93.

Boudewijn Walraven, *Popular Religion in a*
*Confucianized Society*

Financial assistance for gathering materials for this article in Korea was provided by the Netherlands Organization for Scientific Research.

ABBREVIATIONS

AA    Akamatsu Chijō and Akiba Takashi, *Chōsen fūzoku no kenkyū* (Seoul: Ōsaka yagō shoten, 1937–38), 2 vols.

RS    *Richō kakushu bunken fūzoku kankei shiryō satsuyō*, comp. by Chōsen sōtokufu chūsūin (Seoul: Chōsen sōtokufu, 1944).

TY    *Taedong yasŭng (Kugyŏk-)*, 2d ed., ed. and trans. Minjok munhwa ch'ujinhoe (Seoul: Minjok munhwa mun'go kanhaenghoe, 1985), 18 vols.

EPIGRAPH: Hyoch'ŏm's exclamation is reported by his descendant Ŏ Sukkwŏn (1524–54) in *P'aegwan chapki*: *TY*, 1: 737.

1. Popular religion in the Korean context may refer to many things: to the beliefs and practices associated with shamans, to certain forms of Buddhism, and to a range of beliefs that cannot be assigned to any major religious tradition. To keep the term manageable, however, I limit its meaning to the beliefs and practices of shamans and closely related forms of religious activity such as rituals performed by ordinary people addressed to shamanic deities. It is open to discussion whether the mudang may rightfully be called shamans. If a shaman is defined as a religious specialist who derives his or her authority from a socially recognized ability to enter into personal communication with deities and spirits through ecstasy or possession in rituals performed on behalf of others, then the mudang is a shaman.

The mudang are the focus of a study of popular religion in the Chosŏn period that appeared after the present paper was written: Yi P'iryŏng, "Chosŏn hugi ŭi mudang kwa kut," *Chŏngsin munhwa yŏn'gu* 53 (1993): 3–39.

2. The term "civilizing process" is used here in the sense Norbert Elias gave it in his classic pioneering study: *Über den Prozess der Zivilisation. Soziogenetische und psychogenetische Untersuchungen* (Basel: Haus zum Falken, 1939); trans. Edmund Jephcott, in 2 vols.: *The Civilizing Process: The History of Manners* (New York: Urizen Books, 1978) and *Power and Civility: The Civilizing Process 2* (New York: Pantheon Books, 1982). Elias examines the connections among such different things as state formation, tax collection, the suppression of aggressive impulses, and table manners. His use of the term does not imply a value judgment or a deterministic concept of inevitable evolution.

3. Buddhism, for example, increasingly became a form of popular religion because of the lack of elite support. The subsequent rapprochement

between Buddhism and mudang practices deserves investigation, but for lack of space I cannot pursue this topic here.

4. Cf. Peter Burke, *Popular Culture in Early Modern Europe* (Aldershot, Eng.: Wildwood House, 1988), pp. 270–81.

5. One of the most striking examples is the eventual complete acceptance of the Confucian ancestral sacrifice, *chesa*, by all men, irrespective of class.

6. For the notion of cultural capital, see Pierre Bourdieu, *Outline of a Theory of Practice*, trans. Richard Nice (Cambridge: Cambridge University Press, 1991), pp. 171–83.

7. The story by Pak Chiwŏn is included in Yi Kawŏn, comp. and trans., *Yijo hanmun sosŏl sŏn* (Seoul: Minjung sŏgwan, 1961). Significantly, the low-class butcher who wants to become a yangban fails to see the attractions of this lifestyle. The book about yangban etiquette was written by Yi Tŏngmu (1741–93): *Sasojŏl* (2d ed.: Seoul: Myŏngmundang, 1987). Cf. Boudewijn Walraven, "The Confucianization of Korea as a Civilizing Process," in Academy of Korean Studies, comp., *The Universal and Particular Natures of Confucianism* (Sŏngnam: Academy of Korean Studies, 1994), pp. 535–56.

8. This tendency is especially associated with the philosopher Hsün Tzu and reflected in the *Li-chi* (Book of rites); see Patricia Buckley Ebrey, *Confucianism and Family Rituals in Imperial China: A Social History of Writing About Rites* (Princeton: Princeton University Press, 1991), pp. 26–33; Michael Kalton, "Early Yi Dynasty Neo-Confucianism," in Laurel Kendall and Griffin Dix, eds., *Religion and Ritual in Korean Society* (Berkeley: University of California, Institute of Asian Studies, 1987), p. 23.

9. Cf. Irene Bloom, *Knowledge Painfully Acquired: The "K'un-chih chi" by Lo Ch'in-shun* (New York: Columbia University Press, 1987), p. 41. The discussion of this aspect of Neo-Confucian philosophy as understood by Koreans is based on Michael Kalton's ("Early Yi Dynasty Neo-Confucianism") rendering of the views of Kwŏn Kŭn.

10. *T'aejong sillok*, 1: 7b–8a; Boudewijn Walraven, "Confucians and Restless Spirits," in Leonard Blussé and Harriet T. Zurndorfer, eds., *Conflict and Accommodation in Early Modern East Asia: Essays in Honour of Erik Zürcher* (Leiden: E. J. Brill, 1993), pp. 71–93.

11. Yi Chunghwan, *T'aengniji*, in one volume with Pak Chega, *Pukhak ŭi* (Seoul: Taeyang sŏjŏk, 1972), p. 184. Chŏng Mongju was killed by the Yi after he refused to serve the new dynasty.

12. Yi Chunghwan, *T'aengniji*, p. 184. The young girls who served at the shrine claimed that the deity visited them at night.

13. Yi Ik, *Sŏngho sasŏl* (Seoul: Kyŏnghŭi ch'ulp'ansa, 1967), 2: 333–34 ("Kwisin honbaek").

14. Ibid., 1: 114 ("Sŏnghwangmyo"); ibid., 1: 471–72 ("Hasang manghon"); ibid., 1: 520 ("Manghon").

15. Chŏng Yagyong, *Mongminsimsŏ*, in idem, *Chŏng Tasan sŏ* (Seoul: Munhŏn p'yŏnch'an wiwŏnhoe, 1961), 3: 538.

16. Yi Kawŏn, *Yijo hanmun sosŏl sŏn*, pp. 491–99.

17. Ibid., p. 500.

18. My emphasis differs somewhat from that of Kalton, who stresses the contrast with the popular view of spirits; "Early Yi Dynasty Confucianism," pp. 24–25.

19. Ebrey, *Confucianism and Family Ritual*, p. 32: "Hsün Tzu may well have thought that only commoners could believe that sacrifices affected the spirits of the dead, but there seems little doubt that the bulk of the population, including the bulk of the educated, believed in the persistence of conscious spirits of the dead and the ability of their living descendants to influence them or aid them through burial practices and sacrificial rites."

20. Kalton, "Early Yi Dynasty Neo-Confucianism," p. 16.

21. Sŏng Pyŏnghŭi, comp., *Min'gan kyenyŏsŏ* (Seoul: Hyŏngsŏl ch'ulp'ansa, 1982), p. 98 (from *Kyubŏm*, "Guidelines for the Women's Quarters," probably written by a woman in the middle of the eighteenth century).

22. JaHyun Kim Haboush, *A Heritage of Kings: One Man's Monarchy in the Confucian World* (New York: Columbia University Press, 1988), pp. 35–37.

23. It was impossible, therefore, to control the mudang by instituting an examination system for their ordination, such as was devised for Buddhism; cf. *Kyŏngguk taejŏn* (Seoul: Ilchisa, 1978), 3,45b.

24. *Sejong sillok*, 101: 34b–35a; *Tongnip sinmun*, 26/6, 1896 (about a woman possessed by the spirit of the statesman Min T'aeho).

25. The tension created in such instances is inherent in any situation in which a hierarchic organization is confronted with disturbing elements beyond its control. Although a detailed comparison obviously is impossible here, there are strikingly similar tendencies in European and Korean developments. In Europe, too, direct communication between the divine and persons outside the official hierarchy was discouraged. The Catholic church did not deny the possibility of direct intervention of the divine in the lives of individuals through miracles but was increasingly skeptical of concrete claims of miraculous happenings. See R. Muchembled, *Culture populaire et culture des élites dans la France moderne (XVe–XVIIIe siècles)* (Paris: Flammarion, 1978), pp. 266–67.

26. Ch. Dallet, *Histoire de l'église de Corée* (Paris: Victor Palmé, 1874), pp. cxlix–cl.

27. Haboush, *Heritage of Kings*, pp. 7–10; Young-Chan Ro, *The Korean Neo-Confucianism of Yi Yulgok* (Albany: State University of New York Press, 1989), pp. 33–35; p. 35: "moral cultivation was the one way to bring *yin* and *yang* into balance with the mind, harmonize the *ch'i*, and thus correct both society and the natural order."

28. Yi Chunghwan, *T'aengniji*, p. 245.

29. See the following by Park Seong-rae: "Portentography in Korea," *Journal of Social Sciences and Humanities* 46 (1977): 54–71; "Portents in Korean History," *Journal of Social Sciences and Humanities* 47 (1978): 31–92; "Rise of

Confucian Portentology," *Journal of Social Sciences and Humanities* 48 (1978): 1–45; "Portents and Neo-Confucian Politics in Korea, 1392–1519," *Journal of Social Sciences and Humanities* 49 (1979): 53–117.

30. Frits Vos, "A Chinese Book in a Korean Disguise," in *Cahiers d'études coréennes* 5 (1989): 327–50. Cf. also *T'aejo sillok*, 2: 5a; *Sŏngjong sillok*, 86: 16a; Yi Ik, *Sŏngho sasŏl*, 1: 491 ("Poksŏn hwaŭm").

31. Such rituals have been called "magical" and explained as mere concessions to tradition, or to the expectations of the population, by officials who did not really believe in the rituals' efficacy. See Han Ugŭn, "Chosŏn wangjo ch'ogi e issŏsŏ ŭi yugyo inyŏm ŭi silch'ŏn kwa sinang chonggyo: saje munjerŭl chungsim ŭro," *Hanguk saron* 3 (1976): 147–228. I do not think the evidence on this point is convincing. There is material to suggest the contrary as well. See Boudewijn Walraven, "Confucians and Shamans," *Cahiers d'Extrême-Asie* 6 (1991–92): 36–37. Cf. also the remarks made above about the meaning of "belief" in the performance of ritual.

32. Haboush, *Heritage of Kings*, p. 38. Haboush also points out the political advantages to be derived from the performance of such rituals. Cf. Walraven, "Confucians and Restless Spirits." Of course, one should keep in mind that rituals could be performed for several reasons simultaneously (magical, religious, social, or political), or with different motives dominating at different times according to the concrete situation. In any case, such rituals were beyond reproach from a Confucian point of view inasmuch as they were for the public benefit and performed by authorized public officials. They certainly did make sense to the common people, who attributed droughts, epidemics, and other misfortunes to the resentments and anger of spirits and deities and felt that these invisible forces should be pacified by ritual, but this does not mean that from a Confucian point of view they were incorrect.

33. Yi Kyugyŏng, *Oju yŏnmun changjŏn san'go* (Seoul: Tongguk munhwasa, 1959), 2: 380 (*kw*. 43); *Taehan maeil sinbo*, 11/5, 1909.

34. Pak Chiwŏn's story *Yangban chŏn* criticizes the way in which symbolic capital could be transformed into economic benefits. The object of attack in this tale is an impoverished *yangban* who receives grain from the magistrate for no reason other than that his scholarship commands respect.

35. Song Siyŏl, "Kyenyŏsŏ," in Yi Hunsŏk, comp., *Han'guk ŭi yŏhun* (Seoul: Taewŏnsa, 1990), pp. 29–30.

36. Pierre Bourdieu, *La distinction: critique sociale du jugement* (Paris: Les Editions de Minuit, 1979).

37. Chŏng Tasan, *Chŏng Tasan chŏnsŏ*, 3: 447.

38. *Sejong sillok*, 45: 23b–24a.

39. It would, of course, be wrong to deny the peasant moral views and motives, but his need would lend his petitions for material benefits an urgency the yangban would not feel.

40. A yangban vexed by serious illness, for instance, might give up his reservations with regard to the mudang. Cf. Laurel Kendall, *Shamans, Housewives and Other Restless Spirits: Women in Korean Ritual Life* (Honolulu: University of Hawaii Press, 1985), p. 32.

41. Certain sacrifices offered by the court, moreover, seemed to defy a "social" or nonliteral interpretation altogether. Here one may think of the sacrifices to deities worshipped when there was pestilence among horses and cows. See *Yŏngjo sillok*, 31: 10b, 70: 14a,b; *Chŏngjo sillok*, 47: 1b, 2a–2b.

42. In "Confucians and Shamans," pp. 21–44, I list some of the similarities between Confucianism and shamanism. One important point I do not discuss here is the concept of ritual purity.

43. It is possible that in the Three Kingdoms shamans occupied a rather prominent place in society. It has even been suggested that some of the early rulers were shamans. See, e.g., Carter J. Eckert et al., *Korea, Old and New: A History* (Seoul: Ilchokak, 1990), pp. 19, 22–23. Unfortunately, so little is known about the concrete form of rituals in this period that every theory concerning the nature of "shamanism" in the Three Kingdoms is highly speculative. Cf. Yi Nŭnghwa, "Chosŏn musokko," *Kyemyŏng* 19 (1927): 3–5.

44. E.g., *Koryŏsa* (Seoul: Yŏnhŭi taehakkyo, 1955), 17: 16a.

45. Yi Nŭnghwa, "Choson musokko," pp. 7, 8–9; *Koryŏsa*, 85: 17a–18b and 78: 42b; cf. 33: 9a.

46. Han Ugŭn, "Chosŏn wangjo ch'ogi."

47. E.g., *T'aejo sillok*, 2: 6a; *Sejong sillok*, 101: 34b–35a; *Kyŏngguk taejŏn*, 5: 7a, 8a,b.

48. *Sejong sillok*, 49: 12a–14a. Sacrifices were divided into three classes: great, middling, and small. The last two classes had several categories of nature deities, such as gods of streams, seas, and mountains. The review of deities was to decide which gods would qualify to be incorporated in these categories.

49. In China, the Ming and Ch'ing governments from time to time recognized popular cults by conferring titles on certain deities to acknowledge their merits. See Stephan Feuchtwang, *The Imperial Metaphor: Popular Religion In China* (London: Routledge, 1992), p. 160.

50. Deuchler, "Neo-Confucianism in Action," in Kendall and Dix, eds., *Religion and Ritual in Korean Society*, pp. 33–36.

51. There is little information on what this entailed in practice. At least some of the proceeds of the mudang tax seem to have been used for the maintenance of this agency. See *Man'gi yoram*, 2 vols. (Keijō: Chōsen sōtokufu chūsūin, 1937), pp. 309, 443 ("Chaeyongp'yŏn"). Presumably this meant that in times of need, during epidemics for example, the mudang could be summoned for a form of corvée labor. There are indications that mudang tried to escape registration; see *Sejong sillok*, 101: 35a.

52. Yi Ik, *Sŏngho sasŏl*, 1: 114 ("Sŏnghwangmyo"), 1: 217 ("Mu"). For the

tax in general, see also Rim Haksŏng, "Chosŏn sidae muse chedo wa kŭ silt'ae," *Yŏksa minsokhak* 3 (1993): 90-126.

53. *Yukchŏn chorye*, facsimile of the original ed. of 1867 in 2 vols. (Seoul: Kyŏngmunsa, 1979), 1: 410.

54. *Sejong sillok*, 53: 5a-b, 102: 8b; *Sŏngjong sillok*, 98: 28b; *Ch'ugwan chi* (Keijō: Chōsen sōtokufu chūsūin, 1939), pp. 863-64.

55. E.g., *Chungjong sillok*, 10: 27b.

56. *Kyŏngguk taejŏn*, 2: 18b.

57. At the end of the Chosŏn period, people still called mudang who served the women of the royal family *kungmu* (or rather: *nara-mudang*, its purely Korean equivalent), but the term does not, at that time, seem to have been an official appellation.

58. *Sugyo chimnok*, in *Sugyo chibyo* (Keijō: Chōsen sōtokufu chūsūin, 1943), p. 207; see also p. 210 for a prohibition on performing "immoral rituals" (*ŭmsa*) within a radius of ten Korean miles from the capital. For instance, the *Sugyo chimnok* of 1698 contains a decree dating to 1568 which states that *all* mudang *should be expelled from Seoul* (emphasis added).

59. *Chŏngjo sillok*, 1: 44b; *Taejŏn hoet'ong (Kugyŏk -)*, trans. Han'guk kojŏn kugyŏk wiwŏnhoe (Seoul: Koryŏ taehakkyo ch'ulp'anbu, 1960), p. 229.

60. Yi Nŭnghwa, "Chosŏn musokko," p. 15.

61. Ch'oe Kilsŏng, *Han'guk musok non* (Seoul: Hyŏngsŏl ch'ulp'ansa, 1981), pp. 83-90.

62. *Injo sillok*, 36: 29a-b; Murayama Chijun, *Chōsen no fugeki* (Keijō: Chōsen sōtokufu, 1932), p. 175. For an instance of a rain ritual with mudang participation performed on royal command in 1604, see *Ŭngch'ŏn illok, kw* 1, 4th month, 28th day, in *TY*, 11: 16.

63. Yi Kŭngik, *Yŏllyŏsil kisul, (Kugyŏk-)* (Seoul: Minjokmunhwa ch'ujinhoe, 1966), 9: 665. The Office of Rites was under the Ministry of Rites and was charged with practical matters relating to the state rituals (cf. *Taejŏn hoet'ong*, p. 56; *Man'gi yoram*, pp. 87-89, 89-90, 170). It kept the wooden tablets that were used in rituals to represent the deities. The *T'aesang chi* is at present available in a facsimile of the 1873 edition compiled by Yi Kŭnmyŏng (in six *kwŏn*, without pagination) (Seoul: Munhwajae kwalliguk Changsŏgak, 1974). An earlier edition appeared in 1840. The abolition of rain rituals by mudang and *p'ansu* is mentioned near the end of *kwŏn* 4. Yi Ik (*Sŏngho sasŏl*, 1: 217 ["Mu"]) also confirms that the ritual codes did not refer to the employment of mudang.

64. G. H. Jones, "The Spirit Worship of the Koreans," *Transactions of the Korea Branch of the Royal Asiatic Society* 2 (1902): 52-53.

65. Chŏng Yagyong, *Mongminsimsŏ*, 3: 447. When Chŏng mentions the use of shamans in this passage, he refers to their employment in Chinese antiquity.

66. Dallet, *Histoire de l'église de Corée*, p. cxxxix. Cf. a description of a Chinese rain ritual in the nineteenth century in which a local magistrate acts

together with Buddhists and Taoists, and the population also takes part (J. J. M. de Groot, *Jaarlijksche feesten en gebruiken van de Emoy-Chineezen* [Batavia: Bruining, 1881], 1: 53).

67. The material discussed here derives from the chapter on rain prayers in Murayama Chijun, *Sekiten, Kiu, Antaku* (Keijō: Chōsen sōtokufu, 1942), pp. 76–161.

68. The *Taejŏn hoet'ong*, 3: 294, contains a prohibition dating back to 1785 or earlier on the whipping of a mud dragon when praying for rain.

69. I have counted only the localities on which Murayama reports in detail. There are another 120-odd reports in telegraphic style in which mudang are not mentioned at all. Quite often, though, these reports indicate that the local magistrate led the prayers.

70. Murayama, *Sekiten*, pp. 79–81.

71. Ibid., pp. 85–87, 101–104. For Sŏnsan, the source of information is a gazetteer of the pre-colonial period.

72. Murayama, *Sekiten*, pp. 112–113.A special case is Kyŏngju in North Kyŏngsang province. There, during a period of serious drought in 1934, mudang organized rain prayers on their own initiative. It seems clear from the report that this was a new development.

73. Jones, "Spirit Worship of the Koreans," p. 39; Pak Kyehong, *Han'guk minsok yŏn'gu* (Seoul: Hyŏngsŏl ch'ulp'ansa, 1973), pp. 271–72.

74. Although this god wore a name borrowed from China, in practice a *sŏnghwang* was quite different from the Chinese City God, *ch'enghuang* (lit. God of Walls and Moats). Both *Sŏnghwang* and *ch'enghuang* were protectors of places, but the *sŏnghwang*, as a local tutelary god, inherited much of the character of the earlier mountain gods, who were also guardian deities. Cf. David Johnson, "The City-God Cults of T'ang and Sung China," *Harvard Journal of Asiatic Studies* 45, no. 1 (1985): 363–457; and Yu Tongsik, *Han'guk mugyo ŭi yŏksa wa kujo* (Seoul: Yŏnse taehakkyo ch'ulp'anbu, 1975), pp. 179–85.

75. Chŏng Yagyong, *Mongminsimsŏ*, 3: 443; Yi Nŭnghwa, "Chosŏn musokko," p. 47.

76. A truly comprehensive and systematic study of local gazetteers has not yet been carried out.

77. *(Sinjŭng) Tongguk yŏji sŭngnam* (Seoul: Minjok munhwa ch'ujinhoe, 1971), vol. 5, 39: 36a.

78. *Chungjong sillok*, 24: 16a, 25: 45a–b, 26: 46a–47a, 31: 12a.

79. Yi Nŭnghwa, "Chosŏn musokko," p. 7; cf. *Chŏn'guk chiri chi*, 3: 296. In most sources (e.g., *Sejong sillok*, 76: 25b, which concerns the official veneration of the god), this deity appears as a mountain god; this is illustrative of the confusion in Korea between mountain gods and *sŏnghwang*.

80. *Chŭngbo munhŏn pigo* (lithographic ed., Seoul: Tongguk munhwasa, 1959), 61: 25b. There is one earlier reference dating back to 996; see *Koryŏsa*, 90: 3a.

81. *Sejong sillok,* 76: 24a–27a. The same cults are mentioned in *T'aejong sillok,* 28: 14b.

82. *Kukcho orye ŭi* (Seoul: Kyŏngmunsa, 1979), 2: 99a–109a; Walraven, "Confucians and Restless Spirits."

83. Yi Hunsang, *Chosŏn hugi ŭi hyangni* (Seoul: Ilchogak, 1990), p. 164.

84. That, indeed, *sŏnghwang* shrines could be found everywhere by the end of the fifteenth century or the early sixteenth century is confirmed by the gazetteer *Sinjŭng Tongguk yŏji sŭngnam,* the main text of which dates to 1486, although in its definitive form it was published in 1530.

85. *Chŏn'guk chiri chi,* 3: 269.

86. *Chŏngjo sillok,* 35: 31a–b.

87. The popular concept of the *sŏnghwang* might emerge occasionally in epithets used on the wooden tablets representing the deities in the sacrifices. Thus, in one place the *sŏnghwang* was called "General-who-breaks-through-the-lines" (*chŏlch'ung changgun,* an official military rank), which was too reminiscent of the countless spirit-generals of the shamanic pantheon. See Yi Ik, *Sŏngho sasŏl,* 1: 114 ("Sŏnghwangmyo").

88. A comparison of the entries for Koksŏng (where, as we have seen, Sin Sunggyŏm was popularly regarded as the local *sŏnghwang*) in the *Sinjŭng Tongguk yŏji sŭngnam* (39: 36a) and in a later gazetteer, the *Tongguk yŏji chi* (*Chŏn'guk chiri chi,* 3: 348), which probably dates from the mid-seventeenth century, shows an interesting variation in the way the official *sŏnghwang* cult was dissociated from the worship of a personal deity. Whereas the *Sinjŭng Tongguk yŏji sŭngnam* notes only that Sunggyŏm was regarded as *sŏnghwang,* according to the *Tongguk yŏji chi* there was a separate shrine for Sin Sunggyŏm, apart from a regular *sŏnghwang* altar. At the shrine, a local magistrate (probably a descendant of Sin) and a provincial governor during the reign of King Sŏnjo (r. 1567–1608) had local families make sacrifices in spring and autumn. In this way, one could have a regular *sŏnghwang* cult while continuing to venerate Sin Sunggyŏm not so much as a tutelary deity but rather as an examplar of Confucian virtue: Sunggyŏm had sacrificed his own life to save his lord, the first king of Koryŏ. This solution must have had particular appeal for local members of the Sin family.

89. Romeyn Taylor, "Official and Popular Religion," in Kwang-Ching Liu, ed., *Orthodoxy in Late Imperial China* (Berkeley: University of California Press, 1990), pp. 149–53.

90. C. A. Clark, *Religions of Old Korea* (Seoul: Christian Literature Society of Korea, 1961), pp. 202–3.

91. Han Ugŭn, "Chosŏn wangjo ch'ogi," pp. 165–66.

92. Yi Kyugyŏng, *Oju yŏnmun chanjŏn san'go,* 2: 379.

93. Chŏng Yagyong (*Mongminsimsŏ,* 3: 447) mentions the example of Chŏng Ŏnhwang (1597–1672) who suppressed the cult of a Silla princess by setting fire to her shrine.

94. Yi Ik, *Sŏngho sasŏl*, 1: 114 ("Sŏnghwangmyo"); Yi Hongjik, *Sae kuksa sajŏn* (Seoul: Paengmansa, 1975), p. 1087. Yi's campaign is retold, with a new twist, in a mudang song, according to which he destroyed no less than 500 shrines. The gods of the few remaining shrines, however, demonstrated their power, and Yi, duly impressed, returned to the mainland, leaving the final victory to popular religion. In a sense this is historically accurate, since Yi's iconoclasm did not succeed in eradicating the irregular cults, which continue to flourish. Cf. Hyŏn Yongjun, *Chejudo musok charyo sajŏn* (Seoul: Sin'gu munhwasa, 1980), pp. 811–15.

95. *Chŏn'guk chiri chi*, 3: 243, 253.

96. Yi Ik (*Sŏngho sasŏl*, 1: 114 ["Sŏnghwangmyo"]) says that the magistrates did not forbid the worship of *sŏnghwang* by mudang and the people. He indignantly remarks that the reason for allowing irregular cults and the activities of mudang was that they provided the government with income from taxes (ibid., pp. 114, 217 ["Mu"]).

97. Hong Sŏngmo, *Tongguk sesigi*, 7th ed., ed. with three other texts and trans. Yi Sŏkho (Seoul: Üryu munhwasa, 1974), pp. 275–76. Cf. the *Sinjŭng Tongguk yŏji sŭngnam*, vol. 5, 32: 41a.

98. Hong Sŏngmo, *Tongguk sesigi*, p. 259.

99. *Imyŏng chi*, quoted in Yi Hunsang, *Chosŏn hugi ŭi hyangni*, p. 164.

100. This festival is still celebrated at present.

101. Yi Hunsang, *Chosŏn hugi ŭi hyangni*, chap. 1.

102. For an attempt to suppress it (in the fifteenth century), see Ŏ Sukkwŏn, *P'aegwan chapki* in *TY*, 1: 737. For evidence of the survival of the cult into the second half of the Chosŏn period, see Yi Sugwang, *Chibong yusŏl* (Keijō: Chōsen kosho kankōkai, 1915), 2: 205; and Yi Kyugyŏng, *Oju yŏnmun changjŏn san'go*, 2: 380.

103. Hong Sŏngmo, *Tongguk sesigi*, p. 264; about cults in Kunwi (North Kyŏngsang province), Samch'ŏk (Kangwŏn province), and Anbyŏn (South Hamgyŏng province).

104. Yi Hunsang, *Chosŏn hugi ŭi hyangni*, p. 164; *RS*, p. 932; *Ŭpchi* (Seoul: Asea munhwasa, 1981), 1: 195. In the last instance, a cult was resumed after a magistrate had destroyed the shrine because it was believed that the anger of the deity was behind an outbreak of fatal disease.

105. Chang Chugŭn and Ch'oe Kilsŏng, *Kyŏnggi-do chiyŏk musok* (Seoul: Munhwajae kwalliguk, 1967), p. 124.

106. Hwang Hyŏn, *(Chŏnyŏk) Maech'ŏn yarok*, with trans. by Im Pyŏngju (Seoul: Ch'ŏnggu munusa, 1980), 1: 293; also p. 116.

107. The most important source is Murayama Chijun, *Chōsen no burakusai* (Keijō: Chōsen sōtokufu, 1937); also see his *Sekiten*, pp. 162–248. For discussions of village festivals, see Yu Tongsik, *Han'guk mugyo ŭi yŏksa wa kujo*, pp. 238–57; and Ch'oe Kilsŏng, *Han'guk musok ŭi yŏn'gu* (Seoul: Asea munhwasa, 1978), pp. 287–335.

108. Cf. the report on a contemporary village festival by Yi Namsik, "Obongsansŏng sansinje wa tang-kosa," in idem, *Min'gan sinang* (Seoul: Minsokhakhoe, 1989), pp. 348–89.

109. In 1901, a newspaper article (*Cheguk sinmun*, 9/3, 1901) deplored the fact that shamans not only misled ignorant peasants but also were received in the houses of great officials and learned scholars. Attached to the offices of the magistrates in all thirteen provinces and all 350 counties were "official mudang" (*kwanmudang*). When a new magistrate took office, there would always be a ritual during which the mudang prayed for the help of the spirits (*kwisin*) to ensure that the people would prosper and that the official would, for his next appointment, obtain a high post.

110. Cf. Walraven, "Confucians and Shamans."

111. Han Ugŭn, "Chosŏn wangjo ch'ogi," pp. 158–63; Sin Hŭm, *Sangch'on chamnok*, in *TY*, 6: 56; *Sejong sillok*, 101: 34b–35a; Deuchler, "Neo-Confucianism in Action," pp. 52–53.

112. Interestingly, from modern evidence it appears that women were allowed even less scope in Korean ancestor worship than the most widely respected ritual handbook, Chu Hsi's *Chia-li*, permitted. Whereas Chu Hsi prescribed that women make the second offering (Ebrey, *Chu Hsi's Family Rituals* [Princeton: Princeton University Press, 1991] p. 163), this task in Korea was nearly always given to men. See Roger L. Janelli and Dawnhee Yim Janelli, *Ancestor Worship and Korean Society* (Stanford: Stanford University Press, 1982), p. 183. Also see Chang Ch'ŏlsu, *Han'guk chŏnt'ong sahoe ŭi kwanhon sangje*, 3rd ed. (Seoul: Han'guk chŏngsin munhwa yŏn'guwŏn, 1988) pp. 121–25.

113. *RS*, pp. 1402–3.

114. Yi Tŏngmu, *Sasojŏl*, pp. 258–59, 267; cf. Dallet, *Histoire de l'église de Corée*, pp. cvlviii–cxliv, about mudang rituals and sundry superstitious practices: "les maris, pour ne pas compromettre la paix de leur ménage, les tolèrent même en refusant d'y prendre part, de sorte que depuis le palais jusqu'à la dernière cabane, elles sont universellement pratiquées" (the husbands tolerate them for the sake of domestic peace, even if they refuse to take part in them, so that from the palace down to the meanest hovel they are universally practiced).

115. Walraven, "Confucians and Restless Spirits."

116. *Yŏngjo sillok*, 106: 24b. Yi Ik (*Sŏngho sasŏl*, 1: 187 ["Yŏkkwi"]) recognized that spirits were responsible for infectious diseases but thought that the prayers of the "ignorant people" were completely useless. For other views, see Donald Leslie Baker, "*Sirhak* Medicine: Measles, Smallpox, and Chŏng Tasan," *Korean Studies* 14 (1990): 135–66.

117. *Lun-yü* 7: 5 and 7: 35; *Chŏngjong sillok*, 3: 2b; Yi Ik, *Sŏngho sasŏl*, 2: 148–49 ("Pyŏngdo"), p. 165 ("Chilbyŏng haengdo"); *RS*, p. 1308; cf. (*Kyoju*) *Naebang kasa*, comp. Ch'oe T'aeho (Taegu: Hyŏngsŏl ch'ulpansa, 1980), p. 50 (a poem written to transmit Confucian values to women): "Your fate is

decided by Heaven / Follow it and blessed you will be." When members of the royal family were ill, objections against praying apparently carried less weight. Prayers at the royal ancestral hall, the altar of Soil and Grain (*sajik-tan*), or the mountains and rivers recognized as numinous in the official codes were the standard procedure in such cases.

118. Yi Tŏngmu, *Sasojŏl*, p. 266.

119. Ibid.

120. Song Siyŏl, "Kyenyŏsŏ," p. 29; also cf. Yi Tŏngmu, *Sasojŏl*, p. 258.

121. *(Kyoju) Naebang kasa*, p. 96.

122. E.g., *Sejong sillok*, 53: 5a–b.

123. Sŏng, *Min'gan kyenyŏsŏ* (from *Kyubŏm*), pp. 103–4; see also p. 126.

124. Ibid. (from *Yŏja ch'ohak*, "A Primer for Women," by Kim Chongsu, 1761–1831), p. 41.

125. *(Kyoju) Naebang kasa*, pp. 45–69 (most likely from the late nineteenth century).

126. *RS*, p. 1433.

127. Sŏng, *Min'gan kyenyŏsŏ*, p. 40 (*Yŏja ch'ohak*): "It is the task of a woman to be diligent in making clothes and food and doing the house-keeping." The text goes on to say that it is enough if a woman knows *han'gŭl* and that knowledge of Chinese characters only will give her airs.

128. *RS*, pp. 1256–57.

129. *Sukchong sillok*, 14B: 50a–b.

130. *Injo sillok*, 3: 3a. This alerts us to the fact that many yangban sons in their early youth, when still with their mothers, must have been in contact with shaman rituals. It is doubtful that the influence of such childhood experiences was completely eradicated by their formal education. This may be one explanation for the "backsliding" of yangban males in certain circumstances.

131. Divorce, nevertheless, was not a deed to be performed lightly. Cf. Martina Deuchler, "The Tradition: Women During the Yi Dynasty," in Sandra Mattielli, ed., *Virtues in Conflict: Tradition and the Korean Woman Today* (Seoul: RAS, 1977), pp. 34–37.

132. It was not absolutely necessary to seek the help of mudang for "women's problems," since women prayed on their own. There was even an important "Confucian" precedent for praying to obtain a son in that Confucius' parents had done so, but there was no prescribed form for this comparable to that for ancestor rituals. In Korea women would often go to the mountains to pray. Yi Nŭnghwa, *Chosŏn yŏsokko*, reprint with modern trans. (Seoul: Taeyang sŏjŏk, 1973), p. 420–21 (original pagination: 91–92).

133. *Chŏngjo sillok*, 45: 10a.

134. Hong Sŏngmo, *Tongguk sesigi*, pp. 256–57.

135. *AA*, 1: 574–75.

136. *AA* 1: 575–76. The rites for the gods of smallpox, for instance, were to a large extent for children (who had not yet acquired immunity). Corre-

spondingly, in shaman songs, the gods of smallpox, if slighted by the parents, attack the children. Sim Usŏng, "Sonnim kut," *Kiwŏn* 2, no. 1 (1974): 189. Cf. also Kendall, *Shamans, Housewives and Other Restless Spirits*, p. 165.

137. Kendall, *Shamans, Housewives and Other Restless Spirits*, pp. 72, 148.

138. Kang Hanyŏng, ed., *Sin Chaehyo p'ansori sasŏl chip*, 2d ed. (Seoul: Minjung sŏgwan, 1972), pp. 130–31.

139. Hwang Hyŏn, *Maech'ŏn yarok*, pp. 74–75. For an example of mudang ritual for children of the royal household early in the second half of the dynasty, see *Injo sillok*, 39: 19b.

140. Yi Nŭnghwa, "Chosŏn musokko," p. 15. Interestingly, there also exist forms of such adoption in popular Confucianism (see Griffin Mortimer Dix, "The East Asian Country of Propriety: Confucianism in a Korean Village" [Ph.D. diss., University of California, San Diego, 1977], p. 191ff) and other religions. I have seen the long pieces of cloth on which the names of the adoptive children are written in one of the annexes of the Waryongmyo on Namsan and in the Three Sages Hall (Samsŏngdang) of a Buddhist temple, the Hangnimsa. This is evidence of the demand for such divine protection.

141. Sŏng, *Min'gan kyenyŏsŏ*, p. 73 (from *Yŏgye yagŏn*, "Covenant of Rules for Women," by an anonymous author, presumably from the early nineteenth century).

142. Ibid., p. 90 (from *Yŏgye yagŏn*).

143. Ibid., p. 24 (from *Naejŏngp'yŏn*, "Household Management," by Kwŏn Ku, 1672–1749); cf. pp. 12 (*Naejŏngp'yŏn*) and 31–32 (*Yŏja ch'ohak*).

144. This was called *haengch'ae mullim*. Sŏ Taesŏk and Pak Kyŏngsin, *Ansŏng muga* (Seoul: Chimmundang, 1990), pp. 475–82.

145. *(Yŏkchu) Naebang kasa*, p. 67.

146. Cf. Kim Kwang-il, "Kut and the Treatment of Mental Disorders," in Chai-shin Yu and R. Guisso, eds., *Shamanism: The Spirit World of Korea* (Berkeley: Asian Humanities Press, 1988), pp. 131–61.

147. *Sunjo sillok*, 25: 9a–b, 9b–10a.

148. *Taehan maeil sinbo*, 20/6, 1908.

149. Janelli and Janelli, *Ancestor Worship*, p. 151. For evidence from the early twentieth century that a mudang worshipped the spirits of two princesses who had died of smallpox before they had married, see Ellen Salem, "Women Surviving: Palace Life in Seoul after the Annexation," in Mattielli, ed., *Virtues in Conflict*, p. 89.

150. Cf. the use of the term *aedŭl chosang* (child ancestors) in Sŏ and Pak, *Ansŏng muga*, p. 244; see also ibid., p. 243; and Janelli and Janelli, *Ancestor Worship*, pp. 151–53.

151. It is not known, unfortunately, by whom the rituals were performed, and whether it was by men or by women.

152. Walraven, "Confucians and Restless Spirits."

153. Janelli and Janelli (*Ancestor Worship*, pp. 118–19) present an interesting example of Confucian ritual offered to a paternal grandfather's sister who had died without offspring, after a mudang had divined that her resentful spirit had caused the death of several children.

154. Both *ant'aek* and *kosa* were rituals for the housegods, but the exact content of the terms appears to have differed by region. Sometimes the terms seem interchangeable. In certain cases, the difference was in scale (*ant'aek* being more elaborate than *kosa*), in others the time of performance was different (e.g., *kosa* in the tenth month and *ant'aek* at New Year). *Kosa* also has a more general meaning, referring to minor sacrifices of a different nature. See Kim T'aegon, *Han'guk musok yŏn'gu* (Seoul: Chimmundang, 1981), p. 66; and Murayama, *Sekiten*, pp. 276–78.

155. Murayama, *Sekiten*, pp. 287–91. Probably men also participated in some cases when the ritual was *not* Confucianized, an indication of the "in-between" nature of this kind of ritual; see ibid., pp. 258–59.

156. Kendall, *Shamans, Housewives and Other Restless Spirits*, p. 109.

157. Laurel Kendall (ibid., chap. 8) considers modern mudang rituals primarily household, not family, rituals.

158. Yi Nŭnghwa, "Chosŏn musokko," p. 53; *Yŏngjo sillok*, 49: 17a–b; Yi Ik, *Sŏngho sasŏl*, 1: 417 ("Wŏnbi chagyo"); Yi Kŭngik, *Yŏllyŏsil kisul*, 6: 644.

159. Murayama Chijun (*Chōsen no kijin* [Keijō: Chōsen sōtokufu, 1929], pp. 208–9) estimated that for over half of the women so honored the reason to do so was not admiration for their virtue but rather fear for the wrath of their spirits. Since he does not provide a source, it is impossible to judge the reliability of this. However, the existence of a double interpretation of the honors given to chaste women is telling.

160. *Yŏngjo sillok*, 49: 10b–11a.

161. *Sukchong sillok*, 59: 42a, 61: 24a, *T'aesang chi, kw.* 4.

162. Walraven, "Confucians and Restless Spirits."

163. Dix, "Country of Propriety," pp. 163–66.

164. Yi Kwanggyu, *Han'gugin ŭi ilsaeng* (Seoul: Hyŏngsŏl ch'ulp'ansa, 1985), p. 103. The custom of putting rice in the mouth is mentioned in the *Chia-li*, where it is also stated that coins should be placed there. No reference is made, however, to any words spoken in accompaniment. Ebrey, *Chu Hsi's Family Rituals*, p. 77.

165. Peter Brown, *The Cult of the Saints* (Chicago: University of Chicago Press, 1981); Lewis Lancaster, "Elite and Folk: Comments on the Two-Tiered Theory," in George A. DeVos and Takao Sofue, eds., *Religion and Family in East Asia* (Berkeley: University of California Press, 1986), pp. 87–95.

166. B. C. A. Walraven, *Songs of the Shaman: The Ritual Chants of the Korean Mudang* (London: Kegan Paul, 1994).

167. Wing-tsit Chan, "Neo-Confucianism as an Integrative Force in Chinese Life and Thought," in Laurence G. Thompson, ed., *Studia Asiatica* (San Francisco: Chinese Materials Center, 1975), p. 332.

168. Sŏ Taesŏk, *Han'guk muga ŭi yŏn'gu* (Seoul: Munhak sasangsa, 1980), p. 326. The child that is the fruit of his mother's prayers in this song is the Buddha Śākyamuni! (The childless king, in other words, is Śākyamuni's father.)

169. Ibid., p. 325.

170. Sŏ and Pak, *Ansŏng muga*, p. 477.

171. Park Il-young, "Minjung, Schamanismus und Inkulturation" (Ph.D. diss., University of Freiburg, Switzerland, 1988), p. 174.

172. *AA*, 1: 48–49.

173. Walraven, *Songs of the Shaman*, pp. 136–39.

174. For the position of Confucianism as moral orthodoxy in China, see Liu, ed., *Orthodoxy in Late Imperial China*, p. 2; and C. K. Yang, *Religion in Chinese Society* (Berkeley: University of California Press, 1961), chap. 11. In Korea, as in China, Confucian ethics not only affected shamanism. In a book about Zen, a prominent Korean monk devotes more than twenty-five pages to the Three Bonds and the Five Human Relations. Kusan Suryŏn, *Sŏksaja* (Seoul: Puril ch'ulpansa, 3rd ed.: 1987).

175. Sŏ Taesŏk, *Han'guk muga ŭi yŏn'gu*, p. 329.

176. *AA*, 1: 148–49. This does not mean that this cosmology was really important to the mudang, but it is a mark of the prestige of Confucianism.

177. *AA*, 2: 277–93. These texts are discussed by Dieter Eikemeier in an unpublished manuscript: "Beyond Performance: Shamans and Shamans' Courts."

178. *AA*, 2: 277–78, 281.

179. *AA*, 2: 286.

180. The question about the exact "sources of Confucian culture" cannot be answered here. It seems, however, that with the growth of the number of yangban (or those with yangban aspirations) in the later Chosŏn period, few villages were entirely without "civilizing agents." The preponderance of Confucian-style village rituals confirms this supposition.

181. Walraven, *Songs of the Shaman*, chap. 6.

182. *Taehan maeil ilbo*, 30/5, 1906; Cho Hung-youn, *Koreanischer Schamanismus* (Hamburg: Hamburgisches Museum für Völkerkunde, 1982), pp. 27–28. Among modern shamans, few traces remain of this classification.

183. Cf. Arthur P. Wolf and Robert J. Smith, "China, Korea, and Japan," in Kendall and Dix, eds., *Religion and Ritual in Korean Society*, p. 193. In Korea, Taoism was lacking as an institutional force but was available as a creed with the potential to straddle the gap between elite and popular religion.

184. For late imperial China, the use of Buddhist and Taoist priests in wedding and funeral ceremonies is described as a "widespread phenomenon," even though it was condemned by a few purists; see Charlotte Furth, "The Patriarch's Legacy: Household Instructions and the Transmission of Orthodox Values," in Liu, ed. *Orthodoxy in Late Imperial China*, p. 194.

185. James L. Watson, "Standardizing the Gods: The Promotion of T'ien Hou ("Empress of Heaven") Along the South China Coast, 960–1960," in D. Johnson, A. Nathan, and E. Rawski, eds., *Popular Culture in Late Imperial China* (Berkeley: University of California Press, 1985), p. 299.

186. Willem Jan Boot, "The Adoption and Adaptation of Neo-Confucianism in Japan: The Role of Fujiwara Seika and Hayashi Razan" (Ph.D. diss., University of Leiden, 1983), p. 204; Peter Nosco, "Introduction: Neo-Confucianism and Tokugawa Discourse," in idem, ed., *Confucianism and Tokugawa Culture* (Princeton: Princeton University Press, 1984), pp. 8, 10, 24; see also in the same volume, Herman Ooms, "Neo-Confucianism and the Formation of Early Tokugawa Ideology: Contours of a Problem," pp. 59–61.

187. I do not think this is the only factor. There seems to be a correlation, for instance, between religiousness and concern for the family, which may explain why Korean women, whose life is centered around the family, show such religious fervor.

188. Yi Ik, *Sŏngho sasŏl*, 1: 218 ("Mu").

189. They wear women's clothing during rituals; see Kendall, *Shamans, Housewives and Other Restless Spirits*, p. 27. Cf. Yi Ik, *Sŏngho sasŏl*, 1: 458 ("Nammu yŏbok").

190. For a comparative discussion of gender and religion in China, Korea, and Japan, see Wolf and Smith, "China, Korea, and Japan," pp. 191–95.

191. By contrast, mediums in nineteenth-century Europe who possessed enough education to speak in the language of mainstream culture addressed issues that were potentially of public concern. For example, they would convey messages from prominent theologians, which, if taken seriously, would have had great import. Luther appeared in a spiritualistic séance to renounce his doctrine of justification by faith. See Logie Barrow, *Independent Spirits: Spiritualism and English Plebeians, 1850–1910* (London: Routledge and Kegan Paul, 1986), p. 12.

192. Cf. *Sukchong sillok*, 18: 22b, and 19: 22b–23b (the latter about a mudang who was implicated in a movement of Maitreya millenarians).

193. Thus, in Bourdieu's (*Outline of a Theory of Practice*, p. 41) formulation, the power of the mudang, if any, was a "dominated power" that could operate only indirectly by recognizing the authority it used for its own ends.

194. Hwang Hyŏn, *Maech'ŏn yarok*, pp. 191–92, 305, 308–11; Yi Nŭnghwa, "Chosŏn musokko," p. 15.

## Don Baker, *Catholicism in a Confucian World*

This article began as a paper presented at a conference on Confucianism and late Chosŏn Korea held at UCLA in January 1992. Martina Deuchler, JaHyun Kim Haboush, Wm. Theodore de Bary, Peter Bol, Michael Kalton, and others at that conference pointed out weaknesses in my argument that made it less persuasive than it could have been. I have revised that paper in response to their criticisms, but the overall argument that remains and all surviving flaws in it are my sole responsibility.

1. Chŏng Yagyong, *Chŏng Tasan chŏnsŏ* (Seoul: Munhŏn p'yŏnch'an wiwŏnhoe, 1960), "Ch'i yangji pyŏn," 1: 245 (I: 12: 18a).

2. Chŏng, I: 12: 17b–19a. Tasan made a similar evaluation of the ideas of Mo Tzu and Yang Chu and of the impact of their guiding precepts on their followers; see "Maengja youi" (Essential points of the *Mencius*), pp. 660–61 (II: 5: 48b–49a).

3. Donald J. Munro, *The Concept of Man in Early China* (Stanford: Stanford University Press, 1969), p. ix. A similar point is made in Chad Hansen, "Chinese Language, Chinese Philosophy, and 'Truth,'" in *Journal of Asian Studies* 44, no. 3 (1985): 491–519.

4. *Basic Writings of Mo Tzu, Hsün Tzu, and Han Fei Tzu*, trans. Burton Watson (New York: Columbia University Press, 1967), p. 118.

5. Kwang-ching Liu, ed., *Orthodoxy in Late Imperial China* (Berkeley: University of California Press, 1990).

6. James Watson has made a similar argument in Tu Wei-ming et al., eds., *The Confucian World Observed* (Honolulu: East-West Center, 1992), p. 96. Watson argues that "rather than orthodoxy or correct belief, it is orthopraxy or correct practice that matters. It is not what people carry in their heads that matters; it is what they did on the ground that made them Confucian or Chinese or whatever."

7. *Analects* 2: 16.

8. See the translation by Arthur Waley, *The Analects of Confucius* (New York: Vintage Books, 1938), p. 91. "He who sets to work upon a different strand destroys the whole fabric."

9. Chŏng, II: 7: 31a, "Nonŏ ko'gŭmju" (Commentaries, old and recent, on the *Analects*).

10. Sin Hudam (1702–61) debated Catholic ideas with Yi Ik (1681–1763) in 1724, and Sin wrote his "Sŏhak pyŏn," a lengthy analysis of three Catholic missionary publications, shortly thereafter. For more information on Sin and his critical reaction to "Western learning," see my "The Use and Abuse of the Sirhak Label," *Kyohoesa yŏn'gu* 3 (1981): 183–254.

11. For a brief summary of the birth of the Korean Catholic church, see my "The Martyrdom of Paul Yun: Western Religion and Eastern Ritual in 18th Century Korea," *Transactions of the Royal Asiatic Society* 54 (1979): 33–58.

12. Sasoon Yun (Yun Sasun), in *Critical Issues in Neo-Confucian Thought: The Philosophy of Yi T'oegye*, trans. Michael C. Kalton (Seoul: Korea University Press, 1990), p. 31, says that T'oegye conceived of truth as "basically subjective practical knowledge that is directly related to moral conduct." Yun adds (p. 46): "The kind of truth that was T'oegye's main focus is the kind of practical knowledge or truth needed for the practice of morality rather than the objective sort of truth that is 'truth for the sake of truth.'"

13. Yi Ik, "Idan," *Sŏngho sasŏl yusŏn,* ed. An Chŏngbok (Seoul: Myŏngmundang, 1982), pp. 371–72.

14. An Chŏngbok, *Sunamjip* (Seoul: Sŏnggyun'gwan taehakkyo, Taedong munhwa yŏn'guwŏn, 1970), 8: 28b.

15. See, e.g., the discussion in An Chŏngbok's letter to Kwŏn Ch'ŏlsin, ibid., 6: 15b–18b.

16. Ibid., 27b.

17. Hwang Tŏkkil, *Haryŏ sŏnsaeng munjip* (The collected writings of Hwang Tŏkkil) (Seoul: Kyujanggak Collection, n.d.), 9: 35b.

18. An Chŏngbok, *Sunamjip,* 6: 29b.

19. Sin Hudam, "Sŏhakpyŏn," in Yi Manch'ae, ed., *Pyŏgwip'yŏn* (Seoul: Yŏlhwadang, 1971), p. 90.

20. See, e.g., Ricci's *T'ien-chu shih-i,* in Li Chih-tsao, ed., *T'ien-hsüeh ch'u-han* (Taipei: T'ai-wan hsüeh-sheng shu-chü, 1963), 1: 351–636.

21. An Chŏngbok, *Sunamjip,* "Ch'ŏnhak ko," 17: 1a–8a.

22. Elaine Pagels, *The Gnostic Gospels* (New York: Random House, 1979).

23. For a fascinating study of the interplay of Catholic dogma and scientific theory, see Pietro Redoni, *Galileo, Heretic,* trans. Raymond Rosenthal (Princeton: Princeton University Press, 1987).

24. *Taemyŏngnyul chikhae* (reprinted — Seoul: Pŏpchech'ŏ, 1964), pp. 294–95; J. J. M. de Groot, *Sectarianism and Religious Persecution in China* (New York: Paragon Books, 1970), pp. 137, 147. The Ming law code served as the basic penal code of the Chosŏn dynasty.

25. Dan Overmyer, "Attitudes Toward Popular Religion in Ritual Texts of the Chinese State: *The Collected Statutes of the Great Ming," Cahiers d'Extrême-Asie,* no. 5 (1989–1990), pp. 191–221, provides pages of evidence that the Chinese state was concerned much more with controlling the public rituals performed by commoners than with their personal religious beliefs.

26. Liu, *Orthodoxy in Late Imperial China, passim.*

27. For example, see An Chŏngbok's 1784 letter to Kwŏn Ch'ŏlsin, in *Sunamjip,* 6: 29a–b.

28. *Mencius:* 3B: 9.

29. See, e.g., Hong Nagan's letter to Ch'ae Chegong in Yi Kigyŏng, ed., *Pyŏgwip'yŏn* (Seoul: Kyohoesa yŏn'guso, 1979), p. 26.

30. An Chŏngbok, *Sunamjip,* 17: 16a–17a, "Ch'ŏnhak mundap."

31. Martina Deuchler, "Neo-Confucianism: The Impulse for Social Action in Early Yi Korea," *Journal of Korean Studies* 2 (1980): 75–79; Kŭm Changt'ae, "Chungjongjo t'aehaksaeng ŭi pyŏkpul undong," in idem, *Han'guk yugyo ŭi chaejomyŏng,* pp. 199–208.

32. See, e.g.,Yi Ik as cited by An Chŏngbok, *Sunamjip,* 17: 26b.

33. Letter by Yi Hŏn'gyŏng to Hong Yangho before Hong's departure on an official mission to Beijing, in *Kanongjip,* 9: 36a–38a. Also note Pak Chiwŏn's criticism of the arrogant assumption of moral and cultural superiority

some Koreans displayed in China, *Yŏrha ilgi*, in *Yŏnamjip* (Pak Chiwŏn's collected works), 14.la–4a.

34. Kŭm Changt'ae, "T'oegye ŭi Yangmyŏnghak pip'an," in idem, *Han'guk yugyo ŭi chaejomyŏng*, pp. 209–18; Kim Kilhwan, *Chosŏnjo yuhak sasang yŏn'gu* (Seoul: Ilchisa, 1980), pp. 69–76.

35. Martina Deuchler, "Reject the False and Uphold the Straight: Attitudes Toward Heterodox Thought in Early Yi Korea," in Wm. Theodore de Bary and JaHyun Kim Haboush, eds., *The Rise of Neo-Confucianism in Korea* (New York: Columbia University Press, 1985), pp. 375–410, and, in the same volume, Miura Kunio, "Orthodoxy and Heterodoxy in Seventeenth-Century Korea: Song Siyŏl and Yun Hyu," pp. 411–43, discuss sixteenth- and seventeenth-century definitions of orthodoxy in terms of fidelity to the moral and ritual message of the Classics and to the interpretations of those Classics by Chu Hsi. I differ with them only in the emphasis I place on the moral underpinning of those particular definitions of orthodoxy.

36. Michael Kalton, *To Become a Sage* (New York: Columbia University Press, 1988) provides a particularly illuminating glimpse of the ascetic and pessimistic elements in T'oegye's thought, particularly on pp. 24 and 172. Donald Baker, *Chosŏn hugi yugyo wa ch'ŏnju-gyo ŭi taerip* (The confrontation between Confucianism and Catholicism in late Chosŏn dynasty Korea), trans. Kim Seyun (Seoul: Iljogak, 1997) traces the growth of that ascetic and pessimistic strand into the eighteenth century.

37. See, e.g., the letter Kwŏn Ch'ŏlsin wrote to An Chŏngbok saying that no matter how hard he studied Confucian texts and tried to practice Confucian moral discipline, he was unable to makes much progress. *Sunamjip*, 6: 27b.

38. *Chu Tzu yü-lei*, 1: 418 (Taipei: Cheng-chung shu-chü, 1962), cited in Donald J. Munro, *Images of Human Nature: A Sung Portrait* (Princeton: Princeton University Press, 1988), p. 39.

39. An Chŏngbok, *Sunamjip*, 6: 34a.

40. Ibid., 17: 26a.

41. For an illuminating discussion of selfishness and selflessness in Chinese Confucian writings, see Donald Munro, "The Concept of Interest in Chinese Thought," *Journal of the History of Ideas* 41, no. 2 (1980): 179–97.

42. Sin Hudam, "Sŏhakpyŏn" in Yi Manch'ae, *Pyŏgwip'yŏn*, p. 40.

43. Ibid., p. 60. Sin uses *chŏng* instead of *kong* for lack of selfishness here. That is the same *chŏng* used in other contexts to mean orthodoxy.

44. Munro, "The Concept of Interest in Chinese Thought," p. 180.

45. Yi Ik, *Sŏngho sasŏl* (The miscellaneous writings of Yi Ik) (Seoul: Minjok munhwa ch'ujinhoe, 1977–78), 26: 15b–16a.

46. Ibid., 13: 22a–b, 30: 39b–40a.

47. Ibid., 11: 2b.

48. Yi Ik, "Idan," in *Sŏngho sasŏl yusŏn*, pp. 371–72.

49. Yi Ik, *Sŏngho chŏnjip*, 55: 27b, included in *Sŏngho sŏnsaeng munjip* (Seoul: Kyŏngin munhwasa, 1974).

50. Sin Hudam, "Sŏhakpyŏn," in Yi Manch'ae, *Pyŏgwip'yŏn*, pp. 38–103; An Chŏngbok, "Ch'ŏnhak mundap," in *Sunamjip*, 17: 8a–26a; Yi Hŏn'gyŏng, "Ch'ŏnhak mundap," in *Kanongjip*, 22: 39a–44b.

51. Chŏng Yagyong, "Nonŏ ko'gŭmju," in *Chŏng Tasan chŏnsŏ*, II: 7: 31a–b.

52. Yi Hwang, *T'oegye sŏnjip*, trans. Yun Sasun (Seoul: Hyŏnamsa, 1988), p. 368; Michael C. Kalton, *To Become a Sage*, chap. 8, pp. 175–89. T'oegye is citing *Chu Tzu ch'üan-shu*, 85: 6a. The translation here is mine.

53. Chŏng, I: 13: 37b–38a; II: 2: 23a.

54. Ricci, *Ch'ŏnju sirŭi* (Seoul: Kwangdŏksa, 1972), pp. 283–84. This is a Korean reprint of *T'ien-chu shih-i*.

55. Chŏng, II: 3: 6a–7b, 4: 5b–8b.

56. Chan Wing-tsit, trans., *A Sourcebook in Chinese Philosophy* (Princeton: Princeton University Press, 1969), p. 785.

57. Wm. Theodore de Bary, *Neo-Confucian Orthodoxy and the Learning of the Mind-and-Heart* (New York: Columbia University Press, 1981), p. 14.

58. Wing-tsit Chan, "Chu Hsi on T'ien," in idem, *Chu Hsi: New Studies* (Honolulu: University of Hawaii Press, 1989), pp. 184–96; Hoyt C. Tillman, "Consciousness of T'ien in Chu Hsi's Thought," *Harvard Journal of Asiatic Studies* 47, no. 1 (1987): 35, argues, however, that "caution should be exercised in asserting that Chu Hsi never used the word *t'ien* in its meaning of a deity."

59. Yi Hwang, "Chin sŏnghak sipto," in *T'oegye chŏnsŏ* (Seoul: Sŏnggyun'gwan University, Taehan Munhwa yŏn'guso, 1958), 1: 209 (7: 31a).

60. Chŏng, II: 3: 4b–5b.

61. Ibid., 8: 19b.

62. Ibid., 3: 5b, 4: 21a–23b.

63. Ibid., 19: 46a.

64. Ibid., 3: 3b–4a, 3: 30b, 15: 35b.

65. Ch'oe Tonghŭi, "Tasan ŭi sin'gwan," *Han'guk sasang*, no. 15 (1977): 106–34; Han Chongman, "Tasan ŭi ch'ŏn'gwan," *Tasan hakbo* 2 (1979): 121–49; Ha Ubong, "Chŏng Tasan ŭi sŏhakgwan'gye e taehan ilgoch'al," *Kyohoesa yŏn'gu* 1 (1977): 71–112, esp. pp. 97–101.

66. Kang Chaeŏn, "Chŏng Tasan ŭi sŏhakkwan" (Seoul: Minŭmsa, 1990), pp. 58–62. For an English translation of Ricci's catechism, see *The True Meaning of the Lord of Heaven*, trans. Douglas Lancashire and Peter Hu Kuochen, S.J. (St. Louis: Institute of Jesuit Sources, 1985). For Ricci's argument that the god of Catholicism is the god of the Confucian Classics, see pp. 123–31.

67. Chŏng, II: 15: 15b.

68. Ch'oe Sŏgu, "Chŏng Tasan ŭi sŏhak sasang," in idem, *Chŏng Tasan kwa kŭ sidae* (Seoul: Minŭmsa, 1986), pp. 105–37, is the classic exposition of the Tasan-was-a-Catholic argument. For a counterargument, see Kim Sanghong, *Tasanhak yŏn'gu* (Seoul: Kyemyŏng munhwasa, 1990), pp. 11–85.

69. Ch'oe Kibok, "Chosŏnjo Ch'ŏnju kyohoe ŭi chesa kŭmnyŏng kwa Tasan ŭi chosang chesa kwan," in idem, *Han'guk kyohoesa nonmunjip*, II (Seoul: Han'guk kyohoesa yŏn'guso, 1985), pp. 97–198.

70. Charles Dallet, *Histoire de l'église de Corée* (Paris: Victor Palme, 1874), 1: 37–8 (hereafter all subsequent references are to vol. 1).

71. Ibid., pp. 42–53.

72. Ibid., p. 48.

73. Ibid., p. 49.

74. Ibid., p. 47. This statement by Yun is repeated by Governor Chŏng in his report to the throne urging severe punishment for Yun and Kwŏn. See *Chŏngjo sillok*, 33: 55a–56a.

75. Note the statement by Ricci, which Yun had surely read, that "the term 'god' does not refer to morality itself but rather to the Lord from Whom morality originates" (*Ch'ŏnju sirŭi*, p. 65).

76. Dallet, *Histoire*, p. 43.

77. See, e.g., the memorial by Sin Ki in *Chŏngjo sillok*, 33: 43b.

78. *Chŏngjo sillok*, 26: 7a–b.

79. Dallet, *Histoire*, p. 44.

80. Sin Ki, in *Chŏngjo sillok*, 33: 43b, is just one of many who uses this phrase. For more examples of the language used in criticizing Yun and Kwŏn and their Catholic religion, see *Chŏngjo sillok*, 33: 40b–57b *passim*. See also Yi Kigyŏng, ed., *Pyŏgwip'yŏn*, pp. 17–108.

81. See King Chŏngjo's decree of execution; *Chŏngjo sillok*, 33: 57a.

82. See, e.g., Magistrate Sin Sawŏn's October 2, 1791, letter to Hong Na-gan in which he explains that there was nothing wrong with reading Catholic books and that he took action against Yun only after he had clear evidence that Yun had been led by such books to act improperly. Yi Kigyŏng, ed., *Pyŏgwip'yŏn*, pp. 22–25.

83. Note Censor General Kwŏn Igang's memorial of October 29, 1791, which points out that Catholicism is no ordinary *idan* but poses a much more serious threat to the moral foundations of society than any heterodoxy before it. That is why Kwŏn condemns Catholics for using *sasŏl* (perverse language) and mangling moral principles. Yi Kigyŏng, ed., *Pyŏgwip'yŏn*, p. 58.

84. Dallet, *Histoire*, pp. 53–54.

85. Ricci, *Ch'ŏnju sirŭi*, pp. 243–44, states that only someone who believes such Catholic doctrines as the existence of god and of heaven and hell deserves to be called a gentleman, that is to say, someone who is orthodox.

86. Aquinas, *De Veritate* 23: 6, cited in Eric D'Arcy, "Worthy of Worship: A Catholic Contribution," in Gene Outka and John P. Reeder, Jr., eds., *Religion and Morality* (Garden City, N.Y.: Anchor Books, 1973), p. 191.

87. Ricci, *Ch'ŏnju sirŭi*, pp. 76–84.

88. Ibid., p. 81.

89. For more on Ricci's categorical misunderstanding of *li*, see Jacques Gernet, *China and the Christian Impact: A Conflict of Cultures*, trans. Janet Lloyd (New York: Cambridge University Press, 1985), esp. pp. 201–12; and John D. Young, *Confucianism and Christianity: The First Encounter* (Hong Kong: Hong Kong University Press, 1983), esp. pp. 33–35.

90. Ricci, *Ch'ŏnju sirŭi*, p. 76.

91. Tasan tells of Yakchŏn's early involvement with, and later withdrawal from, the infant Korean Catholic church in his "Sŏnjungssi Chŏng Yakchŏn myojimyŏng," in *Chŏng Tasan chŏnsŏ*, I: 15: 38b–42b. Tasan's account of his own involvement can be found in his "Chach'an myojimyŏng," in ibid., I: 16: 1a–30a. Tasan's condemnation of Catholicism can also be found in his responses to his interrogators as recorded in *Ch'uan kŭp kugan* (Seoul: Asea munhwasa, 1978), vol. 25, esp. pp. 13–19, 39–40.

92. *Ch'uan kŭp kugan*, vol. 25, p. 49.

93. Dallet, *Histoire*, pp. 115–25; Hwang Sayŏng, *Hwang Sayŏng paeksŏ*, ed. and trans. Yun Chaeyŏng (Seoul: Chŏngŭmsa, 1975), pp. 48–51.

94. Chŏng Yakchong, *Chugyo yoji* (Seoul: Hwang Sŏktu Luga sŏwŏn, 1984); Hector Diaz, *A Korean Theology: Chu-Gyo Yo-Ji: Essentials of the Lord's Teaching by Chŏng Yagjong Augustine* (Fribourg: Neue Zeitschrift für Missionswissenschaft, 1986), pp. 53–73.

95. A modern Korean translation of the entire text by Ha Sŏngnae is available in the 1984 edition cited in the previous note. Diaz presents a complete English translation alongside the original, *A Korean Theology*, pp. 275–435.

96. Diaz, *A Korean Theology*, pp. 297–301.

97. Ibid., p. 327.

98. *Ch'uan kŭp kugan*, 25: 48; Yi Nŭnghwa, *Chosŏn kidokkyo kŭp oegyosa* (Seoul: Han'gukhak yŏn'guso, 1977), p. 118.

99. Diaz, *A Korean Theology*, pp. 85–107.

100. Dallet, *Histoire*, 2: 168.

101. Chŏng Hasang, *Sang Chaesang sŏ* (Seoul: Asea munhwasa, 1976).

102. Ibid., pp. 3–4.

103. Ibid., pp. 24–25.

104. Ibid., pp. 11–12.

105. Ibid.

106. Ibid., pp. 10–11.

107. Ibid., pp. 8–9.

108. Ibid., pp. 9, 23–24.

109. Ibid., pp. 3, 23.

110. Ibid., p. 18.

111. Yi Kigyŏng, ed. *Pyŏgwip'yŏn*, p. 398.

112. For an in-depth and multifaceted analysis of this conceptual gap dividing Catholicism from Neo-Confucianism, see Jacques Gernet, *China and the Christian Impact: A Conflict of Cultures*.

# Glossary

aedŭl chosang  애들祖上
aegoe  額外
aengnae  額內
An Chŏngbok  安鼎福
An Hyang  安珦
An T'aekchun  安宅駿
An Yu  安裕
Anbong yŏngdang  安峰影堂
Anbyŏn  安邊
Andong  安東
An'gang  安康
Anju  安州
Ansim-sa  安心寺
ant'aek  安宅

Beijing  北京
bushi  武士

Chach'an myojimyŏng  自撰墓誌銘
chadŭk  自得
Ch'ae Chegong  蔡濟恭
chaech'oe  齋衰
ch'ajangja  次長子
ch'amch'oe  斬衰
Chang Chinhwan  張震煥
Chang Chiyŏn  張志淵

Chang Shang-ying  張商英
Chang Yu  張維
*Changam sŏnsaengjip*  丈巖先生集
changja  長子
changnim  장님
Changsŏgak  藏書閣
Ch'angwŏn  昌原
ch'arye  茶禮
chasŏl  自說
*Chasŏlchip*  自說集
Chaŭi  慈懿
Chaŭn  慈恩
Cheju  濟州
chemun  祭文
Ch'en Ch'un  陳淳
cheng  正
Ch'eng  程
Cheng Hsüan  鄭玄
Ch'eng I  程頤
Ch'eng-Chu  程朱
ch'eng-huang  城隍
chesa  祭祀
chi  知
ch'i  氣
ch'i chunghwa  致中和
ch'i k'e  七克
ch'i yangji pyŏn  致良知辨

Chia Kung-yen　賈公彥

*Chia-li*　家禮

Chieh　桀

Ch'ien-lung　乾隆

Chih　跖

chih-chih　致知

ch'iji　致知

ch'ik　則

Ch'ilsŏng　七星

*chin Sŏnghak sipto*　進聖學
十圖

Ch'in Shih-huang　秦始皇

Chinch'ŏn　鎭川

Ch'ing　清

Ch'ing T'ai-tsung　清太宗

Chin'gak Hyesim　眞覺慧諶

Chin'gam Hyeso　眞鑒慧昭

Ching-chai-chen　敬齋箴

Chinju　晉州

chinsa　進師

Chinsan　珍山

*Chin-ssu lu*　近思錄

Chinul　知訥

Chiri　智異

Chiri-san Ssanggye-sa chungch'ang
ki　智異山雙溪寺重創記

chisŏng　至誠

Ch'i-sung　契嵩

ch'iung　窮

Cho　趙

Cho Hŏn　趙憲

Cho Ik　趙翼

Cho Inok　趙仁沃

Cho Kwangjo　趙光祖

Cho Sik　曺植

Cho T'aeŏk　趙泰億

Ch'oe Ch'angdae　崔昌大

Ch'oe Ch'iwŏn (Koun)　崔致遠
(孤雲)

Ch'oe Ch'ung　崔沖

Ch'oe Kibok　崔基福

Ch'oe Myŏnggil　崔鳴吉

*Ch'oe saengwŏn chŏn*　崔生
員傳

Ch'oe Sŏgu　崔奭祐

Ch'oe Sŏkchŏng　崔錫鼎

Ch'oe Tonghŭi　崔東熙

Ch'oe Yŏng　崔塋

Ch'oe Yut'ae　崔有泰

Chogye　曹溪

chŏk Hyu　賊鑴

chŏkcha　嫡子

chŏkt'ong　嫡統

chŏlch'ung changgun　折衝將軍

Chŏlla　全羅

chŏn　傳

ch'ŏn　賤

chon Chu yangijŏk　尊周攘夷狄

chŏng　正

Chŏng Chedu　鄭齊斗

Chŏng Hasang　丁夏祥

Chŏng Ho　鄭澔

Chŏng Kyŏngse　鄭經世

Chŏng Manjo　鄭萬祚

Chŏng Minsi　鄭民始

Chŏng Mongju　鄭夢周

Chŏng Okcha　鄭玉子

Chŏng Ŏnhwang　丁彥璜

chŏng sasŭp　正士習

Chŏng T'aehwa　鄭太和

*Chŏng Tasan chŏnsŏ*　丁茶山全書

*Chŏng Tasan kwa kŭ sidae*　丁茶山
과 그時代

*Chŏng Tasan ŭi Sŏhakkwan*　丁茶山
의 西學觀

*Chŏng Tasan ŭi sŏhakkwan'gye e
taehan ilgoch'al*　丁茶山의
西學關係에對한一考察

*Chŏng Tasan ŭi sŏhak sasang*
丁茶山의 西學思想

Chŏng Tojŏn　鄭道傳

Chŏng Yagyong　丁若鏞

Chŏng Yakchŏn　丁若銓

Chŏng Yakchong (Augustine)
　丁若鍾

Ch'ŏngan　清安

chŏngch'e　正體

chŏnghak　正學

Ch'ŏnghŏ　清虚

Chŏnghŭi　貞熹

chŏnghye ssangsu　定慧雙修

Ch'ongji　總持

Chŏngjo　正祖

*Chŏngjo sillok*　正祖實錄

Chŏngjong　定宗

Ch'ŏngju　清州

chŏngmun　正文

chŏngmyŏng　正名

Ch'ongnam　總南

chŏngsŏng　精誠

chŏngsŏng (ŭl) tŭrida　精誠
　을드리다

chŏngsŏng tŭrigi　精誠 드리기

chŏngsŏng tŭryŏ　精誠 드려

Chŏngsŏng wanghu　貞聖王后

chongt'ong　宗統

chon'gun pisin　尊君卑臣

Chŏngŭp　井邑

chon'gyŏng wido　尊經衛道

*Ch'ŏnhak ko*　天學考

*Ch'ŏnhak mundap*　天學問答

Chŏnju　全州

*Ch'ŏnju sirŭi*　天主實義

ch'ŏnmyŏng　天命

chonsa　尊士

Ch'ŏnt'ae　天台

ch'ŏp　妾

chosang　祖上

ch'osi　初試

Chosŏn　朝鮮

*Chosŏn hugi munhwa undongsa*
　朝鮮後期文化運動史

*Chosŏn hugi tangjaengsa yŏn'gu*
　朝鮮後期黨爭史研究

*Chosŏnjo Ch'ŏnju kyohoe ŭi chesa
　kŭmnyŏng kwa Tasan ŭi chosang
　chesagwan*　朝鮮朝天主教會
　의祭祀禁令과 茶山의 祖上
　祭祀觀

*Chosŏnjo yuhaksasang yŏn'gu*
　朝鮮朝儒學思想研究

*Chosŏn kidokkyo kŭp oegyosa*
　朝鮮基督教及外交史

*Chosŏn sidae chŏngch'isa ŭi
　chaejomyŏng*　朝鮮時代政治史
　의 再照明

*Chosŏn yugyo yŏnwŏn*　朝鮮
　儒教淵源

Chou　周

Chou Wen-mo (Korean: Chu
　Munmo)　周文摸

*Chou-li*　周禮

Chu Hsi　朱熹

Chu Sebung　周世鵬

*Chu Tzu chia-li*　朱子家禮

*Chu Tzu ta-ch'üan*　朱子大全

*Chu Tzu yü-lei*　朱子語類

chüan　卷

*Chuan kŭp kugan*　推安及
　鞠安

*Chuang-tzu*　莊子

*Chugyo yoji*　主教要旨

*Ch'un-ch'iu* (Korean: *Ch'un-ch'u*)
　春秋

*Ch'un-ch'u pojŏn*　春秋補傳

Ch'ungch'ŏng　忠清

Ch'unghyŏn sŏwŏn　忠賢
　書院

chungja　衆子

Chungjong　中宗

*Chungjongjo t'aehaksaeng ŭi pyŏkpul undong* 中宗朝太學生의闢佛運動
Ch'ungnyŏl 忠烈
Chungsin 中神
*Chungyong/Chung-yung* 中庸
*Chungyong changgu ch'aje* 中庸章句次第
*Chungyong Chuja changgu porok* 中庸朱子章句補錄
*Chungyong kaeju* 中庸改註
*Chungyong sŏl* 中庸說
*Chungyong Taehak husŏl* 中庸大學後說
Ch'unhyang 春香

Ha Sŏngnae 河聲來
Ha Ubong 河宇鳳
Haeju 海州
haengch'ae mullim 행채물림
haengjang 行狀
*Hakkyo mobŏm* 學校模範
Ham Yuil 咸有一
Hamgyŏng 咸鏡
Hamhŏ 涵虛
Han (China) 漢
Han (river) 漢江
Han Chongman 韓鍾萬
Han Ugŭn 韓㙯擡
Hangnimsa 鶴林寺
hangnye 學禮
*Han'guk inmyŏng taesajŏn* 韓國人名大事典
*Han'guk kyohoesa nonmunjip* 韓國教會史論文集
*Han'guksa* 韓國史
*Han'guk saron* 韓國史論
*Han'guk sasang* 韓國思想
*Han'guk yuhak non'gu* 韓國儒學論究
*Han'guk yuhaksa* 韓國儒學史
*Han'guk yugyo ŭi chaejomyŏng* 韓國儒教의再照明
*Hansujae sŏnsaengjip* 寒水齋先生集
*Haryo sŏnsaeng munjip* 下廬先生文集
Hideyoshi 秀吉
Hŏ Mok 許穆
hoch'a 胡差
Hoehŏn 晦軒
Hong Kyejŏk 洪啓𤐣
Hong Nagan 洪樂安
Hong Uhaeng 洪禹行
Hong Yangho 洪良浩
Hongmungwan 弘文館
hongp'ae kosa 紅牌告祀
Hŏsaeng chŏn 許生傳
Hŏŭng Pou 虛應普雨
Hsia 夏
*Hsiao-ching* 孝經
*Hsin-ching* 心經
hsing 性
hsüeh-kuei 學規
*Hsün Tzu* 荀子
Huang Kan 黃幹
Hŭiyang-san 曦陽山
Hŭngch'ŏn-sa 興天寺
hwadu 話頭
Hwagok sŏwŏn 花谷書院
hwalgu 活句
*Hwang Sayŏng paeksŏ* 黃嗣永帛書
Hwang Tŏkkil 黃德吉
Hwanghae 黃海
Hwangsan sŏwŏn 黃山書院
Hwaŏm 華嚴
Hwayangdong mukp'ae 華陽洞墨牌
Hwayang sŏwŏn 華陽書院
hwi 諱

hyanggyo 鄉校
hyanggwŏn 鄉權
hyangni 鄉吏
hyangsa (anniversary rites) 享祀
hyangsa (local shrine) 鄉祠
hyangyu 鄉儒
Hyojong 孝宗
hyŏngsik 形式
Hyŏnjong 顯宗
*Hyŏnjŏng-non* 顯正論
*Hyŏnjong sillok* 顯宗實錄
Hyŏnp'ung 玄風
Hyujŏng 休靜

i 理
idan 異端
idu 吏讀
i'gyŏn 異見
i-ki 理氣
*I-li* 儀禮
Im Su'gan 任守幹
Imgo sŏwŏn 臨皐書院
Imje 臨濟
in'ga 印可
Inhyŏn wanghu 仁顯王后
Injo 仁祖
"Injodae chŏngch'i seryŏk ŭi
    tonghyang" 仁祖代政治勢力
    의動向
Injong 仁宗
Insŏn 仁宣
Inyŏl 仁烈
isa 里社
Isan sŏwŏn 伊山書院
Isan wŏn'gyu 伊山院規

Kaesŏng 開城
kaguk pudongnye 家國不同禮
Kang 姜
Kang Chaeŏn 姜在彦

Kang Chujin 姜周鎭
K'ang-hsi 康熙
Kangnŭng 江陵
Kangwŏn 江原
kanhwa Sŏn 看話禪
*Kanongjip* 艮翁集
k'ao-cheng 考証
kapsin 甲申
karye 家禮
kasa 歌辭
kaseja 假世子
ki 氣
Kihŏ Yŏnggyu 騎虛靈圭
Kihwa 己和
Kim Chaero 金在魯
Kim Ch'anghŭp 金昌翕
Kim Ch'anghyŏp 金昌協
Kim Ch'angjip 金昌集
Kim Changsaeng 金長生
Kim Chin'gwi 金鎭龜
Kim Chin'gyu 金鎭圭
Kim Chip 金集
Kim Chongsu 金宗壽
Kim Ilson 金馹孫
Kim Kilhwan 金吉煥
Kim Koengp'il 金宏弼
Kim Manch'ae 金萬埰
Kim Man'gi 金萬基
Kim Man'gŭn 金萬謹
Kim Manjung 金滿重
Kim Sanghŏn 金尚憲
Kim Sanghong 金相洪
Kim Sangyong 金尚容
Kim Sŏkchu 金錫冑
Kim Suhang 金壽恒
Kim Suhong 金壽弘
Kim Suhŭng 金壽興
Kim Wŏnhaeng 金元行
Kim Yongdŏk 金龍德
Kim Yusin 金庾信

ko 格
kogang 考講
kŏguk 去國
kojŭng 考証
Koksŏng 谷城
*Kollyunjip* 昆侖集
kong 公
kongan 公案
kongsim 公心
kongŭi 公議
kopke 곱게
korye 古禮
Koryŏ 高麗
kosa 告祀
Kosan sŏwŏn 孤山書院
Kosŏng 高城
ko-wu 格物
*Kukcho oryeŭi* 國朝五禮儀
kuksa 國師
Kŭm Changt'ae 琴章泰
Kŭmsŏngsan 錦城山
kung (to investigate) 窮
kung (impartial) 公
kungmu 國巫
kunsu 郡守
Kunwi 軍威
Kwanghae 光海
Kwangsan Kim 光山金氏
kwanmudang 官무당
kwayu 科儒
kwi (spirit) 鬼
kwi (noble) 貴
kwisin 鬼神
Kwŏn Ch'ŏlsin 權哲身
Kwŏn Igang 權以綱
Kwŏn Ku 權琛
Kwŏn Kŭn 權近
Kwŏn Sangha 權尚夏
Kwŏn Sangyŏn (James) 權尚然
Kwŏn Sangyu 權尚游

Kwŏn Si 權諰
*kyegamnok* 癸甲錄
kyemi 癸未
kyo 教
*Kyohoesa yŏn'gu* 教會史研究
Kyojong 教宗
Kyojong p'ansa 教宗判事
kyŏk 格
kyŏng 敬
Kyŏnggi 京畿
*Kyŏngguk taejŏn* 經國大典
kyŏnghak 經學
Kyŏnghŏ 鏡虛
Kyŏngjaejam-do 敬齋箴圖
Kyŏngjong 景宗
Kyŏngju 慶州
*Kyŏngmong yogyŏl* 擊夢要訣
kyŏngmul 格物
Kyŏngsan 慶山
Kyŏngsang 慶尚
*Kyŏngsŏ kondŭkp'yŏn* 經書困得編
*Kyŏngsŏ pyŏnŭi* 經書辨疑
kyosaeng 校生

li 理
Li Chih-tsao 李之藻
Li Tung 李侗
liang-chih 良知
*Li-chi* 禮記
Lin-chi 臨濟
Lin-chi Ch'an 臨濟禪
Lo Ts'ung-yen 羅從彥
Lu Hsiang-shan 陸象山
Lu Shih-i 陸世儀
*Lun-yü* 論語

Ma Tsu 媽祖
*Maengja yoŭi* 孟子要義
Min 閔
min 民

Min Am    閔黯
Min Chinhu    閔鎭厚
Min Chŏngjung    閔鼎重
Min T'aeho    閔台鎬
Minam pu    民碞賦
minch'ungdan    愍忠壇
ming    名
Ming    明
Miryang    密陽
Mo-tzu    墨子
Mokch'ŏn    木川
mubu    巫夫
mudang    무당
muga    巫歌
Muhak Chach'o    無學自超
muit'ong    無二統
mul    物
Munhoe sŏwŏn    文會書院
Munhŏn sŏwŏn    文憲書院
Munjong    文宗
Munjŏng    文定
munkwa    文科
Munmyo    文廟
Murayama Chijun    村山智順
Musŏng sŏwŏn    武城書院
Myohyang-san    妙香山
myŏng (fate)    命
myŏng (name)    名
*Myŏnggokchip*    明谷集
Myŏngjong    明宗
*Myŏngjong sillok*    明宗實錄
*Myŏngsim pogam*    明心寶鑑
Myŏngsŏng wanghu    明聖王后

naesil    內實
Naju    羅州
Nam Kuman    南九萬
*Namhwagyŏng chuhae*    南華經
　註解
Namin    南人

Namsan    南山
Namwŏn Yun    南原尹氏
Na'ong Hyegŭn    懶翁惠勤
Noemuk Ch'ŏyŏng    雷默處英
*Non Sabyŏnnok pyŏn*    論思辨錄辨
*Nongamjip*    農巖集
nonhak    論學
*Nonŏ kogŭmju*    論語古今註
Noron    老論
Noryang    露梁
*Nup'an ko*    鏤板考

Ŏ Hyoch'ŏm    魚孝瞻
O Such'ang    吳洙彰
Okch'ŏn    玉川
Okkwa    玉果
Oksan sŏwŏn    玉山書院
ŏllo    言路
ŏn'gwan    言官
*Oryun haengsil to*    五倫行實圖
ŏŭi    語義

Paegundong    白雲洞
Paech'ŏn    白川
*Paekho chŏnsŏ*    白湖全書
Paekho Yun Hyu    白湖
　尹鑴
*Paekho Yun Hyu sasang yŏn'gu*
　白湖尹鑴思想研究
"Paekho Yun Hyu ŭi kyŏngsegwan
　kwa kŭndae chŏngsin"
　白湖尹鑴의 經世觀과
　近代精神
"Paekho Yun Hyu yŏn'gu"
　白湖尹鑴研究
Paekp'a Kŭnsŏng    白坡亘璇
Pai-lu-tung shu-yüan    白鹿
　洞書院
Pak Changwŏn    朴長遠
Pak Chiwŏn    朴趾源

Pak Munsu　朴文秀
Pak P'ilchu　朴弼周
Pak Sech'ae　朴世采
Pak Sedang　朴世堂
"Pak Sedang ŭi sirhak sasang e
　kwanhan yŏn'gu"　朴世堂의
　實學思想에관한研究
"Pak Sŏgye wa pan-Chujahakjŏk
　sasang"　朴西溪와反朱子學
　的思想
Pak T'aebo　朴泰輔
Pak T'aehan　朴泰翰
p'almok　八目
pan　反
pandang　反黨
panggungnye　邦國禮
Pannam Pak　番南朴
p'ansŏ　判書
p'ansu　판수
Pari kongju　바리公主
pien-cheng　辯證
pinso　殯所
Pongam-sa　鳳巖寺
Pongnim　鳳林
pono　保奴
Pŏphŭng-sa　法興寺
Pŏpsŏng　法性
pu-cheng　補正
Pugin　北人
Pugŭn　府根
Puhyu Sŏnsu　浮休善修
puich'am　不二斬
pukpŏl　北伐
P'ungdam Ŭisim　楓潭義諶
P'unggi　豐基
P'ungsŏng　豐城
punhyang sŏlbŏp　焚香說法
purok　附錄
Puryŏng　富寧
Puyong Yŏnggwan　芙蓉靈觀

*Pyŏgwip'yŏn*　闢衛編
Pyŏksong Chiŏm　碧松智嚴
p'yŏn　編
pyŏnp'a　辨破
*Pyŏnp'amun*　辨破文

sa (affair)　事
sa (private, selfish)　私
*Sabyŏnnok*　思辨錄
sach'ŏn　事天
*Sadan ch'ilchŏng insim tosim sŏl*
　四端七情人心道心說
sadang　祠堂
sado　斯道
sado chi nanjŏk　斯道之亂賊
*Saekkyŏng*　稽經
saengwŏn　生員
Saganwŏn　司諫院
sahak　邪學
sajiktan　社稷壇
sajok　士族
sallim　山林
salp'uri　살푸리
Samch'ŏk　三陟
*Samga kwigam*　三家龜鑑
Samgang　三綱
*Samgang haengsil to*　三綱行實圖
Samgang sŏwŏn　三江書院
Samjŏndo　三田渡
samnyŏn sangsik　三年上食
Samsin　삼신
Samsŏngdang　三聖堂
Samsu　三水
samun chi nanjŏk　斯文之亂敵
Samyŏng taesa　泗溟大師
Sangchaesang sŏ　上宰相書
Sangje/Shang-ti　上帝
sangnyun p'aeŭi　傷倫悖義
sansin　山神
sarim　士林

saron　士論

sasŏl　邪說

Sejo　世祖

Sejong　世宗

Seoul　서울

Shenyang　瀋陽

shih (event)　事

shih (reality)　實

*Shih-ching*　詩經

Shih-wu Ch'ing-kung　石屋清珙

*Shu-ching*　書經

Shun　舜

sibi　是非

Sihŭng　始興

sijo　時調

sijŏn　諡典

sil　實

Silla　新羅

*Sillok*　實錄

sillyŏng　神靈

siltŭk　實得

*Simbŏp yoch'o*　心法要抄

simno　心路

sin　神

Sin Hudam　愼後聃

Sin Ki　申耆

Sin Kyŏngjik　愼景稷

Sin Sawŏn　申史源

Sin Sunggyŏm　申崇謙

Sin Wan　申梡

Sinch'ŏn　信川

Sindŏk　神德

sin'gyŏng　新經

Sin'in　神印

*Sinju Todŏkkyŏng*　新註道德經

sinsa myŏngbyŏn　愼思明辨

sinsŏl　新說

sinŭi　新義

Sirhak　實學

Sŏ P'irwŏn　徐必遠

Sŏ Yugu　徐有榘

Sŏak sŏwŏn　西岳書院

"Sŏgye chŏnjip"　西溪全集

*Sŏgye chŏnsŏ*　西溪全書

*Sŏgye chŏrhak ŭi pan-Chujahakjŏk sabyŏn kujo wa sidaesŏng*　西溪哲學의反朱子學的思辨構造와時代性

"Sŏgye ch'osu myop'yo"　西溪樵叟墓表

sogyŏng　소경

*Sohak*　小學

*Sŏhakpyŏn*　西學辨

Sohyŏn　昭顯

Sohyŏn sŏwŏn　紹賢書院

Sŏin　西人

sŏin　庶人

sŏja　庶子

Sŏkch'ŏndong　石泉洞

Sŏkkyŏn　石堅

Sŏksil sŏwŏn　石室書院

sŏl　說

Sŏn　禪

*Sŏn Kyo kyŏl*　禪教訣

*Sŏn Kyo sŏk*　禪教釋

sŏnang　서낭

sŏnangsin　서낭신

sŏng (nature)　性

sŏng (sincerity)　誠

Song Chun'gil　宋浚吉

Sŏng Hon　成渾

Sŏng Kyŏngch'ang　成慶昌

Song Siyŏl　宋時烈

*Sŏn'ga kwigam*　禪家龜鑑

Sŏnggyun'gwan　成均館

*Sŏnghak chipyo*　聖學集要

*Sŏnghak sipto*　聖學十圖

Sŏngho　星湖

*Sŏngho chŏnjip*　星湖全集

*Sŏngho sasŏl*　星湖僿說

*Sŏngho sasŏl yusŏn*　星湖僿說
　類選

*Sŏngho sŏnsaeng munjip*　星湖
　先生文集

*Sŏngho Yi Ik yŏn'gu*　星湖李瀷
　研究

sŏnghwang　城隍

sŏnghwangdang　城隍堂

sŏnghwang-sa　城隍祠

*Songja taejŏn*　宋子大全

Sŏngjong　成宗

Sŏngju　星州

Sŏngnihak　性理學

Sŏngsan Yissi　星山李氏

Sŏnjo　宣祖

Sŏnjong　禪宗

Sŏnjungssi Chŏng Yakchŏn
　myojimyŏng　先仲氏丁
　若銓墓誌銘

*Sŏnmun sugyŏng*　禪門手鏡

sŏnsaeng　先生

Sŏnsan　善山

sŏnyu　先儒

sŏp'a chi ryu　庶派之流

sŏphwangje　攝皇帝

Sŏsomun　小西門

Soron　少論

sŏryu　庶流

Sŏsan taesa　西山大師

sŏson　庶孫

Sosu sŏwŏn　紹修書院

sŏwŏn　書院

*Sŏwŏn tŭngnok*　書院謄錄

Ssanggye sŏwŏn　雙溪書院

*Ssu-k'u ch'üan-shu*　四庫全書

*Ssu-pien lu*　四辨錄

sudŭk sup'il　隨得隨筆

*Sugyo chimnok*　受教輯錄

Sukchong　肅宗

*Sukchong sillok*　肅宗實錄

*Sukchong sillok pogwŏl chŏngo*
　肅宗實錄補闕正誤

"Sukchongdae kapsul hwan'guk
　kwa chŏngbyŏn ch'amyo
　kyech'ŭng punsŏk"
　肅宗代甲戌換局과政變參
　與階層分析

*Sunamjip*　順庵集

Sung　宋

Sungin　崇仁

Sunhŭng　順興

*Ta Ming-lü*　大明律

*Ta-hsüeh*　大學

*Taedong munhwa yŏn'gu*　大東
　文化研究

T'aego Pou　太古普愚

Taegwan　大關

*Taehak*　大學

*Taehak changgu poyu*　大學章句
　補遺

"Taehak chŏnp'yŏn taeji ansŏl"
　大學全編大旨按說

*Taehak kobon pyŏllok*　大學古本
　別錄

Taeja-am　大慈庵

taejangbu　大丈夫

T'aejo　太祖

T'aejong　太宗

*Taemyŏngnyul chikhae*　大明
　律直解

taesahŏn　大司憲

*T'aesang chi*　太常誌

T'aesangsi　太常寺

Tai Chen　戴震

T'ang　唐

tangbŏl　黨伐

t'angp'yŏng　蕩平

Tanjong　端宗

*Tao-te ching*　道德經

tao-t'ung  道統
Tasan  茶山
*Tasan hakpo*  茶山學報
*Tasan ŭi ch'ŏn'gwan*  茶山의天觀
*Tasan ŭi sin'gwan*  茶山의神觀
*Tasanhak ŭi t'amgu*  茶山學의
  探究
*Tasanhak yŏn'gu*  茶山學研究
*T'ien-chu shih-i*  天主實義
T'ien Hou  天后
*T'ien-hsüeh ch'u-han*  天學初函
to  道
To Sinjing  都慎徽
Tobong sŏwŏn  道峰書院
Todong sŏwŏn  道東書院
T'oegye  退溪
*T'oegye chŏnsŏ*  退溪全書
*T'oegye sŏnjip*  退溪選集
*T'oegye ŭi Yangmyŏnghak pip'an*
  退溪의陽明學批判
*To'gokchip*  陶谷集
tohak  道學
*Tohak yŏllyu sok*  道學源流續
tojejo  都提調
*Tok Sangsŏ*  讀尚書
Tŏkch'ŏn sŏwŏn  德川書院
*Toksŏ'gi*  讀書記
toktae  獨對
Tokugawa  德川
Tollyŏngbu  敦寧府
Tonam sŏwŏn  遯岩書院
t'ongbyŏn  痛辨
*Tongguk sesigi*  東國歲
  時記
Tongju  東州
tongsin  洞神
*T'ongsŏl*  通說
T'ongyŏng  統營
Tosan sŏwŏn  陶山書院
Tseng-tzu  曾子

Tŭkt'ong Kihwa  得通己和
Tzu-hsia  子夏
Tzu-lu  子路
Tzu-ssu  子思

ŭiri  義理
ŭiri chi sil  義理之實
ŭisŭnggun  義僧軍
ŭmsa  淫祀
Ŭnbyŏng chŏngsa  隱屏精舍

Wang An-shih  王安石
Wang Po  王柏
Wang Yang-ming  王陽明
wangsa  王師
Wansan Ch'oe  完山崔
Waryongmyo  臥龍廟
wiho  衛護
Wŏlchŏ Toan  月渚道安
Wŏn Tup'yo  元斗杓
wŏndon sinhae  圓頓信解
Wŏnjŏk-am  圓寂菴
wŏn'yu  院儒
wŏnno  院奴
wu  物
Wu San-kuei  吳三桂

yain  野人
Yakch'ŏnjip  藥泉集
Yakkuk  藥局
yang  陽
Yang Chu  陽朱
Yang Shih  陽時
yangban  兩班
*Yangban chŏn*  兩班傳
Yang-ch'i  楊岐
yangji  良知
Yangju  揚州
Yao  堯
Yean  禮安

*Yegi yup'yŏn*　禮記類編
*Yegi yup'yŏn pyŏnnon*　禮記
　類編辨論
Yejong　睿宗
yesong　禮訟
Yi　李
Yi Chae　李縡
Yi Changgyŏng　李長庚
Yi Chinyang　李眞養
Yi Chŏngyŏng　李正英
Yi Chunghwan　李重煥
Yi Ch'unhŭi　李春熙
Yi Hajin　李夏鎭
Yi Hangbok　李恒福
Yi Hasŏng　李廈成
Yi Hŏn'gyŏng　李獻慶
Yi Hŭijae　李曦載
Yi Hwang　李滉
Yi Hyŏngsang　李衡詳
Yi I　李珥
Yi Ik　李瀷
Yi Ingmyŏng　李翼明
Yi Inyŏp　李寅燁
Yi Kigyŏng　李基慶
Yi Kijin　李箕鎭
Yi Kwal　李适
Yi Kwangjŏk　李光廸
Yi Kwanmyŏng　李觀命
Yi Kyoak　李喬岳
Yi Kyŏngsŏk　李景奭
Yi Kyŏngyŏ　李敬輿
Yi Kyubo　李奎報
Yi Manch'ae　李晚采
Yi Mansŏng　李晚成
Yi Minyŏng　李敏英
Yi Nŭnghwa　李能和
Yi Ok　李鈺
Yi Ŏnjŏk　李彦瓅
Yi Pangŏn　李邦彦
Yi Pokhyu　李福休

Yi Pyŏngdo　李丙燾
Yi Saek　李穡
Yi Sajŭng　李思曾
Yi Sik　李植
Yi Sŏnggye　李成桂
Yi Sŏngmu　李成茂
Yi Suhae　李壽海
Yi Suk　李䎘
Yi Sŭnghun (Peter Lee)　李承薰
Yi Sunsin　李舜臣
Yi T'aejin　李泰鎭
Yi T'an　李坦
Yi T'oegye　李退溪
Yi Tŏgon　李德溫
Yi Tŏkhyŏng　李德泂
Yi Tŏksu　李德壽
Yi Tŏngmu　李德懋
Yi Ŭihyŏn　李宜顯
Yi Ŭnsun　李銀順
Yi Wŏnik　李元翼
Yi Yŏ　李畬
Yi Yulgok　李栗谷
*Yijo tangjaengsa yŏn'gu*　李朝
　黨爭史研究
*Yi-lo yüan-yüan lu*　伊洛淵源錄
yin　陰
yŏdan　厲壇
yŏgwi　厲鬼
yŏje　厲祭
*Yŏksa hakpo*　歷史學報
yŏllyŏ　烈女
yŏmt'oe　恬退
*Yŏnamjip*　燕巖集
*Yŏnbo*　年譜
yŏng　靈
Yŏngch'ŏn　永川
Yŏngjo　英祖
yŏngjŏng　影幀
Yŏngnam　嶺南
Yŏnsan　連山

Yŏnsan'gun    燕山君
*Yŏrha ilgi*    熱河日記
Yu Hongnyŏl    柳洪烈
Yu Hŭich'un    柳希春
Yu Hyŏngwŏn    柳馨遠
Yu Ŏnmyŏng    俞彥明
Yu Sangun    柳尚運
Yu Sŏngnyong    柳成龍
Yu Yŏnghŭi    劉英姬
*Yüan-chüeh ching* 圓覺經
*Yuhak yŏn'gu*    儒學研究
Yujŏm-sa    榆岾寺
Yujŏng    惟政
Yukkyŏng    六經

Yun Chaeyŏng    尹在瑛
Yun Chich'ung (Paul)    尹持忠
Yun Chŭng    尹拯
Yun Hyu    尹鑴
Yun Sasun    尹絲淳
Yun Segi    尹世紀
Yun Sŏkhwan    尹錫煥
Yun Sŏndo    尹善道
Yun Sŏn'gŏ    尹宣擧
Yun Yangnae    尹陽來
yurim    儒林
yurim kongŭi    儒林公議
yusaeng    儒生

# Index

*Harvard East Asian Monographs*
(* out-of-print)

# Harvard East Asian Monographs

*18. Frank H. H. King (ed.) and Prescott Clarke, *A Research Guide to China-Coast Newspapers, 1822–1911*

19. Ellis Joffe, *Party and Army: Professionalism and Political Control in the Chinese Officer Corps, 1949–1964*

*20. Toshio G. Tsukahira, *Feudal Control in Tokugawa Japan: The Sankin Kōtai System*

21. Kwang-Ching Liu, ed., *American Missionaries in China: Papers from Harvard Seminars*

22. George Moseley, *A Sino-Soviet Cultural Frontier: The Ili Kazakh Autonomous Chou*

23. Carl F. Nathan, *Plague Prevention and Politics in Manchuria, 1910–1931*

*24. Adrian Arthur Bennett, *John Fryer: The Introduction of Western Science and Technology into Nineteenth-Century China*

25. Donald J. Friedman, *The Road from Isolation: The Campaign of the American Committee for Non-Participation in Japanese Aggression, 1938–1941*

26. Edward LeFevour, *Western Enterprise in Late Ching China: A Selective Survey of Jardine, Matheson and Company's Operations, 1842–1895*

27. Charles Neuhauser, *Third World Politics: China and the Afro-Asian People's Solidarity Organization, 1957–1967*

28. Kungtu C. Sun, assisted by Ralph W. Huenemann, *The Economic Development of Manchuria in the First Half of the Twentieth Century*

*29. Shahid Javed Burki, *A Study of Chinese Communes, 1965*

30. John Carter Vincent, *The Extraterritorial System in China: Final Phase*

31. Madeleine Chi, *China Diplomacy, 1914–1918*

*32. Clifton Jackson Phillips, *Protestant America and the Pagan World: The First Half Century of the American Board of Commissioners for Foreign Missions, 1810–1860*

33. James Pusey, *Wu Han: Attacking the Present through the Past*

34. Ying-wan Cheng, *Postal Communication in China and Its Modernization, 1860–1896*

35. Tuvia Blumenthal, *Saving in Postwar Japan*

36. Peter Frost, *The Bakumatsu Currency Crisis*

37. Stephen C. Lockwood, *Augustine Heard and Company, 1858–1862*

38. Robert R. Campbell, *James Duncan Campbell: A Memoir by His Son*

39. Jerome Alan Cohen, ed., *The Dynamics of China's Foreign Relations*

40. V. V. Vishnyakova-Akimova, *Two Years in Revolutionary China, 1925–1927*, tr. Steven L. Levine

*41. Meron Medzini, *French Policy in Japan during the Closing Years of the Tokugawa Regime*

# Harvard East Asian Monographs

# Harvard East Asian Monographs